MANUAL

INTRODUCTORY

BUSINESS

FORECASTING

Paul Newbold
University of Illinois, Champaign

Theodore Bos
University of Alabama, Birmingham

HG60AX
PUBLISHED BY
SOUTH-WESTERN PUBLISHING CO.
CINCINNATI, OH   WEST CHICAGO, IL   DALLAS, TX   LIVERMORE, CA

ISBN: 0-538-80248-0

1 2 3 4 5 6 7 BB 4 3 2 1 0 9

Printed in the United States of America

Contents

Chapter 1

BUSINESS FORECASTING: BEYOND THE CRYSTAL BALL

Contents of Chapter 1

Chapter 2

A REVIEW OF SOME BASIC CONCEPTS
IN STATISTICS

Contents of Chapter 2

Answers to Exercises at End of Chapter.

2.1   The random variable X has a normal distribution with mean 50 and standard deviation 10.
  (a)   The probability is 0.10 that this random variable takes a value less than what number?
  (b)   The random variable Y is defined by $Y = 250 - 3X$.   Find the mean and standard deviation of Y.

------- Answer to 2.1 --------

(a)   [From Section 2.2, subsection *The Normal Distribution*]

$$\alpha = P(Z < -z_\alpha)$$

$$\alpha = P((X-\mu)/\sigma < -z_\alpha)$$

$$\alpha = P(X < \mu - \sigma z_\alpha)$$

$$0.10 = P(X < 50 - 10 \times 1.282)$$

$$0.10 = P(X < 37.18)$$

Answer to (a) is 37.18

(b)   [From Section 2.2, subsection *Expected Values, Mean, and Variance*]

Since $Y = 250 - 3X$, then $\mu_Y = 250 - 3\mu_X = 250 - 3\times 50 = 100$, and
$\sigma_Y = 3\sigma_X = 3\times 10 = 30$.

Note: At the end of the subsection *Expected Values, Mean, and Variance*, instead of
$\sigma_Y = B\sigma_X$, the formula should strictly be $\sigma_Y = +\sqrt{B^2}\,\sigma_X$.

****

2.2   A particular brand of lightbulb has a lifetime whose distribution is normal with mean
1,500 hours and standard deviation 300 hours.

(a)   The probability is 0.05 that one of these lightbulbs has a lifetime of more than how
many hours?
(b)   Four of these lightbulbs are chosen at random. The probability is 0.05 that their
average lifetime is more than how many hours?

------- Answer to 2.2 --------

(a)   [From Section 2.2, subsection *The Normal Distribution*]

$$\alpha = P(Z > z_\alpha)$$

$$0.05 = P(Z > 1.645)$$

$$0.05 = P((X-\mu)/\sigma > 1.645)$$

$$0.05 = P(X > 1,500 + 1.645\times 300)$$

Answer to (a) is 1,993.5.

(b)   [From Section 2.3, *Sampling and Sampling Distributions*]

$$\alpha = P(Z > z_\alpha)$$

$$0.05 = P(Z > 1.645)$$

$$0.05 = P((X-\mu)/\sigma_{\bar{X}} > 1.645)$$

where $\sigma_{\bar{X}} = \sigma/\sqrt{n} = 300/\sqrt{4} = 150$

$$0.05 = P(X > 1,500 + 1.645\times 150)$$

Answer to (b) is 1,746.75.

****

2.3   A mutual fund has a very large portfolio of stocks. A random sample of nine of these showed the following percentage returns over a year. [See text for data]. Assume that the population distribution is normal.

(a)   Find the sample mean.
(b)   Find the sample variance.
(c)   Find the sample standard deviation.
(d)   Find a 99% confidence interval for the population mean.
(e)   Find a 95% confidence interval for the population variance.
(f)   Find a 90% confidence interval for the population standard deviation.

------- Answer to 2.3 --------

From the data: $n = 9$, $\Sigma X = 94$, $\Sigma X^2 = 1170.32$, and $\Sigma(X - \bar{X})^2 = 188.5422$.

[Parts (a), (b), and (c) are from Section 2.3, *Sampling and Sampling Distributions*]

(a) $\bar{X} = 10.444$

(b) $s^2 = 23.568$ [Note that if one is using LOTUS 123, the @var(range) calculates the population variance, and so the sample variance is @var(range)*$n/(n-1)$.

(c) $s = 4.855$

[Parts (d), (e), and (f) are from Section 2.4, subsection *Confidence Intervals*]

(d)   The appropriate t distribution has $(n - 1)$ degrees of freedom. Since $n = 9$, t_8 will be used.

$$0.99 = P(-3.355 < t_8 < 3.355) = P(-3.355 < (\bar{X}-\mu)/(s/\sqrt{n}) < 3.355)$$

or $$\bar{X} - 3.355s/\sqrt{n} < \mu < \bar{X} + 3.355s/\sqrt{n}$$

or $$10.444 - 3.355\times4.855/\sqrt{9} < \mu < 10.444 + 3.355\times4.855/\sqrt{9}$$

or, the 99% confidence interval for the population mean is: $5.014 < \mu < 15.873$.

(e)   The appropriate χ^2 distribution has $(n - 1)$ degrees of freedom. Since $n = 9$, χ_8^2 will be used.

$$0.95 = P(2.18 < \chi_8^2 < 17.53) = P(2.18 < (n - 1)s^2/\sigma^2 < 17.53)$$

or $$(n - 1)s^2/17.53 < \sigma^2 < (n - 1)s^2/2.18$$

or $$8\times23.568/17.53 < \sigma^2 < 8\times23.568/2.18$$

or $10.756 < \sigma^2 < 86.488$ is the 95% confidence interval of the population variance.

(f)   Since $n = 9$, χ_8^2 will be used.

$$0.90 = P(2.73 < \chi_8^2 < 15.51) = P(2.73 < (n-1)s^2/\sigma^2 < 15.51)$$

or $$(n-1)s^2/15.51 < \sigma^2 < (n-1)s^2/2.73$$

or $$8\times23.568/15.51 < \sigma^2 < 8\times23.568/2.73$$

or $12.156 < \sigma^2 < 69.064$ is the 90% confidence interval of the population variance.

and thus, taking the square roots of the above limits, the 90% confidence interval of the population standard deviation is: $3.487 < \sigma < 8.310$.

****

2.4   Carefully explain why a 95% confidence interval for a population parameter will be wider than a 90% confidence interval for that parameter based on the same information.

------- Answer to 2.4 --------

[From Section 2.4, subsection *Confidence Intervals*]

Quoting the text — "Notice that the 95% confidence interval is wider than the 90% confidence interval. This result is quite general. Based on the same information, the greater the probability content the wider will be the confidence interval for any population parameter. This is to be expected; the surer we want to be that a computed interval will contain the parameter, the wider the interval that will be required."

****

2.5 A random sample of twelve automobiles showed the following figures for miles achieved on a gallon of gas. [See text for data]. Assume the population distribution is normal.

 (a) Find the sample mean.
 (b) Find the sample variance.
 (c) Find the sample standard deviation.
 (d) Find a 90% confidence interval for the population mean.
 (e) Find a 90% confidence interval for the population standard deviation.

------- Answer to 2.5 --------

From the data: $n = 12$, $\Sigma X = 232.9$, $\Sigma X^2 = 4514.1$, and $\Sigma(X - \bar{X})^2 = 13.2867$.

[Parts (a), (b), and (c) are from Section 2.3, *Sampling and Sampling Distributions*]

(a) $\bar{X} = 19.367$

(b) $s^2 = 1.208$ [Note that if one is using LOTUS 123, the @var(range) calculates the population variance, and so the sample variance is @var(range)*n/(n-1).

(c) $s = 1.099$

[Parts (d) and (e) are from Section 2.4, subsection *Confidence Intervals*]

(d) The appropriate t distribution has $(n - 1)$ degrees of freedom. Since $n = 12$, t_{11} will be used.

$$0.90 = P(-1.796 < t_{11} < 1.796) = P(-1.796 < (\bar{X}-\mu)/(s/\sqrt{n}) < 1.796)$$

or $$\bar{X} - 1.796s/\sqrt{n} < \mu < \bar{X} + 1.796s/\sqrt{n}$$

or $$19.367 - 1.796\times1.099/\sqrt{12} < \mu < 19.367 + 1.796\times1.099/\sqrt{12}$$

or, the 99% confidence interval for the population mean is: $18.797 < \mu < 19.937$.

(e) The appropriate χ^2 distribution has $(n - 1)$ degrees of freedom. Since $n = 12$, χ_{11}^2 will be used.

$$0.90 = P(4.57 < \chi_{11}^2 < 19.68) = P(4.57 < (n - 1)s^2/\sigma^2 < 19.68)$$

or $$(n - 1)s^2/19.68 < \sigma^2 < (n - 1)s^2/4.57$$

or $$11\times1.208/19.68 < \sigma^2 < 11\times1.208/4.57$$

or $0.675 < \sigma^2 < 2.908$ is the 90% confidence interval for the population variance.

and thus, taking the square roots of the above limits, the 90% confidence interval of the population standard deviation is: $0.822 < \sigma < 1.705$.

****

2.6   A random sample of n observations, X_1, X_2, . . ., X_n, is taken from a population with mean μ. Let $\bar{X}$ denote the sample mean.

(a)   Show that

$$\sum_{i=1}^{n}(X_i - \bar{X}) = 0$$

(b)   Using the result in (a), show that if $\hat{\mu}$ is any number

$$\sum_{i=1}^{n}(X_i - \hat{\mu})^2 = \sum_{i=1}^{n}[(X_i - \bar{X}) + (\bar{X} - \hat{\mu})]^2 = \sum_{i=1}^{n}(X_i - \bar{X})^2 + n(\bar{X} - \hat{\mu})^2$$

(c)   Using the result in (b), show that the sum of squared discrepancies

$$S = \sum_{i=1}^{n}(X_i - \hat{\mu})^2 \quad \text{is smallest when} \quad \hat{\mu} = \bar{X}.$$

------- Answer to 2.6 --------

(a)   Since $\bar{X} = \Sigma X/n$, and $n\bar{X} = \Sigma X$, therefore $\sum_{i=1}^{n}(X_i - \bar{X}) = \Sigma X_i - \Sigma \bar{X} = \Sigma X_i - n\bar{X} = 0$.

(b)
$$\sum_{i=1}^{n}(X_i - \hat{\mu})^2 = \Sigma(X - \bar{X})^2 + 2\Sigma(X - \bar{X})(\bar{X} - \hat{\mu}) + \Sigma(\bar{X} - \hat{\mu})^2$$

$$= \sum_{i=1}^{n}(X_i - \bar{X})^2 + n(\bar{X} - \hat{\mu})^2$$

where, as $\hat{\mu}$ is a constant, and as $\Sigma(X - \bar{X}) = 0$, then

$$2\Sigma(X_i - \bar{X})(\bar{X} - \hat{\mu}) = 0$$

(c)   Using the answer to part (b), $\Sigma(\bar{X} - \hat{\mu})^2$ cannot be negative: its smallest value must occur when $\hat{\mu} = \bar{X}$.

Hence this value of $\hat{\mu}$ must minimize $\sum_{i=1}^{n}(X_i - \bar{X})$.

****

2.7 A random number of n observations, X_1, X_2, ..., X_n, is taken from a population with mean μ and variance σ^2. Let

$$\hat{\mu} = c_1X_1 + c_2X_2 + \ldots + c_nX_n$$

where the c_i are fixed numbers be an estimator of μ.

(a) Show that $\hat{\mu}$ is an unbiased estimator of μ if and only if $c_1 + c_2 + \ldots + c_n = 1$

(b) Show that the variance of $\hat{\mu}$ is $(c_1^2 + c_2^2 + \ldots + c_n^2)\sigma^2$

(c) Show that
$$\sum_{i=1}^{n}c_i^2 = \sum_{i=1}^{n}[(c_i - n^{-1}) + n^{-1}]^2$$
$$= \sum_{i=1}^{n}(c_i - n^{-1})^2 + 2n^{-1}\sum_{i=1}^{n}(c_i - n^{-1}) + n^{-1}$$
$$= \sum_{i=1}^{n}(c_i - n^{-1})^2 + n^{-1}$$

if $\hat{\mu}$ is an unbiased estimator of μ.

(d) Using the results in (b) and (c), show that if $\hat{\mu}$ is an unbiased estimator of μ, its variance is smallest if

$$c_i = n^{-1} \; ; \; i = 1, 2, \ldots, n$$

that is, $\hat{\mu}$ is the sample mean $\bar{X}$.

------- Answer to 2.7 --------

(a) [From Section 2.4, subsection *Models and Forecasts*]

Since $E(\hat{\mu}) = \mu$, if $\hat{\mu}$ is to be unbiased, then

$$E(\hat{\mu}) = E(c_1X_1 + c_2X_2 + \ldots + c_nX_n) = \mu$$

$$c_1E(X_1) + c_2E(X_2) + \ldots + c_nE(X_n) = \mu$$

or $$c_1\mu + c_2\mu + \ldots + c_n\mu = \mu$$

if and only if $$(c_1 + c_2 + \ldots + c_n)\mu = \mu$$

or, in other words, $(c_1 + c_2 + \ldots + c_n) = 1$ if and only if $\hat{\mu}$ is unbiased.

(b) The variance of $\hat{\mu}$, $\text{Var}(\hat{\mu}) = c_1^2\text{Var}(X_1) + c_2^2\text{Var}(X_2) + \ldots + c_n^2\text{Var}(X_n)$
$$= (c_1^2 + c_2^2 + \ldots + c_n^2)\sigma^2$$

since $\text{Var}(X_1) = \text{Var}(X_2) = \ldots = \text{Var}(X_n) = \sigma^2$.

(c)   The second term on the RHS of the second line of expressions in part (c) of the exercise,

$$2n^{-1} \sum_{i=1}^{n}(c_i - n^{-1}) = 0$$

only if $\Sigma c_i = 1$ (since $\Sigma n^{-1} = 1$)

and so, $\Sigma c_i^2 = \sum_{i=1}^{n}(c_i - n^{-1})^2 + n^{-1}$ only if $\hat{\mu}$ is an unbiased estimator of μ.

(d) $\text{Var}(\hat{\mu}) = (c_1^2 + c_2^2 + \ldots + c_n^2)\sigma^2 = \sigma^2(\Sigma c_i^2)$

and since $\Sigma c_i^2 = \sum_{i=1}^{n}(c_i - n^{-1})^2 + n^{-1}$ (from part(c)) if $\hat{\mu}$ is an unbiased estimator of μ

then $\text{Var}(\hat{\mu}) = \sigma^2[\sum_{i=1}^{n}(c_i - n^{-1})^2 + n^{-1}]$, if $\hat{\mu}$ is an unbiased estimator of μ.

Therefore, if $\hat{\mu}$ is an unbiased estimator of μ, $\text{Var}(\hat{\mu})$ is smallest when $\sum_{i=1}^{n}(c_i - n^{-1})^2 = 0$

or when $c_i = n^{-1}$; $i = 1, 2, \ldots, n$.

****

2.8   Refer to Exercise 2.3, A tenth observation is to be drawn from this population.
(a)   Find a point forecast for the new observation.
(b)   Find a 95% confidence interval forecast for the new observation.

------- Answer to 2.8 --------

(a)   The point estimate for the new (the 10*th*) observation is $\hat{X}_{10} = \bar{X} = 10.444$

(b) $0.95 = P(-2.306 < t_8 < 2.306)$

and so $0.95 = P(-2.306 < (\hat{X}_{10} - X_{10})/s((n+1)/n)^{1/2} < 2.306)$

or $0.95 = P(\hat{X}_{10} - 2.306\, s(10/9)^{1/2} < X_{10} < \hat{X}_{10} + 2.306\, s(10/9)^{1/2}$

$10.444 - 2.306 \times 4.855(10/9)^{1/2} < X_{10} < 10.444 + 2.306 \times 4.855(10/9)^{1/2}$

and so the 95% confidence interval for the new (the 10*th*) observation is –1.357 to 22.245.

****

2.9   Refer to Exercise 2.5. A thirteenth observation is to drawn from this population.
      (a)   Find a point forecast for the new observation.
      (b)   Find a 90% confidence interval forecast for the new observation.

------- Answer to 2.9 --------

(a)   The point estimate for the new (the 13th) observation is $\hat{X}_{13} = \bar{X} = 19.367$

(b) $0.90 = P(-1.796 < t_{11} < 1.796)$

      and so $0.90 = P(-1.796 < (\hat{X}_{13} - X_{13})/s((n+1)/n)^{\frac{1}{2}} < 1.796)$

      or $0.90 = P(\hat{X}_{13} - 1.796\ s(13/12)^{\frac{1}{2}} < X_{13} < \hat{X}_{13} + 1.796\ s(13/12)^{\frac{1}{2}}$

            $19.367 - 1.796 \times 1.099(13/12)^{\frac{1}{2}} < X_{13} < 19.367 + 1.796 \times 1.099(13/12)^{\frac{1}{2}}$

      and so the 95% confidence interval for the new (the 13th) observation is 17.313 to 21.421.

****

2.10   A chain store group has a very large number of retail outlets. For a random sample of ten of these outlets, the following figures were found for percentage sales growth over the last year. [See text for data.]
Assume the population distribution is normal.
  (a)   Find the sample mean.
  (b)   Find the sample variance.
  (c)   Find the sample standard deviation.
  (d)   Test at the 5% level the null hypothesis that the population mean growth is at least 10%.
  (e)   Test at the 5% level the null hypothesis that the population standard deviation is at most 2%.

------- Answer to 2.10 --------

From the data: $n = 10$, $\Sigma X = 85.3$, $\Sigma X^2 = 789.13$, and $\Sigma(X - \bar{X})^2 = 61.521$

[Parts (a), (b), and (c) are from Section 2.3, *Sampling and Sampling Distributions*]

    (a) $\bar{X} = 8.530$ (b) $s^2 = 6.836$ (c) $s = 2.615$

[Parts (d) and (e) are from Section 2.5, *Hypothesis Testing*]

(d) H_0: $\mu \geq 10$

              H_1: $\mu < 10$

Since $n = 10$, we have $(n - 1) = 9$ degrees of freedom for the t-test.

Decision rule: Reject H_0 if $t_{calc} < -t_{9,.05}$

$t_{calc} = (\bar{X} - \mu_0)/(s/\sqrt{n}) = (8.530 - 10)/(2.615/\sqrt{10}) = -1.778$.

Since $t_{calc} = -1.778 > t_{9,.05} = -1.833$, and therefore, do not reject the null hypothesis – it is possible that the population mean growth is at least 10% – or, in other words, there is not enough statistical information to reject the null hypothesis.

(e) H_0: $\sigma \leq 2$ or H_0: $\sigma^2 \leq 4$

                                     H_1: $\sigma^2 > 4$

Since $n = 10$, we have $(n - 1) = 9$ degrees of freedom for this χ^2 test.

Decision rule: Reject H_0 if $\chi^2_{calc} > \chi^2_{9,.05}$

$\chi^2_{calc} = (n - 1)s^2/\sigma^2_0 = 9 \times 6.836/4 = 15.381$

Since $\chi^2_{calc} = 15.381 < \chi^2_{9,.05} = 16.92$

do not reject the null hypothesis that the population variance is less than 4% – or, in other words, that the population standard deviation is less than 2%.

****

2.11 Carefully explain why, if a null hypothesis is rejected against some alternative at the 5% significance level, then using the same data this same null hypothesis will be rejected against the same alternative at the 10% significance level.

------- Answer to 2.11 --------

[From Section 2.5, *Hypothesis Testing*]

If a null hypothesis can be rejected (given a particular data set) at the 5% level of significance, then it can be rejected at any level of significance above 5%. Similarly if a null hypothesis can be rejected (given a particular data set) at the 10% level of significance, then that null can be rejected at any level of significance above 10%. Thus if a null is rejected at the 5% level, then it can also be rejected at any level above 5%, and thus it can be rejected at the 10% level of significance.

****

2.12 Forecasts of earnings per share for major corporations are made by large numbers of financial analysts. For a random sample of eight analysts, the following forecasts, in dollars, for earnings per share of a particular corporation were found. [See text for data]. Assume the population distribution is normal.
   (a)   find the sample mean.
   (b)   Find the sample variance.
   (c)   Find the sample standard deviation.
   (d)   Test at the 5% level against a two-sided alternative the null hypothesis that the population mean is $12 per share.
   (e)   Test at the 5% level the null hypothesis that the population standard deviation is at most $2.

------- Answer to 2.12 --------

From the data: $n = 8$, $\Sigma X = 100.6$, $\Sigma X^2 = 1296.54$, and $\Sigma(X - \bar{X})^2 = 31.495$.

[Parts (a), (b), and (c) are from Section 2.3, *Sampling and Sampling Distributions*]

   (a) $\bar{X} = 12.575$ (b) $s^2 = 4.4993$ (c) $s = 2.1212$

[Parts (d) and (e) are from Section 2.5, *Hypothesis Testing*]

(d) H_0: $\mu = 12$

                       H_1: $\mu \neq 12$

Since $n = 8$, we have $(n - 1) = 7$ degrees of freedom for the t-test.

Decision rule: Reject H_0 if $t_{calc} < -t_{7,.025}$ or $t_{calc} > t_{7,.025}$

$t_{calc} = (\bar{X} - \mu_0)/(s/\sqrt{n}) = (12.575 - 12)/(2.121/\sqrt{8}) = 0.767$.

Since $t_{calc} = 0.767$ is between $-t_{7,.025} = -2.365$ and $t_{7,.025} = 2.365$, and therefore, do not reject the null hypothesis – it is possible that the population mean is $12 – or, in other words, there is not enough statistical information to reject the null hypothesis.

(e) H_0: $\sigma \leq 2$ or H_0: $\sigma^2 \leq 4$

                                                                 H_1: $\sigma^2 > 4$

Since $n = 8$, we have $(n - 1) = 7$ degrees of freedom for this χ^2 test.

Decision rule: Reject H_0 if $\chi^2_{calc} > \chi^2_{7,.05}$

$\chi^2_{calc} = (n - 1)s^2/\sigma^2_0 = 7 \times 4.499/4 = 7.873$.

Since $\chi^2_{calc} = 7.873 < \chi^2_{7,.05} = 14.07$

do not reject the null hypothesis that the population variance is less than 4 – or, in other words, that the population standard deviation is less than $2.

****

Chapter 3

CORRELATION AND
THE LINEAR REGRESSION MODEL

Contents of Chapter 3

Answers to Exercises at End of Chapter.

3.1   The sample correlation is $r = c_{XY}/s_X s_Y$

Show that the statistic (3.1.4) for testing the null hypothesis that the population correlation is zero can be written

$$t = r/\{(1-r^2)/(n-2)\}^{1/2} = (n-2)^{1/2}\{c_{XY}/s_X s_Y\}/(s_X^2 s_Y^2 - c_{XY}^2)^{1/2}$$

------- Answer to 3.1 --------

[From Section 3.1, *Correlation*]

Since $r = c_{XY}/s_X s_Y$,

$$t = r/\{(1-r^2)/(n-2)\}^{1/2} = (n-2)^{1/2}(c_{XY}/s_X s_Y)/(1 - c_{XY}^2/s_X^2 s_Y^2)^{1/2}$$

Multiplying both the numerator and denominator by $s_X s_Y$ (or $(s_X^2 s_Y^2)^{1/2}$), one gets

$$t = (n-2)^{1/2} c_{XY}/(s_X^2 s_Y^2 - c_{XY}^2)^{1/2}$$

****

3.2   Let a and b denote the least squares estimates of the intercept and slope parameters of the linear regression line

(a)   Show that the fitted line $\hat{Y} = a + bX$

       passes through the point of the sample means $(\bar{X}, \bar{Y})$

(b)   Denoting by $e_t = Y_t - \hat{Y}_t$

       the residuals from the fitted line, show that $\sum_{t=1}^{n} e_t = 0.$

------- Answer to 3.2 --------

[From Section 3.3, *Fitting the Linear Regression Model*]

(a)   If $\hat{Y} = a + bX$ passes through the point $(\bar{X}, \bar{Y})$ then substituting the point into this equation $\bar{Y} = a + b\bar{X}$ which is identical (after re-arranging terms) to the formula for a, the least squares estimate of the intercept, *ie.* $a = \bar{Y} - b\bar{X}.$

(b)   Since $e_t = Y_t - \hat{Y},$ summing both left and right sides for $t = 1, 2, \ldots, n$

$$\sum_{t=1}^{n} e_t = \sum_{t=1}^{n} (Y_t - \hat{Y}_t) = \Sigma(Y_t - a - bX) = \Sigma Y_t - na - b\Sigma X = n(\bar{Y} - a - b\bar{X}) = 0,$$

as $a = \bar{Y} - b\bar{X}$ (which is the formula for the least squares estimator of the intercept),

or $\bar{Y} - a - b\bar{X} = 0.$

****

3.3   Let a and b denote the least squares estimates of the intercept and slope parameters of the linear regression line, and let

$$Y_t = \hat{Y}_t + e_t = (a + bX_t) + e_t$$

(a)   Show that $\hat{Y}_t - \bar{Y} = b(X_t - \bar{X})$

       and hence that $\sum_{t=1}^{n} (\hat{Y}_t - \bar{Y})^2 = b^2 \sum_{t=1}^{n} (X_t - \bar{X})^2$

(b)   Show that $\sum_{t=1}^{n} e_t^2 = \sum_{t=1}^{n} [(Y_t - \bar{Y}) - b(X_t - \bar{X})]^2 = \sum_{t=1}^{n} (Y_t - \bar{Y})^2 - b^2 \sum_{t=1}^{n} (X_t - \bar{X})^2$

(c)   Using the results (a) and (b), deduce the sums of squares decomposition

$$SST = SSR + SSE$$

(d)   Using (a), show that the coefficient of determination is

$$R^2 = SSR/SST = [\sum_{t=1}^{n} (X_t - \bar{X})(Y_t - \bar{Y})]^2 / \sum_{t=1}^{n} (X_t - \bar{X})^2 \sum_{t=1}^{n} (Y_t - \bar{Y})^2$$

       and hence that the coefficient of determination is the square of the sample correlation coefficient.

------- Answer to 3.3 --------

[From Section 3.3, *Fitting the Linear Regression Model*]

(a) $\hat{Y}_t = a + bX_t$ is the formula for the fitted regression line

and $\bar{Y} = a + b\bar{X}$ since $a = \bar{Y} - b\bar{X}$.

Subtract the latter from the former equation to get $(\hat{Y}_t - \bar{Y}) = b(X_t - \bar{X})$.

Square both sides of this equation, and then sum all such terms for $t = 1, 2, \ldots, n$, to get

$$\sum_{t=1}^{n}(\hat{Y}_t - \bar{Y})^2 = b^2 \sum_{t=1}^{n}(X_t - \bar{X})^2$$

(b) Since $e_t = Y_t - a - bX_t$ and since $\bar{Y} - a - b\bar{X} = 0$,

then $e_t = (Y_t - \bar{Y}) - b(X_t - \bar{X})$ which after summing becomes

$$\sum_{t=1}^{n}e_t^2 = \sum_{t=1}^{n}[(Y_t - \bar{Y}) - b(X_t - \bar{X})]^2$$

$$= \sum_{t=1}^{n}[(Y_t - \bar{Y})^2 - 2b(X_t - \bar{X})(Y_t - \bar{Y}) + b^2(X_t - \bar{X})]$$

$$= \sum_{t=1}^{n}(Y_t - \bar{Y})^2 - 2b\sum_{t=1}^{n}(X_t - \bar{X})(Y_t - \bar{Y}) + b^2\sum_{t=1}^{n}(X_t - \bar{X})^2$$

and since $b = \sum_{t=1}^{n}(X_t - \bar{X})(Y_t - \bar{Y}) / \sum_{t=1}^{n}(X_t - \bar{X})^2$

or $\sum_{t=1}^{n}(X_t - \bar{X})(Y_t - \bar{Y}) = b\sum_{t=1}^{n}(X_t - \bar{X})^2$

and so, $\sum_{t=1}^{n}e_t^2 = \sum_{t=1}^{n}(Y_t - \bar{Y})^2 - 2b^2\sum_{t=1}^{n}(X_t - \bar{X})^2 + b^2\sum_{t=1}^{n}(X_t - \bar{X})^2$

or $\sum_{t=1}^{n}e_t^2 = \sum_{t=1}^{n}(Y_t - \bar{Y})^2 - b^2\sum_{t=1}^{n}(X_t - \bar{X})^2$

(c) [From Section 3.3, subsection *Sum of Squares Decomposition and the Coefficients of Determination*]

Since $\sum_{t=1}^{n}e_t^2 = \sum_{t=1}^{n}(Y_t - \bar{Y})^2 - b^2\sum_{t=1}^{n}(X_t - \bar{X})^2$ (from (b) above),

and since $\sum_{t=1}^{n}(\hat{Y}_t - \bar{Y})^2 = b^2\sum_{t=1}^{n}(X_t - \bar{X})^2$ (from (a) above),

then $\sum_{t=1}^{n}e_t^2 = \sum_{t=1}^{n}(Y_t - \bar{Y})^2 - \sum_{t=1}^{n}(\hat{Y}_t - \bar{Y})^2$

The three terms that make up this equation, are defined in the text as SSE, SST, and SSR respectively. Thus the above equation can be written as SSE = SST − SSR, which after re-arrangement is equal to the formula

$$SST = SSR + SSE$$

(d)   Since $\text{SSR} = \sum\limits_{t=1}^{n}(\hat{Y}_t - \bar{Y})^2$,   from (a), it is also true that $\text{SSR} = b^2 \sum\limits_{t=1}^{n}(X_t - \bar{X})^2$.

Thus

$$R^2 = b^2\, \Sigma(X_t - \bar{X})^2 / \Sigma(Y_t - \bar{Y})^2$$

$$= [\Sigma(X_t - \bar{X})(Y_t - \bar{Y})]^2\, \Sigma(X_t - \bar{X})^2 \,/\, [\Sigma(X_t - \bar{X})^2]^2\, \Sigma(Y_t - \bar{Y})^2$$

$$= [\Sigma(X_t - \bar{X})(Y_t - \bar{Y})]^2 \,/\, \Sigma(X_t - \bar{X})^2\, \Sigma(Y_t - \bar{Y})^2 = r^2,$$

by definintion.

****

3.4   For a sample of 20 observations, the correlation between percentage price inflation over a year and the rate of interest at the beginning of the year is 0.684. In this sample, what percentage of the variability in percentage price inflation is explained by its linear relationship with beginning of year interest rate?

------- Answer to 3.4 --------

[From Section 3.1, *Correlation*]

Since the correlation, r = 0.684 therefore the coefficient of determination, $R^2 = r^2 = 0.684^2 = 0.468$. Hence 46.8% of the variability in percentage price inflation is explained by its linear relationship with beginning of year interest rate.

****

3.5 The following linear regression model was estimated through the least squares from a sample of 18 annual observations:

$$\hat{Y} = 1.284 + 0.237\,X$$
$$\quad\;\;(0.681)\quad(0.102)$$

where the figures in parentheses below parameter estimates are the corresponding estimates' standard errors, and

Y = Annual percentage change in value of a firm's sales
X = Annual percentage change in the firm's advertising expenditures

(a) Interpret the estimated slope of the regression line.
(b) Find a 95% confidence interval for the slope of the population regression line.

------- Answer to 3.5 --------

(a) [From Section 3.2, *The Linear Regression Model*]

Since $b = 0.237$, a one percentage increase in the firm's annual advertising expenditures will result in an expected 0.237% increase in the firm's annual sales.

(b) [From Section 3.4, *Inference about the Linear Regression Model*]

The 95% confidence interval for the slope of the population regression model is

$$b - t_{16,0.025}s_b \;<\; \beta \;<\; b + t_{16,0.025}s_b$$

since $n = 18$, and so we have $n - 2 = 16$ degrees of freedom. Thus the 95% confidence interval is

$$0.237 - 2.120 \times 0.102 \;<\; \beta \;<\; 0.237 + 2.120 \times 0.102$$

or
$$0.021 \;<\; \beta \;<\; 0.453$$

****

3.6 The following linear regression model was estimated through least squares from a sample of 22 annual observations:

$$\hat{Y} = 7.124 - 0.708\,X$$
$$\quad\;\;(2.316)\quad(0.259)$$

where figures in parentheses below parameter estimates are the corresponding estimated standard errors, and

Y = Percentage of the labor force unemployed at the end of the year
X = Percentage growth in gross national product during the year

(a) Interpret the estimated slope of the regression line.
(b) Test at the 5% level the null hypothesis that the slope of the population regression line is zero against the alternative that the true slope is negative.
(c) Find and interpret the coefficient of determination for this regression.

------- Answer to 3.6 --------

(a)   [From Section 3.2, *The Linear Regression Model*]

Since $b = -0.708$, a one percentage increase in gross national product during a year will result in an expected decrease of 0.708% in the unemployment rate at the end of the year.

(b)   [From Section 3.4, *Inference about the Linear Regression Model*]

$$H_0: \beta \geq 0$$

$$H_1: \beta < 0$$

Decision Rule: Reject H_0 if $t_{calc} < -t_{20,0.05}$ (since $n = 22$, there are $(n - 2) =$ 20 degrees of freedom for this test).

$t_{calc} = (b - 0)/s_b = -0.708/0.259 = -2.734$, and $-t_{20,0.05} = -1.725$.

Since $t_{calc} = -2.734 < -t_{20,0.05} = -1.725$ then reject H_0, the evidence suggests that the slope of the population regression line is negative.

(c)   [From Section 3.3, subsection *Sum of Squares Decomposition and the Coefficients of Determination*]

It is known that the t-test that the population correlation coefficient is significantly different from zero gives rise to the same calculated t-value as the t-test that the population slope is significantly different from zero. See Exercise 3.8c.

Thus $$t = {}^r/\{(1-r^2)/(n-2)\}^{1/2} = t = (b - 0)/s_b$$

and after squaring both formulae, and noting that $r^2 = R^2$

$$b^2/s_b^2 = (n - 2) R^2 / (1 - R^2)$$

Multiply through both sides by s_b^2 and $(1 - R^2)$,

$$b^2(1 - R^2) = (n - 2) s_b^2 R^2$$

Re-arrange terms, so that R^2 is on the right-hand-side

$$b^2 = R^2 [b^2 + (n - 2)s_b^2]$$

or $$R^2 = b^2 / [b^2 + (n - 2)s_b^2]$$

For this exercise we have $R^2 = (-0.708)^2 / [(-0.708)^2 + 20\times0.259^2] = 0.272$.

Hence 27.2% of the variability in percentage growth in GNP is explained by its linear relationship with the percentage of the labor force unemployed at the end of the year, in the sample.

****

3.7 The accompanying table shows, for a period of 23 months, the rate of return (Y) on the stock of Illinois Power Company and a stock market index rate of return (X).

(a) Find by least squares the sample regression of Y on X, and interpret the slope of the fitted regression line.

(b) Find and interpret the coefficient of determination for the fitted regression.

(c) Find the sample correlation between the rate of return on the stock of Illinois Power and the rate of return on the market index.

(d) Find the 95% confidence interval for the slope of the population regression line.

(e) Test at the 1% level against a two-sided alternative the null hypothesis that the slope of the population regression line is one.

(f) Test at the 1% level against a two-sided alternative the null hypothesis that the intercept of the population regression line is zero, and interpret your finding.

(g) Find a point forecast of the rate of return on the stock of Illinois Power next month, if the rate of return on the market index is expected to be 0.04.

(h) Find and discuss the implications of a 95% prediction interval for the rate of return on the stock of Illinois Power next month if the rate of return on the market index is expected to be 0.04.

------- Answer to 3.7 --------

[From Section 3.3, *Fitting the Linear Regression Model*]

This exercise is best done on a spreadsheet, rather than on a statistics program. Working it on a spreadsheet forces the student to be responsible for the formulas. See the spreadsheet accompanying this page.

	A	B	C	D	E	F	G	H
1	t	X	Y	(X-XBAR)	(X-XBAR)²	(Y-YBAR)²	Y HAT	e(t)²
2				*(Y-YBAR)				
3	1	-0.0763	-0.0800	0.00657	0.00651	0.00663	-0.0833	0.000011
4	2	0.0595	0.0751	0.00406	0.00304	0.00543	0.0593	0.000249
5	3	-0.0026	0.0588	-0.00040	0.00005	0.00329	-0.0059	0.004188
6	4	-0.0997	-0.1042	0.01099	0.01083	0.01115	-0.1079	0.000014
7	5	-0.0615	-0.0194	0.00137	0.00434	0.00043	-0.0678	0.002341
8	6	-0.0503	-0.0593	0.00332	0.00299	0.00369	-0.0560	0.000011
9	7	0.0746	0.1513	0.01053	0.00493	0.02247	0.0752	0.005796
10	8	0.0498	0.0365	0.00159	0.00206	0.00123	0.0491	0.000159
11	9	0.0428	0.0211	0.00076	0.00148	0.00039	0.0418	0.000427
12	10	-0.0157	-0.0276	0.00058	0.00040	0.00084	-0.0197	0.000063
13	11	0.0522	0.1099	0.00519	0.00229	0.01177	0.0516	0.003394
14	12	0.0615	0.0415	0.00229	0.00326	0.00161	0.0614	0.000396
15	13	0.0493	0.0368	0.00159	0.00202	0.00125	0.0486	0.000139
16	14	0.0149	-0.0740	-0.00079	0.00011	0.00569	0.0125	0.007476
17	15	0.0440	0.1118	0.00438	0.00157	0.01219	0.0430	0.004729
18	16	0.0340	-0.1207	-0.00362	0.00088	0.01491	0.0325	0.023479
19	17	-0.0364	-0.0458	0.00192	0.00166	0.00223	-0.0414	0.000019
20	18	0.0042	0.0103	0.00000	0.00000	0.00008	0.0012	0.000082
21	19	-0.0406	-0.0678	0.00311	0.00202	0.00479	-0.0458	0.000483
22	20	0.0419	0.0146	0.00050	0.00141	0.00017	0.0408	0.000688
23	21	-0.0057	0.0466	-0.00046	0.00010	0.00204	-0.0092	0.003111
24	22	-0.0396	-0.0685	0.00307	0.00193	0.00489	-0.0448	0.000563
25	23	0.0002	-0.0147	0.00007	0.00002	0.00026	-0.0030	0.000137
26								
27	SUM	0.10050	0.03230	0.05662	0.05390	0.11743		0.05795
28	AVG	0.00437	0.00140					

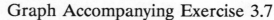

Graph Accompanying Exercise 3.7

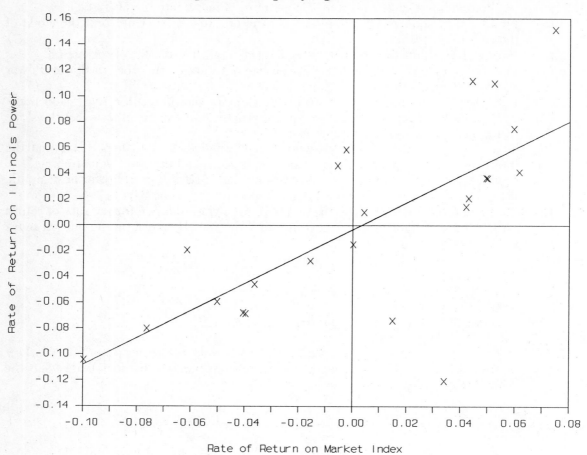

(a)   [From Section 3.3, *Fitting the Linear Regression Model*]

$$b = \sum_{t=1}^{n}(X_t - \bar{X})(Y_t - \bar{Y}) \Big/ \sum_{t=1}^{n}(X_t - \bar{X})^2 = 0.05662/0.05390 = 1.050361$$

$$a = \bar{Y} - b\bar{X} = 0.00140 - 1.050361 \times 0.00437 = -0.00318$$

(b)   [From Section 3.3, subsection *Sums of Squares Decomposition and the Coefficient of Determination*]

$$R^2 = [\sum_{t=1}^{n}(X_t - \bar{X})(Y_t - \bar{Y})]^2 \Big/ \sum_{t=1}^{n}(X_t - \bar{X})^2 \sum_{t=1}^{n}(Y_t - \bar{Y})^2$$

$$= 0.05662^2/(0.05390 \times 0.11743) = 0.506453$$

Hence 50.6% of the variability in the rate of return of the stock of Illinois Power Company is explained by its linear relationship with the stock market index rate of return, in this sample.

(c) [From Section 3.1, *Correlation*]

$$r = [\sum_{t=1}^{n}(X_t - \bar{X})(Y_t - \bar{Y})] \ / \ [\sum_{t=1}^{n}(X_t - \bar{X})^2 \sum_{t=1}^{n}(Y_t - \bar{Y})^2]^{\frac{1}{2}}$$

$$= \ 0.05662/(0.05390 \times 0.11743)^{\frac{1}{2}} \ = \ 0.711655$$

(One could also find as $r = (R^2)^{\frac{1}{2}}$).

(d) [From Section 3.4, *Inference about the Linear Regression Model*]

Before the confidence interval for the population slope can be calculated, we need several quantities:

(i) $s^2 = \Sigma e_t^2/(n-2) = 0.05795/21 = 0.002760$

(ii) $s_b = (s^2/\Sigma(X_t - \bar{X})^2)^{\frac{1}{2}} = (0.002760/0.05390)^{\frac{1}{2}} = 0.226268$

(iii) $t_{21,0.025} = 2.080$ (since we have $(n - 2)$ degrees of freedom)

and now, the limits for this confidence interval are:

$$b \ \pm \ t_{21,0.025} \ s_b \quad \text{or} \quad 1.050361 \ \pm \ 2.080 \times 0.226268$$

or the 95% confidence interval for the slope is from 0.5797 to 1.5210.

(e) [From Section 3.4, *Inference about the Linear Regression Model*]

$$H_0: \ \beta = 1$$
$$H_1: \ \beta \neq 1$$

Decision Rule: Reject H_0 if $|t_{calc}| > t_{21,0.005}$

$t_{calc} = (b - 1)/s_b = (1.050361 - 1)/0.226268 = 0.223$ while $t_{21,0.005} = 2.831.$

Since $t_{calc} = 0.223 < t_{21,0.005} = 2.831$ do not reject H_0, there is not enough statistical evidence to suggest that β is not equal to one.

(f) [From Section 3.4, *Inference about the Linear Regression Model*]

$$H_0: \ \alpha = 0$$
$$H_1: \ \alpha \neq 0$$

Decision Rule: Reject H_0 if $|t_{calc}| > t_{21,0.005}$

$s_a = \{s^2[1/n + \bar{X}^2/\Sigma(X_t-\bar{X})^2]\}^{\frac{1}{2}} = \{.002760(1/23 + 0.00437^2/0.05390)\}^2 = 0.0109984$

$t_{calc} = (a - 0)/s_a = -0.00318/0.0109984 = -0.290$ while $t_{21,0.005} = 2.831.$

Since $|t_{calc}| = 0.290 < t_{21,0.005} = 2.831$ do not reject the null hypothesis, there is not enough statistical evidence to suggest that α is not equal to zero.

(g)   [From Section 3.5, *Forecasting from the Fitted Linear Regression Model*]

If the rate of return on the market index is 0.04, then the rate of return on the stock of Illinois Power,

$$\hat{Y} = a + bX = -0.00318 + 1.050361 \times 0.04 = 0.0388291$$

(h)   [From Section 3.5, *Forecasting from the Fitted Linear Regression Model*]

The 95% prediction interval is $\hat{Y} \pm t_{n-2} \{[1 + 1/n + (X - \bar{X})^2/\Sigma(X_t - \bar{X})^2] s^2\}^{\frac{1}{2}}$

or $0.0388 \pm 2.080 \{[1 + 1/23 + (0.04 - 0.00437)^2/0.05390]0.002760\}^{\frac{1}{2}}$

or from -0.074 to 0.152.

Since this prediction interval for this rate of return is anywhere from a negative number to a positive number, one cannot be certain of a positive rate of return. Further, the interval is wide resulting from the fact that the data is not closely clustered around the sample regression line – see the accompanying graph, and note that the measure for the closeness of the association between the two variables, R^2 is only 50.6%.

                    ****

3.8   Let s_X and s_Y denote the sample standard deviations, and c_{XY} the sample covariance.

(a)   Show that the unbiased estimator (3.3.2) of the variance of the error term in the linear regression model can be written

$$s^2 = \sum_{t=1}^{n} e_t^2/(n - 2) = (s_Y^2 - b^2 s_X^2)(n - 1)/(n - 2)$$
$$= (s_X^2 s_Y^2 - c_{XY}^2)(n - 1)/[(n - 2)s_X^2]$$

(b)   Using the result in (a), show that the statistic for testing that the slope of the population regression line is zero can be written

$$t = b/s_b = b(n - 1)^{\frac{1}{2}} s_X/s$$
$$= (n - 2)^{\frac{1}{2}} c_{XY} / (s_X^2 s_Y^2 - c_{XY}^2)^{\frac{1}{2}}$$

(c)   Comparing the results in Exercises 3.1 and part (b) of this exercise deduce that the tests for no linear association based on the sample correlation coefficient and the slope of the sample regression line are equivalent.

------- Answer to 3.8 --------

[From Sections 3.3 and 3.4]

(a)
$$s^2 = \Sigma e_t^2/(n-2) = \Sigma(Y_t - a - bX_t)^2/(n-2).$$

Let's focus on the numerator. Since $a = \bar{Y} - b\bar{X}$,

$$\Sigma(Y_t - a - bX_t)^2 = \Sigma[(Y_t - a - bX_t) - (\bar{Y} - a - b\bar{X})]^2$$

$$= \Sigma[(Y_t - \bar{Y}) - b(X_t - \bar{X})]^2$$

$$= \Sigma(Y_t - \bar{Y})^2 - 2b\,\Sigma(X_t - \bar{X})(Y_t - \bar{Y}) + b^2\,\Sigma(X_t - \bar{X})^2$$

and since $b = \Sigma(X_t - \bar{X})(Y_t - \bar{Y})/\Sigma(X_t - \bar{X})^2$,

$$= \Sigma(Y_t - \bar{Y})^2 - 2b^2\,\Sigma(X_t - \bar{X})^2 + b^2\,\Sigma(X_t - \bar{X})^2$$

$$= \Sigma(Y_t - \bar{Y})^2 - b^2\,\Sigma(X_t - \bar{X})^2$$

$$= (n-1)\,[s_Y^2 - b^2\,s_X^2].$$

Therefore
$$\Sigma(X_t - \bar{X})(Y_t - \bar{Y}) = b\,\Sigma(X_t - \bar{X})^2.$$

Putting this result for the numerator into the formula for s^2, one gets

$$s^2 = (n-1)[s_Y^2 - b^2\,s_X^2]/(n-2)$$

where since $b = c_{XY}/s_X^2$, and so $b^2 = c_{XY}^2/s_X^4$

$$s^2 = (n-1)[s_Y^2 - c_{XY}^2/s_X^2]/(n-2)$$

or
$$s^2 = (s_X^2 s_Y^2 - c_{XY}^2)(n-1)/[(n-2)s_X^2]$$

(b) Since $s_b = s/[\Sigma(X_t - \bar{X})^2]^{1/2}$ and $(n-1)s_X^2 = \Sigma(X_t - \bar{X})^2$

then $s_b = s/[s_X(n-1)^{1/2}]$

Therefore $t = b/s_b = b\,(n-1)^{1/2}\,s_X/s.$

Since $b = c_{XY}/s_X^2$, and $s = (s_X^2 s_Y^2 - c_{XY}^2)^{1/2}(n-1)^{1/2}/[(n-2)^{1/2}\,s_X]$

$$t = c_{XY}\,(n-1)^{1/2}\,/\,(s_X\,s) = c_{XY}\,(n-1)^{1/2}\,(n-2)^{1/2}\,s_X\,/\,[s_X\,(s_X^2 s_Y^2 - c_{XY}^2)^{1/2}\,(n-1)^{1/2}$$

$$= c_{XY}\,(n-2)^{1/2}\,/\,(s_X^2 s_Y^2 - c_{XY}^2)^{1/2}$$

(c) This is fairly obvious, as the t value is exercise 3.1 is for a test of no linear association based on the sample correlation coefficient, while the t value in exercise 3.8b is for the same test based on the slope of the sample regression line.

****

3.9   The accompanying table shows 22 annual observations on retail sales per household (Y) and disposable income per household (X), both in constant dollars, in the United States.
   (a)   Find by least squares the sample regression of retail sales on disposable income, and interpret the slope of the fitted regression line.
   (b)   Find and interpret the coefficient of determination for the fitted regression.
   (c)   Find a 95% confidence interval for the slope of the population regression line.
   (d)   Test at the 1% level the null hypothesis that the slope of the population regression line is zero against the alternative that it is positive.
   (e)   Find a point forecast for retail sales per household next year if it is expected that disposable income per household next year will be $12,600.
   (f)   Find and discuss the implications of a 95% prediction interval for retail sales per household next year if it is expected that disposable income per household next year will be $12,600.

------- Answer to 3.9 --------

[From Section 3.3, *Fitting the Linear Regression Model*]

This exercise is best done on a spreadsheet, rather than on a statistics program. Working it on a spreadsheet forces the student to be responsible for the formulas. See the next page for the spreadsheet accompanying this exercise.

(a)   [From Section 3.3, *Fitting the Linear Regression Model*]

$$b = \sum_{t=1}^{n}(X_t - \bar{X})(Y_t - \bar{Y}) / \sum_{t=1}^{n}(X_t - \bar{X})^2 = 13,004,501/34,086,319 = 0.381516$$

$$a = \bar{Y} - b\bar{X} = 6,042.41 - 0.381516\times10,799.05 = 1,922.392$$

Graph Accompanying Exercise 3.9

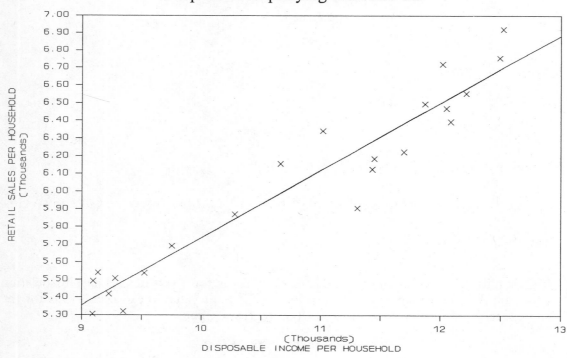

	A	B	C	D	E	F	G	H
1	t	X	Y	(X-XBAR)	(X-XBAR)²	(Y-YBAR)²	Y HAT	e(t)²
2				*(Y-YBAR)				
3	1	9098	5492	936271	2893556	302950	5393.43	9715.69
4	2	9138	5540	834524	2759072	252415	5408.69	17241.67
5	3	9094	5305	1257316	2907180	543772	5391.91	7552.61
6	4	9282	5507	812240	2301427	286663	5463.63	1880.88
7	5	9229	5418	980351	2465043	389887	5443.41	645.69
8	6	9347	5320	1048971	2108436	521875	5488.43	28368.49
9	7	9525	5538	642640	1623192	254429	5556.34	336.34
10	8	9756	5692	365493	1087944	122787	5644.47	2259.12
11	9	10282	5871	88626	267336	29381	5845.15	668.35
12	10	10662	6157	-15704	18781	13131	5990.12	27847.61
13	11	11019	6342	65896	48380	89755	6126.33	46515.52
14	12	11307	5907	-68782	258018	18336	6236.20	108374.1
15	13	11432	6124	51643	400631	6657	6283.89	25565.40
16	14	11449	6186	93328	422441	20618	6290.38	10894.69
17	15	11697	6224	163060	806322	32975	6384.99	25918.99
18	16	11871	6496	486229	1149087	205745	6451.38	1991.15
19	17	12018	6718	823515	1485850	456423	6507.46	44326.83
20	18	12523	6921	1514651	2972019	771922	6700.13	48785.07
21	19	12053	6471	537434	1572402	183690	6520.81	2481.41
22	20	12088	6394	453185	1661404	123616	6534.17	19646.73
23	21	12215	6555	725805	2004927	262749	6582.62	762.83
24	22	12494	6755	1207809	2872871	507786	6689.06	4347.74
25								
26	SUM		237579	132933	13004501	34086319	5397561		436127
27	AVG		10799.05	6042.41					

(b) [From Section 3.3, subsection *Sums of Squares Decomposition and the Coefficient of Determination*]

$$R^2 = [\sum_{t=1}^{n}(X_t - \bar{X})(Y_t - \bar{Y})]^2 \; / \; \sum_{t=1}^{n}(X_t - \bar{X})^2 \sum_{t=1}^{n}(Y_t - \bar{Y})^2$$

$$= 13{,}004{,}501^2/(34{,}086{,}319 \times 5{,}397{,}561) = 0.919199$$

Hence 91.9% of the variability in annual retail sales per household is explained by its linear relationship with the disposable income per household, in this sample.

(c) [From Section 3.4, *Inference about the Linear Regression Model*]

Before the confidence interval for the population slope can be calculated, we need several quantities:

(i) $s^2 = \Sigma e_t^2/(n-2) = 436{,}127/20 = 21{,}806.35$

(ii) $s_b = (s^2/\Sigma(X_t - \bar{X})^2)^{\frac{1}{2}} = (21{,}806.35/34{,}086{,}319)^{\frac{1}{2}} = 0.025293$

(iii) $t_{20,0.025} = 2.086$ (since we have $(n - 2)$ degrees of freedom)

and now, the limits for this confidence interval are: $b \pm t_{21,0.025} \, s_b$

or

$$0.381516 \pm 2.086 \times 0.025293$$

or the 95% confidence interval for the slope is from 0.3288 to 0.4343.

(d)   [From Section 3.4, *Inference about the Linear Regression Model*]

$$H_0: \quad \beta \leq 0$$
$$H_1: \quad \beta > 0$$

Decision Rule: Reject H_0 if $t_{calc} > t_{20,0.01}$

$t_{calc} = (b - 0)/s_b = (.381516 - 0)/0.025293 = 15.084$ while $t_{20,0.01} = 2.528$.

Since $t_{calc} = 15.084 > t_{20,0.01} = 2.528$ reject H_0, one can be quite certain that the population regression slope is positive.

(e)   [From Section 3.5, *Forecasting from the Fitted Linear Regression Model*]

If disposable income per household is \$12,600, then it is expected that retail sales per household,

$\hat{Y} = a + bX = 1{,}922.392 + 0.381516 \times 12{,}600 = 6{,}729.50$

(f)   [From Section 3.5, *Forecasting from the Fitted Linear Regression Model*]

The 95% prediction interval is

$$\hat{Y} \pm t_{n\text{-}2} \{[1 + 1/n + (X - \bar{X})^2/\Sigma(X_t - \bar{X})^2] \, s^2\}^{\frac{1}{2}}$$

$$6729.50 \pm 2.086 \{[1 + 1/22 + (12{,}600 - 10{,}799.05)^2/34{,}086{,}319]21{,}806.35\}^{\frac{1}{2}}$$

or from   \$6,400.81 to \$7,058.20.

This interval can be interpreted as saying we are 95% confident that if disposable income per household is \$12,600, then one can expect that retail sales per household for that year would be somewhere between \$6,400.81 and \$7,058.20. Since the data points are reasonably close to the estimated regression line (given the R^2 of 91.9%) and since the predicted point is among the observed data points (and hence fairly close to the middle of the data set) the interval is fairly narrow.

****

3.10 The accompanying table shows, for a period of 23 months, the rate of return (Y) on the stock of Vulcan Materials Corporation and a stock market index rate of return (X).
   (a)   Estimate by least squares the regression of Y on X, and interpret the slope of the sample regression line.
   (b)   Find and interpret the coefficient of determination for the fitted regression line.
   (c)   Find the sample correlation between the rate of return on the stock of Vulcan Materials and the rate of return on the market index.
   (d)   Find a 90% confidence interval for the slope of the population regression line.
   (e)   Test at the 1% level against a two-sided alternative the null hypothesis that the slope of the population regression line is one.
   (f)   Test at the 1% level against a two-sided alternative the null hypothesis that the intercept of the population regression line is zero, and interpret your findings.

(g) Find a point forecast for the rate of return on the stock of Vulcan Materials next month, if the rate of return on the market index is expected to be 0.04.

(h) Find and discuss the implications of a 95% prediction interval for the rate of return on the stock of Vulcan Materials next month if the rate of return on the market index is expected to be 0.04.

------- Answer to 3.10 --------

[From Section 3.3, *Fitting the Linear Regression Model*]

This exercise is best done on a spreadsheet, rather than on a statistics program. Working it on a spreadsheet forces the student to be responsible for the formulas. See this page for the accompanying spreadsheet.

(a) [From Section 3.3, *Fitting the Linear Regression Model*]

$$b = \sum_{t=1}^{n}(X_t - \bar{X})(Y_t - \bar{Y}) / \sum_{t=1}^{n}(X_t - \bar{X})^2 = 0.03922/0.05390 = 0.727616$$

$$a = \bar{Y} - b\bar{X} = 0.01644 - 1.050361 \times 0.00437 = 0.013259$$

	A	B	C	D (X-XBAR)*(Y-YBAR)	E (X-XBAR)²	F (Y-YBAR)²	G Y HAT	H e(t)²
1	t	X	Y					
3	1	-0.0763	0.0368	-0.00164	0.00651	0.00041	-0.0423	0.006250
4	2	0.0595	0.0142	-0.00012	0.00304	0.00001	0.0566	0.001794
5	3	-0.0026	0.1748	-0.00110	0.00005	0.02508	0.0114	0.026710
6	4	-0.0997	-0.1429	0.01658	0.01083	0.02539	-0.0593	0.006992
7	5	-0.0615	-0.0764	0.00612	0.00434	0.00862	-0.0315	0.002017
8	6	-0.0503	0.0376	-0.00116	0.00299	0.00045	-0.0233	0.003714
9	7	0.0746	0.1015	0.00597	0.00493	0.00724	0.0675	0.001153
10	8	0.0498	0.0855	0.00314	0.00206	0.00477	0.0495	0.001296
11	9	0.0428	0.0182	0.00007	0.00148	0.00000	0.0444	0.000687
12	10	-0.0157	-0.0833	0.00200	0.00040	0.00995	0.0018	0.007248
13	11	0.0522	0.0390	0.00108	0.00229	0.00051	0.0512	0.000150
14	12	0.0615	0.0500	0.00192	0.00326	0.00113	0.0580	0.000064
15	13	0.0493	0.0952	0.00354	0.00202	0.00620	0.0491	0.002122
16	14	0.0149	-0.0761	-0.00097	0.00011	0.00856	0.0241	0.010040
17	15	0.0440	0.0471	0.00122	0.00157	0.00094	0.0453	0.000003
18	16	0.0340	0.1236	0.00318	0.00088	0.01148	0.0380	0.007328
19	17	-0.0364	0.0050	0.00047	0.00166	0.00013	-0.0132	0.000332
20	18	0.0042	-0.0547	0.00001	0.00000	0.00506	0.0163	0.005043
21	19	-0.0406	-0.0158	0.00145	0.00202	0.00104	-0.0163	0.000000
22	20	0.0419	-0.0588	-0.00282	0.00141	0.00566	0.0437	0.010516
23	21	-0.0057	0.0682	-0.00052	0.00010	0.00268	0.0091	0.003491
24	22	-0.0396	0.0000	0.00072	0.00193	0.00027	-0.0156	0.000242
25	23	0.0002	-0.0106	0.00011	0.00002	0.00073	0.0134	0.000576
27	SUM	0.10050	0.37810	0.03922	0.05390	0.12631		0.09777
28	AVG	0.00437	0.01644					

Graph Accompanying Exercise 3.10

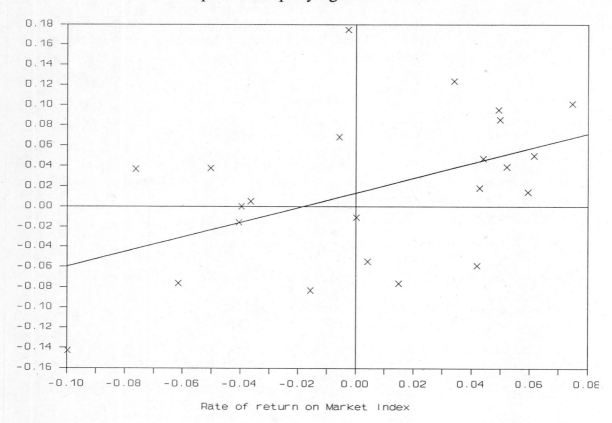

Rate of return on Market Index

(b) [From Section 3.3, subsection *Sums of Squares Decomposition and the Coefficient of Determination*]

$$R^2 = [\sum_{t=1}^{n}(X_t - \bar{X})(Y_t - \bar{Y})]^2 \, / \, \sum_{t=1}^{n}(X_t - \bar{X})^2 \sum_{t=1}^{n}(Y_t - \bar{Y})^2$$

$$= 0.03922^2/(0.05390 \times 0.12631) = 0.225943$$

Hence 22.6% of the variability in the rate of return of the stock of Vulcan Materials is explained by its linear relationship with the stock market index rate of return, in this sample.

(c) [From Section 3.1, *Correlation*]

$$r = [\sum_{t=1}^{n}(X_t - \bar{X})(Y_t - \bar{Y})] \, / \, [\sum_{t=1}^{n}(X_t - \bar{X})^2 \sum_{t=1}^{n}(Y_t - \bar{Y})^2]^{1/2}$$

$$= 0.03922/(0.05390 \times 0.12631)^{1/2} = 0.475335$$

(d)   [From Section 3.4, *Inference about the Linear Regression Model*]

Before the confidence interval for the population slope can be calculated, we need several quantities:

(i) $s^2 = \Sigma e_t^2/(n-2) = 0.09777/21 = 0.004656$

(ii) $s_b = (s^2/\Sigma(X_t - \bar{X})^2)^{1/2} = (0.004656/0.05390)^{1/2} = 0.293886$

(iii) $t_{21,0.05} = 1.721$ (since we have $(n-2)$ degrees of freedom)

and now, the limits for this confidence interval are: $b \pm t_{21,0.025}\, s_b$
or 0.727616 ± 1.721×0.293886

or the 95% confidence interval for the slope is from 0.2218 to 1.2334.

(e)   [From Section 3.4, *Inference about the Linear Regression Model*]

$$H_0: \beta = 1$$
$$H_1: \beta \neq 1$$

Decision Rule: Reject H_0 if $|t_{calc}| > t_{21,0.005}$

$t_{calc} = (b - 1)/s_b = (0.727616 - 1)/0.293886 = -0.927$ while $t_{21,0.005} = 2.831$.

Since $t_{calc} = -0.927 < t_{21,0.005} = 2.831$ do not reject H_0, there is not enough statistical evidence to suggest that β is not equal to one.

(f)   [From Section 3.4, *Inference about the Linear Regression Model*]

$$H_0: \alpha = 0$$
$$H_1: \alpha \neq 0$$

Decision Rule: Reject H_0 if $|t_{calc}| > t_{21,0.005}$

$s_a = \{s^2[1/n + \bar{X}^2/\Sigma(X_t-\bar{X})^2]\}^{1/2} = \{.004656(1/23 + 0.00437^2/0.05390)\}^2 = 0.0142852$

$t_{calc} = (a - 0)/s_a = 0.013259/0.0142852 = 0.928$ while $t_{21,0.005} = 2.831$.

Since $|t_{calc}| = 0.928 < t_{21,0.005} = 2.831$ do not reject the null hypothesis, there is not enough statistical evidence to suggest that α is not equal to zero.

(g)   [From Section 3.5, *Forecasting from the Fitted Linear Regression Model*]

If the rate of return on the market index is 0.04, then the rate of return on the stock of Vulcan Materials,

$$\hat{Y} = a + bX = 0.013259 + 0.727616\times0.04 = 0.0423644$$

(h)   [From Section 3.5, *Forecasting from the Fitted Linear Regression Model*]

The 95% prediction interval is

$$\hat{Y} \pm t_{n-2} \{[1 + 1/n + (X - \bar{X})^2/\Sigma(X_t - \bar{X})^2]\, s^2\}^{\frac{1}{2}}$$

$$0.0423644 \pm 2.080 \{[1 + 1/23 + (0.04 - 0.00437)^2/0.05390]0.004656\}^{\frac{1}{2}}$$

or from   −0.104 to 0.189.

Since this prediction interval for this rate of return is anywhere from a negative number to a positive number, one cannot be certain of a positive rate of return. Further, the interval is wide resulting from the fact that the data is not closely clustered around the sample regression line − see the accompanying graph, and note that the measure for the closeness of the association between the two variables, R^2 is only 22.6%.

****

Chapter 4

THE MULTIPLE REGRESSION MODEL

Contents of Chapter 4

Answers to questions at end of chapter.

4.1 The accompanying table shows 25 annual observations on percentage profit margin (Y), net revenues per deposit dollar (X_1), and number of offices (X_2) for U.S. savings and loan associations. Assume a model of the form

$$Y_t = \alpha + \beta_1 X_{1t} + \beta_2 X_{2t} + \epsilon_t$$

where ϵ_t is a random error term

(a) Fit by least squares the multiple regression model, and interpret the parameter estimates.
(b) Find and interpret the coefficient of determination.
(c) Find a 95% confidence interval for the parameter β_1.
(d) Test at the 5% significance level the null hypothesis

$$H_0: \ \beta_2 = 0$$

against the alternative hypothesis

$$H_1: \ \beta_2 < 0$$

(e) Test at the 1% significance level the null hypothesis

$$H_0: \ \beta_1 = \beta_2 = 0$$

(f) Test at the 5% significance level the null hypothesis that the error terms are not correlated with one another, against the alternative they follow a first order autoregressive process with positive parameter.
(g) It is expected that, in the next two years, the independent variables will take the values

$$X_{1,26} = 4.70 \ ; \ X_{1,27} = 4.80 \ ; \ X_{2,26} = 9,350 \ ; \ X_{2,27} = 9,400$$

Find point forecasts of percentage profit margins for savings and loan associations in these two years.

------- Answer to 4.1 --------

(a)   LOTUS 123 Spreadsheet: Used /Data Regression

	A	B	C	D	E	F	G	H	I	J
1	t	Y	X1	X2	Yhat	e(t)²	(Y-Ybar)²	(Yhat-Ybar)²	(e(t)-e(t-1))²	
2	1	0.75	3.92	7298	0.6765	0.0054	0.0057	0.0000		
3	2	0.71	3.61	6855	0.7133	0.0000	0.0013	0.0015	0.0059	
4	3	0.66	3.32	6636	0.6991	0.0015	0.0002	0.0006	0.0013	
5	4	0.61	3.07	6506	0.6722	0.0039	0.0041	0.0000	0.0005	
6	5	0.70	3.06	6450	0.6838	0.0003	0.0007	0.0001	0.0062	
7	6	0.72	3.11	6402	0.7076	0.0002	0.0021	0.0011	0.0000	
8	7	0.77	3.21	6368	0.7398	0.0009	0.0091	0.0043	0.0003	
9	8	0.74	3.26	6340	0.7586	0.0003	0.0043	0.0071	0.0024	
10	9	0.90	3.42	6349	0.7943	0.0112	0.0509	0.0144	0.0154	
11	10	0.82	3.42	6352	0.7936	0.0007	0.0212	0.0142	0.0063	
12	11	0.75	3.45	6361	0.7984	0.0023	0.0057	0.0154	0.0056	
13	12	0.77	3.58	6369	0.8273	0.0033	0.0091	0.0234	0.0001	
14	13	0.78	3.66	6546	0.8022	0.0005	0.0112	0.0163	0.0012	
15	14	0.84	3.78	6672	0.7992	0.0017	0.0274	0.0156	0.0040	
16	15	0.79	3.82	6890	0.7544	0.0013	0.0134	0.0064	0.0000	
17	16	0.70	3.97	7115	0.7340	0.0012	0.0007	0.0035	0.0048	
18	17	0.68	4.07	7327	0.7049	0.0006	0.0000	0.0009	0.0001	
19	18	0.72	4.25	7546	0.6930	0.0007	0.0021	0.0003	0.0027	
20	19	0.55	4.41	7931	0.6351	0.0072	0.0155	0.0015	0.0126	
21	20	0.63	4.49	8097	0.6127	0.0003	0.0020	0.0038	0.0105	
22	21	0.56	4.70	8468	0.5701	0.0001	0.0131	0.0109	0.0008	
23	22	0.41	4.58	8717	0.4796	0.0048	0.0699	0.0379	0.0035	
24	23	0.51	4.69	8991	0.4375	0.0053	0.0270	0.0561	0.0202	
25	24	0.47	4.71	9179	0.3954	0.0056	0.0418	0.0778	0.0000	
26	25	0.32	4.78	9318	0.3774	0.0033	0.1256	0.0882	0.0174	
27										
28	SUM					0.0625	0.4640	0.4015	0.1218	
29	AVG	0.674				SSE	SST	SSR	Numerator	
30									of Durbin-Watson	

```
                          Regression Output:
            Constant                     1.5644967711
            Std Err of Y Est             0.0533022172
            R Squared                    0.8652960677
            No. of Observations                    25
            Degrees of Freedom                     22

            X Coefficient(s)0.2371974  -0.000249079
            Std Err of Coef.0.0555593   0.0000320485
            t-ratios        4.2692616  -7.771949195

            R Squared       0.8652960   0.8652960677

            F calc          70.660570

            d                1.9483048
```

MINITAB Output (User input is underlined)

```
MTB > read '\subdir\ch04q01.prn' c1 c2 c3
      25 ROWS READ
  ROW     C1      C2      C3

    1    0.75    3.92    7298
    2    0.71    3.61    6855
    3    0.66    3.32    6636
    4    0.61    3.07    6506
    .    .    .

MTB > name c1 'Y', c2 'X1', c3 'X2'
MTB >
MTB > regress c1 2 c2 c3;
SUBC> predict 4.70 9350;
SUBC> predict 4.80 9400;
SUBC> dw.
```

The regression equation is
Y = 1.56 + 0.237 X1 -0.000249 X2

```
Predictor        Coef         Stdev      t-ratio
Constant       1.56450       0.07940      19.70
X1             0.23720       0.05556       4.27
X2            -0.00024908   0.00003205    -7.77


s = 0.05330     R-sq = 86.5%     R-sq(adj) = 85.3%
```

Analysis of Variance

```
SOURCE        DF          SS          MS
Regression     2       0.40151     0.20076
Error         22       0.06250     0.00284
Total         24       0.46402


SOURCE        DF       SEQ SS
X1             1       0.22990
X2             1       0.17161
```

Unusual Observations

```
Obs.     X1          Y      Fit  Stdev.Fit   Residual    St.Resid
  9     3.42     0.9000   0.7943    0.0147     0.1057       2.06R
```

R denotes an obs. with a large st. resid.

Durbin-Watson statistic = 1.95

```
    Fit   Stdev.Fit        95% C.I.            95% P.I.
 0.3504     0.0301   ( 0.2879, 0.4129)   ( 0.2234, 0.4775)

 0.3617     0.0286   ( 0.3024, 0.4210)   ( 0.2363, 0.4871)
```

The estimated multiple regression model is:

$$Y_t = 1.56450 + 0.23720\,X_{1t} - 0.000249\,X_{2t}$$

Interpretation of parameter estimates:

If net revenues per deposit dollar (X_{1t}) increases by one unit, then percentage profit margin (Y_t) will increase by 0.23720 percentage points, when the number of offices is fixed.

If the number of offices (X_{2t}) increases by one, then percentage profit margin (Y_t) will decrease by 0.000249 percentage points, when net revenues are fixed.

(b) From the outputs above, the coefficient of determination (R^2) is 86.5%. This means that the above estimated linear equation explains 86.5% of the variation of percentage profit margin.

(c) The 95% confidence interval for β_1 is

$$b_1 \pm t_{n-k-1,0.025}\, s_{\beta 1} = 0.23720 \pm 2.074 \times 0.05556 = 0.12197 \text{ to } 0.35243$$

since the appropriate t has $n - k - 1 = 25 - 2 - 1 = 22$ degrees of freedom, and $t_{22,0.025} = 2.074$.

(d) H_0: $\beta_2 \geq 0$ (there is a not a negative relationship between the number of offices, X_{2t}, and percentage profit margin, Y_t)
    H_1: $\beta_2 < 0$ (there is a negative relationship between the number of offices, X_{2t}, and percentage profit margin, Y_t)

Decision Rule: Reject H_0 if $t_{calc} < -t_{n-k-1}$

$$t_{calc} = (b_2 - \beta_{2,0})/s_{\beta 2}$$
$$= (-0.000249 - 0)/0.0003205 = -7.77 \text{ (see the above computer results also)}$$

Since $t_{calc} = -7.77 < -t_{n-k-1} = -t_{22} = -2.074$ reject H_0, β_2 is not positive or zero.

(e) H_0: $\beta_1 = \beta_2 = 0$

    H_1: at least one $\beta_i \neq 0$

Decision Rule: Reject H_0 if $F_{calc} > F_{k,n-k-1,0.01}$

$$F_{calc} = (SSR/K) / (SSE/(n - K - 1)) = (0.40151/2) / (0.06250/22) = 70.66$$

Since $F_{calc} = 70.66 > F_{k,n-k-1,0.01} = F_{2,22,0.01} = 5.72$, reject the null hypothesis that these two variables explain nothing of the variation in the dependent variable.

(f) H_0: $\rho \leq 0$

       H_1: $\rho > 0$

       Decision Rule:
       (i)   Reject H_0 if $d < d_{L,0.05}$
       (ii)   One does not have enough statistical information to reject H_0 if $d > d_{U,0.05}$
       (iii) The Durbin-Watson test is inconclusive if $d_{L,0.05} < d < d_{U,0.05}$

       $d = \Sigma(e_t - e_{t-1})^2 / \Sigma e_t^2 = 0.1218/0.0625 = 1.95$ (see Lotus 123 spreadsheet above)

       $d_{L,0.05} = 1.21$ and $d_{U,0.05} = 1.55$ ($n=25$, $K=2$) from the Appendix TABLE A.5.

       Since $d = 1.95 > d_{U,0.05} = 1.55$, one does not have enough statistical information to
       reject the null hypothesis that there is not positive autocorrelation. Thus, one normally
       says that such a regression does not have positively autocorrelated errors.

(g) $Y_{26} = 1.56450 + 0.23720\, X_{1,26} - 0.000249\, X_{2,26}$

            $= 1.56450 + 0.23720 \times 4.70 - 0.000249 \times 9350 = 0.3504$

       $Y_{27} = 1.56450 + 0.23720\, X_{1,27} - 0.000249\, X_{2,27}$

            $= 1.56450 + 0.23720 \times 4.80 - 0.000249 \times 9400 = 0.3617$

                    ****

4.2   (a)   When an important independent variable is omitted from a regression model, quite misleading results can emerge. This is the problem of specification bias. Using the data of Exercise 4.1, fit by least squares the simple linear regression of Y on X_1, and comment on the results.

(b)   If an important independent variable is omitted from a regression model, this can be reflected in strongly autocorrelated error terms. Comment on the value of the Durbin-Watson test statistic from the fitted regression in part(a), and on the implications of this result.

------- Answer to 4.2 --------

(a)   Below is the MINITAB output of the regression Y_t on X_{1t}. The data is from Exercise 4.1 above, and this output (or PC session) is a continuation of the MINITAB work in the exercise above. Again user input is underlined.

```
MTB >
MTB > regress c1 1 c2;
SUBC> dw.

The regression equation is
Y = 1.33 - 0.169 X1

Predictor        Coef        Stdev       t-ratio
Constant       1.3262       0.1386         9.57
X1            -0.16913      0.03559        -4.75

s = 0.1009      R-sq = 49.5%      R-sq(adj) = 47.4%

Analysis of Variance

SOURCE        DF          SS           MS
Regression    1        0.22990      0.22990
Error        23        0.23412      0.01018
Total        24        0.46402

Durbin-Watson statistic = 0.85
```

The results of this regression are in sharp contrast to the results in exercise 4.1. The R^2 dropped from 86.5% to 49.5%. The coefficient of X_{1t} was positive and significant in the exercise 4.1, and now it is significant and negative.

(b)   A test for positive autocorrelation on the residuals of this regression yield different results.

$d_{L,0.05} = 1.29$, $d_{U,0.05} = 1.45$ ($n=25$, $K=1$)

Since $d = 0.85 < d_{L,0.05} = 1.29$, reject the null hypothesis of non-positive autocorrelation, and accept the alternative of positive autocorrelated errors.

The presence of significant positive autocorrelation in the regression of Y_t on X_{1t}, suggests that one or more important variables have been omitted from this equation. (These results are caused by the fact the X_{1t} and X_{2t} are highly correlated leading to multicollinearity in the full regression).

****

4.3   Refer to the data of Table 4.1, and to the fitted regression (4.3.1). It is expected that, in
       the next two years, the independent variables will take the values

$X_{1,21} = 3.8$; $X_{2,21} = 0.700$; $X_{3,21} = 1.670$

$X_{1,22} = 3.8$; $X_{2,22} = 0.700$; $X_{3,22} = 1.670$

Find point forecasts of days of incapacity due to sickness per person for these two years.

------- Answer to 4.3 --------

In the text equation (4.3.1) is

$\log(\hat{Y}) = 2.714 - 0.030 \log X_1 + 0.316 \log X_2 + 0.401 \log X_3$

Note that these logs are natural logs.

Thus $\hat{Y}_{21} = \exp(2.714 - 0.030 \ln X_{1,21} + 0.316 \ln X_{2,21} + 0.401 \ln X_{3,21}$

or $\hat{Y}_{21} = \exp(2.714 - 0.030 \ln(3.8) + 0.316 \ln(0.700) + 0.401 \ln(1.670) = 11.094$

Similarly $\hat{Y}_{22} = \exp(2.714 - 0.030 \ln X_{1,22} + 0.316 \ln X_{2,22} + 0.401 \ln X_{3,22}$

or $\hat{Y}_{22} = \exp(2.714 - 0.030 \ln(4.0) + 0.316 \ln(0.690) + 0.401 \ln(1.680) = 10.901$

****

4.4   Sometimes, when the estimated value of a regression parameter is small in magnitude, compared with the estimated standard error, an analyst will drop the corresponding variable from the regression, and re-estimate the model. Following inspection of (4.3.1), estimate the regression of $\log Y$ on $\log X_2$ and $\log X_3$ and, discuss the results. Using the same values for future values of the independent variables as in Exercise 4.3. obtain from the new fitted model point forecasts of days of incapacity due to sickness per person for the next two years. Compare these with the forecasts of Exercise 4.3.

------- Answer to 4.4 --------

Variable	Regression 1	2	3
Constant	2.71448	2.69818	2.85039
$Ln(X_1)$	-0.03012		
(p value)	(0.4685)		
$Ln(X_2)$	0.31604	0.29818	0.37631
(p value)	(0.0000)	(0.0000)	(0.0000)
$Ln(X_3)$	0.40117	0.32907	
(p value)	(0.0592)	(0.0693)	
R squared	0.91961	0.91684	0.89845
d	1.734	1.611	1.751
d_L	1.00	1.10	1.20
d_U	1.68	1.54	1.41
Y_{21}	15.9152	15.8090	15.1223
Y_{22}	15.8565	15.7723	15.0406

Exhibit to accompany answer to Exercise 4.4

In the box accompanying this answer, are the results of the regression with all three independent variables, with the two variables requested in this exercise, and (for further comparison) with just the log of X_2. The last regression was done for comparitive purposes, as the variable X_3 is not significant at the 5% level in regression 2.

The forecasts of the dependent variable for the next two periods for the first two regressions are very close. The corresponding forecasts for the third regression are slightly different from those of the first two regressions. This is somewhat disconcerting since the third regression is not that different from the other two. The R^2 dropped only slightly from regressions two to three. The Durbin-Watson statistic shows no significant autocorrelation in any – but this is especially important in the third, for (given exercise 4.2) if $\ln(X_3)$ were quite important the Durbin-Watson statistic could show significant autocorrelation (a piece of information we cannot use since the data does not support it).

****

4.5   Refer to the data of Table 4.3, and to the model (4.4.9) fitted to these data. It is expected that, in the next two quarters, the independent variables will take the values

$$X_{1,35} = 106.0 \; ; \; X_{1,36} = 105.0 \; ; \; X_{2,36} = 0.9400$$

Obtain point forecasts of Japanese quantity of imports in these two quarters.

------- Answer to 4.5 --------

From the model (4.4.9) or from the printout in Exhibit 4.2, the estimated regression equation is

$$\log(\hat{Y}_t) = 0.50434 + 0.26071 \log X_{1t} - 0.10781 \log X_{2t} + 0.62594 \log Y_{t-1}$$

Note that these logs are natural logs.

$$\hat{Y}_{35} = \exp(0.50434 + 0.26071 \log X_{1,35} - 0.10781 \log X_{2,35} + 0.62594 \log Y_{34})$$

$$= \exp[0.50434 + 0.26071 \log(106.0) - 0.10781 \log(0.90) + 0.62594 \log(108.2)]$$

$$= 105.995$$

Similarly,

$$\hat{Y}_{36} = \exp(0.50434 + 0.26071 \log X_{1,36} - 0.10781 \log X_{2,36} + 0.62594 \log \hat{Y}_{35})$$

$$= \exp[0.50434 + 0.26071 \log(105.0) - 0.10781 \log(0.94) + 0.62594 \log(105.995)]$$

$$= 103.892$$

****

4.6 (a) In Section 4.4 we considered separately the possibilities of adaptive expectations and partial adjustment models. It is entirely possible that these phenomena could occur jointly. Let Y_t denote the actual value of a dependent variable, and X_t the actual value of an independent variable, at time t. Denote by Y_t^* the desired value for the dependent variable at time t, and by X_t^* the expectation per period of future values of the independent variable, formed at time t. Assume that the desired level of the dependent variable is related to the expected value of the independent variable by

$$Y_t^* = \delta + \lambda X_t^* \tag{1}$$

that expectations of the independent variable are formed through

$$X_t^* = (1 - \gamma)X_t + \gamma X_{t-1}^* \tag{2}$$

and that the partial adjustment mechanism for the dependent variable

$$Y_t - Y_{t-1} = (1 - \omega)(Y_t^* - Y_{t-1}) + u_t \tag{3}$$

holds. In these expressions, δ, λ, γ, and ω are fixed parameters, and u_t is a random error term with mean zero. Show that these three equations imply

$$Y_t = \alpha + \beta X_t + \gamma_1 Y_{t-1} + \gamma_2 Y_{t-2} + \epsilon_t$$

where $\alpha = \delta(1 - \omega)(1 - \gamma)$; $\beta = \lambda(1 - \omega)(1 - \gamma)$; $\gamma_1 = (\omega + \gamma)$; $\gamma_2 = -\omega\gamma$

and

$$\epsilon_t = u_t - \gamma u_{t-1}$$

(b) Following from this discussion of part (a), fit to the data of Table 4.3 the model

$$\log Y_t = \alpha + \beta_1 X_{1t} + \beta_2 X_{2t} + \gamma_1 Y_{t-1} + \gamma_2 Y_{t-2} + \epsilon_t$$

and discuss the results.

------- Answer to 4.6 --------

(a) Substituting the value for Y_t^* from equation [1] into equation [3],

$$Y_t - Y_{t-1} = (1 - \omega)(\delta + \lambda X_t^* - Y_{t-1}) - u_t$$

$$Y_t - Y_{t-1} = (1 - \omega)\delta + (1 - \omega)\lambda X_t^* - (1 - \omega)Y_{t-1} + u_t$$

From this equation, subtract γ times the once lagged version of itself

$$(Y_t - Y_{t-1}) - \gamma(Y_{t-1} - Y_{t-2}) = (1 - \gamma)(1 - \omega)\delta - (1 - \omega)Y_{t-1} + \gamma(1 - \omega)Y_{t-2}$$
$$+ (1 - \omega)\lambda X_t^* - (1 - \omega)\gamma\lambda X_{t-1}^* + u_t - \gamma u_{t-1}$$

$$Y_t = (1 - \gamma)(1 - \omega)\delta + (\gamma + \omega)Y_{t-1} - \omega\gamma Y_{t-2} + (1 - \omega)\lambda(X_t^* - \gamma X_{t-1}^*) + u_t - \gamma u_{t-1}$$

From equation [2], $X_t^* - \gamma X_{t-1}^* = (1 - \gamma)X_t$

and so, after substitution, the above equation becomes,

$$Y_t = (1 - \gamma)(1 - \omega)\delta + (\gamma + \omega)Y_{t-1} - \omega\gamma Y_{t-2} + (1 - \omega)(1 - \gamma)\lambda X_t + u_t - \gamma u_{t-1}$$

(b)   The regression results from the requested regression are shown below. The output is
from an SPSS session in which Cochrane-Orcutt estimates were requested. We are
spared some anguish here as the autocorrelation coefficient (γ in this case) is quite
insignificantly different from zero. That is the calculated t value is (rho divided by its
standard error) = 0.03675/0.19232 which is clearly much less than one (which is less than
the appropriate critical value - whatever it is). Furthermore several of the variables have
insignificant coefficients. See the last column, the one headed by "SIG T". This column
actually displays the p values. Whenever a p value is above α, say 5%, the estimated
coefficient is insignificantly different from zero. If everything were significant (or close)
we would have to worry about how these coefficients relate to those in the adaptive
expectations and partial adjustment models <u>with two X variables</u> − part (a) of the
exercise only has one, and the extension seems far from trivial.

```
FINAL PARAMETERS:

Estimate of Autocorrelation Coefficient

Rho                       .03675093
Standard Error of Rho     .19232008
Mean Squared Error        .00136403

Cochrane-Orcutt Estimates

Multple R                 .83099672
R-Squared                 .69055555
Adjusted R-Squared        .63104701
Standard Error            .04098615
Durbin-Watson            1.7480915

              Analysis of Variance:

             DF    Sum of Squares      Mean Square
Regression    4        .09746835         .02436709
Residuals    26        .04367649         .00167986

           Variables in the Equation:

                    B         SEB        BETA           T        SIG T
LNPRC        .22370039   .12118547    .30010331   1.8459341    .07631808
LNRGNP      -.13622772   .04969175   -.38293235  -2.7414555    .01091731
LNIMP1       .30952220   .19401612    .31022633   1.5953427    .12272067
LNIMP2       .41036315   .19282697    .44753206   2.1281419    .04296821
CONSTANT     .24171750   .57570441        .         .4198639    .67803425

           *****************************
```

4.7   In Section 4.6, we discuss separately the forecasting of future values of a dependent variable from models with a lagged dependent variable, and from models with first order autoregressive errors. From this discussion, it is possible to see how point forecasts of a dependent variable should be derived from a model with both lagged dependent variable and first order autoregressive errors. Consider the model

$$Y_t = \alpha + \beta_1 X_{1t} + \ldots + \beta_k X_{kt} + \gamma Y_{t-1} + \epsilon_t \quad ; \quad \epsilon_t = \rho \epsilon_{t-1} + a_t$$

where the errors a_t have mean zero, constant variance, and are uncorrelated with one another. Assuming that suitable estimates of the parameters α, β_1, . . ., β_k, γ, ρ are available, explain how you would obtain conditional point forecasts of future values of the dependent variable.

------- Answer to 4.7 --------

From the equation (above) subtract ρ times the first of the equation, and rearrange terms to get

$$Y_t = \alpha(1 - \rho) + \beta_1(X_{1t} - \rho X_{1,t-1}) + \ldots + \beta_k(X_{kt} - \rho X_{k,t-1}) + (\gamma + \rho)Y_{t-1} - \gamma\rho Y_{t-2} + a_t$$

Thus,

$$\hat{Y}_{n+1} = \alpha(1 - \rho) + \beta_1(X_{1,n+1} - \rho X_{1n}) + \ldots + \beta_k(X_{k,n+1} - \rho X_{kn}) + (\gamma + \rho)Y_n - \gamma\rho Y_{n-1}$$

and so on, where these forecasts are conditional on the values entered for the $X_{i,n+1}$. The value of $\hat{Y}_{n+1}$ is then used (on the right-hand-side of the equation) to predict $\hat{Y}_{n+2}$.

****

4.8   (a)   The linear trend model $Y_t = \alpha + \beta t + \epsilon_t$

is to be fitted by least squares to the time series $Y_1, Y_2, \ldots, Y_n$. Show that the least squares estimates of the parameters β and α are, respectively,

$$b = 12 \, \Sigma \, tY_t \, / \, [n(n2 - 1)] \; - \; 6\bar{Y}/(n - 1)$$

where $\bar{Y}$ is the sample mean of the Y_t, and

$$a = \bar{Y} - b \, (n + 1)/2$$

(b)   The exponential trend model is to be fitted in the form

$$\log Y_t = \alpha + \beta t + \epsilon_t$$

to the time series $Y_1, Y_2, \ldots, Y_n$. Find expressions for the least squares estimates of β and α.

------- Answer to 4.8 --------

(a)   From chapter 3.3 $b = \Sigma(X_t - \bar{X})(Y_t - \bar{Y}) \, / \, \Sigma(X_t - \bar{X})^2$, but since X_t is now replaced by t,

$$b = \Sigma(t - \bar{t})(Y_t - \bar{Y}) \, / \, \Sigma(t - \bar{t})^2$$

Since it can easily be shown that $\Sigma t = \tfrac{1}{2}n(n + 1)$ and that $\bar{t} \, \Sigma Y = n\bar{t}\bar{Y}$,   the numerator becomes

$$\Sigma(t - \bar{t})(Y_t - \bar{Y}) = \Sigma tY - \bar{Y}\Sigma t - \bar{t}\,\Sigma Y + n\bar{t}\bar{Y} = \Sigma tY - \bar{Y}\Sigma t = \Sigma tY - \tfrac{1}{2}\bar{Y}n(n + 1)$$

Furthermore, the denominator $\Sigma(t - \bar{t})^2 = n(n^2 - 1)/12$.

This follows since $\Sigma t^2 = n(n+1)(2n+1)/6$

Thus

$$b = \{\Sigma tY - \tfrac{1}{2}\bar{Y}n(n + 1)\} \, / \, \{n(n^2 - 1)/12\} = 12 \, \Sigma \, tY_t \, / \, [n(n2 - 1)] \; - \; 6\bar{Y}/(n - 1).$$

In chapter 3.3, $a = \bar{Y} - b\bar{X} = \bar{Y} - b\bar{t} = \bar{Y} - \tfrac{1}{2}(n + 1)b$

(b)   The only difference between this case and the one above, is the the dependent variable is logged -- that is, Y_t is replaced by $(\log Y_t)$. So the formula for b above, becomes

$$b = 12 \, \Sigma \, (t \log Y_t) \, / \, [n(n2 - 1)] \; - \; 6\Sigma(\log Y_t)/[n(n - 1)]$$

$$b = [12/n(n2 - 1)] \log(\textstyle\prod_t Y_t^t) \; - \; [6/n(n - 1)] \log(\textstyle\prod_t Y_t)$$

$$b = \log[\textstyle\prod_t (Y_t^A - Y_t^B)] \quad \text{where} \quad A = 12t/n(n2 - 1) \;\text{and}\; B = 6/n(n - 1)$$

$$b = \log[\textstyle\prod_t (Y_t^C)]$$

where $C = 12t/n(n2 - 1) - 6/n(n - 1) = 6(2t - n - 1)/[n(n^2 - 1)]$

Also $a = \log(\textstyle\prod_t Y_t) - b \, (n + 1)/2$

****

4.9 The multiple regression model (4.1.2), with K independent variables, is estimated by least squares from a sample of n observations. Let R^2 be the coefficient of determination and $\bar{R}^2$ the corrected coefficient of determination.

(a) Show that $R^2 = 1 - [(n - K - 1)/(n - 1)] (1 - \bar{R}^2)$

(b) Show that $\bar{R}^2 = 1 - [(n - 1)/(n - K - 1)] (1 - R^2)$

(c) Show that the statistic (4.3.3) for testing the null hypothesis that all of the partial regression coefficients are zero can be written

$$F = [(n - K - 1)/K] [\bar{R}^2/(1 - \bar{R}^2)] + 1/(1 - \bar{R}^2)$$

------- Answer to 4.9 --------

(a) We have that $R^2 = SSR/SST = 1 - SSE/SST$ [1]

and $\bar{R}^2 = 1 - [SSE/(n - k - 1)] / [SST/(n - 1)]$ [2]

From equation [1] we have that $SSE/SST = 1 - R^2$

and so equation [2] becomes $\bar{R}^2 = 1 - [SSE/SST] [(n - 1)/(n - k - 1)]$

or $\bar{R}^2 (n - k - 1)/(n - 1) = (n - k - 1)/(n - 1) - SSE/SST$

or, by using the implication of [1] above

$$\bar{R}^2 (n - k - 1)/(n - 1) = (n - k - 1)/(n - 1) - (1 - R^2)$$ [3]

Re-arranging equation [3] yields

$$R^2 = 1 + \bar{R}^2 (n - k - 1)/(n - 1) - (n - k - 1)/(n - 1)$$

$$R^2 = 1 - (1 - \bar{R}^2)(n - k - 1)/(n - 1)$$ ....QED for (a)

(b) Re-arranging equation [3] so that $\bar{R}^2$ is on the left-hand-side, yields

$$\bar{R}^2 = 1 - (1 - R^2)(n - 1)/(n - k - 1)$$ ....QED for (b)

(c)   The proof of this is not straight forward. If one works forward from the formula for F by replacing the values of R^2 by appropriate expressions involving $\bar{R}^2$, one finds another (also correct) formula for F involving $\bar{R}^2$ instead of R^2. Let us show this first so that no-one need try it themselves.

From equation (4.3.3) of the text, $F = [(n - k - 1) R^2] / [k (1 - R^2)]$

From part (a) above we have $R^2 = 1 - (1 - \bar{R}^2)(n - k - 1)/(n - 1)$

This implies that $1 - R^2 = (1 - \bar{R}^2)(n - k - 1)/(n - 1)$

Dividing the latter by the former one gets

$$R^2/(1 - R^2) = (n - 1) / [(n - k - 1)(1 - \bar{R}^2)] - 1$$

Multiplying both sides by $(n - k - 1)/k$, leaves the left-hand-side equal to F

$$F = [(n - k - 1)/k] R^2/(1 - R^2)$$

$$= [(n - 1)/k] [1/(1 - \bar{R}^2)] - (n - k - 1)/k \qquad [1]$$

As mentioned above, although this expression is also a formula for F in terms of $\bar{R}^2$, it is not the one asked for, and furthermore is not very helpful in finding the other formula. We will now attack the problem in another way -- perhaps the way it was first discovered. We will let the new formula for F (ie., the one involving $\bar{R}^2$) be a linear transformation of the term

$[(n - k - 1)/k] \bar{R}^2/(1 - \bar{R}^2)$ which is like the formula for F except it has $\bar{R}^2$ instead of R^2.

Thus, let $[(n - k - 1)/k] R^2/(1 - R^2) = \mathbf{A} [(n - k - 1)/k] \bar{R}^2/(1 - \bar{R}^2) + \mathbf{B}$ [2]

where, to prove our case, we must prove that $\mathbf{A} = 1$, and $\mathbf{B} = 1/(1 - \bar{R}^2)$.

Using equation [1] above, we can replace the LHS of equation [2], so that no terms include R^2.

$[(n - 1)/k] [1/(1 - \bar{R}^2)] - (n - k - 1)/k = \mathbf{A} [(n - k - 1)/k] \bar{R}^2/(1 - \bar{R}^2) + \mathbf{B}$

Multiply both sides by $k (1 - \bar{R}^2)$

$$(n - 1) - (n - k - 1) (1 - \bar{R}^2) = \mathbf{A} (n - k - 1) \bar{R}^2 + \mathbf{B} k(1 - \bar{R}^2)$$

$$n - 1 - n + k + 1 + n\bar{R}^2 - k\bar{R}^2 - \bar{R}^2 = \mathbf{A}n\bar{R}^2 - \mathbf{A}k\bar{R}^2 - \mathbf{A}\bar{R}^2 + \mathbf{B}k - \mathbf{B}k\bar{R}^2$$

By cancelling out, and then collecting terms, one gets

$$\bar{R}^2(n - k - 1) + k = \mathbf{A}\bar{R}^2(n - k - 1) + \mathbf{B}k(1 - \bar{R}^2)$$

from which it is clear that $\mathbf{A}$ must equal 1, and $\mathbf{B}$ must equal $1/(1 - \bar{R}^2)$.

****

4.10 The following regression was fitted by ordinary least squares to 30 annual observations on time series data

$$\log \hat{Y}_t = 1.31 - 0.27 \log X_{1t} + 0.53 \log X_{2t} - 0.82 \log X_{3t} \quad ; \quad \bar{R}^2 = 0.615 \quad ; \quad d = 0.496$$
$$\qquad\qquad\qquad (0.17) \qquad\qquad (0.21) \qquad\qquad (0.30)$$

where Y_t = Number of business failures
$\quad\quad\;\; X_{1t}$ = Volume of industrial production
$\quad\quad\;\; X_{2t}$ = Short term interest rate
$\quad\quad\;\; X_{3t}$ = Value of new business orders placed

Figures in brackets below parameter estimates are the corresponding estimated standard errors

(a) Interpret, in the context of the assumed model, the estimated parameter on $\log X_{3t}$.
(b) Interpret the corrected coefficient of determination, $\bar{R}^2$.
(c) Briefly explain why $\bar{R}^2$ might be preferred to for purposes of interpretation.
(d) What null hypothesis can be tested through the Durbin-Watson statistic? Carry out this test for the present problem, using a 1% significant level.
(e) Given your findings in (d), what are the consequences of proceeding with the ordinary least squares-estimated model? Explain what you would do next.
(f) Estimate the correlation between adjacent error terms in this model

------- Answer to 4.10 --------

(a) If X_3, the value of new business orders placed, increases by one percent, then the number of business failures will decrease by 0.82%, all else remaining fixed.

(b) A value of the corrected coefficient of determination is difficult to interpret if not in comparison to another. By itself, one can only say that, at 0.615, the corrected coefficient of determination for this equation is not exceedingly great, but it is not bad either.

(c) $\bar{R}^2$, the corrected coefficient of determination, might be preferred to R^2 as $\bar{R}^2$ measures the strength of the association between the dependent variable and the set of independent variables regardless of the number of independent variables used. The is not true of R^2 which increases as the number of independent variables increases.

(d) The null hypothesis of the Durbin-Watson test is that adjacent errors of a regression equation are not positively correlated.

H_0: $\rho = 0$

H_1: $\rho > 0$

The test statistic, d, is given to be 0.496. (Since d is not greater than 2, we leave it as is).

The values from the Durbin-Watson table for d_L and d_U when $n = 30$, $k = 3$ for α of 1% are 1.01 and 1.42, respectively.

Since $d = 0.496 < d_L = 1.01$ the null hypothesis is rejected in favor of the alternative that adjacent errors are positively correlated.

(e)   If one were to continue with the OLS estimates, one must understand that all test results are suspect (are likely to yield misleading results), and forecasts from this model are inefficient (since the errors, although assumed to be nonforecastable, are forecastable).

(f)   In the text we are told that $d \simeq 2(1 - r)$, where r is sample correlation between adjacent errors. One can easily work out that this means that $r \simeq 1 - d/2$.
In this case that means that $r \simeq 1 - 0.496/2 = 0.752$.

****

4.11 The following regression was fitted by ordinary least squares to 32 annual observations on time series data

$$\log \hat{Y}_t = 2.52 - 0.62 \log X_{1t} + 0.92 \log X_{2t} + 0.61 \log X_{3t} + 0.16 \log X_{4t} \ ;$$
$$\qquad\qquad (0.28) \qquad\quad (0.38) \qquad\quad (0.21) \qquad\quad (0.12)$$

$$R^2 = 0.638 \ ; \ d = 0.615$$

where figures in brackets below parameter estimates are the corresponding estimated standard errors, and

Y_t = Quantity of U.S. wheat exported
X_{1t} = Price of U.S. wheat on world markets
X_{2t} = Quantity of U.S. wheat harvested
X_{3t} = Measure of income in countries purchasing U.S. wheat
X_{4t} = Price of barley on world markets

(a)   Interpret, in the context of the assumed model, the estimated parameter on $\log X_{1t}$.
(b)   Interpret the coefficient of determination, R^2.
(c)   Find the corrected coefficient of determination, $\bar{R}^2$.
(d)   Test the null hypothesis that the regression errors are not correlated with one another against the alternative that they obey a first order autoregressive model with positive parameter.
(e)   Given your findings in (d), is it possible with the information provided to validly test the null hypothesis that, all else equal, income in countries purchasing U.S. wheat has no impact on the quantity of U.S. wheat exported.

------- Answer to 4.11 --------

(a)   If X_1, the price of U.S. wheat on world markets, increases by one percent, then the expected quantity of U.S. wheat exported will decrease by 0.62%, all else remaining fixed.

(b)   Since R^2 is given as 0.638, then one can say that the estimated regression line explains 63.8% of the variation in the log of the quantity of wheat exported, in this sample.

(c)   From exercise 4.9 we have

$$\bar{R}^2 = 1 - [(n - 1)/(n - K - 1)] \, (1 - R^2)$$

$$= 1 - [(32-1)/(32-4-1)] \, (1-0.638) \;=\; 0.584$$

(d) H_0: $\rho = 0$

        H_1: $\rho > 0$

The test statistic, d, is given to be 0.615. (Since d is not greater than 2, we leave it as is).

The values from the Durbin-Watson table for d_L and d_U when $n = 32$, $k = 4$ for α of 5% (as α is not specified) are 1.01 and 1.42, respectively.

Since $d = 0.615 < d_L = 1.01$ the null hypothesis is rejected in favor of the alternative that adjacent errors are positively correlated.

(e)   No, as the errors are autocorrelated, all test results derived from this estimation are likely to yield misleading results.

****

4.12 An agricultural economist believes that the amount of beef consumed (Y) in tons in a year in the United States depends on the price of beef (X_1) in dollars per pound, the price of pork (X_2) in dollars per pound, the price of chicken (X_3) in dollars per pounds, and income per household (X_4) in current dollars. The following sample regression was obtained through ordinary least squares, using time series of 30 annual observations:

$$\log \hat{Y}_t = 0.044 - 0.529 \log X_{1t} + 0.217 \log X_{2t} + 0.193 \log X_{3t} + 0.416 \log X_{4t} \ ;$$
$$\qquad\qquad\quad (0.168)\qquad\quad (0.103)\qquad\quad (0.106)\qquad\quad (0.163)$$

$$R^2 = 0.704 \ ; \ d = 1.758$$

where figures in brackets below parameter estimates are the corresponding estimated standard errors.

(a) Interpret, in the context of the assumed model, the estimated parameter on $\log X_{2t}$.
(b) Find and interpret a 90% confidence interval for the parameter on $\log X_{1t}$ in the true regression.
(c) Test the null hypothesis that the four variables ($\log X_{1t}$, $\log X_{2t}$, $\log X_{3t}$, $\log X_{4t}$) do not, as a set, have any linear influence on $\log Y_t$.
(d) Carefully explain the value of calculating the Durbin-Watson d statistic in time series regressions. What can be learned from that statistic in the present case?

------- Answer to 4.12 --------

(a) If X_2, the price of pork, increases by one percent, then the amount of beef consumed will increase by 0.217 percent, all else remaning fixed.

(b) The 90% confidence interval for β_1 is:

$$b_1 \pm t_{25,0.05} \ s_{b_1} \ = \ -0.529 \pm 1.708 \times 0.168$$

or; $-0.816 < \beta_1 < -0.242$

Thus the 90% confidence interval for the effect of a one percent increase in the price of beef on the amount of beef consumed, all else equal, is from a decrease of 0.816% to a decrease of 0.242%.

(c) H_0: $\beta_1 = \beta_2 = \beta_3 = \beta_4 = 0$

H_1: at least one $\beta_i \neq 0$

Decision Rule: Reject H_0 if $F_{calc} > F_{k,n-k-1,0.05}$ (Since no level of significance was given, using an α of 5%).

$$F_{calc} = (R^2/K) \ / \ ((1 - R^2)/(n - K - 1)) \ = \ (0.704/4) \ / \ ((1 - 0.704)/25) \ = \ 14.865$$

Since $F_{calc} = 14.865 > F_{k,n-k-1,0.05} = F_{4,25,0.05} = 2.76$, reject the null hypothesis that these four variables do not, as a set, have any linear influence on $\log Y_t$.

(d) The value of the Durbin-Watson statistic d is that if it shows that the regression's errors are not autocorelated, then all tests (actually, all estimates dependent on the estimated error variance – the standard errors, R^2, and SSE) are reliable. On the other hand, if the Durbin-Watson statistic shows that the regression's errors are autocorrelated, then all test statistics are unreliable.

$$H_0: \ \rho = 0$$

$$H_1: \ \rho > 0$$

The test statistic, d, is given to be 1.758.

The values from the Durbin-Watson table for d_L and d_U when $n = 30$, $k = 4$ for α of 5% (since α is not given) are 1.14 and 1.74, respectively.

Since $d = 1.758 > d_U = 1.74$ the null hypothesis is not rejected. That is, there is not significant evidence of positively autocorrelated errors. Given the discussion above, all tests derived from the regression's estimates are reliable.

****

4.13 A market researcher is interested in the average amount of money per year spent by college students on clothing. From 25 years of annual data the following estimated regression was obtained through ordinary least squares

$$Y_t = 50.72 + 0.124\,X_{1t} + 0.271\,X_{2t} + 0.451\,Y_{t-1} + \epsilon_t \ ; \ d = 1.821$$
$$\qquad\quad (0.047) \qquad (0.213) \qquad (0.136)$$

where figures in brackets below coefficient estimates are the corresponding estimated standard errors, and

Y_t = Expenditure per student on clothes, in real dollars
X_{1t} = Disposable income per student (after the payment of tuition, fees, room and board), in real dollars
X_{2t} = Index of advertising, aimed at the student market, on clothes

(a) Test at the 5% level, against the obvious one-sided alternative, the null hypothesis that, all else equal, advertising does not affect expenditures on clothes in this market.
(b) Find a 95% confidence interval for the parameter on X_{1t} in the true regression model.
(c) With advertising level held fixed, what would be the expected impact over time of a $1 increase in real disposable income per student on clothing expenditure?
(d) Test the null hypothesis that the error terms ϵ_t are autocorrelated against he alternative that they follow a first order autoregressive model with positive parameter.

------- Answer to 4.13 --------

(a) H_0: $\beta_2 = 0$

           H_1: $\beta_2 \neq 0$

Decision rule: Reject H_0 if $t_{calc} < -t_{n-k-1,0.025}$ or $> t_{n-k-1,0.025}$

$t_{calc} = (b_1 - \beta_{1,0})/s_{b_1} = (0.124 - 0)/0.047 = 2.638$

$t_{n-k-1,0.025} = t_{25-3-1,0.025} = t_{21,0.025} = 2.080$

Since $t_{calc} = 2.638 > t_{21,0.025} = 2.080$, reject H_0, and thus, all else equal, advertising does affect clothing expenditures.

(b)   The 95% confidence interval for β_1 is:

       $b_1 \pm t_{21,0.025} s_{b_1} = 0.124 \pm 2.080 \times 0.047$

   or; $0.026 < \beta_1 < 0.222$

(c)   [From Chapter 4.4 Subsection *Fitting Data to a Model with a Lagged Dependent Variable*]

A one unit increase in X_1 will lead to an estimated $b_1/(1-b_3)$ change in Y (where b_3 is the estimated coefficient of Y_{t-1}). Thus, with the advertising level fixed, the expected impact over time of a \$1 increase in real disposable income per student on clothing expenditure is \$0.226.

(d) H_0: $\rho = 0$

           H_1: $\rho > 0$

The test statistic, d, is given to be 1.821. Note that in this regression there is a lagged dependent variable thus one must calculate Durbin's h statistic.

Decision rule: Reject H_0 if $h > 1.645$ (using an α of 5%).

First calculate $r = 1 - d/2 = 1 - 1.821/2 = 0.0895$.

Then, $h = r[n/(1 - ns_c^2)]^{1/2}$ See the text at equation 4.5.10.

$h = 0.0895[25/(1 - 25 \times 0.136^2)]^{1/2} = 0.610$

Since $h = 0.610 < 1.645$, do not reject H_0, there is not enough information to reject the null hypothesis of no autocorrelation.

****

4.14   The accompanying table shows 36 annual observations on real imports (Y_t) and real gross national product (X_t) in the United States. Consider the log linear lagged dependent variable model

$$\log Y_t = \alpha + \beta \log X_t + \gamma \log Y_{t-1} + \epsilon_t$$

(a)   Fit by least squares the log linear lagged dependent variable model, and write a full report on your findings, including a test for autocorrelated errors.

(b)   It is expected that, in the next three years, real gross national product will

$$X_{37} = 3900 \; ; \; X_{38} = 4020 \; ; \; X_{39} = 4100$$

Predict real imports for these years.

------- Answer to 4.14 --------

On the next page is a *LOTUS 123* spreadsheet that yields the regression results for the logged data. The lines were added by a word processor.

(a)   The worksheet tells us that the estimated regression equation is:

$$\log Y_t = -3.135 + 0.570 \log X_t + 0.753 \log Y_{t-1} + \epsilon_t \; ; \; R^2 = .992 \; ; \; d = 2.145$$
$$ (0.140) (0.064)$$

The right side of the spreadsheet (columns G..L) involves the calculation of d, the Durbin-Watson statistic, and Durbin's h statistic for testing autocorrelation in the presence of a lagged dependent variable. The test for autocorrelation is necessary as otherwise the tests on the coefficients and the equation are suspect.
The spreadsheet calculates h twice, once using the approximation from d (as described in the text) – see cells G16..L16. Above this, is the proper calculation of r using a regression in which an intercept of zero was forced. The h from this is calculated in cell L13. It is somewhat different from the approximation in cell L16. Both values though are well inside the acceptance region (h is distributed as the standard normal under the null, and hence the aceeptance region is from -1.96 to $+1.96$ at the 5% level of confidence). Thus there should be no suspicion of overinflated test results from the above estimated equation.
The estimated equation is very good, the R^2 is extremely large at .992, thus relating that this equation explains 99.2% of the variation in the log of real imports. Therefore the F test for the significance of the equation yields a calculated F of 2,107 which is well within the rejection region of the test that the independent variables do not explain Y. Similarly, both variables significantly explain Y, since both t values are far above a critical value of say 2.576 (using a 1% level of significance).
One can interpret the estimated coefficients as follows. The first year effect on real imports of a 1% increase in real GNP is 0.570%, while the full effect is $0.570/(1-0.753)$ = 2.31%.

(b)   The prediction for the years numbered 37, 38, and 39 are shown on the spreadsheet, first in logged form in cells D55..D57, which are transformed back (with the @exp(..) function) in cells B55..B57.

	A	B	C	D	E	F	G	H	I	J	K	L
1	Regression for part (a) of Exercise 4.14						Regression for calculation of r					
2												
3		Y range: D20..D54						Y range: G21..G54				
4		X range: E20..F54						X range: G20..G53				
5												
6		Regression Output:						Regression Output:				
7		Constant			-3.13509			Constant			0	
8		Std Err of Y Est			0.061502			Std Err of Y Est			0.059939	
9		R Squared			0.992464			R Squared			0.006146	
10		No. of Observations			35			No. of Observations			34	
11		Degrees of Freedom			32			Degrees of Freedom			33	
12												
13		X Coefficient(s)	0.570281	0.753279				X Coefficient(s)	-0.08050	> > h =		-0.515
14		Std Err of Coef.	0.140338	0.064390				Std Err of Coef.	0.172433			
15		t calc	4.063610	11.69854								
16		F calc	2107.355				d =	2.145	r =	-0.072 > > h =		-0.464
17												

t	Y	X	log(Y)	log(X)	log(Y(t-1))	e(t)		e(t)²
1	62.9	1380.0	4.14	7.23			[e-e(t-1)]²	
2	64.8	1435.3	4.17	7.27	4.14	0.041		0.0017
3	61.7	1416.2	4.12	7.26	4.17	-0.023	0.0041	0.0005
4	66.6	1494.9	4.20	7.31	4.12	0.060	0.0068	0.0036
5	70.8	1525.7	4.26	7.33	4.20	0.052	0.0001	0.0027
6	71.9	1551.1	4.28	7.35	4.26	0.012	0.0016	0.0001
7	71.0	1539.3	4.26	7.34	4.28	-0.008	0.0004	0.0001
8	77.2	1629.1	4.35	7.40	4.26	0.053	0.0037	0.0028
9	77.5	1665.2	4.35	7.42	4.35	-0.019	0.0051	0.0004
10	76.4	1708.7	4.34	7.44	4.35	-0.051	0.0010	0.0026
11	82.0	1799.4	4.41	7.50	4.34	0.001	0.0027	0.0000
12	84.8	1873.3	4.44	7.54	4.41	-0.041	0.0018	0.0017
13	90.0	1973.3	4.50	7.59	4.44	-0.037	0.0000	0.0014
14	98.4	2087.5	4.59	7.64	4.50	-0.025	0.0002	0.0006
15	111.7	2208.4	4.72	7.70	4.59	0.003	0.0008	0.0000
16	117.1	2271.3	4.76	7.73	4.72	-0.061	0.0041	0.0038
17	130.6	2365.6	4.87	7.77	4.76	-0.011	0.0025	0.0001
18	137.4	2423.3	4.92	7.79	4.87	-0.056	0.0020	0.0032
19	143.9	2416.2	4.97	7.79	4.92	-0.047	0.0001	0.0022
20	148.9	2484.8	5.00	7.82	4.97	-0.063	0.0003	0.0040
21	168.2	2608.5	5.13	7.87	5.00	0.005	0.0047	0.0000
22	196.3	2744.0	5.28	7.92	5.13	0.039	0.0011	0.0015
23	250.1	2729.3	5.52	7.91	5.28	0.168	0.0166	0.0282
24	219.8	2695.0	5.39	7.90	5.52	-0.136	0.0927	0.0186
25	252.0	2826.7	5.53	7.95	5.39	0.070	0.0428	0.0049
26	282.0	2958.6	5.64	7.99	5.53	0.054	0.0003	0.0029
27	309.3	3115.1	5.73	8.04	5.64	0.032	0.0005	0.0010
28	346.3	3192.3	5.85	8.07	5.73	0.062	0.0009	0.0038
29	372.4	3187.2	5.92	8.07	5.85	0.050	0.0001	0.0025
30	371.6	3248.7	5.92	8.09	5.92	-0.018	0.0046	0.0003
31	335.7	3166.0	5.82	8.06	5.92	-0.103	0.0073	0.0106
32	345.1	3279.1	5.84	8.10	5.82	-0.019	0.0071	0.0004
33	410.6	3501.4	6.02	8.16	5.84	0.097	0.0134	0.0093
34	403.9	3607.4	6.00	8.19	6.02	-0.068	0.0270	0.0046
35	422.3	3713.3	6.05	8.22	6.00	-0.027	0.0016	0.0007
36	462.6	3818.0	6.14	8.25	6.05	0.014	0.0017	0.0002
37	494.32	3900	6.203	8.269	6.14			
38	528.71	4020	6.270	8.299				
39	562.46	4100	6.332	8.319				

Chapter 5

AN INTRODUCTION TO TIME SERIES AND THEIR COMPONENTS

Contents of Chapter 5

Answers to Exercises at End of Chapter.

5.1   What is meant in saying that a time series can be viewed as being made up of components? Provide examples of business and economic time series in which you would expect to find strong evidence of (i) trend (ii) seasonality (iii) irregularity.

------- Answer to 5.1 --------

(i)   Series that show strong <u>trend</u> are those measuring some aspect of economic activity – for example, GNP, money supply, personal income.

(ii) Series that are expected to show strong <u>seasonality</u> are concerned with sales measured on a monthly, or quarterly basis – for example, retail sales, unemployment, and even GNP (remember that many of the most important economic series measured and reported by the Federal Government are deseasonalized before reporting).

(iii) Series that show a strong <u>irregularity</u> are, for example, prices arrived at in financial and commodity markets – for example, interest rates, exchange rates, price of grain.

****

5.2   The table shows per capita national product (in constant dollars) in the United States over a period of 24 years. [See the text or the spreadsheet below for the data].

(a)   Graph this time series and discuss its behavior.
(b)   Compute the series of simple centered 5-point moving averages. Graph this smoothed series and discuss its properties.

------- Answer to 5.2 --------

	A	B	C
1	t	GNP p.c.	5-point MA
2			
3	1	9,896	
4	2	10,281	
5	3	10,741	10,715.8
6	4	11,233	11,093.4
7	5	11,428	11,427.8
8	6	11,784	11,635.8
9	7	11,953	11,782.0
10	8	11,781	11,981.6
11	9	11,964	12,214.4
12	10	12,426	12,375.8
13	11	12,948	12,515.2
14	12	12,760	12,714.6
15	13	12,478	12,915.6
16	14	12,961	13,124.6
17	15	13,431	13,409.0
18	16	13,993	13,712.2
19	17	14,182	13,942.8
20	18	13,994	13,979.4
21	19	14,114	13,973.6
22	20	13,614	14,091.4
23	21	13,964	14,307.4
24	22	14,771	14,558.2
25	23	15,074	
26	24	15,368	

In the time period shown GNP per capita goes through several cycles with dips (recession?) in years 8-9, 13-14, and 20-21. The 5-point moving average smooths out these cycles quite well and conveys to the reader that GNP per capita follows (except for occasional ups and downs) a fairly consistent long term, broken only here in periods 17, 18 and 19 when it experienced stable growth.

Graph Accompanying Excercise 5.2

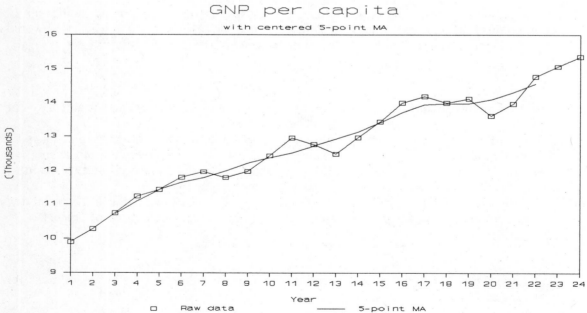

GNP per capita
with centered 5-point MA

(Thousands)

Year

□   Raw data   ——— 5-point MA

5.3   The table shows the base interest rates of United Kindom banks over 32 quarters. [See the text or the accompanying spreadshhet for the data].
(a)   Graph this time series and discuss its behavior over these eight years.
(b)   Compute the series of simple centered 5-point moving averages. Graph this smoothed series and discuss its behavior.

------- Answer to 5.3 -------

	A	B	C	D
1	Year	Qtr	UK Interest	5-point MA
2			Rates	
3	1	1		
4	1	2	12.43	
5	1	3	14.00	
6	1	4	15.41	15.168
7	2	1	17.00	15.892
8	2	2	17.00	16.136
9	2	3	16.05	15.766
10	2	4	15.22	14.766
11	3	1	13.56	13.834
12	3	2	12.00	13.656
13	3	3	12.34	13.378
14	3	4	15.16	13.240
15	4	1	13.83	13.110
16	4	2	12.87	12.578
17	4	3	11.35	11.710
18	4	4	9.68	10.940
19	5	1	10.82	10.266
20	5	2	9.98	9.796
21	5	3	9.50	9.642
22	5	4	9.00	9.256
23	6	1	8.91	9.440
24	6	2	8.89	9.542
25	6	3	10.90	10.364
26	6	4	10.01	11.118
27	7	1	13.11	11.684
28	7	2	12.68	11.804
29	7	3	11.72	12.262
30	7	4	11.50	11.728
31	8	1	12.30	11.192
32	8	2	10.44	11.020
33	8	3	10.00	10.882
34	8	4	10.86	
35	9	1	10.81	

For the time period shown, UK base interest rate is strongly irregular. The 5-point moving average seems to provide just enough smoothing to be able to tell the series' local trend – that is, where it is actually heading rather than where is seems to be heading given the last month or two.

Graph Accompanying Exercise 5.3

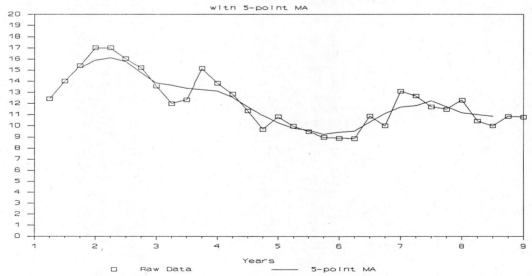

UK Base Interest Rate
with 5-point MA

5.4   A smoothed series is to be calculated from a series X_t ($t = 1, 2, \ldots, n$) through a 5×3 moving average. Find an expression for the smoothed series in terms of the original observations on X_t.

------- Answer to 5.4 --------

$$X \qquad\qquad\qquad \text{3-point MA}$$

$$
\begin{array}{ll}
X_{t-3} & \\
X_{t-2} & (X_{t-3} + X_{t-2} + X_{t-1})/3 \\
X_{t-1} & (X_{t-2} + X_{t-1} + X_t)/3 \\
X_t & (X_{t-1} + X_t + X_{t+1})/3 \\
X_{t+1} & (X_t + X_{t+1} + X_{t+2})/3 \\
X_{t+2} & (X_{t+1} + X_{t+2} + X_{t+3})/3 \\
X_{t+3} & \\
\end{array}
$$

The 5-point moving average of the 3-point moving average for period t, is the addition of the 5 expressions in the second column.

$$X_t^{**} = (X_{t-3} + 2\,X_{t-2} + 3\,X_{t-1} + 3\,X_t + 3\,X_{t+1} + 2\,X_{t+2} + X_{t+3})/15$$

****

5.5   The table shows the evolution of the value of the United States dollar in terms of number of dollars per International Monetary Fund special drawing right over a period of 30 months. [See text or the spreadsheet below for the data].
   (a)   Graph this series and discuss its behavior.
   (b)   Compute the series of simple centered 5-point moving averages. Graph this smoothed series and comment on its behavior.
   (c)   Compute the series of 3×3 moving averages. Graph this smoothed series and discuss its properties.

------- Answer to 5.5 --------

	A	B	C	D	E
1	YearMth		Data	5-pt MA	3x3 MA
2	1	1	0.975		
3	1	2	0.959		
4	1	3	0.991	0.9818	0.9823
5	1	4	0.991	0.9864	0.9887
6	1	5	0.993	1.0020	0.9983
7	1	6	0.998	1.0108	1.0089
8	1	7	1.037	1.0244	1.0254
9	1	8	1.035	1.0402	1.0408
10	1	9	1.059	1.0592	1.0579
11	1	10	1.072	1.0714	1.0726
12	1	11	1.093	1.0866	1.0877
13	1	12	1.098	1.1060	1.1033
14	2	1	1.111	1.1192	1.1191
15	2	2	1.156	1.1358	1.1378
16	2	3	1.138	1.1448	1.1480
17	2	4	1.176	1.1582	1.1582

	A	B	C	D	E
1	YearMth		Data	5-pt MA	3x3 MA
18	2	5	1.143	1.1678	1.1643
19	2	6	1.178	1.1816	1.1790
20	2	7	1.204	1.1890	1.1931
21	2	8	1.207	1.1978	1.2022
22	2	9	1.213	1.2042	1.2046
23	2	10	1.187	1.2080	1.2041
24	2	11	1.210	1.2202	1.2146
25	2	12	1.223	1.2304	1.2307
26	3	1	1.268	1.2502	1.2527
27	3	2	1.264	1.2694	1.2699
28	3	3	1.286	1.2822	1.2837
29	3	4	1.306	1.2842	1.2896
30	3	5	1.287		
31	3	6	1.278		

For the time period shown both the 5-point and the 3×3 moving average smooth out the irregularities in the data quite well. They show a steady trend in the series. The slight difference in the two moving averages is that the 3×3 moving average weighs the current observation higher than those 1 and 2 observations away. That is, the weights for the 3×3 MA are 1-2-3-2-1, while the weights for the 5-point are the same for the same 5 observations.

Graph Accompanying Exercise 5.5

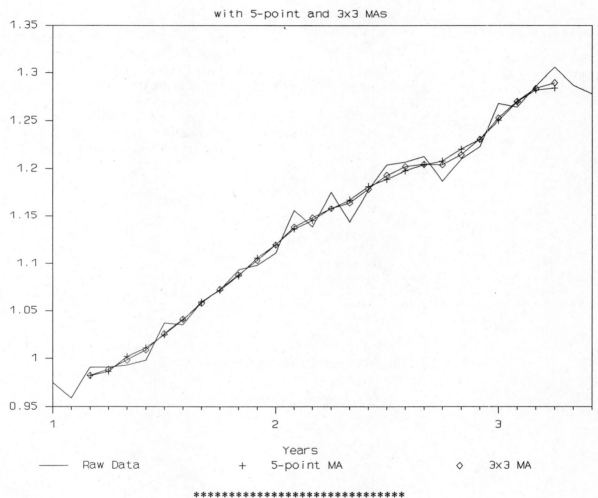

No. of US dollars per IMF drawing right

with 5-point and 3x3 MAs

Years

——— Raw Data   +   5-point MA   ◇   3×3 MA

****

5.6   The table shows percentage annual change in the consumer price index in the United
      States over 21 years. [See text or the spreadsheet below for the data].
      (a)   Graph this time series and discuss its behavior.
      (b)   Calculate the series of simple centered 5-point moving averages. Graph this
            smoothed series and comment on its behavior.
      (c)   Compute the series of 3×3 moving averages. Graph the series and comment on the
            resulting picture.

------- Answer to 5.6 --------

	A Year	B CPI % chg	C 5-point M	D 3x3 MA
1	Year	CPI	5-point M	3x3 MA
2		% chg		
3	1	1.6		
4	2	3.1		
5	3	2.8	3.42	3.333
6	4	4.2	4.28	4.222
7	5	5.4	4.52	4.833
8	6	5.9	4.62	4.956
9	7	4.3	5.02	4.767
10	8	3.3	6.14	5.311
11	9	6.2	6.78	6.733
12	10	11.0	7.08	8.078
13	11	9.1	7.72	8.178
14	12	5.8	8.00	7.467
15	13	6.5	8.06	7.411
16	14	7.6	8.94	8.633
17	15	11.3	9.86	10.333
18	16	13.5	9.80	10.856
19	17	10.4	8.92	9.456
20	18	6.2	7.52	7.067
21	19	3.2	5.54	4.956
22	20	4.3		
23	21	3.6		

Over the time period the change in the CPI
goes through several ups and downs. This
exercise shows much more clearly the
difference (noted in the last exercise) between
the 5-point and the 3×3 moving averages. The
5-point MA results in a smoother series than
the 3×3 MA because the 3×3 weights the
current observation heavier than the 5-point
MA.

Graph Accompanying Exercise 5.6

Annual Percentage Change in the CPI

with 5-pt and 3x3 MAs

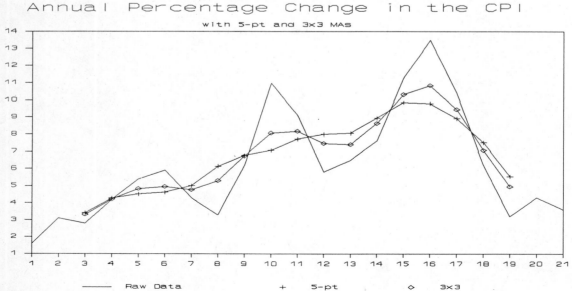

| | Raw Data | + | 5-pt | ◇ | 3×3 |

5.7   The table shows seven years of quarterly observations on the price of aluminum in U.S. cents per pound. [See text or the spreadsheet below for the data].
(a)   Draw a graph of this time series and discuss its behavior.
(b)   Compute the series of 3×3 moving averages. Draw a graph of the smoothed series and comment on what is revealed.

------- Answer to 5.7 --------

	A Year	B Qtr	C Data	D 3x3 MA
1	Year	Qtr	Data	3x3 MA
2	1	1	93.2	
3	1	2	81.3	
4	1	3	78.6	77.222
5	1	4	69.0	70.578
6	2	1	65.4	64.967
7	2	2	58.9	59.489
8	2	3	54.1	55.078
9	2	4	50.7	51.167
10	3	1	48.8	48.089
11	3	2	43.7	45.589
12	3	3	43.5	45.456
13	3	4	43.9	48.489
14	4	1	54.6	55.144
15	4	2	64.8	62.300
16	4	3	71.6	67.444
17	4	4	70.0	68.167
18	5	1	68.0	64.967
19	5	2	59.5	59.367
20	5	3	50.1	53.989
21	5	4	49.6	50.711
22	6	1	49.4	49.033
23	6	2	49.1	47.956
24	6	3	45.6	47.256
25	6	4	44.7	47.833
26	7	1	51.5	49.778
27	7	2	53.1	51.489
28	7	3	52.3	
29	7	4	51.8	

In the time period shown aluminum price falls steadily, rises about to half of what it was, and then falls again, only to increase a little at the end. There are less ups and downs than the series in the last exercise. The most important difference between this series and the one in the last exercise is that there is more time (distance, or observations) between one trough and the next peak. This will make it impossible for a 3×3 (or 5-point) MA to smooth out the dips and peaks. This is clear from the graph. A much longer span is necessary to smooth out the obvious dip and peak − try 7, 9 and 11-point moving averages. The 11-point MA smooths it out the dip and peak in years 3 and 4. This goes far to demonstrate that if a particular MA is to be effective, then the span of the moving average should be from one peak (or dip) to the next. This graph shows what looks like cyclical bebehavior.

Graph Accompanying Exercise 5.7

Aluminum Price
with 3x3 MA

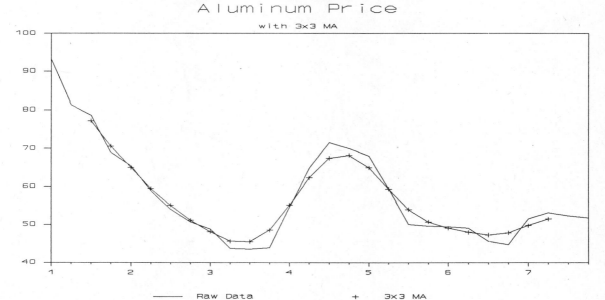

Raw Data   +   3x3 MA

5.8   What is meant by the seasonal adjustment of a time series? What is the value of having access to seasonally adjusted data?

------- Answer to 5.8 --------

By "seasonal adjustment of a time series", or deseasonalization, one means that the seasonal component of the data has been essentially removed.   See the first five paragraphs of section 5.5 of the text for pros and cons of seasonal adjustment.   One salient sentence giving weight to the usefulness of seasonal adjustment is: "... seasonal adjustment forms a valuable part of a *preliminary*, or *exploratory*, data analysis, allowing through graphical inspection a useful visual feel for time series data, perhaps as a prelude to performing a more sophisticated analysis."

****

5.9   The table shows quarterly earnings per share of a corporation over a period of seven years. [See text or the spreadsheet below for the data].
(a)   Using a 2×4 moving average, estimate the trend component, and graph the resulting series.
(b)   Using the seasonal index method, obtain and graph the series of seasonally adjusted earnings per share.
(c)   What can be learned from the components estimates for this time series?

------- Answer to 5.9 --------

Graph Accompanying Exercise 5.9
Quarterly Earnings Per Share

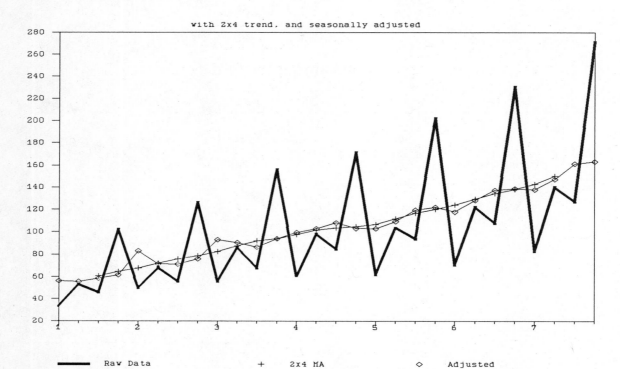

with 2x4 trend, and seasonally adjusted

Raw Data   +   2x4 MA   ◇   Adjusted

	A	B	C	D	E	F	G
1	YearQtr		Data	4-pt MA	2x4 MA	Seasonal	Seasonally
2						Indices	Adjusted
3	1	1	34				56.39
4	1	2	53	58.75			55.70
5	1	3	46	62.75	60.75	0.7572	58.46
6	1	4	102	66.50	64.63	1.5783	61.49
7	2	1	50	69.00	67.75	0.7380	82.93
8	2	2	68	75.00	72.00	0.9444	71.47
9	2	3	56	76.50	75.75	0.7393	71.17
10	2	4	126	81.00	78.75	1.6000	75.96
11	3	1	56	84.00	82.50	0.6788	92.88
12	3	2	86	91.50	87.75	0.9801	90.39
13	3	3	68	92.50	92.00	0.7391	86.42
14	3	4	156	95.50	94.00	1.6596	94.05
15	4	1	60	99.75	97.63	0.6146	99.52
16	4	2	98	103.50	101.63	0.9643	103.00
17	4	3	85	104.00	103.75	0.8193	108.02
18	4	4	171	105.50	104.75	1.6325	103.09
19	5	1	62	107.75	106.63	0.5815	102.84
20	5	2	104	115.50	111.63	0.9317	109.30
21	5	3	94	117.75	116.63	0.8060	119.46
22	5	4	202	122.25	120.00	1.6833	121.78
23	6	1	71	125.75	124.00	0.5726	117.76
24	6	2	122	132.75	129.25	0.9439	128.22
25	6	3	108	135.75	134.25	0.8045	137.25
26	6	4	230	140.25	138.00	1.6667	138.66
27	7	1	83	145.00	142.63	0.5819	137.67
28	7	2	140	155.25	150.13	0.9326	147.14
29	7	3	127				161.40
30	7	4	271				163.38
31							
32				QUARTER			
33		Year	1	2	3	4	TOTALS
34		1			0.7572	1.5783	
35		2	0.7380	0.9444	0.7393	1.6000	
36		3	0.6788	0.9801	0.7391	1.6596	
37		4	0.6146	0.9643	0.8193	1.6325	
38		5	0.5815	0.9317	0.8060	1.6833	
39		6	0.5726	0.9439	0.8045	1.6667	
40		7	0.5819	0.9326			
41							
42	Median		0.5983	0.9442	0.7808	1.6460	3.9693
43	Index		0.6029	0.9515	0.7869	1.6587	4.0000

In retrospect, although the raw data contains a strong seasonal pattern which is increasing in size (a sign that a the seasonal pattern is better estimated with a multiplicative than an additive model), it is now clear that the drop from each fourth quarter to the next first quarter is growing faster than constant proportional rate (assumed by the multiplicative model). This is shown by the seasonally adjusted series for the first quarters of years 2 and 3 are above the smoothed data; while the corresponding values for the first quarters in years 5, 6 and 7 are below the smoothed series. Another way to view this, is to say that the seasonal effect is changing (that is, not best represented by a median) -- see how the estimated values of the first quarter index is increasing through time -- cells C35..C40.

****

5.10 The table shows quarterly earnings per share of a corporation over a period of seven years. [See text or the spreadsheet below for the data].
   (a)   Draw a graph of this series and discuss its behavior.
   (b)   Using a 2×4 moving average, estimate the trend component, and graph the resulting series.
   (c)   Using the seasonal index method, obtain and graph the series of seasonally adjusted earnings per share.
   (d)   What can be learned from the components estimates for this time series?

------- Answer to 5.10 --------

Graph Accompanying Exercise 5.10
Quarterly Earnings Per Share

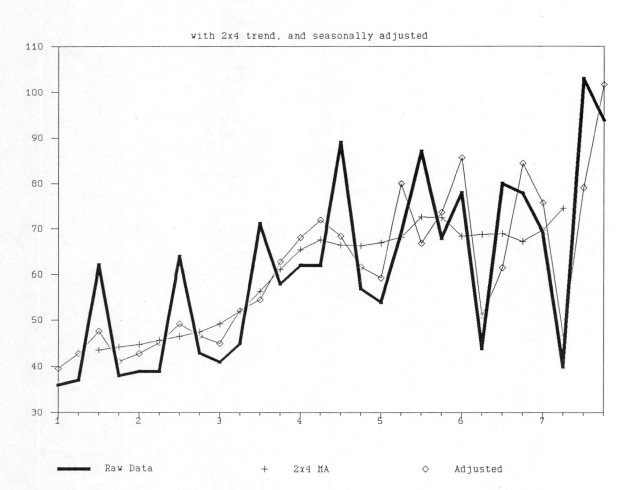

	A	B	C	D	E	F	G
1	YearQtr		Data	4-pt MA	2x4 MA	Seasonal	Seasonally
2						Indices	Adjusted
3	1	1	36				39.52
4	1	2	37	43.25			42.87
5	1	3	62	44.00	43.63	1.4212	47.63
6	1	4	38	44.50	44.25	0.8588	41.11
7	2	1	39	45.00	44.75	0.8715	42.81
8	2	2	39	46.25	45.63	0.8548	45.19
9	2	3	64	46.75	46.50	1.3763	49.17
10	2	4	43	48.25	47.50	0.9053	46.52
11	3	1	41	50.00	49.13	0.8346	45.01
12	3	2	45	53.75	51.88	0.8675	52.15
13	3	3	71	59.00	56.38	1.2594	54.55
14	3	4	58	63.25	61.13	0.9489	62.74
15	4	1	62	67.75	65.50	0.9466	68.06
16	4	2	62	67.50	67.63	0.9168	71.84
17	4	3	89	65.50	66.50	1.3383	68.37
18	4	4	57	67.25	66.38	0.8588	61.66
19	5	1	54	66.75	67.00	0.8060	59.28
20	5	2	69	69.50	68.13	1.0128	79.96
21	5	3	87	75.50	72.50	1.2000	66.84
22	5	4	68	69.25	72.38	0.9396	73.56
23	6	1	78	67.50	68.38	1.1408	85.62
24	6	2	44	70.00	68.75	0.6400	50.99
25	6	3	80	67.75	68.88	1.1615	61.46
26	6	4	78	66.75	67.25	1.1599	84.38
27	7	1	69	72.50	69.63	0.9910	75.74
28	7	2	40	76.50	74.50	0.5369	46.35
29	7	3	103				79.13
30	7	4	94				101.69
31							

			QUARTER				
32				QUARTER			
33		Year	1	2	3	4	TOTALS
34		1			1.4212	0.8588	
35		2	0.8715	0.8548	1.3763	0.9053	
36		3	0.8346	0.8675	1.2594	0.9489	
37		4	0.9466	0.9168	1.3383	0.8588	
38		5	0.8060	1.0128	1.2000	0.9396	
39		6	1.1408	0.6400	1.1615	1.1599	
40		7	0.9910	0.5369			
41							
42	Median		0.9090	0.8611	1.2989	0.9224	3.9915
43	Index		0.9110	0.8630	1.3017	0.9244	4.0000

After year 4, the series changes its character. It would be nice to have a couple more years of data to see if the possible new pattern, in years 6 and 7, continues. It is fairly obvious that the value of the adjustment process is very small when it comes to trying to use the last two years of adjusted data – the low second quarter is the actual data is repeated in the adjusted series.

****

5.11 The table shows the value of quarterly sales of a corporation over a period of six years.
      [See text or the spreadsheet below for the data].
      (a)   Graph this series and discuss its properties.
      (b)   Using a 2×4 moving average, estimate the trend component, and graph this series.
      (c)   Using the seasonal index method, obtain and graph the series of seasonally adjusted
             sales values.
      (d)   What can be learned from the components estimates for this time series?

------- Answer to 5.11 --------

Graph Accompanying Exercise 5.11
Quarterly Sales

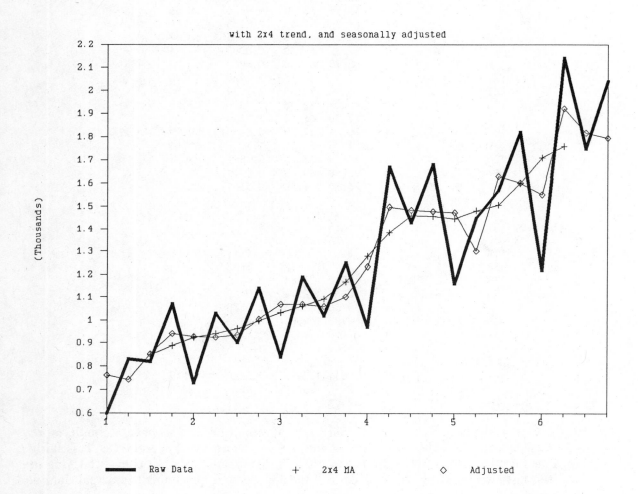

with 2x4 trend, and seasonally adjusted

Raw Data   +   2x4 MA   ◇   Adjusted

	A	B	C	D	E	F	G
1	YearQtr		Data	4-pt MA	2x4 MA	Seasonal	Seasonally
2						Indices	Adjusted
3	1	1	600				762.86
4	1	2	830	830.00			744.73
5	1	3	820	862.50	846.25	0.9690	851.43
6	1	4	1070	912.50	887.50	1.2056	941.98
7	2	1	730	932.50	922.50	0.7913	928.15
8	2	2	1030	950.00	941.25	1.0943	924.18
9	2	3	900	977.50	963.75	0.9339	934.50
10	2	4	1140	1017.50	997.50	1.1429	1003.61
11	3	1	840	1047.50	1032.50	0.8136	1068.00
12	3	2	1190	1075.00	1061.25	1.1213	1067.75
13	3	3	1020	1107.50	1091.25	0.9347	1059.10
14	3	4	1250	1227.50	1167.50	1.0707	1100.45
15	4	1	970	1330.00	1278.75	0.7586	1233.29
16	4	2	1670	1437.50	1383.75	1.2069	1498.43
17	4	3	1430	1485.00	1461.25	0.9786	1484.81
18	4	4	1680	1430.00	1457.50	1.1527	1479.00
19	5	1	1160	1465.00	1447.50	0.8014	1474.86
20	5	2	1450	1500.00	1482.50	0.9781	1301.04
21	5	3	1570	1515.00	1507.50	1.0415	1630.18
22	5	4	1820	1687.50	1601.25	1.1366	1602.25
23	6	1	1220	1732.50	1710.00	0.7135	1551.15
24	6	2	2140	1787.50	1760.00	1.2159	1920.15
25	6	3	1750				1817.08
26	6	4	2040				1795.93
27							
28				QUARTER			
29		Year	1	2	3	4	TOTALS
30		1			0.9690	1.2056	
31		2	0.7913	1.0943	0.9339	1.1429	
32		3	0.8136	1.1213	0.9347	1.0707	
33		4	0.7586	1.2069	0.9786	1.1527	
34		5	0.8014	0.9781	1.0415	1.1366	
35		6	0.7135	1.2159			
36							
37							
38	Median		0.7913	1.1213	0.9690	1.1429	4.0245
39	Index		0.7865	1.1145	0.9631	1.1359	4.0000

The irregular component of this data is larger than we have seen so far in these seasonal adjustment exercises. When this happens you worry that your sample is too small and that the estimates of the seasonal indexes are biased by the large irregular occurrences.

****

5.12 The table shows quarterly product sales over a period of seven years. [See text or the spreadsheet below for the data].
   (a)   Graph this series and discuss its properties.
   (b)   Using a 2×4 moving average, estimate the trend component, and graph this series.
   (c)   Using the seasonal index method, obtain and graph the series of seasonally adjusted product sales.
   (d)   What can be learned from the components estimates for this time series?

------- Answer to 5.12 --------

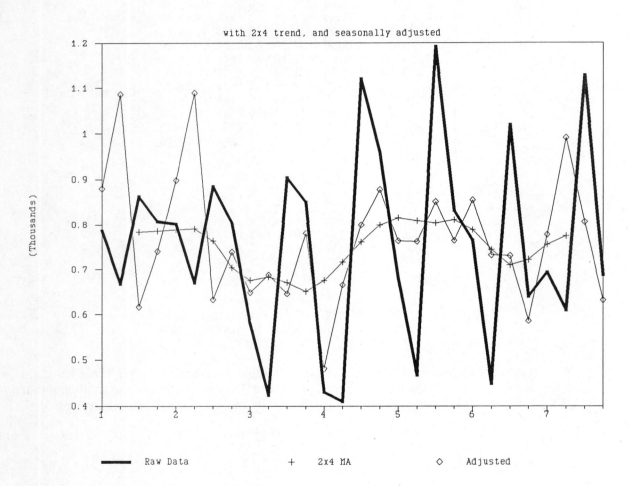

Quarterly Sales

with 2x4 trend, and seasonally adjusted

	A	B	C	D	E	F	G
1	YearQtr		Data	4-pt MA	2x4 MA	Seasonal	Seasonally
2						Indices	Adjusted
3	1	1	786				880.00
4	1	2	668	781.00			1086.31
5	1	3	863	785.00	783.00	1.1022	616.14
6	1	4	807	785.50	785.25	1.0277	739.53
7	2	1	802	791.00	788.25	1.0174	897.91
8	2	2	670	790.50	790.75	0.8473	1089.56
9	2	3	885	734.75	762.63	1.1605	631.85
10	2	4	805	673.00	703.88	1.1437	737.69
11	3	1	579	677.75	675.38	0.8573	648.24
12	3	2	423	689.25	683.50	0.6189	687.89
13	3	3	904	652.00	670.63	1.3480	645.41
14	3	4	851	648.50	650.25	1.3087	779.85
15	4	1	430	702.50	675.50	0.6366	481.42
16	4	2	409	729.25	715.88	0.5713	665.12
17	4	3	1120	792.00	760.63	1.4725	799.63
18	4	4	958	806.75	799.38	1.1984	877.90
19	5	1	681	824.75	815.75	0.8348	762.44
20	5	2	468	793.50	809.13	0.5784	761.07
21	5	3	1192	814.25	803.88	1.4828	851.03
22	5	4	833	809.50	811.88	1.0260	763.35
23	6	1	764	766.75	788.13	0.9694	855.37
24	6	2	449	718.25	742.50	0.6047	730.17
25	6	3	1021	700.75	709.50	1.4390	728.95
26	6	4	639	740.75	720.75	0.8866	585.57
27	7	1	694	768.00	754.38	0.9200	777.00
28	7	2	609	780.25	774.13	0.7867	990.36
29	7	3	1130				806.77
30	7	4	688				630.48
31							
32				QUARTER			
33		Year	1	2	3	4	TOTALS
34		1			1.1022	1.0277	
35		2	1.0174	0.8473	1.1605	1.1437	
36		3	0.8573	0.6189	1.3480	1.3087	
37		4	0.6366	0.5713	1.4725	1.1984	
38		5	0.8348	0.5784	1.4828	1.0260	
39		6	0.9694	0.6047	1.4390	0.8866	
40		7	0.9200	0.7867			
41							
42	Median	0.8886	0.6118	1.3935	1.0857	3.9796	
43	Index	0.8932	0.6149	1.4007	1.0912	4.0000	

In this series, the size of the seasonal component varies through time. Also, after seasonal adjustment, it seems that the irregular component is also unusually large. It is hard to believe that any other more sophisticated adjustment process will take care of such quickly changing seasonality (if indeed that is happening).

Chapter 6

EXPONENTIAL SMOOTHING ALGORITHMS

Contents of Chapter 6

Answers to questions at end of chapter.

6.1   Discuss the limitations of forecasting future values of a time series as the average of all past values. Why might weighted averages be preferred? Explain how simple exponential smoothing involves, in effect, a particular scheme of weighted averages.

------- Answer to 6.1 --------

Even if there is no clear trend (or seasonality) in a time series, the general level of the last several periods may be clearly different from, and preferrable to, the simple average of all the available data.

If the recent data is at a different level from that of most of the previous data, a weighted average will be preferred - with the most recent data having larger weights than data further into the past.

The simple exponential algorithm is developed in equations (6.2.1) to (6.2.4). Similarly equation (6.2.1) with its exponentially declining weights can be derived from equation (6.2.4), the smoothing algorithm, by repetitive substitution of L_{t-s} for $s = 1,2,...,$infinity.

****

6.2   Suppose that the series X_t is to be predicted through simple exponential smoothing. Let L_t denote the estimate of the level, and e_t the error made in the prediction of X_t at time $t-1$. If α denotes the smoothing constant, show that

$$L_{t-1} - (1-\alpha)L_{t-2} = \alpha X_{t-1} = X_t - (1-\alpha)X_{t-1} - [e_t - (1-\alpha)e_{t-1}]$$

and hence that $X_t - X_{t-1} = e_t - (1-\alpha)e_{t-1}.$

------- Answer to 6.2 --------

$L_{t-1} - (1-\alpha)L_{t-2} = \alpha X_{t-1}$ is a re-arrangement of

$L_{t-1} = \alpha X_{t-1} + (1-\alpha)L_{t-2}$ which is the simple smoothing algorithm lagged one period.

$$L_{t-1} - (1-\alpha)L_{t-2} = X_t - (1-\alpha)X_{t-1} - [e_t-(1-\alpha)e_{t-1}]$$

where, since e_t = actual – forecast = $X_t - L_{t-1}$, the LHS $L_{t-1} - (1-\alpha)L_{t-2}$ can be written as

$(X_t-e_t) - (1-\alpha)(X_{t-1}-e_{t-1})$ which is equal to the RHS.

Therefore, $\alpha X_{t-1} = X_t - (1-\alpha)X_{t-1} - [e_t - (1-\alpha)e_{t-1}]$

which when re-arranged with X's on the LHS and e's on the RHS yields:

$$X_t - X_{t-1} = e_t - (1-\alpha)e_{t-1}.$$

****

6.3   The accompanying table shows the percent of building expenditures to gross national product in the United States over a period of twenty five years.

(a)   Use simple exponential smoothing, with smoothing constant 0.5, to predict future values of this series.

(b)   Graph the time series, together with forecasts for the next five years.

------- Answer to 6.3 --------

Note that the e(t)² (column E) and LOTUS 123 /Data Table 1 (range G8..H17) were not requested in this problem. The results of the Data Table 1 show that the larger the α (or in other words, the larger the weight on recent observations) the smaller the error sum of squares will be. This is happening since the data trends downwards, and so the last observation will usually be a better forecast of the next period than any weighted average of the past data. This cries out for a better smoothing technique. See Exercise 6.8.

	A	B	C	D	E	F	G	H	I
1			0.5	= ALPHA					
2		Expenditures							
3	Year	X(t)	L(t)	f(t,1)	e(t)²				
4									
5	1	11.4	11.40				Forecast	SSE	
6	2	10.8	11.10	11.40	0.36		equals:	7.78	
7	3	10.8	10.95	11.10	0.09				
8	4	10.7	10.83	10.95	0.06			7.78	
9	5	10.9	10.86	10.83	0.01		0.1	25.10	
10	6	10.6	10.73	10.86	0.07		0.2	13.98	
11	7	10.7	10.72	10.73	0.00		0.3	10.43	
12	8	10.1	10.41	10.72	0.38		0.4	8.77	
13	9	9.8	10.10	10.41	0.37		0.5	7.78	
14	10	10.0	10.05	10.10	0.01		0.6	7.05	
15	11	10.0	10.03	10.05	0.00		0.7	6.47	
16	12	9.7	9.86	10.03	0.11		0.8	5.97	
17	13	10.3	10.08	9.86	0.19		0.9	5.54	
18	14	10.6	10.34	10.08	0.27				
19	15	10.6	10.47	10.34	0.07				
20	16	9.8	10.14	10.47	0.45				
21	17	8.8	9.47	10.14	1.78				
22	18	8.9	9.18	9.47	0.32				
23	19	9.2	9.19	9.18	0.00				
24	20	9.7	9.45	9.19	0.26				
25	21	9.7	9.57	9.45	0.06				
26	22	8.8	9.19	9.57	0.60				
27	23	8.1	8.64	9.19	1.18				
28	24	7.6	8.12	8.64	1.09				
29	25	7.9	8.01	8.12	0.05				
30	26			8.01					
31	27			8.01					
32	28			8.01					
33	29			8.01					
34	30			8.01					

****

Graph Accompanying Exercise 6.3

Building Expenditures to GNP

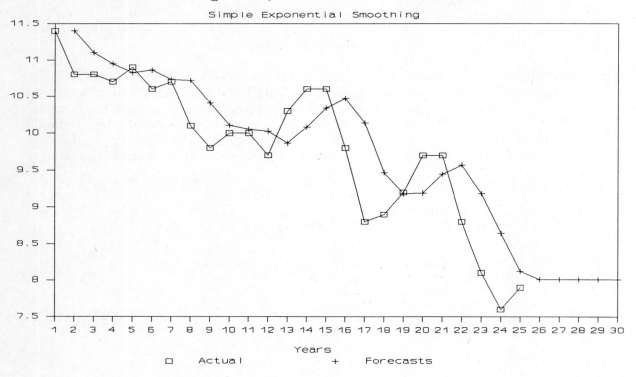

Simple Exponential Smoothing

Years

□   Actual   +   Forecasts

Graph Aaccompanying Exercise 6.4

Housing Starts per 1,000 People

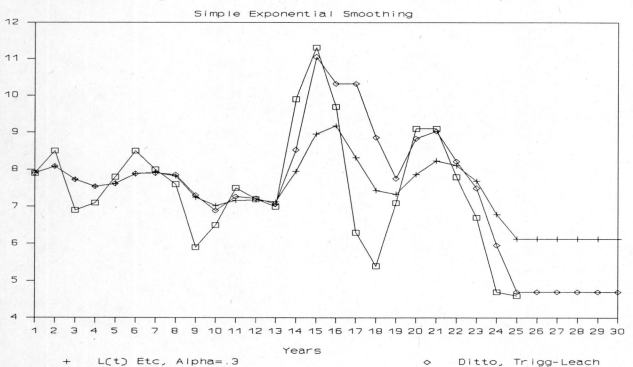

Simple Exponential Smoothing

Years

+   L(t) Etc, Alpha=.3   ◇   Ditto, Trigg-Leach

6.4 The accompanying table shows private housing starts per thousand of population in the United States over a period of twenty five years.

(a) Use simple exponential smoothing, with smothing constant 0.3, to predict future values of this series.

(b) Graph the time series, together with forecasts for the next five years.

(c) Use the method of Trigg and Leach, with $\delta = 0.1$, to derive forecasts through simple exponential smoothing with an adaptive smoothing constant.

------- Answer to 6.4 --------

	A	B	C	D	E	F	G	H	I
1									
2		Housing	0.3 = ALPHA		0.1 = DELTA				
3		Starts							
4	Year	X(t)	L(t)	e(t)	E(t)	D(t)	TS(t)	ALPHA	L(t)
5									
6	1	7.9	7.90						7.90
7	2	8.5	8.08	0.60				0.30	8.08
8	3	6.9	7.73	-1.18				0.30	7.73
9	4	7.1	7.54	-0.63				0.30	7.54
10	5	7.8	7.62	0.26				0.30	7.62
11	6	8.5	7.88	0.88				0.30	7.88
12	7	8.0	7.92	0.12	-0.11	0.61	-0.18	0.18	7.90
13	8	7.6	7.82	-0.30	0.07	0.44	0.15	0.15	7.86
14	9	5.9	7.25	-1.96	-0.20	0.70	-0.28	0.28	7.30
15	10	6.5	7.02	-0.80	-0.41	0.81	-0.51	0.51	6.90
16	11	7.5	7.17	0.60	-0.47	0.76	-0.62	0.62	7.27
17	12	7.2	7.18	-0.07	-0.51	0.75	-0.68	0.68	7.22
18	13	7.0	7.12	-0.22	-0.49	0.73	-0.67	0.67	7.07
19	14	9.9	7.96	2.83	0.47	0.91	0.52	0.52	8.53
20	15	11.3	8.96	2.77	1.18	1.30	0.91	0.91	11.05
21	16	9.7	9.18	-1.35	0.79	1.45	0.55	0.55	10.31
22	17	6.3	8.32	-4.01	0.00	2.24	0.00	0.00	10.31
23	18	5.4	7.44	-4.91	-0.94	3.17	-0.29	0.29	8.86
24	19	7.1	7.34	-1.76	-1.85	2.96	-0.63	0.63	7.76
25	20	9.1	7.87	1.34	-2.14	2.68	-0.80	0.80	8.83
26	21	9.1	8.24	0.27	-1.82	2.46	-0.74	0.74	9.03
27	22	7.8	8.11	-1.23	-1.26	1.90	-0.66	0.66	8.22
28	23	6.7	7.68	-1.52	-0.58	1.22	-0.47	0.47	7.50
29	24	4.7	6.79	-2.80	-0.79	1.43	-0.55	0.55	5.96
30	25	4.6	6.13	-1.36	-1.33	1.43	-0.93	0.93	4.70
31	26		6.13						4.70
32	27		6.13						4.70
33	28		6.13						4.70
34	29		6.13						4.70
35	30		6.13						4.70
36									
37			<< Part (a) >>	<< Part (c)					>>

****

6.5 Exponential smoothing is used to provide forecasting algorithms that are not explicitly based on the specification of a formal statistical model. Discuss the consequences, and some of the difficulties that can arise, in the absence of a formal model.

------- Answer to 6.5 --------

See sections 6.6 and 6.7 of text.
Because no formal class of generating model is assumed, exponential smoothing
(a)   lacks a systematic approach to model selection, and
(b)   lacks a convincing methodology for checking the appropriateness of the chosen algorithm (this includes convincing statistical tests and confidence intervals for forecasts).

****

6.6 The accompanying table shows the United States 6-month treasury bill rate over thirty consecutive months.

(a)   Use simple exponential smoothing, with smoothing constants 0.2, 0.4, 0.6, 0.8 to predict future values of this time series.
(b)   Which value of the smoothing constant would you chose for further forecasting?

------- Answer to 6.6 --------

Graph Accompanying Exercise 6.6

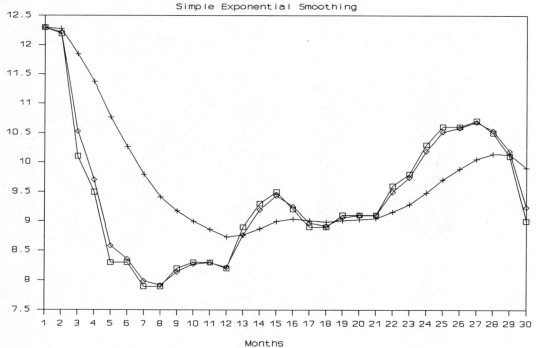

US Six Month Treasury Bill Rate

Simple Exponential Smoothing

□   Actual   +   Smooth (Alpha=0.2)   ◇   Smooth (Alpha=0.8)

	A	B	C	D	E	F	G	H	I
2		Rate	0.2	0.4	0.6	0.8			
3	Month	X(t)	L(t)	L(t)	L(t)	L(t)			
5	1	12.3	12.3	12.3	12.3	12.3			
6	2	12.2	12.3	12.3	12.2	12.2			
7	3	10.1	11.8	11.4	11.0	10.5			
8	4	9.5	11.4	10.6	10.1	9.7			
9	5	8.3	10.8	9.7	9.0	8.6			
10	6	8.3	10.3	9.1	8.6	8.4			
11	7	7.9	9.8	8.6	8.2	8.0			
12	8	7.9	9.4	8.3	8.0	7.9			
13	9	8.2	9.2	8.3	8.1	8.1			
14	10	8.3	9.0	8.3	8.2	8.3			
15	11	8.3	8.9	8.3	8.3	8.3			
16	12	8.2	8.7	8.3	8.2	8.2			
17	13	8.9	8.8	8.5	8.6	8.8			
18	14	9.3	8.9	8.8	9.0	9.2			
19	15	9.5	9.0	9.1	9.3	9.4			
20	16	9.2	9.0	9.1	9.2	9.2			
21	17	8.9	9.0	9.0	9.0	9.0			
22	18	8.9	9.0	9.0	9.0	8.9			
23	19	9.1	9.0	9.0	9.0	9.1			
24	20	9.1	9.0	9.1	9.1	9.1			
25	21	9.1	9.0	9.1	9.1	9.1			
26	22	9.6	9.2	9.3	9.4	9.5			
27	23	9.8	9.3	9.5	9.6	9.7			
28	24	10.3	9.5	9.8	10.0	10.2			
29	25	10.6	9.7	10.1	10.4	10.5			
30	26	10.6	9.9	10.3	10.5	10.6			
31	27	10.7	10.0	10.5	10.6	10.7			
32	28	10.5	10.1	10.5	10.5	10.5			
33	29	10.1	10.1	10.3	10.3	10.2			
34	30	9.0	9.9	9.8	9.5	9.2			

	A	B	C	D	E	F	G	H	I
37		Rate	0.2	0.4	0.6	0.8			
38	Month	X(t)	e(t)²	e(t)²	e(t)²	e(t)²		Data Table 1	
40	1	12.3							44.88
41	2	12.2	0.01	0.01	0.01	0.01		0.1	76.06
42	3	10.1	4.75	4.67	4.58	4.49		0.2	44.88
43	4	9.5	5.49	3.59	2.12	1.05		0.3	31.16
44	5	8.3	9.46	5.46	3.18	1.97		0.4	23.51
45	6	8.3	6.05	1.97	0.51	0.08		0.5	18.69
46	7	7.9	5.61	1.54	0.47	0.21		0.6	15.43
47	8	7.9	3.59	0.55	0.08	0.01		0.7	13.13
48	9	8.2	1.48	0.02	0.04	0.08		0.8	11.48
49	10	8.3	0.76	0.00	0.03	0.02		0.9	10.28
50	11	8.3	0.49	0.00	0.00	0.00		0.95	9.83
51	12	8.2	0.43	0.01	0.01	0.01		0.99	9.52
52	13	8.9	0.03	0.41	0.45	0.46			
53	14	9.3	0.29	0.62	0.45	0.29			
54	15	9.5	0.40	0.45	0.22	0.09			
55	16	9.2	0.04	0.01	0.01	0.06			
56	17	8.9	0.02	0.06	0.12	0.12			
57	18	8.9	0.01	0.02	0.02	0.00			
58	19	9.1	0.01	0.01	0.02	0.03			
59	20	9.1	0.01	0.00	0.00	0.00			
60	21	9.1	0.01	0.00	0.00	0.00			
61	22	9.6	0.31	0.28	0.26	0.25			
62	23	9.8	0.42	0.27	0.16	0.09			
63	24	10.3	1.03	0.65	0.44	0.31			
64	25	10.6	1.24	0.62	0.32	0.17			
65	26	10.6	0.79	0.22	0.05	0.01			
66	27	10.7	0.66	0.15	0.04	0.01			
67	28	10.5	0.20	0.00	0.02	0.03			
68	29	10.1	0.00	0.15	0.20	0.19			
69	30	9.0	1.28	1.77	1.64	1.41			

Sum of squared one-step ahead forecasts
44.88 23.51 15.43 11.48

(b)   Since the smoothing constant 0.8 gives rise to the smallest sum of squared one step ahead forecasts, one would prefer this value among those considered for further forecasting.

FURTHER COMMENTS: After looking at the graph of these one step ahead forecasts, and knowing that the best smoothing constant is close to one, it is clear that local trend is important. Hence let's try Holt's exponential smoothing.

	A	B	C	D	E	F	G	H	I
1									
2					9.23 = forecast SSE				
3		Rate	0.8	0.5					
4	Month	X(t)	L(t)	T(t)	e(t)²				
5									
6	1	12.3		0.0					
7	2	12.2	12.2	-0.1					
8	3	10.1	10.5	-0.9	4.00				
9	4	9.5	9.5	-0.9	0.01				
10	5	8.3	8.4	-1.1	0.08				
11	6	8.3	8.1	-0.7	0.99				
12	7	7.9	7.8	-0.5	0.21				
13	8	7.9	7.8	-0.2	0.32				
14	9	8.2	8.1	0.0	0.44				
15	10	8.3	8.3	0.1	0.05				
16	11	8.3	8.3	0.1	0.00				
17	12	8.2	8.2	0.0	0.04				
18	13	8.9	8.8	0.3	0.43				
19	14	9.3	9.2	0.4	0.07				
20	15	9.5	9.5	0.3	0.01				
21	16	9.2	9.3	0.1	0.42				
22	17	8.9	9.0	-0.1	0.25				
23	18	8.9	8.9	-0.1	0.00				
24	19	9.1	9.0	0.0	0.11				
25	20	9.1	9.1	0.0	0.00				
26	21	9.1	9.1	0.0	0.00				
27	22	9.6	9.5	0.2	0.22				
28	23	9.8	9.8	0.2	0.01				
29	24	10.3	10.2	0.4	0.07				
30	25	10.6	10.6	0.4	0.00				
31	26	10.6	10.7	0.2	0.13				
32	27	10.7	10.7	0.1	0.03				
33	28	10.5	10.6	0.0	0.14				
34	29	10.1	10.2	-0.2	0.22				
35	30	9.0	9.2	-0.6	0.99				
36									
37									
38	Data Table 2 (with restricted search to save space)								
39									
40	8.44 = Minimum value in 2 way table								
41									
42	9.23	0.1	0.3	0.5	0.6	0.7	0.8	0.9	
43	0.8	11.27	10.24	9.23	8.89	8.66	8.54	8.51	
44	0.9	10.08	9.26	8.61	8.46	8.44	8.53	8.73	
45	0.99	9.36	8.78	8.49	8.56	8.79	9.19	9.79	

Since a large smoothing constant for the trend component leads to smaller sum of squared one step ahead forecasts, this is a better alternative than simple exponential smoothing.

****

6.7 Suppose that the series X_t is to be predicted through Holt's linear trend algorithm, with smoothing constants α and β. Let L_t and T_t denote the estimates of level and slope, and e_t the error made in the prediction of X_t at time $(t-1)$.

(a) Show that
$$T_{t-1} - 2T_{t-2} + T_{t-3} = \alpha\beta(e_{t-1} - e_{t-2})$$

(b) Show that
$$L_{t-1} - 2L_{t-2} + L_{t-3} = \alpha\beta e_{t-2} + \alpha(e_{t-1} - e_{t-2})$$

(c) Using the results in (a) and (b), show that
$$X_t - 2X_{t-1} + X_{t-2} = e_t - (2-\alpha-\alpha\beta)e_{t-1} + (1-\alpha)e_{t-2}$$

------- Answer to 6.7 --------

Given the equations:
$$L_t = \alpha X_t + (1-\alpha)(L_{t-1} + T_{t-1}) \tag{6.3.1a}$$

and
$$T_t = \beta(L_t - L_{t-1}) + (1-\beta)T_{t-1} \tag{6.3.1b}$$

the text arrives at the error form of the algorithm:
$$L_t = L_{t-1} + T_{t-1} + \alpha e_t \tag{6.3.3a}$$

and
$$T_t = T_{t-1} + \alpha\beta e_t \tag{6.3.3b}$$

(a) Re-arrange (6.3.3b) so that: $T_t - T_{t-1} = \alpha\beta e_t$.

Lag this equation by one: $T_{t-1} - T_{t-2} = \alpha\beta e_{t-1}$.

Subtract the latter from the former, to get: $T_t - 2T_{t-1} + T_{t-2} = \alpha\beta(e_t - e_{t-1})$

which is equivalent to the equation in Exercise 6.7a, except this is for one period ahead.

(b) Similarly, re-arrange (6.3.3a) so that:

$L_t - L_{t-1} = T_{t-1} + \alpha e_t$ and lag by one period; $L_{t-1} - L_{t-2} = T_{t-2} + \alpha e_{t-1}$ Subtract the latter from the former, to get:

$$L_t - 2L_{t-1} + L_{t-2} = T_{t-1} - T_{t-2} + \alpha(e_t - e_{t-1})$$

and since, $T_{t-1} - T_{t-2} = \alpha\beta e_{t-1}$, which was arrived at above:

$$L_t - 2L_{t-1} + L_{t-2} = \alpha\beta e_{t-1} + \alpha(e_t - e_{t-1})$$

which is equivalent to the equation in Exercise 6.7b, again except that this is for one period ahead.

(c) Since $$e_t = X_t - (L_{t-1} - T_{t-1}), \; X_t = e_t + L_{t-1} - T_{t-1}$$

Subtract the once lagged version of this equation away from itself to get;

$X_t - X_{t-1} = e_t - e_{t-1} + L_{t-1} - L_{t-2} - (T_{t-1} - T_{t-2})$ and again subtract the once lagged version of this equation from itself to get, after re-arranging:

$$X_t - 2X_{t-1} + X_{t-2} = e_t - 2e_{t-1} + e_{t-2} + L_{t-1} - 2L_{t-2} + L_{t-3} - (T_{t-1} - 2T_{t-2} + T_{t-3})$$

Using the results in parts (a) and (b), the RHS becomes:

$$e_t - 2e_{t-1} + e_{t-2} + \alpha\beta e_{t-2} + \alpha(e_{t-1} - e_{t-2}) + \alpha\beta(e_{t-1} - e_{t-2})$$

which after collecting like terms becomes identical to the RHS of the equation in part (c).

****

6.8 Consider again the data of Exercise 6.3 on the percent of building expenditures to gross national product.

(a)   Use Holt's linear trend algorithm, with smoothing constants $\alpha = 0.4$, $\beta = 0.5$, to obtain forecasts for the next five years.

(b)   Faced with such a time series, discuss how you would decide whether to use simple exponential smoothing or Holt's linear trend algorithm.

------- Answer to 6.8 --------

Graph Accompanying Exercise 6.8
Building Expenditure to GNP
Holt's Linear Trend Algorithm

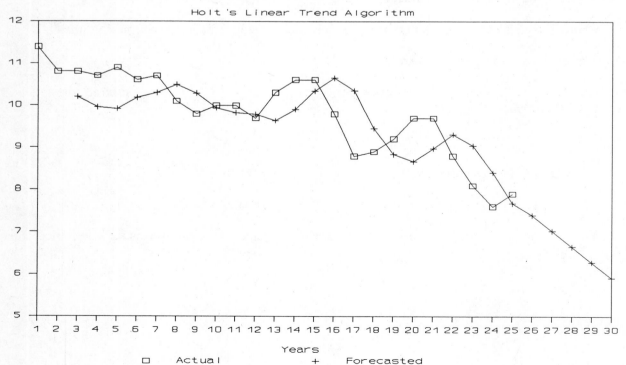

	A	B	C	D	E	F	G
1							
2						Forecast	
3			ALPHA	BETA		SSE	
4			0.4	0.5		10.53	
5		Expenditures					
6	Year	X(t)	L(t)	T(t)	f(t,1)	e(t)²	
7							
8	1	11.4					
9	2	10.8	10.80	-0.60			
10	3	10.8	10.44	-0.48	10.20	0.36	
11	4	10.7	10.26	-0.33	9.96	0.55	
12	5	10.9	10.31	-0.14	9.92	0.95	
13	6	10.6	10.35	-0.05	10.18	0.18	
14	7	10.7	10.46	0.03	10.29	0.16	
15	8	10.1	10.33	-0.05	10.49	0.15	
16	9	9.8	10.09	-0.14	10.28	0.23	
17	10	10.0	9.97	-0.13	9.94	0.00	
18	11	10.0	9.90	-0.10	9.83	0.03	
19	12	9.7	9.76	-0.12	9.80	0.01	
20	13	10.3	9.90	0.01	9.64	0.44	
21	14	10.6	10.19	0.15	9.92	0.47	
22	15	10.6	10.44	0.20	10.34	0.07	
23	16	9.8	10.31	0.03	10.64	0.71	
24	17	8.8	9.72	-0.28	10.34	2.37	
25	18	8.9	9.23	-0.38	9.45	0.30	
26	19	9.2	8.99	-0.31	8.84	0.13	
27	20	9.7	9.08	-0.11	8.67	1.06	
28	21	9.7	9.27	0.04	8.98	0.53	
29	22	8.8	9.10	-0.06	9.30	0.25	
30	23	8.1	8.66	-0.25	9.04	0.88	
31	24	7.6	8.09	-0.41	8.41	0.66	
32	25	7.9	7.76	-0.37	7.67	0.05	
33	26				7.40		
34	27				7.03		
35	28				6.66		
36	29				6.29		
37	30				5.92		
38							
39	Data Table 2.						
40							
41	10.53	0.1	0.2	0.3	0.4	0.5	0.7	0.9
42	0.1	117.332	66.7860	50.1064	42.6605	36.9376	26.6875	19.6289
43	0.3	20.4773	14.6064	12.1774	11.0522	10.7434	11.4897	13.3217
44	0.5	11.3064	9.59755	9.33406	9.65533	10.2819	11.8812	13.3589
45	0.7	8.39087	7.81140	7.97152	8.36399	8.81073	9.53056	9.79369
46	0.9	6.75785	6.50673	6.65941	6.88285	7.07147	7.21066	7.06993

This two way table shows that the minimum one step ahead forecast SSE occurs when α is large, and β is 0.2. (α varies by row, and β by column).

****

6.9 The accompanying table shows anthracite production, in thousands of tons, over a period of twenty five years.

(a) Use Holt's linear trend algorithm, with smoothing constants $\alpha = 0.3$, $\beta = 0.4$, to predict this time series.

(b) Graph the series together with forecasts for the next five years.

------- Answer to 6.9 --------

	A	B	C	D	E	F	G
1	Anthracite Production (Thousand Net Tons)						
2						Forecast	
3			ALPHA	BETA		SSE	
4			0.3	0.4		44.15	
5							
6	t	X(t)	L(t)	T(t)	f(t,1)	e(t)²	
7							
8	1	20.6					
9	2	18.8	18.80	-1.80			
10	3	17.4	17.12	-1.75	17.00	0.16	
11	4	16.9	15.83	-1.57	15.37	2.35	
12	5	18.3	15.47	-1.08	14.26	16.33	
13	6	17.2	15.23	-0.75	14.39	7.91	
14	7	14.9	14.61	-0.70	14.49	0.17	
15	8	12.9	13.61	-0.82	13.91	1.03	
16	9	12.3	12.64	-0.88	12.79	0.24	
17	10	11.5	11.69	-0.91	11.77	0.07	
18	11	10.5	10.69	-0.94	10.78	0.08	
19	12	9.7	9.74	-0.95	9.75	0.00	
20	13	8.7	8.76	-0.96	8.79	0.01	
21	14	7.1	7.59	-1.04	7.80	0.49	
22	15	6.7	6.59	-1.03	6.55	0.02	
23	16	6.3	5.79	-0.94	5.57	0.54	
24	17	6.4	5.32	-0.75	4.85	2.40	
25	18	6.2	5.05	-0.56	4.56	2.68	
26	19	6.2	5.01	-0.35	4.50	2.89	
27	20	6.7	5.27	-0.11	4.66	4.17	
28	21	5.4	5.24	-0.08	5.16	0.06	
29	22	5.8	5.35	0.00	5.16	0.41	
30	23	5.4	5.36	0.01	5.35	0.00	
31	24	4.2	5.02	-0.14	5.37	1.37	
32	25	4.0	4.62	-0.24	4.88	0.78	
33	26				4.38		
34	27				4.14		
35	28				3.90		
36	29				3.65		
37	30				3.41		
38							
39	Data Table 2.						
40							
41	44.15	0.1	0.2	0.3	0.4	0.5	0.7	0.9
42	0.1	614.38	300.01	168.08	110.89	85.36	71.30	75.07
43	0.3	95.15	54.26	45.48	44.15	44.52	44.45	42.79
44	0.5	45.85	32.96	30.68	30.37	30.50	31.56	33.64
45	0.7	30.93	25.03	24.27	24.49	25.01	26.37	27.65
46	0.9	24.17	20.98	20.80	21.21	21.77	23.01	24.30

Graph Accompanying Exercise 6.9

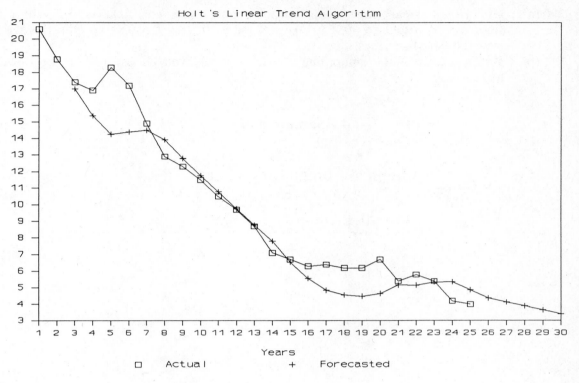

This two way table (α varies by row, and β by column) shows that the minimum one step ahead forecast SSE occurs when α is large, and β is 0.3.

****

6.10 The accompanying table shows the number of active oil wells (in thousands) in the United
      States over a period of 30 years.

(a)   Use Holt's linear trend algorithm with all sixteen combinations of values of
      smoothing constants, $\alpha = 0.2, 0.4, 0.6, 0.8$ and $\beta = 0.2, 0.4, 0.6, 0.8$ to predict this series
      over the next five years.

(b)   Which values of the smoothing constants would you choose to use for further
      forecasting.

------- Answer to 6.10 --------

Graph Accompanying Exercise 6.9

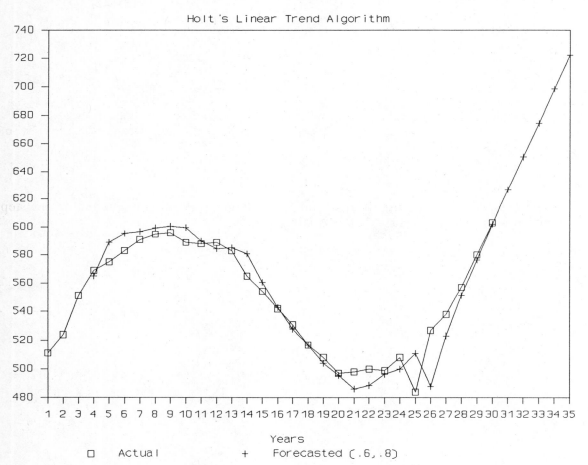

Number of Active Oilwells in US

Holt's Linear Trend Algorithm

□   Actual   +   Forecasted (.6,.8)

	A	B	C	D	E	F	G	H
1	Number of Active Oil Wells in US							
2						Average forecast		
3			ALPHA	BETA		SSE		
4			0.6	0.8		139.2		
5								
6	Year	X(t)	L(t)	T(t)	f(t,1)	e(t)²		
7								
8	1	511						
9	2	524	524.0	13.00				
10	3	551	545.4	19.72				
11	4	569	567.4	21.58	565.1	15.1		
12	5	575	580.6	14.85	589.0	196.9		
13	6	583	588.0	8.87	595.5	155.3		
14	7	591	593.3	6.06	596.9	34.2		
15	8	595	596.8	3.95	599.4	19.4		
16	9	596	597.9	1.69	600.7	22.2		
17	10	589	593.2	-3.39	599.6	111.7		
18	11	588	588.7	-4.27	589.8	3.4		
19	12	589	587.2	-2.09	584.5	20.6		
20	13	583	583.8	-3.10	585.1	4.4		
21	14	565	571.3	-10.65	580.7	247.7		
22	15	554	556.7	-13.84	560.6	44.1		
23	16	542	542.3	-14.23	542.8	0.7		
24	17	531	529.8	-12.84	528.1	8.4		
25	18	517	517.0	-12.84	517.0	0.0		
26	19	508	506.5	-11.00	504.2	14.7		
27	20	497	496.4	-10.26	495.5	2.3		
28	21	498	493.3	-4.56	486.1	141.0		
29	22	500	495.5	0.87	488.7	127.9		
30	23	499	497.9	2.14	496.3	7.1		
31	24	508	504.8	5.94	500.1	62.7		
32	25	484	494.7	-6.91	510.8	717.0		
33	26	527	511.3	11.91	487.8	1536.5		
34	27	538	532.1	19.00	523.2	218.2		
35	28	557	554.6	21.83	551.1	34.9		
36	29	580	578.6	23.53	576.5	12.5		
37	30	603	602.6	23.95	602.1	0.8		
38	31				626.6			
39	32				650.6			
40	33				674.5			
41	34				698.5			
42	35				722.4			
43								
44								
45	Data Table 2							
46								
47	139.2	0.2	0.4	0.6	0.8			
48	0.2	2246.4	1435.2	772.3	455.9			
49	0.4	669.1	339.0	212.7	167.5			
50	0.6	328.3	190.6	148.8	139.2			
51	0.8	223.9	158.3	148.0	157.3			

The two table (range A47..E51) has α varying by row, and β by column. Since the sum of squared of one step ahead forecast errors is the smallest when $\alpha=0.6$ and $\beta=0.8$ (for the 16 combinations tried), one would choose this combination for further forecasting.

****

6.11 The accompanying table shows plant and equipment expenditures in billions of dollars in the United States over a period of seven years.

(a)   Use the Holt-winters algorithm with additive seasonality, and with smoothing constants $\alpha = 0.5$, $\beta = 0.2$, $\gamma = 0.3$ to derive forecasts for the next eight quarters.
(b)   Repeat part (a), but now assuming multiplicative seasonality

------- Answer to 6.11 --------

	A	B	C	D	E	F	G	H
1	Holt-Winters with additive seasonality							
2	Plant & Equipment Expenditures: Billions of Dollars							
3								
4				ALPHA	BETA	GAMMA		
5				0.5	0.2	0.3		
6								
7	Year	Qtr	X(t)	L(t)	T(t)	F(t)		
8								
9	1	1	19.38			-2.73		
10	1	2	22.01			-0.10		
11	1	3	21.86			-0.25		
12	1	4	25.20	22.11	0.00	3.09		
13	2	1	21.50	23.17	0.21	-2.41		
14	2	2	24.73	24.11	0.36	0.11		
15	2	3	25.04	24.88	0.44	-0.13		
16	2	4	28.48	25.36	0.45	3.10		
17	3	1	24.10	26.16	0.52	-2.31		
18	3	2	28.16	27.36	0.66	0.32		
19	3	3	28.23	28.19	0.69	-0.08		
20	3	4	31.92	28.85	0.68	3.09		
21	4	1	25.82	28.83	0.54	-2.52		
22	4	2	28.43	28.74	0.42	0.13		
23	4	3	27.79	28.51	0.29	-0.27		
24	4	4	30.74	28.23	0.17	2.92		
25	5	1	25.87	28.39	0.17	-2.52		
26	5	2	29.70	29.07	0.27	0.28		
27	5	3	30.41	30.01	0.41	-0.07		
28	5	4	34.52	31.01	0.52	3.10		
29	6	1	29.20	31.63	0.54	-2.49		
30	6	2	33.73	32.81	0.67	0.47		
31	6	3	34.82	34.19	0.81	0.14		
32	6	4	38.06	34.98	0.81	3.09		
33	7	1	32.35	35.32	0.71	-2.63		
34	7	2	37.89	36.72	0.85	0.68		
35	7	3	38.67	38.05	0.95	0.28		
36	7	4	44.91	40.41	1.23	3.51	44.91	
37	8	1					39.01	
38	8	2					43.55	
39	8	3					44.38	
40	8	4					48.84	
41	9	1					43.93	
42	9	2					48.47	
43	9	3					49.30	
44	9	4					53.76	

	A	B	C	D	E	F	G	H
1	Holt-Winters with multiplicative seasonality							
2				ALPHA	BETA	GAMMA		
3				0.5	0.2	0.3		
4								
5	Year	Qtr	X(t)	L(t)	T(t)	F(t)		
6								
7	1	1	19.38			0.88		
8	1	2	22.01			1.00		
9	1	3	21.86			0.99		
10	1	4	25.20	22.11	0.00	1.14		
11	2	1	21.50	23.32	0.24	0.89		
12	2	2	24.73	24.20	0.37	1.00		
13	2	3	25.04	24.95	0.45	0.99		
14	2	4	28.48	25.19	0.40	1.14		
15	3	1	24.10	26.34	0.55	0.90		
16	3	2	28.16	27.48	0.67	1.01		
17	3	3	28.23	28.29	0.70	0.99		
18	3	4	31.92	28.53	0.61	1.13		
19	4	1	25.82	28.95	0.57	0.90		
20	4	2	28.43	28.84	0.43	1.00		
21	4	3	27.79	28.61	0.30	0.99		
22	4	4	30.74	28.04	0.13	1.12		
23	5	1	25.87	28.52	0.20	0.90		
24	5	2	29.70	29.17	0.29	1.01		
25	5	3	30.41	30.13	0.42	0.99		
26	5	4	34.52	30.67	0.45	1.12		
27	6	1	29.20	31.80	0.58	0.90		
28	6	2	33.73	32.93	0.69	1.01		
29	6	3	34.82	34.33	0.83	1.00		
30	6	4	38.06	34.54	0.71	1.12		
31	7	1	32.35	35.50	0.76	0.91		
32	7	2	37.89	36.84	0.88	1.02		
33	7	3	38.67	38.19	0.97	1.00		
34	7	4	44.91	39.70	1.08	1.12	44.91	
35	8	1					36.98	
36	8	2					42.57	
37	8	3					43.10	
38	8	4					49.32	
39	9	1					40.89	
40	9	2					46.96	
41	9	3					47.43	
42	9	4					54.15	

Graph Accompanying Exericse 6.11

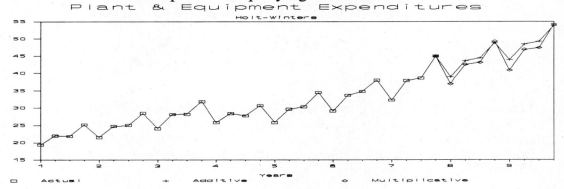

Plant & Equipment Expenditures
Holt-Winters

□ Actual   + Additive   ◇ Multiplicative

6.12   Suppose that, in general exponential smoothing, a constant predictor

$$\hat{X}_t(h) = a(t) \quad ; \quad h = 1, 2, \cdots$$

is required. The value of $a(t)$ is chosen to minimize

$$S = \sum_{j=0}^{t-1} \delta^j [X_{t-j} - a(t)]^2 \quad ; \quad 0 < \delta < 1$$

(a)   Show that the value of $a(t)$ for which S is a minimum is

$$a(t) = (1-\delta) \sum_{j=0}^{t-1} \delta^j X_{t-j} / (1-\delta^t)$$

and hence that

$$a(t-1) = (1-\delta) \sum_{j=0}^{t-2} \delta^j X_{t-1-j} / (1-\delta^{t-1})$$

(b)   Show that

$$a(t) - \delta a(t-1) \simeq (1-\delta) \ X_t$$

provided that t is moderately large, so that we can take $\delta^t \simeq \delta^{t-1} \simeq 0$.

(c)   Discuss the result in (b) in terms of the simple exponential smoothing algorithm.

------- Answer to 6.12 --------

(a)   Differentiate S with respect to $a(t)$, and set equal to zero for S's maximum:

$$\frac{dS}{da(t)} = -\ \sum 2\delta^j \ [X_{t-j} - a(t)] = 0$$

so that
$$\sum_{j=0}^{t-1} \delta^j \ X_{t-j} = \sum_{j=0}^{t-1} \delta^j \ a(t)$$

where $\sum_{j=0}^{t-1} \delta^j = (1-\delta^t)/(1-\delta)$

and so re-arranging the previous equation we get the solution.

(b)   When t is moderately large, then δ^t is approximately zero, and hence

$$a(t) = (1-\delta) \ [X_t + \delta^1 X_{t-1} + \delta^2 X_{t-2} + \cdots + \delta^{t-1} X_1]$$

and so
$$\delta a(t) = (1-\delta) \qquad [\delta^1 X_{t-1} + \delta^2 X_{t-2} + \cdots + \delta^t X_0]$$

and thus
$$a(t) - \delta a(t) = (1-\delta) \ X_t$$

(c)   This last statement is nothing more than the simple exponential smoothing algorithm - ie, if one replaces $a(t)$ with L_t and re-arranges terms.   Thus one can say the simple exponential smoothing forecast is a constant predictor which minimizes a weighted average (with weights exponentially declining from the present to the past) of the past prediction errors.

****

6.13 The accompanying table shows monthly retail sales of apparel, in billions of dollars, over four years.

 (a) Use the Holt-Winters algorithm with additive seasonality, and with smoothing constants $\alpha = 0.2$, $\beta = 0.4$, $\gamma = 0.3$ to derive forecasts for the next twelve months.
 (b) Repeat part (a), but now assuming multiplicative seasonality.

------- Answer to 6.13 --------

Graph Accompanying Exercise 6.13
Retail Sales of Apparel

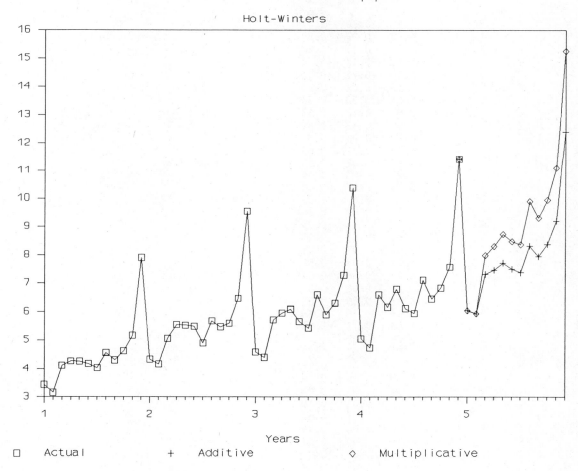

	A	B	C	D	E	F	G	H
1	Holt-Winters with additive seasonality							
2				ALPHA	BETA	GAMMA		
3			APPAREL	0.2	0.4	0.3		
4								
5	Year	Month	X(t)	L(t)	T(t)	F(t)		
6								
7	1	1	3.43			-1.07		
8	1	2	3.15			-1.35		
9	1	3	4.12			-0.38		
10	1	4	4.27			-0.23		
11	1	5	4.26			-0.24		
12	1	6	4.18			-0.32		
13	1	7	4.04			-0.46		
14	1	8	4.56			0.06		
15	1	9	4.31			-0.19		
16	1	10	4.62			0.12		
17	1	11	5.17			0.67		
18	1	12	7.91	4.50	0.00	3.41		
19	2	1	4.34	4.68	0.07	-0.85		
20	2	2	4.17	4.91	0.13	-1.17		
21	2	3	5.06	5.12	0.17	-0.29		
22	2	4	5.55	5.39	0.21	-0.11		
23	2	5	5.53	5.63	0.22	-0.20		
24	2	6	5.49	5.84	0.22	-0.33		
25	2	7	4.9	5.92	0.16	-0.63		
26	2	8	5.68	5.99	0.12	-0.05		
27	2	9	5.47	6.02	0.09	-0.30		
28	2	10	5.59	5.98	0.04	-0.03		
29	2	11	6.47	5.98	0.02	0.62		
30	2	12	9.55	6.03	0.03	3.44		
31	3	1	4.59	5.93	-0.02	-1.00		
32	3	2	4.4	5.85	-0.05	-1.25		
33	3	3	5.72	5.84	-0.03	-0.24		
34	3	4	5.96	5.87	-0.01	-0.05		
35	3	5	6.09	5.94	0.03	-0.10		
36	3	6	5.66	5.97	0.03	-0.33		
37	3	7	5.42	6.01	0.03	-0.62		
38	3	8	6.6	6.16	0.08	0.09		
39	3	9	5.9	6.24	0.08	-0.31		
40	3	10	6.31	6.32	0.08	-0.03		
41	3	11	7.27	6.45	0.10	0.68		
42	3	12	10.38	6.63	0.13	3.54		
43	4	1	5.05	6.62	0.07	-1.17		
44	4	2	4.73	6.55	0.02	-1.42		
45	4	3	6.59	6.62	0.04	-0.17		
46	4	4	6.17	6.57	0.00	-0.16		
47	4	5	6.79	6.64	0.03	-0.02		
48	4	6	6.12	6.62	0.01	-0.38		
49	4	7	5.95	6.62	0.01	-0.63		
50	4	8	7.11	6.70	0.04	0.19		
51	4	9	6.45	6.74	0.04	-0.31		
52	4	10	6.83	6.80	0.04	-0.01		
53	4	11	7.57	6.85	0.05	0.69		
54	4	12	11.43	7.10	0.13	3.77	11.43	11.43
55	5	1					6.06	6.04
56	5	2					5.93	5.93
57	5	3					7.31	7.99
58	5	4					7.46	8.30
59	5	5					7.72	8.73
60	5	6					7.49	8.47
61	5	7					7.36	8.36
62	5	8					8.31	9.90
63	5	9					7.95	9.31
64	5	10					8.37	9.95
65	5	11					9.20	11.10
66	5	12					12.41	15.26

Note that the data in column H is copied from the next spreadsheet which accomplishes the multiplicative seasonality version. It is put in above for direct comparison, and for graphing.

	A	B	C	D	E	F	G	H
1	Holt-Winters with multiplicative seasonality							
2				ALPHA	BETA	GAMMA		
3			APPAREL	0.2	0.4	0.3		
4								
5	Year	Month	X(t)	L(t)	T(t)	F(t)		
6								
7	1	1	3.43			0.76		
8	1	2	3.15			0.70		
9	1	3	4.12			0.92		
10	1	4	4.27			0.95		
11	1	5	4.26			0.95		
12	1	6	4.18			0.93		
13	1	7	4.04			0.90		
14	1	8	4.56			1.01		
15	1	9	4.31			0.96		
16	1	10	4.62			1.03		
17	1	11	5.17			1.15		
18	1	12	7.91	4.50	0.00	1.76		
19	2	1	4.34	4.74	0.10	0.81		
20	2	2	4.17	4.56	-0.01	0.76		
21	2	3	5.06	4.47	-0.05	0.98		
22	2	4	5.55	4.46	-0.03	1.04		
23	2	5	5.53	4.46	-0.02	1.03		
24	2	6	5.49	4.46	-0.01	1.02		
25	2	7	4.9	4.36	-0.05	0.97		
26	2	8	5.68	4.39	-0.02	1.10		
27	2	9	5.47	4.40	-0.01	1.04		
28	2	10	5.59	4.43	0.01	1.10		
29	2	11	6.47	4.61	0.08	1.22		
30	2	12	9.55	5.31	0.33	1.77		
31	3	1	4.59	5.27	0.18	0.83		
32	3	2	4.4	5.08	0.03	0.79		
33	3	3	5.72	5.04	0.00	1.03		
34	3	4	5.96	5.02	-0.01	1.08		
35	3	5	6.09	5.02	0.00	1.09		
36	3	6	5.66	4.94	-0.03	1.06		
37	3	7	5.42	4.82	-0.07	1.01		
38	3	8	6.6	4.90	-0.01	1.17		
39	3	9	5.9	4.88	-0.01	1.09		
40	3	10	6.31	4.94	0.02	1.15		
41	3	11	7.27	5.17	0.10	1.28		
42	3	12	10.38	5.94	0.37	1.76		
43	4	1	5.05	5.89	0.20	0.84		
44	4	2	4.73	5.66	0.03	0.81		
45	4	3	6.59	5.67	0.02	1.07		
46	4	4	6.17	5.57	-0.03	1.09		
47	4	5	6.79	5.57	-0.02	1.13		
48	4	6	6.12	5.46	-0.06	1.08		
49	4	7	5.95	5.31	-0.09	1.05		
50	4	8	7.11	5.36	-0.03	1.22		
51	4	9	6.45	5.33	-0.03	1.13		
52	4	10	6.83	5.38	0.00	1.19		
53	4	11	7.57	5.56	0.07	1.30		
54	4	12	11.43	6.44	0.39	1.77	11.43	
55	5	1					6.04	
56	5	2					5.93	
57	5	3					7.99	
58	5	4					8.30	
59	5	5					8.73	
60	5	6					8.47	
61	5	7					8.36	
62	5	8					9.90	
63	5	9					9.31	
64	5	10					9.95	
65	5	11					11.10	
66	5	12					15.26	

6.14   Suppose that the simple constant predictor

$$\hat{X_t}(h) = L(t) \quad ; \quad h = 1, 2, \cdots$$

is to be used, with L_t taken as the unweighted average of all available observations

$$L_t = (X_1 + X_2 + \cdots + X_t)/t$$

Show that $\qquad\qquad L_t = t^{-1} X_t + (t - 1)t^{-1}L_{t-1}$

Compare this with simple exponential smoothing.

------- Answer to 6.14 --------

$$L_t = t^{-1} (X_1 + X_2 + \cdots + X_t)$$

and thus $\qquad\qquad L_{t-1} = (t-1)^{-1} (X_1 + X_2 + \cdots + X_{t-1})$

or $\qquad\qquad (t-1)t^{-1} L_{t-1} = t^{-1} (X_1 + X_2 + \cdots + X_{t-1})$

Substituting this into the first equation -- for the appropriate parts of the RHS, one gets

$$L_t = t^{-1} X_t + (t-1)t^{-1}L_{t-1}$$

This is the same as simple exponential smoothing, <u>if</u> the smoothing constant, $\alpha = t^{-1}$. This cannot occur of course, since the smoothing constant does not change through time. Also, as similar as the two situations seem to be when expressed this way, neither is ever a special case of the other, and thus are never identical. Nevertheless, it is interesting to compare one's favorite smoothing constant (α) for a particular data set with t^{-1} (the inverse of the number of observations).

Note also that, as t becomes moderately large,

$$L_t \simeq L_{t-1}$$

which is simple exponential smoothing with $\alpha = 0$.

****

Chapter 7

ARIMA MODELS: THE BOX-JENKINS APPROACH TO FORECASTING

Contents of Chapter 7

In our experience most students will have access to an electronic spreadsheet on a personal computer. These will serve the student well for most of the material in this text – that is, all except for the selection, estimation, and checking of an ARIMA model. It is difficult to write computer programs to estimate ARIMA models, and thus the available programs are expensive. Although the procedure is cumbersome and although exact results will not be obtained, if an ARIMA model has no moving average terms, it can be estimated with a multiple regression program. Or, if the model has only one or two parameters, one can similarly get close by doing a one or two parameter grid search on a spreadsheet. This still leaves many possibly interesting models to be estimated by a name program (MINITAB, SAS, SPSS etc). The student may have access to such a program at school. For the students that have access to a PC at work, or at home, but do not have an ARIMA estimation program, we include here a program written in BASIC that will calculate the autocorrelations and partial autocorrelations. This can be used in the model selection phase.

Note it is not the intent that this program be elegant or computationally fast. It serves to calculate autocorrelations. Also, since written in BASIC it can be easily altered to the user's tastes in input/output and other needs (differencing, for example).

The program, called ACF.BAS, is listed in Exhibit M7.1 (see the next page).

The following notes are to point out various features of this program to those inclined to tinker with it. Please note the dimensions on line 100. Alter them if you have particular needs which are not met by these array sizes. Also, note that the program not only puts the results on the screen, but also puts them in a file called ACF.TMP into the default directory. See lines 180 and 480.

The input data file is currently expected to contain only raw data (no dates etc.). Each observation will normally be on a new line. The program will prompt you for the name of the input data file. It will also prompt you for the number of autocorrelations you want calculated and displayed. (Note that processing time grows exponentially as the number of auto-correlations to be calculated increases.)

The formulas for the calculations are the sample correlation version of equation (7.4.1) on page 230. The procedure for calculating the partial autocorrelations is explained near equation (7.5.8) on pp. 239-40. The program sets up a symmetrical matrix A whose elements are sample autocorrelations calculated on lines 220–260. A is inverted in place in lines 320–450, and used to calculate the partial autocorrelations on line 460.

```
100 DIM X(240), RHO(36), A(36,36), B(36,36)
110 'In line 100 the maximum number of observations is 240, and
120 'the maximum number of autocorrelations is 36.
130 '
140 CLS
150 INPUT "Input file";IFILE$
160 PRINT : INPUT "Maximum number of (partial) autocorrelations ";MAXAUTO
170 OPEN IFILE$ FOR INPUT AS #1
180 OPEN "acf.tmp" FOR OUTPUT AS #2
190 N=0 : SUM=0
200 N=N+1 : INPUT #1, X(N) : SUM=SUM+X(N) : IF EOF(1) <> -1 GOTO 200
210 XBAR=SUM/N : PRINT : PRINT "The number of observations is ";N
220 SD=0 : FOR T%=1 TO N : SD=SD+(X(T%)-XBAR)*(X(T%)-XBAR) : NEXT
230 PRINT : PRINT "  K   ACF      PACF"
240 FOR TAU%=1 TO MAXAUTO : SN=0
250 FOR T%=TAU%+1 TO N : SN=SN+(X(T%)-XBAR)*(X(T%-TAU%)-XBAR) : NEXT
260 RHO(TAU%)=SN/SD
270 FOR I=1 TO TAU% : A(I,I)=1 : NEXT
280 FOR I=1 TO TAU% : FOR J=I+1 TO TAU% : A(I,J)=RHO(J-I) : A(J,I)=RHO(J-I)

290 NEXT : NEXT
300 K=TAU%
310 '
320 ' ****** I N V E R T  (MATRIX "A" IN PLACE)
330 PMIN=1E-08 : IE = 0 : DET = 1
340 FOR ICOL=1 TO K : PIVOT=A(ICOL,ICOL) : DET=PIVOT*DET : A(ICOL,ICOL)=1!
350 IF(ABS(PIVOT) < PMIN) GOTO 430
360 FOR L=1 TO K : A(ICOL,L)=A(ICOL,L)/PIVOT : NEXT L
370 FOR L1=1 TO K
380 IF (L1 = ICOL) GOTO 410
390 T=A(L1,ICOL) : A(L1,ICOL)=0!
400 FOR L=1 TO K : A(L1,L)=A(L1,L)-A(ICOL,L)*T : NEXT L
410 NEXT L1 : NEXT ICOL
420 GOTO ^G50
430 IE=1 : PRINT "Problems with inversion" : STOP
440 '
450 ' ********* E N D   O F   I N V E R T
460 PACF=0 : FOR I=1 TO TAU% : PACF=PACF+A(TAU%,I)*RHO(I) : NEXT
470 PRINT USING " ## ##.### ##.###";TAU%;RHO(TAU%);PACF
480 PRINT #2, USING " ## ##.### ##.###";TAU%;RHO(TAU%);PACF
490 NEXT TAU%
500 SYSTEM
```

Exhibit M7.1
BASIC program that calculates ACFs and PACFs

Answers to questions at end of chapter.

7.1   The accompanying table gives 57 annual observations on building expenditures as a percentage of gross national product in the United States. Fit autoregressive models of all orders up to five. Select one of these fitted models for forecasting, and predict the next six values of this series.

------- Answer to 7.1 -------

The following is part of the SPSS output of the AR estimations for this problem. The forecasts for the next six periods for each of the models appears at the end of this output.

Both the AIC and SBC are minimized for the model AR(2). Given the AR(2)'s two significant coefficients it is clearly preferable to the AR(3), AR(4), and AR(5). Yet the forecasts for the series derived from the AR(2), AR(3), AR(4), and AR(5) are quite similar. See the accompanying clipped SPSS output and graph. The AR(1) is clearly the odd man out. This might be compared to the mis-specification of a regression model.

```
AR(1)                   --------------------

Standard error          1.1324912
Log likelihood          -87.639486
AIC                     179.27897
SBC                     183.36507

             Variables in the Model:

                     B          SEB      T-RATIO   APPROX. PROB.
AR1           .8633807    .06434466   13.418063      0.0
CONSTANT     9.4427244    .99333485    9.506084      0.0

AR(2)                   --------------------

Standard error          .98221932
Log likelihood          -79.290165
AIC                     164.58033
SBC                     170.70948

             Variables in the Model:

                     B          SEB      T-RATIO   APPROX. PROB.
AR1          1.2955643    .11488128   11.277419      0.0
AR2          -.5077917    .11460206   -4.430912      .00004638
CONSTANT     9.3390885    .59929915   15.583350      0.0
```

AR(3)   -------------------

Standard error   .9911009
Log likelihood   -79.286943
AIC   166.57389
SBC   174.74609

Variables in the Model:

	B	SEB	T-RATIO	APPROX. PROB.
AR1	1.2824954	.13575397	9.447203	0.0
AR2	-.4744255	.21249331	-2.232661	.02981909
AR3	-.0257318	.13581391	-.189464	.85045308
CONSTANT	9.3369075	.59101925	15.797975	0.0

AR(4)   -------------------

Standard error   .99160359
Log likelihood   -78.831099
AIC   167.6622
SBC   177.87745

Variables in the Model:

	B	SEB	T-RATIO	APPROX. PROB.
AR1	1.2863292	.13581664	9.471072	0.0
AR2	-.4135909	.22219382	-1.861397	.06834511
AR3	-.1910144	.22264569	-.857930	.39486852
AR4	.1287169	.13579121	.947903	.34756348
CONSTANT	9.3534437	.66851147	13.991448	0.0

AR(5)   -------------------

Standard error   .99908541
Log likelihood   -78.75266
AIC   169.50532
SBC   181.76363

Variables in the Model:

	B	SEB	T-RATIO	APPROX. PROB.
AR1	1.2953501	.13810454	9.379489	0.0
AR2	-.4256500	.22539596	-1.888454	.06465920
AR3	-.2172915	.23166680	-.937948	.35269207
AR4	.2094921	.22604839	.926758	.35841760
AR5	-.0626194	.13834791	-.452623	.65273970
CONSTANT	9.3472804	.64174744	14.565357	0.0

Case#	BUILDING RAW DATA	FIT1 AR(1)	FIT2 AR(2)	FIT3 AR(3)	FIT4 AR(4)	FIT5 AR(5)
48	9.80	10.44	10.33	10.33	10.31	10.26
49	8.80	9.75	9.30	9.30	9.30	9.31
50	8.90	8.89	8.41	8.40	8.38	8.38
51	9.20	8.97	9.04	9.02	9.07	9.09
52	9.70	9.23	9.38	9.38	9.51	9.48
53	9.70	9.66	9.88	9.88	9.88	9.82
54	8.80	9.66	9.62	9.63	9.63	9.63
55	8.10	8.89	8.46	8.47	8.41	8.41
56	7.60	8.28	8.01	8.00	7.95	7.97
57	7.90	7.85	7.72	7.71	7.77	7.79
58	.	8.11	8.36	8.35	8.38	8.35
59	.	8.29	8.80	8.80	8.87	8.82
60	.	8.45	9.14	9.15	9.19	9.12
61	.	8.59	9.35	9.38	9.34	9.30
62	.	8.70	9.46	9.49	9.37	9.38
63	.	8.80	9.49	9.52	9.35	9.41

End of SPSS output.

The following is a listing of the SPSS "include" file that produced the original of the above output.

```
set beep off.
set more off.
set length = 80 / eject = on.
set boxstring = "-:+".

set listing = "ch07q01.lis".

title 'EXERCISE 7.1'

data list file = "ch07q01.prn" / tmp 1-10.
compute building=tmp.

predict 58 thru 63.
arima variables = building / model = (1,0,0) constant.
compute fit1=fit#1.

predict 58 thru 63.
arima variables = building / model = (2,0,0) constant.
compute fit2=fit#1.

predict 58 thru 63.
arima variables = building / model = (3,0,0) constant.
compute fit3=fit#1.

predict 58 thru 63.
arima variables = building / model = (4,0,0) constant.
compute fit4=fit#1.

predict 58 thru 63.
arima variables = building / model = (5,0,0) constant.
compute fit5=fit#1.

list building fit1 fit2 fit3 fit4 fit5 / format = numbered.
```

Graph Accompanying Exercise 7.1
Building expenditures
as a percentage of GNP

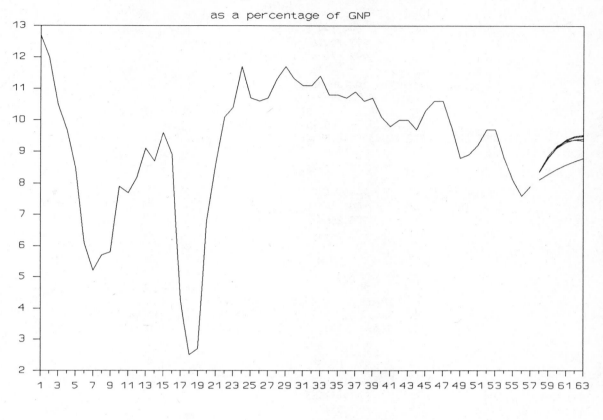

****

7.2   The accompanying table shows 120 monthly observations on soybean price, in dollars per ton, at Decatur, Illinois. Fit autoregressive models of all orders up to five. Choose one of these fitted models for forecasting, and predict price for the next six months.

------- Answer to 7.2 -------

The following is part of the SPSS output of the AR estimations for this problem. The forecasts for the next six periods for each of the models appears at the end of this output.

The AR(2) model has the lowest SBC while the AR(4) has the lowest AIC. The AR(2) is cleaner, or is more parsimonious. Nonetheless the AR(2) and the AR(4) models produce very similar forecasts. Note the the AR(5) also produces forecasts similar to these two.

```
AR(1)              --------------------

Standard error        14.918208
Log likelihood       -494.39998
AIC                   992.79996
SBC                   998.37495

         Variables in the Model:

                 B         SEB      T-RATIO    APPROX. PROB.
AR1          .89899     .039975   22.489105       0.0
CONSTANT  178.64823   12.581562   14.199209       0.0

AR(2)              --------------------

Standard error        14.572459
Log likelihood       -491.13348
AIC                   988.26697
SBC                   996.62944

         Variables in the Model:

                 B         SEB      T-RATIO    APPROX. PROB.
AR1         1.10760     .089247   12.410566       0.0
AR2         -.23219     .090040   -2.578788       .01115410
CONSTANT  177.89767   10.245443   17.363590       0.0

AR(3)              --------------------

Standard error        14.434712
Log likelihood       -489.52563
AIC                   987.05126
SBC                   998.20123

         Variables in the Model:

                 B         SEB      T-RATIO    APPROX. PROB.
AR1         1.06997    .0906660   11.801246       0.0
AR2         -.05170    .1344765    -.384437       .70135808
AR3         -.16379    .0917820   -1.784579       .07694375
CONSTANT  177.47842   8.8184225   20.125869       0.0

AR(4)              --------------------

Standard error        14.330119
Log likelihood       -488.19155
AIC                   986.3831
SBC                  1000.3206

         Variables in the Model:

                 B         SEB      T-RATIO    APPROX. PROB.
AR1         1.09216     .091241   11.969963       0.0
AR2         -.04130     .133231    -.309964       .75714880
AR3         -.32523     .133411   -2.437777       .01630874
AR4          .15277     .092534    1.650936       .10147993
CONSTANT  177.68340   10.311751   17.231157       0.0
```

```
AR(5)                    --------------------

Standard error      14.385015
Log likelihood      -488.14582
AIC                 988.29165
SBC                 1005.0166
```

Variables in the Model:

	B	SEB	T-RATIO	APPROX. PROB.
AR1	1.08708	.092768	11.718295	0.0
AR2	-.03095	.137380	-.225309	.82214230
AR3	-.32379	.134044	-2.415553	.01729995
AR4	.11791	.137461	.857754	.39282855
AR5	.03281	.094207	.348304	.72825414
CONSTANT	177.73526	10.715045	16.587449	0.0

Case#	SOYBEAN RAW DATA	FIT1 AR(1)	FIT2 AR(2)	FIT3 AR(3)	FIT4 AR(4)	FIT5 AR(5)
117	232.70	229.04	237.70	238.22	240.86	240.81
118	227.50	227.24	225.41	231.34	230.75	231.34
119	225.10	222.57	220.11	218.77	213.36	213.23
120	218.00	220.41	218.66	216.80	218.23	217.05
121	.	214.03	211.36	210.18	211.96	212.28
122	.	210.45	205.64	202.57	205.64	206.37
123	.	207.24	200.86	196.00	200.94	201.98
124	.	204.35	196.89	190.64	196.94	198.32
125	.	201.76	193.60	186.50	193.89	195.48
126	.	199.42	190.88	183.41	191.30	193.05

See the material for the answer for Exercise 7.1 (above) to find out which SPSS commands are used to produce this type of output.

Graph Accompanying Exercise 7.2

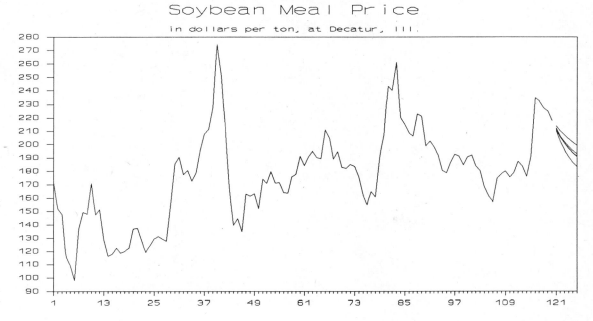

Soybean Meal Price
in dollars per ton, at Decatur, Ill.

7.3   The accompanying table shows 168 monthly observations on the price in cents per bushel of No. 2 yellow corn at Chicago, Illinois. Fit autoregressive models of all orders up to five. Select one of these fitted models for forecasting, and predict price for the next six months.

------- Answer to 7.3 -------

The following is part of the SPSS output of the AR estimations for this problem. The forecasts for the next six periods for each of the models appears at the end of this output.

The AIC is smallest for the AR(3), while the SBC is smallest for the AR(1). Unlike the results in Exercises 7.1 and 7.2, the forecasts produced by these two models are not close to the average forecasts – in fact, the forecasts from the AR(1) track higher than the others, while those from the AR(3) fall lower than the others.

```
AR(1)                   --------------------

Standard error          16.358411
Log likelihood          -708.47845
AIC                     1420.9569
SBC                     1427.2048

          Variables in the Model:

                    B          SEB       T-RATIO    APPROX. PROB.
AR1          .97873       .015006    65.221314     0.0
CONSTANT  238.43676    47.701223     4.998546      .00000148

AR(2)                   --------------------

Standard error          16.218075
Log likelihood          -706.51139
AIC                     1419.0228
SBC                     1428.3947

          Variables in the Model:

                    B          SEB       T-RATIO    APPROX. PROB.
AR1         1.12829      .076918    14.668709      0.0
AR2         -.15460      .077403    -1.997352      .04743093
CONSTANT  238.91797    40.615285     5.882464      .00000002

AR(3)                   --------------------

Standard error          16.153382
Log likelihood          -705.3328
AIC                     1418.6656
SBC                     1431.1615

          Variables in the Model:

                    B          SEB       T-RATIO    APPROX. PROB.
AR1         1.10947      .077582    14.300608      0.0
AR2         -.02007      .117255     -.171167      .86430323
AR3         -.12010      .078143    -1.536913      .12624140
CONSTANT  239.54694    35.949429     6.663442      0.0
```

```
AR(4)                   -------------------

Standard error          16.201293
Log likelihood          -705.32306
AIC                     1420.6461
SBC                     1436.2659

             Variables in the Model:

                   B          SEB       T-RATIO    APPROX. PROB.
AR1           1.11090      .078319     14.184218       0.0
AR2           -.01962      .117636     -.166795       .86773825
AR3           -.13436      .117910    -1.139484       .25617281
AR4            .01290      .079019      .163304       .87048149
CONSTANT    239.49977    36.553302     6.552069       0.0

AR(5)                   -------------------

Standard error          16.160952
Log likelihood          -704.43867
AIC                     1420.8773
SBC                     1439.6211

             Variables in the Model:

                   B          SEB       T-RATIO    APPROX. PROB.
AR1           1.10892      .078126     14.194034       0.0
AR2           -.00567      .117786     -.048133       .96166968
AR3           -.13134      .117612    -1.116758       .26575121
AR4           -.10153      .118062     -.859992       .39106473
AR5            .10370      .078836     1.315431       .19022341
CONSTANT    239.15565    41.029854     5.828820       .00000003


Case#  CORNPRC    FIT1      FIT2      FIT3      FIT4      FIT5
       RAW DATA   AR(1)     AR(2)     AR(3)     AR(4)     AR(5)

  165   355.00   353.50    357.25    356.23    356.24    356.29
  166   349.00   352.52    351.79    354.68    354.79    354.86
  167   361.00   346.65    345.18    344.68    344.37    345.26
  168   332.00   358.39    359.64    358.23    358.31    355.78
  169     .      330.01    325.07    326.54    326.65    327.35
  170     .      328.06    321.73    319.62    319.59    321.29
  171     .      326.16    319.03    315.53    315.90    316.56
  172     .      324.29    316.51    311.80    312.29    316.15
  173     .      322.47    314.08    308.57    309.23    313.98
  174     .      320.68    311.72    305.54    306.30    312.34
```

See the material for the answer for Exercise 7.1 (above) to find out which SPSS commands are used to produce this type of output.

Graph Accompanying Exercise 7.3
Corn Price

in cts/bushel of #2 yellow at Chicago

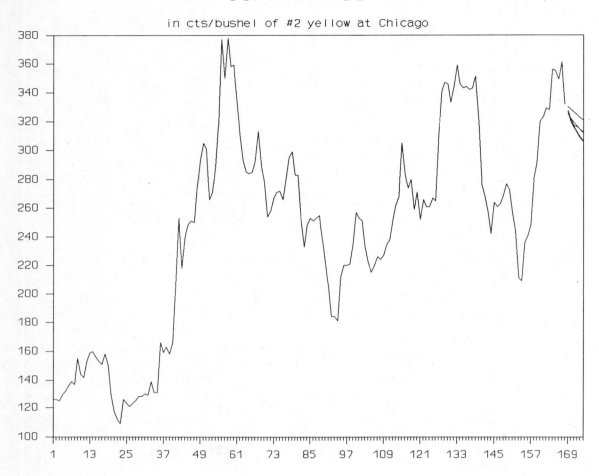

****

7.4   The time series X_t is generated by the first order autoregressive model

$$X_t = C + \phi_1 X_{t-1} + a_t$$

Show that, standing at time n, the forecast of X_{n+h} is given by

$$\hat{X}_n(h) = (1 + \phi_1 + \ldots + \phi_1^{h-1})C + \phi_1^h X_n$$

Discuss the behavior of this predictor when $|\phi_1| < 1$, as h becomes large.

------- Answer to 7.4 -------

Since
$$X_t = C + \phi_1 X_{t-1} + a_t$$

$$\hat{X}_n(1) = \hat{X}_{n+1} = C + \phi_1 X_n$$

Also $\qquad \hat{X}_n(2) = \hat{X}_{n+2} = C + \phi_1 \hat{X}_{n+1} = C + C\phi_1 + \phi_1^2 X_n$

Further $\quad \hat{X}_n(3) = \hat{X}_{n+3} = C + \phi_1 \hat{X}_{n+2} = C + C\phi_1 + C\phi_1^2 + \phi_1^3 X_n$

and so, by induction $\quad \hat{X}_n(h) = C(1 + \phi_1 + \phi_1^2 + \ldots + \phi_1^{h-1}) + \phi_1^h X_n$

If $S = (1 + \phi_1 + \phi_1^2 + \ldots + \phi_1^{h-1}) = (1 - \phi_1^h)/(1 - \phi_1)$

then, as h becomes large, $S = 1/(1 - \phi_1)$ approximately.

So, as h becomes large, $\hat{X}_n(h) = C/(1 - \phi_1)$

Or, in other words, as the forecast becomes further away from the last observation, the value of the forecast will converge to the constant $C/(1 - \phi_1)$ which is the mean of the time series.

****

7.5 The accompanying exhibit shows the first 10 sample autocorrelations and sample partial autocorrelations for a non-seasonal stationary time series of 120 observations. Discuss the problem of selecting an appropriate model to fit to this series.

Exhibit accompanying Exercise 7.5

Autocorrelations: Partial Autocorrelations:

```
     Auto- Stand.                            Pr-Aut- Stand.
Lag  Corr. Err. -.25  0  .25  .5  .75  1  Lag Corr. Err. -.25  0  .25  .5  .75
 1
               --+----+----+----+----+----+          --+----+----+----+----+----+
  1  .754  .090   .  :*** .***********      1  .754  .091   .  :*** .**********
  2  .613  .090   .  :*** .********         2  .102  .091   .  :** .
  3  .482  .089   .  :*** .******           3 -.024  .091   .  *   .
  4  .405  .089   .  :*** .****             4  .055  .091   .  :*  .
  5  .346  .089   .  :*** .***              5  .029  .091   .  :*  .
  6  .383  .088   .  :*** .****             6  .209  .091   .  :****
  7  .316  .088   .  :*** .**               7 -.127  .091  .***:  .
  8  .262  .087   . :**.**                  8 -.040  .091   .  *:  .
  9  .179  .087   . :**.*                   9 -.072  .091   .  *:  .
 10  .155  .087   . :***                   10  .062  .091   .  :*  .
```

------- Answer to 7.5 -------

Since the autocorrelations decay somewhat exponentially and since the partial autocorrelations are all insignificantly different from zero except for the one at the first lag, the time series that give rise to these autocorrelations can clearly be represented by an AR(1) $\equiv$ ARIMA(1,0,0) model.

****

7.6   The accompanying exhibit shows the first 10 sample autocorrelations and sample partial autocorrelations for a non-seasonal stationary time series of 120 observations. Discuss the problem of selecting an appropriate model to fit to this series.

Exhibit accompanying Exercise 7.6

Autocorrelations: Partial Autocorrelations:

```
      Auto- Stand.                                      Pr-Aut- Stand.
Lag   Corr.  Err.   -.5 -.25   0   .25        Lag   Corr.   Err.   -.5 -.25   0   .25
             ---+----+----+----+-                            ---+----+----+----+-
 1   -.239  .090        *.***:   .              1  -.239   .091        *.***:   .
 2   -.264  .090        *.***:   .              2  -.341   .091      ***.***:   .
 3    .063  .089          :*   .                3  -.123   .091        . **:   .
 4   -.156  .089        .***:   .               4  -.321   .091       **.***:   .
 5    .019  .089          . *   .               5  -.207   .091        ****:   .
 6    .065  .088          . :*  .               6  -.209   .091        ****:   .
 7    .008  .088          . *   .               7  -.161   .091        .***:   .
 8    .125  .087          . :***                8   .003   .091        . *   .
 9   -.091  .087         .**:   .               9  -.091   .091        . **:   .
10    .003  .087          . *   .              10   .033   .091        . :*  .
```

------- Answer to 7.6 -------

These autocorrelations are clearly generated by a time series that can be adequately represented by an MA(2). That is, all autocorrelations of order higher than two are insignificant from zero, while the <u>partial</u> autocorrelations do not abruptly cut off (after lag 2). The model is an MA(2) ≡ ARIMA(0,0,2).

****

7.7   The accompanying exhibit shows the first 10 sample autocorrelations and sample partial autocorrelations for a non-seasonal stationary time series of 120 observations. Discuss the problem of selecting an appropriate model to fit to this series.

Exhibit accompanying Exercise 7.7

Autocorrelations: Partial Autocorrelations:

```
      Auto- Stand.                                      Pr-Aut- Stand.
Lag   Corr.  Err.  -.25  0  .25  .5  .75       Lag   Corr.   Err.  -.25  0  .25  .5  .75
            --+----+----+----+----+--                        --+----+----+----+----+--
 1    .748  .090   .  :***.**********           1   .748   .091   .  :***.**********
 2    .750  .090   .  :***.**********           2   .433   .091   .  :***.*****
 3    .712  .089   .  :***.**********            3   .196   .091   .  :****
 4    .600  .089   .  :***.********             4  -.149   .091   .***:   .
 5    .575  .089   .  :***.*******              5  -.019   .091   .  *   .
 6    .522  .088   .  :***.******               6   .022   .091   .  *   .
 7    .478  .088   .  :***.******               7   .041   .091   .  :*  .
 8    .456  .087   .  :**.******                8   .035   .091   .  :*  .
 9    .456  .087   .  :**.******                9   .116   .091   .  :**  .
10    .373  .087   .  :**.****                 10  -.142   .091   .***:   .
```

------- Answer to 7.7 -------

Since the partial autocorrelations cut off after lag 3 while the autocorrelations decay slowly, it would seem that a good model would be an AR(3) ≡ ARIMA(3,0,0). It may also be useful to try an ARIMA(2,0,1) and an ARIMA(1,0,2). This is much less clear-cut than the previous two exercises. Some experimentation is therefore desirable.

7.8   Fit the data in Excercise 7.1 on building expenditures an appropriate non-seasonal ARIMA model, and use the fitted model to obtain forecasts for the next six months.

------- Answer to 7.8 -------

To find out which models might be appropriate, the autocorrelation and partial autocorrelation functions for the raw and first differences of the data are necessary. The following output is from SPSS:

```
Autocorrelations:   BUILDING                    Partial Autocorrelations:   BUILDING

       Auto- Stand.                                    Pr-Aut- Stand.
Lag    Corr.  Err.  -.25   0   .25   .5   .75   1    Lag  Corr.  Err.  -.5 -.25   0   .25   .5   .75   1
                    ---+----+----+----+----+----+                     -+----+----+----+----+----+----+
  1    .835  .129    .   :****.************         1   .835  .132     .    :****.************
  2    .564  .128    .   :****.******              2  -.438  .132   ****.****:    .
  3    .304  .127    .   :****.*                   3  -.030  .132     .  *:    .
  4    .128  .126    .   :***  .                    4   .076  .132     .   :**   .
  5    .037  .124    .   :*    .                    5   .009  .132     .   *     .
  6    .020  .123    .   *     .                    6   .060  .132     .   :*    .
  7    .043  .122    .   :*    .                    7   .024  .132     .   *     .
  8    .102  .121    .   :**   .                    8   .122  .132     .   :**   .
  9    .148  .119    .   :***  .                    9  -.037  .132     .  *:    .
 10    .171  .118    .   :***  .                   10   .029  .132     .   :*    .
 11    .176  .117    .   :****.                    11   .060  .132     .   :*    .
 12    .124  .116    .   :**   .                   12  -.176  .132     .****:    .
 13    .017  .114    .   *     .                   13  -.110  .132     .  **:    .
 14   -.112  .113    .  **:    .                   14  -.069  .132     .   *:    .
```

Plot Symbols: Autocorrelations *   Two Standard Error Limits .

Total cases: 57   Computable first lags: 56

```
Autocorrelations:   BUILDING                    Partial Autocorrelations:   BUILDING

Transformations:  difference (1)                Transformations:  difference (1)

       Auto- Stand.                                    Pr-Aut- Stand.
Lag    Corr.  Err.  -.25   0   .25   .5   .75   1    Lag  Corr.  Err.  -.5 -.25   0   .25   .5   .75   1
                    ---+----+----+----+----+----+                     -+----+----+----+----+----+----+
  1    .402  .130    .   :****.***                  1   .402  .134     .   :****.***
  2    .037  .129    .   :*    .                    2  -.148  .134     . ***:    .
  3   -.253  .128  *****:      .                    3  -.257  .134   *****:      .
  4   -.233  .127  *****:      .                    4  -.029  .134     .  *:    .
  5   -.150  .125    . ***:     .                    5  -.052  .134     .  *:    .
  6   -.108  .124    .  **:     .                    6  -.127  .134     . ***:    .
  7   -.155  .123    . ***:     .                    7  -.180  .134     .****:    .
  8    .041  .122    .   :*     .                    8   .154  .134     .   :***
  9    .007  .120    .   *      .                    9  -.155  .134     . ***:    .
 10    .089  .119    .   :**    .                   10   .021  .134     .   *     .
 11    .185  .118    .   :****.                     11   .199  .134     .   :****
 12    .153  .116    .   :***  .                    12  -.014  .134     .   *     .
 13    .083  .115    .   :**   .                    13  -.002  .134     .   *     .
 14    .004  .114    .   *     .                    14   .071  .134     .   :*    .
```

Plot Symbols: Autocorrelations *   Two Standard Error Limits .

Total cases: 57   Computable first lags after differencing: 55

Several ARIMA models are possible: (a) ARIMA(2,0,0), since the PACF of the raw data dies after two significant lags; (b) ARIMA(1,1,0) and; alternatively; (c) ARIMA(0,1,1) since there is only one significant lag on either the ACF or the PACF. Of models (b) and (c), (b), the AR(1) on the first differences is probably better than the MA(1) since the insignificant correlations on the PACF are generally smaller than the corresponding correlations on the ACF. Below is part of the SPSS output from the estimation of these models.

ARIMA(2,0,0) with constant

Standard error   .98221932

Log likelihood   -79.290165
AIC   164.58033
SBC   170.70948

Variables in the Model:

	B	SEB	T-RATIO	APPROX. PROB.
AR1	1.2955643	.11488128	11.277419	0.0
AR2	-.5077917	.11460206	-4.430912	.00004638
CONSTANT	9.3390885	.59929915	15.583350	0.0

Autocorrelations: ERR#1

Lag	Auto- Corr.	Stand. Err.	-.25 0 .25
1	-.033	.129	. *: .
2	.033	.128	. :* .
3	-.086	.127	. **: .
4	-.014	.126	. * .
5	-.030	.124	. *: .
6	.077	.123	. :** .

ARIMA(1,1,0)

Standard error   1.0608806

Log likelihood   -82.356242
AIC   166.71248
SBC   168.73784

Variables in the Model:

	B	SEB	T-RATIO	APPROX. PROB.
AR1	.40079296	.12301661	3.2580393	.00192554

Autocorrelations: ERR#1

Lag	Auto- Corr.	Stand. Err.	-.25 0 .25
1	.062	.130	. :* .
2	-.020	.129	. * .
3	-.257	.128	*****: .
4	-.132	.127	. ***: .
5	-.045	.125	. *: .
6	-.003	.124	. * .

ARIMA(0,1,1)

Standard error   1.0673547

Log likelihood   -82.680169
AIC   167.36034
SBC   169.38569

Variables in the Model:

	B	SEB	T-RATIO	APPROX. PROB.
MA1	-.36268447	.12611957	-2.8757192	.00572380

Autocorrelations: ERR#1

Lag	Auto- Corr.	Stand. Err.	-.25 0 .25
1	.069	.130	. :* .
2	.098	.129	. :** .
3	-.255	.128	*****: .
4	-.127	.127	. ***: .
5	-.112	.125	. **: .
6	-.012	.124	. * .

According to the SBC, the ARIMA(1,1,0) model is best, while according to the AIC the ARIMA(2,0,0) is best. It should be noted that both the ARIMA(1,1,0) and ARIMA(0,1,1) models left seemingly significant autocorrelations in the errors at lag three. Both ARIMA(3,1,0) and ARIMA(0,1,3) models were run and found to be inferior to the ARIMA(1,1,0) and ARIMA(0,1,1) models, respectively.

The three models estimated are similarly good. Their forecasts are shown below.

Case#	BUILDING	FIT200C	FIT110	FIT011
54	8.80	9.62	9.70	9.64
55	8.10	8.46	8.44	8.49
56	7.60	8.01	7.82	7.96
57	7.90	7.72	7.40	7.47
58	.	8.36	8.02	8.06
59	.	8.80	8.07	8.06
60	.	9.14	8.09	8.06
61	.	9.35	8.10	8.06
62	.	9.46	8.10	8.06
63	.	9.49	8.10	8.06

****

7.9 Fit the data in Excercise 7.2 on soybean meal price an appropriate non-seasonal ARIMA model, and use the fitted model to obtain forecasts for the next six months.

------- Answer to 7.9 -------

To find out which models might be appropriate, the autocorrelation and partial autocorrelation functions for the raw and first differences of the data are necessary. The following output is from SPSS:

```
Autocorrelations:  SOYBEAN                    Partial Autocorrelations:  SOYBEAN

     Auto- Stand.                                  Pr-Aut- Stand.
Lag  Corr.  Err.  -.25  0  .25  .5  .75  1    Lag  Corr.  Err.  -.25  0  .25  .5  .75  1
                  --+----+----+----+----+         --+----+----+----+----+----+
 1   .895  .090      :*** .**************     1   .895  .091         :*** .**************
 2   .754  .090      :*** .***********        2  -.235  .091    * .***:   .
 3   .593  .089      :*** .********           3  -.162  .091    .***:    .
 4   .469  .089      :*** .*****              4   .127  .091    .  :***  .
 5   .375  .089      :*** .***                5   .025  .091    .  :*    .
 6   .327  .088      :*** .***                6   .100  .091    .  :**   .
 7   .310  .088      :*** .**                 7   .070  .091    .  :*    .
 8   .299  .087     .:** .***                 8  -.049  .091    . *:     .
 9   .288  .087     .:** .***                 9   .026  .091    .  :*    .
10   .258  .087     .:** .**                 10  -.065  .091    . *:     .
11   .214  .086     .:** .*                  11  -.043  .091    . *:     .
12   .152  .086     .:***                    12  -.059  .091    . *:     .
13   .105  .085     . :**.                   13   .059  .091    .  :*    .
14   .081  .085     . :**.                   14   .074  .091    .  :*    .
15   .080  .085     . :**.                   15   .007  .091    .  *     .
16   .080  .084     . :**.                   16  -.063  .091    . *:     .
17   .091  .084     . :**.                   17   .060  .091    .  :*    .
18   .110  .083     . :**.                   18   .074  .091    .  :*    .
19   .131  .083     . :***                   19   .029  .091    .  :*    .
20   .134  .083     . :***                   20  -.057  .091    . *:     .
21   .114  .082     . :**.                   21  -.071  .091    . *:     .
22   .087  .082     . :**.                   22   .020  .091    .  *     .
23   .054  .081     . :* .                   23  -.015  .091    .  *     .
24   .034  .081     . :* .                   24   .018  .091    .  *     .

Plot Symbols:      Autocorrelations *    Two Standard Error Limits .

Total cases:  120    Computable first lags:  119
```

Autocorrelations: SOYBEAN   Partial Autocorrelations: SOYBEAN

Transformations: difference (1)   Transformations: difference (1)

	Auto-	Stand.								Pr-Aut-	Stand.					
Lag	Corr.	Err.	-.25	0	.25	.5	.75	1	Lag	Corr.	Err.	-.25	0	.25	.5	.75	1

```
       Auto- Stand.                              Pr-Aut- Stand.
Lag    Corr.  Err. -.25   0   .25  .5  .75   1   Lag  Corr.  Err. -.25   0   .25  .5  .75   1
                   --+----+----+----+----+----+                  --+----+----+----+----+----+
  1    .166  .091    .   :***.                    1   .166  .092    .   :***.
  2    .099  .090    .   :**  .                    2   .073  .092    .   :*   .
  3   -.204  .090  ****:    .                      3  -.239  .092  *.***:    .
  4   -.158  .089   .***:    .                      4  -.104  .092    . **:    .
  5   -.172  .089   .***:    .                      5  -.094  .092    . **:    .
  6   -.128  .089   .***:    .                      6  -.120  .092    . **:    .
  7   -.035  .088    .  *:    .                     7  -.033  .092    .  *:    .
  8   -.013  .088    .   *    .                     8  -.058  .092    .  *:    .
  9    .116  .087    .   :**.                       9   .057  .092    .   :*   .
 10    .071  .087    .   :* .                      10  -.000  .092    .   *    .
 11    .085  .087    .   :**.                      11   .012  .092    .   *    .
 12   -.077  .086   .**:    .                      12  -.100  .092    . **:    .
 13   -.121  .086   .**:    .                      13  -.107  .092    . **:    .
 14   -.085  .085   .**:    .                      14  -.009  .092    .   *    .
 15   -.011  .085    .  *    .                     15   .015  .092    .   *    .
 16   -.068  .085    . *:    .                     16  -.124  .092    . **:    .
 17   -.062  .084    . *:    .                     17  -.104  .092    . **:    .
 18   -.011  .084    .  *    .                     18  -.034  .092    .  *:    .
 19    .078  .083    .   :**.                      19   .027  .092    .   :*   .
 20    .116  .083    .   :**.                      20   .027  .092    .   :*   .
 21    .045  .082    .   :* .                      21  -.042  .092    .  *:    .
 22    .016  .082    .   :* .                      22  -.013  .092    .   *    .
 23   -.067  .082    . *:    .                     23  -.046  .092    .  *:    .
 24   -.091  .081   .**:    .                      24  -.082  .092    . **:    .
```

Plot Symbols: Autocorrelations *   Two Standard Error Limits .

Total cases: 120   Computable first lags after differencing: 118

Several models are suggested by these ACFs and PACFs: (a) ARIMA(2,0,0) with constant (least likely, as the ACF and PACF of the the first differences are quieter – fewer and smaller insignificant lags); (b) ARIMA(1,1,0); or (c) ARIMA(0,1,1). The ARIMA(1,1,0) is more likely than the ARIMA(0,1,1) since the PACF of the first differences is "quieter" than the corresponding ACF.

ARIMA(2,0,0) with constant

Standard error   14.572459

Log likelihood   -491.13348
AIC   988.26697
SBC   996.62944

Variables in the Model:

	B	SEB	T-RATIO	APPROX. PROB.
AR1	1.10760	.089247	12.410566	0.0
AR2	-.23219	.090040	-2.578788	.01115410
CONSTANT	177.89767	10.245443	17.363590	0.0

Autocorrelations: ERR#1

Lag	Corr.	Err.	-.25 0 .25
1	-.027	.090	. *: .
2	.179	.090	. :****
3	-.121	.089	. **: .
4	-.009	.089	. * .
5	-.061	.089	. *: .
6	-.056	.088	. *: .

ARIMA(1,1,0)

Standard error   15.037772

Log likelihood   -490.92521
AIC   983.85042
SBC   986.62954

Variables in the Model:

	B	SEB	T-RATIO	APPROX. PROB.
AR1	.16844962	.09079449	1.8552846	.06605146

Autocorrelations: ERR#1

Lag	Corr.	Err.	-.25 0 .25
1	-.014	.091	. * .
2	.111	.090	. :** .
3	-.205	.090	****: .
4	-.102	.089	. **: .
5	-.134	.089	.***: .
6	-.101	.089	. **: .

ARIMA(0,1,1)

Standard error   15.078827

Log likelihood   -491.24454
AIC   984.48907
SBC   987.26819

Variables in the Model:

	B	SEB	T-RATIO	APPROX. PROB.
MA1	-.13526618	.09130930	-1.4814064	.14116354

Autocorrelations: ERR#1

Lag	Corr.	Err.	-.25 0 .25
1	.018	.091	. * .
2	.124	.090	. :** .
3	-.206	.090	****: .
4	-.112	.089	. **: .
5	-.145	.089	.***: .
6	-.108	.089	. **: .

According to both the SBC and the AIC, the ARIMA(1,1,0) model is best. The forecasts for the next six months for each of the models is shown below.

Case#	SOYBEAN	FIT200C	FIT110	FIT011
117	232.70	237.70	242.01	240.27
118	227.50	225.41	232.36	231.68
119	225.10	220.11	226.62	226.94
120	218.00	218.66	224.70	224.85
121	.	211.36	216.80	217.07
122	.	205.64	216.60	217.07
123	.	200.86	216.57	217.07
124	.	196.89	216.56	217.07
125	.	193.60	216.56	217.07
126	.	190.88	216.56	217.07

7.10 Fit the data in Excercise 7.3 on corn price an appropriate non-seasonal ARIMA model, and use the fitted model to obtain forecasts for the next six months.

------- Answer to 7.10 -------

To find out which models might be appropriate, the autocorrelation and partial autocorrelation functions for the raw and first differences of the data are necessary. The following output is from SPSS:

```
Autocorrelations:    CORNPRC              Partial Autocorrelations:   CORNPRC

        Auto- Stand.                              Pr-Aut- Stand.
 Lag    Corr.  Err. -.25   0   .25  .5   .75  1.   Lag   Corr.  Err. -.25   0   .25  .5   .75   1
                    --+----+----+----+----+----+                        --+----+----+----+----+----+
  1     .961  .076    .  :**.****************      1     .961  .077    .  :**.****************
  2     .912  .076    .  :**.***************       2    -.152  .077   ***: .
  3     .858  .076    .  :**.**************        3    -.075  .077    . *: .
  4     .805  .076    .  :**.*************         4    -.011  .077    . * .
  5     .758  .076    .  :**.************          5     .055  .077    . :* .
  6     .713  .075    .  :**.***********           6    -.007  .077    . * .
  7     .670  .075    .  :**.**********            7    -.030  .077    . *: .
  8     .629  .075    .  :**.**********            8     .005  .077    . * .
  9     .596  .075    .  :**.*********             9     .072  .077    . :* .
 10     .560  .074    .  :**.********             10    -.074  .077    . *: .
 11     .523  .074    .  :**.*******             11    -.052  .077    . *: .
 12     .492  .074    .  :**.*******             12     .088  .077    . :**.
 13     .455  .074    .  :**.******              13    -.112  .077   .**: .
 14     .422  .073    .  :**.*****              14     .032  .077    . :* .
 15     .392  .073    .  :**.*****              15     .006  .077    . * .
 16     .364  .073    .  :**.****               16     .020  .077    . * .
 17     .339  .073    .  :**.****               17    -.011  .077    . * .
 18     .314  .072    .  :**.***                18    -.027  .077    . *: .
 19     .282  .072    .  :**.***                19    -.106  .077   .**: .
 20     .248  .072    .  :**.**                 20    -.010  .077    . * .
```

Plot Symbols: Autocorrelations *   Two Standard Error Limits .

Total cases: 168   Computable first lags: 167


```
Autocorrelations:    CORNPRC              Partial Autocorrelations:   CORNPRC

Transformations:  difference (1)          Transformations:  difference (1)

        Auto- Stand.                              Pr-Aut- Stand.
 Lag    Corr.  Err. -.25   0   .25  .5   .75  1    Lag   Corr.  Err. -.25   0   .25  .5   .75   1
                    --+----+----+----+----+----+                        --+----+----+----+----+----+
  1     .129  .077    .  :***                      1     .129  .077    .  :***
  2     .109  .076    .  :**.                       2     .094  .077    .  :**.
  3    -.014  .076    .  * .                        3    -.039  .077    . *: .
  4    -.121  .076   .**: .                         4    -.129  .077   ***: .
  5     .002  .076    .  * .                        5     .038  .077    . :* .
  6    -.018  .076    .  * .                        6     .005  .077    . * .
  7    -.049  .075    . *: .                        7    -.059  .077    . *: .
  8    -.091  .075   .**: .                         8    -.097  .077   .**: .
  9     .067  .075    .  :* .                        9     .112  .077    . :**.
 10     .049  .075    .  :* .                       10     .051  .077    . :* .
 11    -.042  .074    . *: .                        11    -.100  .077   .**: .
 12     .147  .074    .  :***                       12     .142  .077    . :***
 13    -.061  .074    . *: .                         13    -.052  .077    . *: .
 14    -.012  .074    .  * .                         14    -.033  .077    . *: .
 15    -.068  .073    . *: .                         15    -.081  .077   .**: .
 16    -.111  .073   .**: .                          16    -.052  .077    . *: .
 17    -.022  .073    .  * .                         17     .018  .077    . * .
 18     .068  .073    .  :* .                        18     .082  .077    . :**.
 19    -.022  .072    .  * .                         19    -.077  .077   .**: .
 20     .026  .072    .  :* .                        20     .038  .077    . :* .
```

Plot Symbols: Autocorrelations *   Two Standard Error Limits .

Total cases: 168   Computable first lags after differencing: 166

These ACFs and PACFs suggest that attempting any model on the first differences of the data is futile – an AR(1) on the first differences turns out to be insignificant. The obvious model from the PACF of the raw data is an AR(2) with a constant term. Below is portion of the SPSS output for this model.

The results for the AR(1) are shown for comparison purposes. Oddly enough, even though the ARIMA(1,1,0) is insignificant at the 5% level, the AIC and SBC both are lower for it than for the ARIMA(2,0,0) with constant. Perhaps the most plausible model of all is the simple random walk: ARIMA(0,1,0).

ARIMA(2,0,0) with constant

Standard error	16.218075
Log likelihood	-706.51139
AIC	1419.0228
SBC	1428.3947

Variables in the Model:

	B	SEB	T-RATIO	APPROX. PROB.
AR1	1.12829	.076918	14.668709	0.0
AR2	-.15460	.077403	-1.997352	.04743093
CONSTANT	238.91797	40.615285	5.882464	.00000002

Autocorrelations: ERR#1

Lag	Auto- Corr.	Stand. Err.	-.25 0 .25 --+----+----+-
1	-.015	.076	. * .
2	.089	.076	. :**.
3	-.001	.076	. * .
4	-.083	.076	.**: .
5	.023	.076	. * .
6	.000	.075	. * .

ARIMA(1,1,0)

Standard error	16.226612
Log likelihood	-701.84311
AIC	1405.6862
SBC	1408.8042

Variables in the Model:

	B	SEB	T-RATIO	APPROX. PROB.
AR1	.13681056	.07762249	1.7625117	.07982335

Autocorrelations: ERR#1

Lag	Auto- Corr.	Stand. Err.	-.25 0 .25 --+----+----+-
1	-.017	.077	. * .
2	.096	.076	. :**.
3	-.012	.076	. * .
4	-.123	.076	.**: .
5	.019	.076	. * .
6	-.011	.076	. * .

Forecasts

Case#	CORNPRC	FIT200C	FIT110
165	355.00	357.25	359.83
166	349.00	351.79	354.86
167	361.00	345.18	348.18
168	332.00	359.64	362.64
169	.	325.07	328.03
170	.	321.73	327.49
171	.	319.03	327.42
172	.	316.51	327.41
173	.	314.08	327.40
174	.	311.72	327.40

****

7.11 The time series X_t is generated by the second order moving average model

$$X_t - \mu = a_t - \theta_1 a_{t-1} - \theta_2 a_{t-2}$$

Show that its autocorrelations are given by

$$\rho_1 = -\theta_1(1 - \theta_2)/(1 + \theta_1^2 + \theta_2^2)$$

$$\rho_2 = -\theta_2/(1 + \theta_1^2 + \theta_2^2)$$

$$\rho_k = 0 \ ; \ k = 3, 4, \ldots$$

------- Answer to 7.11 -------

Since
$$X_t - \mu = a_t - \theta_1 a_{t-1} - \theta_2 a_{t-2}$$

therefore
$$\text{Var}(X_t) = \gamma_0 = \text{E}(a_t - \theta_1 a_{t-1} - \theta_2 a_{t-2})^2$$

$$\gamma_0 = \text{E}(a_t^2 - 2\theta_1 a_t a_{t-1} - 2\theta_2 a_t a_{t-2} + 2\theta_1 \theta_2 a_{t-1} a_{t-2} + \theta_1^2 a_{t-1}^2 + \theta_2^2 a_{t-2}^2)$$

$$\gamma_0 = \text{E}(a_t^2) + \text{E}(\theta_1^2 a_{t-1}^2) + \text{E}(\theta_2^2 a_{t-2}^2) \ \text{ since } \text{E}(a_t a_{t-s}) = 0 \text{ for all } s \neq 0.$$

$$\gamma_0 = (1 + \theta_1^2 + \theta_2^2)\sigma_a^2$$

Also $\text{Cov}(X_t X_{t-1}) = \gamma_1 = \text{E}(a_t - \theta_1 a_{t-1} - \theta_2 a_{t-2})(a_{t-1} - \theta_1 a_{t-2} - \theta_2 a_{t-3})$

Note again that $\text{E}(a_t a_{t-s}) = 0$ for all $s \neq 0$.

Thus $\gamma_1 = \text{E}(-\theta_1 a_{t-1}^2 + \theta_1 \theta_2 a_{t-2}^2) = -\theta_1(1 - \theta_2)\sigma_a^2$

And so, $\rho_1 = \gamma_1/\gamma_0 = -\theta_1(1 - \theta_2)/(1 + \theta_1^2 + \theta_2^2)$

Also $\text{Cov}(X_t X_{t-2}) = \gamma_2 = \text{E}(a_t - \theta_1 a_{t-1} - \theta_2 a_{t-2})(a_{t-2} - \theta_1 a_{t-3} - \theta_2 a_{t-4})$

$$\gamma_2 = \text{E}(-\theta_2 a_{t-2}^2) = -\theta_2 \sigma_a^2$$

And so, $\rho_2 = \gamma_2/\gamma_0 = -\theta_2/(1 + \theta_1^2 + \theta_2^2)$

Now for the third autocorrelation:

$$\text{Cov}(X_t X_{t-3}) = \gamma_3 = \text{E}(a_t - \theta_1 a_{t-1} - \theta_2 a_{t-2})(a_{t-3} - \theta_1 a_{t-4} - \theta_2 a_{t-5})$$

Since this expression will yield no terms of the type $\text{E}(a_{t-s}^2)$, its value is zero. Furthermore then all autocorrelations for orders of three or higher will be zero for a second order moving average process.

****

7.12 The accompanying table shows an index of the prices received by farmers for all crops over a period of 62 years. Fit an appropriate non-seasonal ARIMA model to the logarithms of these data, and predict prices for the next six years.

------- Answer to 7.12 -------

To find out which models might be appropriate, the autocorrelation and partial autocorrelation functions for the raw and first differences of the logged data are necessary. The output starting on the next page is from SPSS:

Graph Accompanying Exercise 7.12
Crop Price Index

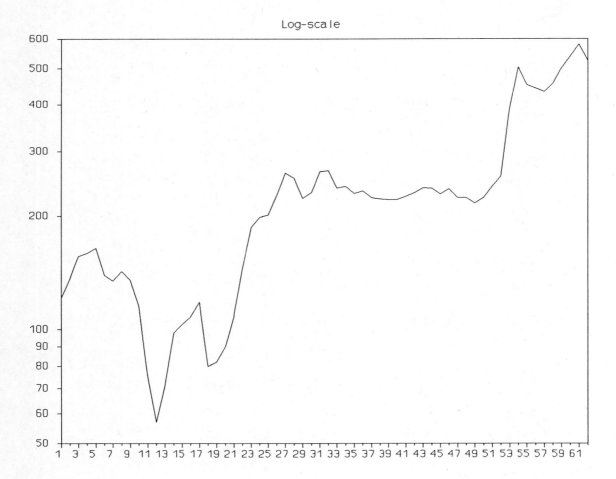

Log-scale

Autocorrelations: CROP_PI

Transformations: natural log

```
        Auto- Stand.
Lag     Corr.  Err.  -.25   0    .25   .5   .75    1
                     --+----+----+----+----+----+
  1     .932   .124    .   :****.************
  2     .835   .123    .   :****.***********
  3     .750   .122    .   :****.*********
  4     .680   .121    .   :****.********
  5     .627   .120    .   :****.*******
  6     .574   .119    .   :****.******
  7     .509   .118    .   :****.*****
  8     .434   .117    .   :****.****
  9     .349   .116    .   :****.**
 10     .277   .114    .   :****.*
 11     .220   .113    .   :****.
 12     .163   .112    .   :***.
 13     .119   .111    .   :** .
 14     .092   .110    .   :** .
 15     .067   .109    .   :*  .
 16     .054   .108    .   :*  .
```

Partial Autocorrelations: CROP_PI

Transformations: natural log

```
        Pr-Aut- Stand.
Lag     Corr.   Err.  -.25   0    .25   .5   .75    1
                      --+----+----+----+----+----+
  1     .932    .127    .   :****.************
  2    -.263    .127  *****:    .
  3     .100    .127    .   :** .
  4     .013    .127    .    * .
  5     .075    .127    .   :** .
  6    -.081    .127    .  **:  .
  7    -.087    .127    .  **:  .
  8    -.087    .127    .  **:  .
  9    -.104    .127    .  **:  .
 10     .047    .127    .   :*  .
 11    -.012    .127    .    *  .
 12    -.079    .127    .  **:  .
 13     .089    .127    .   :** .
 14     .070    .127    .   :*  .
 15    -.018    .127    .    *  .
 16     .080    .127    .   :** .
```

Plot Symbols: Autocorrelations *   Two Standard Error Limits .

Total cases: 62   Computable first lags: 61

Autocorrelations: CROP_PI

Transformations: natural log, difference (1)

```
        Auto- Stand.
Lag     Corr.  Err.  -.25   0    .25   .5   .75    1
                     --+----+----+----+----+----+
  1     .378   .125    .   :****.***
  2    -.098   .124    .  **:   .
  3    -.175   .123    . ***:   .
  4    -.194   .122    .****:   .
  5    -.044   .121    .   *:   .
  6     .112   .120    .   :**  .
  7     .139   .119    .   :*** .
  8    -.001   .117    .    *   .
  9    -.081   .116    .  **:   .
 10    -.091   .115    .  **:   .
 11    -.107   .114    .  **:   .
 12    -.076   .113    .  **:   .
 13    -.096   .112    .  **:   .
 14    -.072   .111    .   *:   .
 15    -.162   .109    .***:    .
 16    -.192   .108   ****:    .
```

Partial Autocorrelations: CROP_PI

Transformations: natural log, difference (1)

```
        Pr-Aut- Stand.
Lag     Corr.   Err.  -.25   0    .25   .5   .75    1
                      --+----+----+----+----+----+
  1     .378    .128    .   :****.***
  2    -.281    .128  *.****:    .
  3    -.027    .128    .   *:   .
  4    -.161    .128    . ***:   .
  5     .077    .128    .   :**  .
  6     .048    .128    .   :*   .
  7     .053    .128    .   :*   .
  8    -.093    .128    .  **:   .
  9     .002    .128    .    *   .
 10    -.042    .128    .   *:   .
 11    -.068    .128    .   *:   .
 12    -.062    .128    .   *:   .
 13    -.134    .128    . ***:   .
 14    -.032    .128    .   *:   .
 15    -.231    .128  *****:    .
 16    -.114    .128    .  **:   .
```

Plot Symbols: Autocorrelations *   Two Standard Error Limits .

Total cases: 62   Computable first lags after differencing: 60

The PACF of the logged data has a large significant spike at lag 1 -- this indicates the need for taking first differences. The ACF and PACF of the first differences of the logged data are nearly the same, except that the ACF is quieter than the PACF -- indicating that an MA is probably better than an AR. The two possible models are therefore (a) ARIMA(0,1,1), and (b) ARIMA(2,1,0). Using both the AIC and SBC the ARIMA(0,1,1) is better than the ARIMA(2,1,0). Below are portions of the SPSS output for these models.

ARIMA(0,1,1)

Standard error	.12773899
Log likelihood	39.291128
AIC	-76.582257
SBC	-74.471383

Variables in the Model:

	B	SEB	T-RATIO	APPROX. PROB.
MA1	-.54957511	.10960546	-5.0141217	.00000505

Autocorrelations: ERR#1

Lag	Auto-Corr.	Stand.Err.	-.25 0 .25
1	-.023	.125	. * .
2	-.052	.124	. *: .
3	-.088	.123	. **: .
4	-.155	.122	. ***: .
5	-.007	.121	. * .
6	.066	.120	. :* .

ARIMA(2,1,0)

Standard error	.12884648
Log likelihood	39.283742
AIC	-74.567484
SBC	-70.345737

Variables in the Model:

	B	SEB	T-RATIO	APPROX. PROB.
AR1	.50579446	.12597096	4.0151673	.00017039
AR2	-.27238218	.12600584	-2.1616632	.03471263

Autocorrelations: ERR#1

Lag	Auto-Corr.	Stand.Err.	-.25 0 .25
1	-.015	.125	. * .
2	-.062	.124	. *: .
3	.058	.123	. :* .
4	-.148	.122	. ***: .
5	-.021	.121	. * .
6	.050	.120	. :* .

Forecasts

Case#	CROP_PI	FIT011	FIT210
59	501.00	476.10	471.01
60	539.00	515.24	518.07
61	580.00	552.52	545.15
62	524.00	595.68	590.04
63	.	488.35	487.93
64	.	488.35	483.84
65	.	488.35	491.23
66	.	488.35	496.15
67	.	488.35	496.60
68	.	488.35	495.48

****

7.13 The accompanying table shows the United Kingdom--United States exchange rate, in terms of dollars per pound, over a period of 144 months. Fit an appropriate non-seasonal ARIMA model to this series, and predict the exchange rate for the next six months.

------- Answer to 7.13 -------

To find out which models might be appropriate, the autocorrelation and partial autocorrelation functions for the raw and first differences of this series are necessary. The following output is from SPSS:

Graph Accompanying Exercise 7.13

UK:US Exchange Rate

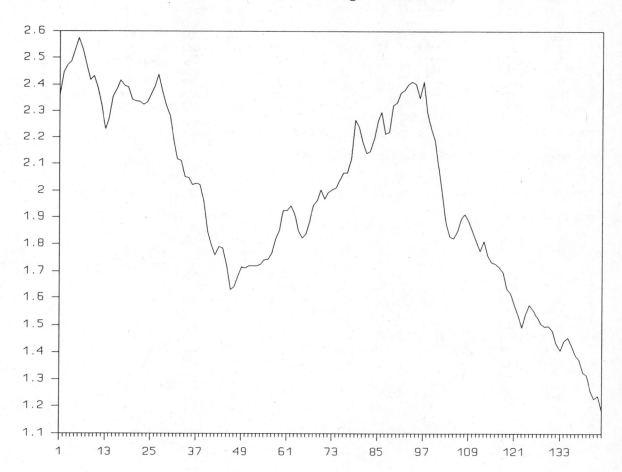

Autocorrelations: US2UK

```
      Auto- Stand.
Lag   Corr.  Err.  -.25   0   .25  .5  .75   1
                   --+----+----+----+----+----+
  1   .969   .082    . :**.***************
  2   .931   .082    . :**.***************
  3   .889   .082    . :**.**************
  4   .848   .082    . :**.*************
  5   .807   .081    . :**.************
  6   .763   .081    . :**.************
  7   .721   .081    . :**.***********
  8   .681   .080    . :**.***********
  9   .643   .080    . :**.**********
 10   .605   .080    . :**.*********
 11   .564   .080    . :**.********
 12   .520   .079    . :**.*******
 13   .477   .079    . :**.*******
 14   .435   .079    . :**.******
 15   .394   .078    . :**.*****
 16   .353   .078    . :**.****
 17   .311   .078    . :**.***
 18   .269   .077    . :**.**
 19   .226   .077    . :**.**
 20   .183   .077    . :**.*
 21   .139   .076    . :***
 22   .091   .076    . :**.
 23   .044   .076    . :* .
 24  -.001   .076    . * .
```

Partial Autocorrelations: US2UK

```
      Pr-Aut- Stand.
Lag   Corr.   Err.  -.25   0   .25  .5  .75   1
                    --+----+----+----+----+----+
  1    .969   .083    . :**.***************
  2   -.128   .083    ***: .
  3   -.071   .083    . *: .
  4   -.007   .083    . * .
  5   -.014   .083    . * .
  6   -.067   .083    . *: .
  7    .013   .083    . * .
  8    .003   .083    . * .
  9    .003   .083    . * .
 10   -.044   .083    . *: .
 11   -.058   .083    . *: .
 12   -.075   .083    . *: .
 13    .003   .083    . * .
 14   -.008   .083    . * .
 15   -.029   .083    . *: .
 16   -.018   .083    . * .
 17   -.059   .083    . *: .
 18   -.026   .083    . *: .
 19   -.059   .083    . *: .
 20   -.023   .083    . * .
 21   -.056   .083    . *: .
 22   -.096   .083    .**: .
 23   -.013   .083    . * .
 24   -.024   .083    . * .
```

Plot Symbols: Autocorrelations * Two Standard Error Limits .

Total cases: 144 Computable first lags: 143

Autocorrelations: US2UK

Transformations: difference (1)

```
      Auto- Stand.
Lag   Corr.  Err.  -.25   0   .25  .5  .75   1
                   --+----+----+----+----+----+
  1   .400   .083    . :**.*****
  2   .115   .082    . :**.
  3   .020   .082    . * .
  4   .029   .082    . :* .
  5   .078   .082    . :**.
  6   .056   .081    . :* .
  7  -.017   .081    . * .
  8   .009   .081    . * .
  9   .061   .080    . :* .
 10   .129   .080    . :***
 11   .166   .080    . :***
 12   .086   .079    . :**.
 13  -.034   .079    . *: .
 14  -.107   .079    .**: .
 15  -.105   .079    .**: .
 16   .055   .078    . :* .
 17   .038   .078    . :* .
 18   .118   .078    . :**.
 19   .056   .077    . :* .
 20  -.021   .077    . * .
 21   .068   .077    . :* .
 22   .037   .076    . :* .
 23   .007   .076    . * .
 24  -.052   .076    . *: .
```

Partial Autocorrelations: US2UK

Transformations: difference (1)

```
      Pr-Aut- Stand.
Lag   Corr.   Err.  -.25   0   .25  .5  .75   1
                    --+----+----+----+----+----+
  1    .400   .084    . :**.*****
  2   -.054   .084    . *: .
  3   -.008   .084    . * .
  4    .035   .084    . :* .
  5    .066   .084    . :* .
  6   -.003   .084    . * .
  7   -.052   .084    . *: .
  8    .045   .084    . :* .
  9    .055   .084    . :* .
 10    .090   .084    . :**.
 11    .090   .084    . :**.
 12   -.015   .084    . * .
 13   -.080   .084    .**: .
 14   -.087   .084    .**: .
 15   -.051   .084    . *: .
 16    .127   .084    . :***
 17   -.033   .084    . *: .
 18    .149   .084    . :***
 19   -.034   .084    . *: .
 20   -.068   .084    . *: .
 21    .080   .084    . :**.
 22   -.061   .084    . *: .
 23    .015   .084    . * .
 24   -.038   .084    . *: .
```

Plot Symbols: Autocorrelations * Two Standard Error Limits .

Total cases: 144 Computable first lags after differencing: 142

The PACF of the raw data has a large (close to one) significant spike at lag one indicating the need for taking first differences. As for the first differences, both the ACF and PACF have a significant spike at lag one but the PACF is just a little quieter than the ACF, thus an AR(1) may be more appropriate than an MA(1). Partial results for both models are shown below.

ARIMA(1,1,0)

Standard error	.04204784
Log likelihood	250.64878
AIC	-499.29755
SBC	-496.33471

Variables in the Model:

	B	SEB	T-RATIO	APPROX. PROB.
AR1	.43167169	.07599621	5.6801736	.00000008

Autocorrelations: ERR#1

Lag	Auto-Corr.	Stand. Err.	-.25 0 .25
1	-.004	.083	. * .
2	-.057	.082	. *: .
3	-.046	.082	. *: .
4	-.006	.082	. * .
5	.066	.082	. :* .
6	.052	.081	. :* .

ARIMA(0,1,1)

Standard error	.04246537
Log likelihood	249.25243
AIC	-496.50486
SBC	-493.54201

Variables in the Model:

	B	SEB	T-RATIO	APPROX. PRO
MA1	-.39841227	.07785281	-5.1175064	.000001

Autocorrelations: ERR#1

Lag	Auto-Corr.	Stand. Err.	-.25 0 .25
1	.029	.083	. :* .
2	.114	.082	. :**.
3	-.025	.082	. * .
4	.023	.082	. * .
5	.052	.082	. :* .
6	.056	.081	. :* .

Forecasts

Case#	US2UK	FIT110	FIT011
141	1.26	1.31	1.32
142	1.23	1.23	1.23
143	1.24	1.21	1.22
144	1.18	1.24	1.25
145	.	1.16	1.16
146	.	1.15	1.16
147	.	1.14	1.16
148	.	1.14	1.16
149	.	1.14	1.16
150	.	1.14	1.16

Both models are very similar, but as was gleaned from the ACFs and PACFs, the ARIMA(1,1,0) is the better of the two models.

****

7.14 The time series X_t is generated by the model ARIMA(0, 1, 1) model

$$X_t - X_{t-1} = a_t - \theta_1 a_{t-1}$$

Show that, standing at time n, the optimal forecasts of $\hat{X}_n(h)$ are the same for all $h = 1, 2, \ldots$

------- Answer to 7.14 -------

The equation for the ARIMA(0, 1, 1) model written above can be written as

$$X_t = X_{t-1} + a_t - \theta_1 a_{t-1}$$

Since the best forecast of white noise (a_{n+1}) is zero, the forecasts

$$\hat{X}_n(1) = \hat{X}_{n+1} = X_n - \theta_1 \hat{a}_n$$

Further $\hat{X}_n(2) = \hat{X}_{n+2} = \hat{X}_{n+1}$ which from above is equal to $X_n - \theta_1 \hat{a}_n$

Therefore, similarly $\hat{X}_n(h) = X_n$ for all $h \geq 1$.

See Chapter 9.2.

****

7.15 The time series X_t is generated by the ARIMA(0, 2, 2) model

$$(1 - B)^2 X_t = (1 - \theta_1 B - \theta_2 B^2) a_t$$

Let $\hat{X}_n(h)$ denote the optimal forecast of X_{n+h} made at time n. Show that

$$\hat{X}_n(h) = 2\hat{X}_n(h-1) - \hat{X}_n(h-2) \ ; \ h = 3, 4, \ldots$$

Hence show that the forecast function is a linear trend

$$\hat{X}_n(h) = \alpha + \beta h \ ; \ h = 1, 2, 3, \ldots$$

where $\alpha = 2\hat{X}_n(1) - \hat{X}_n(2) \ ; \ \beta = \hat{X}_n(2) - \hat{X}_n(1)$

------- Answer to 7.15 (first part) -------

The first forecast is $\hat{X}_n(1) = \hat{X}_{n+1} = 2X_n - X_{n-1} - \theta_1 \hat{a}_n - \theta_2 \hat{a}_{n-1}$

The second is $\hat{X}_n(2) = \hat{X}_{n+2} = 2\hat{X}_n(1) - X_n - \theta_2 \hat{a}_n$

while the third is $\hat{X}_n(3) = \hat{X}_{n+3} = 2\hat{X}_n(2) - \hat{X}_n(1)$

Clearly, at this point the forecasts no longer include in-sample error terms, thus

$$\hat{X}_n(h) = 2\hat{X}_n(h-1) - \hat{X}_n(h-2) \quad \text{for } h = 3, 4, \ldots$$

------- Answer to 7.15 (second part) -------

Going back to the fourth forecast

$$\hat{X}_n(4) \;=\; 2\hat{X}_n(3) - \hat{X}_n(2) \;=\; 2[2\hat{X}_n(2) - \hat{X}_n(1)] - \hat{X}_n(2) \;=\; 3\hat{X}_n(2) - 2\hat{X}_n(1)$$

$$\hat{X}_n(5) \;=\; 2\hat{X}_n(4) - \hat{X}_n(3) \;=\; 2[3\hat{X}_n(2) - 2\hat{X}_n(1)] - [2\hat{X}_n(2) - \hat{X}_n(1)] \;=\; 4\hat{X}_n(2) - 3\hat{X}_n(1)$$

Thus $\quad \hat{X}_n(h) \;=\; (h-1)\hat{X}_n(2) - (h-2)\hat{X}_n(1) \;=\; h[\hat{X}_n(2) - \hat{X}_n(1)] + 2\hat{X}_n(1) - \hat{X}_n(2)$

From this equation it is clear that we can replace

$[\hat{X}_n(2) - \hat{X}_n(1)]$ with β, and $[2\hat{X}_n(1) - \hat{X}_n(2)]$ with α to get

$$\hat{X}_n(h) = \alpha + \beta h \quad ; \quad h = 3, 4, \ldots$$

where $\qquad\qquad \alpha = 2\hat{X}_n(1) - \hat{X}_n(2) \quad ; \quad \beta = \hat{X}_n(2) - \hat{X}_n(1)$

****

7.16 The accompanying exhibit shows the first 40 sample partial autocorrelations for a monthly stationary time series of 240 observations. Discuss the problem of selecting an appropriate model to fit to this series.

<u>Exhibit acompanying Exercise 7.16</u>

Autocorrelations: Partial Autocorrelations:

Lag	Auto- Corr.	Stand. Err.	plot		Lag	Pr-Aut- Corr.	Stand. Err.	plot
			-.25 0 .25 .5 .75 1					-.25 0 .25 .5 .75 1
1	.510	.064	. :** .*******		1	.510	.065	. :** .*******
2	.186	.064	. :** .*		2	-.099	.065	.**: .
3	.044	.064	. :* .		3	-.013	.065	. * .
4	-.104	.064	.**: .		4	-.144	.065	***: .
5	-.172	.064	***: .		5	-.068	.065	. *: .
6	-.161	.063	***: .		6	-.036	.065	. *: .
7	-.123	.063	.**: .		7	-.020	.065	. * .
8	-.067	.063	. *: .		8	-.001	.065	. * .
9	.091	.063	. :**		9	.149	.065	. :***
10	.201	.063	. :** .*		10	.095	.065	. :**.
11	.325	.063	. :** .****		11	.211	.065	. :** .*
12	.532	.063	. :** .********		12	.383	.065	. :** .*****
13	.194	.063	. :** .*		13	-.355	.065	****.**: .
14	-.080	.062	**: .		14	-.098	.065	.**: .
15	-.189	.062	**.*: .		15	-.103	.065	.**: .
16	-.180	.062	**.*: .		16	.114	.065	. :**
17	-.203	.062	**.*: .		17	-.066	.065	. *: .
18	-.146	.062	*.*: .		18	.023	.065	. * .
19	-.062	.062	.*: .		19	-.021	.065	. * .
20	-.003	.062	. * .		20	.022	.065	. * .
21	.096	.061	. :**		21	-.056	.065	. *: .
22	.169	.061	. :*.*		22	.020	.065	. * .
23	.179	.061	. :*.**		23	-.049	.065	. *: .
24	.196	.061	. :*.**		24	-.064	.065	. *: .
25	-.009	.061	. * .		25	.016	.065	. * .
26	-.183	.061	**.*: .		26	-.005	.065	. * .
27	-.255	.061	***.*: .		27	-.030	.065	. *: .
28	-.211	.060	**.*: .		28	-.098	.065	.**: .
29	-.235	.060	***.*: .		29	-.115	.065	.**: .
30	-.131	.060	*.*: .		30	.053	.065	. :*
31	-.017	.060	. * .		31	.017	.065	. * .
32	.017	.060	. * .		32	-.064	.065	. *: .
33	.046	.060	. :*.		33	-.055	.065	. *: .
34	.068	.060	. :*.		34	-.052	.065	. *: .
35	.033	.059	. :*.		35	-.026	.065	. *: .
36	-.015	.059	. * .		36	-.037	.065	. *: .
37	-.144	.059	*.*: .		37	-.065	.065	. *: .
38	-.174	.059	*.*: .		38	.094	.065	. :**.
39	-.166	.059	*.*: .		39	.030	.065	. :*
40	-.092	.059	**: .		40	.041	.065	. :* .

Plot Symbols: Autocorrelations *   Two Standard Error Limits .
Total cases: 240   Computable first lags: 239

------- Answer to 7.16 -------

This is obviously a pure autoregressive model for both the regular (lags less than 12) and seasonal (lags thereafter), since the partial autocorrelations cutoff at low regular and seasonal lags. The data can be represented well by an ARIMA(1,0,0)(1,0,0) since there is only one significant regular lag (lag one), and significant lags at 12 and 13. The significant lag at lag 13 is only an echo of the significant partial autocorrelation at lag 1.

****

7.17 The accompanying exhibit shows the first 40 sample partial autocorrelations for a monthly stationary time series of 240 observations. Discuss the problem of selecting an appropriate model to fit to this series.

<u>Exhibit to accompany Exercise 7.17</u>

Autocorrelations: Partial Autocorrelations:

```
     Auto- Stand.                                    Pr-Aut- Stand.
Lag  Corr.  Err. -1  -.75  -.5 -.25   0   .25    Lag  Corr.  Err. -1  -.75  -.5 -.25   0   .25
                 +----+----+----+----+----+-                      +----+----+----+----+----+-
 1  -.443  .064           ******.**:   .          1  -.443  .065           ******.**:   .
 2   .086  .064              . :**.                2  -.137  .065              ***:   .
 3  -.007  .064              . * .                 3  -.032  .065              .*:   .
 4  -.161  .064           ***:  .                  4  -.210  .065           *.**:   .
 5   .074  .064              . :*                   5  -.121  .065              **:   .
 6  -.023  .063              . * .                  6  -.063  .065              .*:   .
 7  -.030  .063              . *: .                 7  -.096  .065              .**:   .
 8   .126  .063              . :***                 8   .050  .065              . :*
 9   .022  .063              . * .                  9   .139  .065              . :***
10  -.068  .063              . *: .                10   .012  .065              . * .
11   .221  .063              . :**.*              11   .270  .065              . :**.**
12  -.467  .063           ******.**:              12  -.294  .065           ***.**:   .
13   .198  .063              . :**.*              13  -.162  .065              ***:   .
14  -.041  .062              .*: .                 14  -.062  .065              .*:   .
15  -.066  .062              .*: .                 15  -.125  .065              **:   .
16   .172  .062              . :*.*               16  -.043  .065              .*:   .
17  -.099  .062             **: .                  17  -.070  .065              .*:   .
18   .052  .062              . :*.                 18  -.035  .065              .*:   .
19  -.018  .062              . * .                 19  -.075  .065              .**:   .
20  -.024  .062              . * .                 20   .039  .065              . :*
21  -.051  .061              .*: .                 21  -.002  .065              . * .
22   .060  .061              . :*.                 22   .020  .065              . :*
23  -.107  .061             **: .                  23   .045  .065              . :*
24   .091  .061              . :**               24  -.175  .065           ***:   .
25   .027  .061              . :*.                 25  -.020  .065              . * .
26  -.072  .061              .*: .                 26  -.089  .065              .**:   .
27   .150  .061              . :*.*               27   .019  .065              . :*
28  -.119  .060             **: .                  28   .040  .065              . :*
29   .043  .060              . :*.                 29  -.008  .065              . * .
30   .003  .060              . *.                  30   .044  .065              . :*
31  -.048  .060              .*: .                 31  -.031  .065              . *: .
32   .019  .060              . * .                 32   .004  .065              . * .
33   .021  .060              . * .                 33  -.024  .065              . * .
34  -.019  .060              . * .                 34   .006  .065              . * .
35   .128  .059              . :*.*               35   .137  .065              . :***
36  -.097  .059             **: .                  36  -.092  .065              .**:   .
37  -.017  .059              . * .                 37  -.020  .065              . * .
38   .067  .059              . :*.                 38  -.028  .065              . *: .
39  -.065  .059      $! $   .*: .                  39   .113  .065              . :j*.
40   .037  .059              . :*.               040   .070  .065              . :* .
```

Plot Symbols: Autocorrelations *   Two Standard Error Limits .
Total cases: 240   Computable first lags: 239

------- Answer to 7.17 -------

The regular portion can clearly be represented by an MA(1), since the autocorrelations cutoff cleaner (at lag 1) than the partial autocorrelations (lag two is also significant). It would seems that the seasonal part of the ARIMA model to represent this model is also an MA(1). The reason for this are the significant partial autocorrelations at 12 <u>and</u> 24; while the autocorrelations only have the significant lag at 12 (13 being an echo of the significant spike at lag 1).

Thus it is quite likely that the underlying data can be best represented by an ARIMA(0,0,1)(0,0,1).

7.18 The accompanying table shows the index of industrial production in the United States over
      168 months. Fit an appropriate non-seasonal ARIMA model to these data, and predict
      the index for the next twelve months.

------- Answer to 7.18 -------

To find out which models might be appropriate, the autocorrelation and partial
autocorrelation functions for the undifferenced, first differences, first seasonal differences,
and first differences of the first seasonal differences of this series are necessary. The
following output is from SPSS:

Graph Accompanying Exercise 7.18

Industrial Production

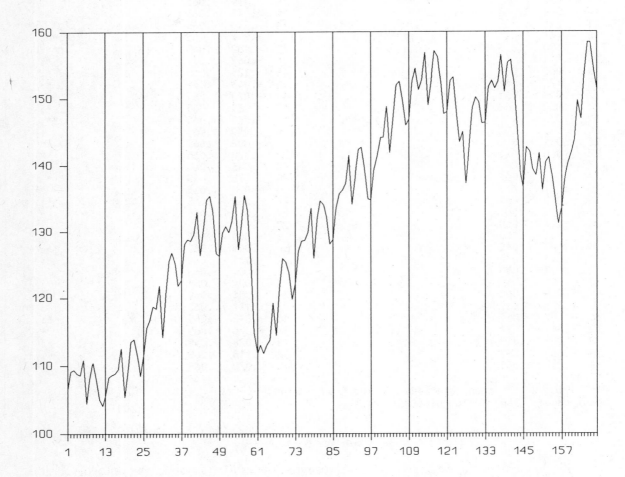

```
Autocorrelations:   IP_ALL              Partial Autocorrelations:   IP_ALL

     Auto- Stand.                             Pr-Aut- Stand.
Lag  Corr.  Err.   0  .25  .5  .75  1    Lag  Corr.  Err.   0  .25  .5  .75  1
                 ---+----+----+----+----+              ---+----+----+----+----+
  1  .955   .076 .  :**.****************   1   .955   .077 .  :**.****************
  2  .911   .076 .  :**.***************    2  -.011   .077 .  *  .
  3  .878   .076 .  :**.***************    3   .107   .077 .  :**.
  4  .851   .076 .  :**.**************     4   .050   .077 .  :* .
  5  .824   .076 .  :**.*************      5  -.002   .077 .  *  .
  6  .797   .075 .  :**.*************      6   .09   .077 .  *  .
  7  .762   .075 .  :**.************       7  -.101   .077 .**: .
  8  .730   .075 .  :**.************       8   .007   .077 .  *  .
  9  .700   .075 .  :**.***********        9  -.011   .077 .  *  .
 10  .677   .074 .  :**.***********       10   .068   .077 .  :* .
 11  .671   .074 .  :**.**********        11   .182   .077 .  :**.*
 12  .673   .074 .  :**.**********        12   .126   .077 .  :***
 13  .627   .074 .  :**.**********        13  -.509   .077 .**: .
 14  .588   .073 .  :**.*********         14   .131   .077 .  :***
 15  .566   .073 .  :**.********          15   .107   .077 .  :**.
 16  .553   .073 .  :**.********          16   .055   .077 .  :* .
 17  .540   .073 .  :**.********          17   .005   .077 .  *  .
 18  .526   .072 .  :**.********          18  -.006   .077 .  *  .
 19  .502   .072 .  :**.*******           19  -.048   .077 .  *: .
 20  .480   .072 .  :**.*******           20   .006   .077 .  *  .
 21  .460   .072 .  :**.******            21   .020   .077 .  *  .
 22  .447   .071 .  :**.******            22   .045   .077 .  :* .
 23  .448   .071 .  :**.******            23   .045   .077 .  :* .
 24  .456   .071 .  :**.******            24   .024   .077 .  *  .
 25  .418   .071 .  :**.*****             25  -.262   .077 .**: .
 26  .386   .071 .  :**.*****             26   .062   .077 .  :* .
 27  .368   .070 .  :**.****              27   .008   .077 .  *  .
 28  .358   .070 .  :**.****              28   .028   .077 .  :* .
 29  .346   .070 .  :**.****              29  -.028   .077 .  *: .
 30  .330   .070 .  :**.****              30  -.039   .077 .  *: .
 31  .303   .069 .  :**.***               31  -.045   .077 .  *: .
 32  .280   .069 .  :**.***               32   .049   .077 .  :* .
 33  .260   .069 .  :**.**                33   .009   .077 .  *  .
 34  .246   .068 .  :**.**                34   .004   .077 .  *  .
 35  .245   .068 .  :**.**                35   .022   .077 .  *  .
 36  .250   .068 .  :**.**                36  -.002   .077 .  *  .

Plot Symbols:     Autocorrelations *    Two Standard Error Limits .

Total cases:  168    Computable first lags:  167
```

Autocorrelations: IP_ALL   Partial Autocorrelations: IP_ALL

Transformations: difference (1)   Transformations: difference (1)

```
      Auto- Stand.                                    Pr-Aut- Stand.
Lag   Corr.  Err.  -.25   0   .25  .5  .75   1    Lag  Corr.  Err. 5 -.25   0   .25  .5
                   --+----+----+----+----+----+                     ---+----+----+----+----+---
  1  -.019  .077        .    *    .                   1  -.019  .077         .    *   .
  2  -.212  .076      *.**:   .                       2  -.213  .077       *.**:   .
  3  -.102  .076       .**:   .                       3  -.116  .077        .**:   .
  4   .039  .076        .  :* .                        4  -.015  .077         .    *   .
  5   .057  .076        .  :* .                        5   .013  .077         .    *   .
  6   .032  .076        .  :* .                        6   .030  .077         .   :* .
  7   .044  .075        .  :* .                        7   .069  .077         .   :* .
  8   .001  .075        .   * .                        8   .029  .077         .   :* .
  9  -.142  .075      ***:   .                         9  -.119  .077        .**:   .
 10  -.271  .075     **.**:   .                        10  -.292  .077      ***.**:   .
 11  -.115  .074       .**:   .                        11  -.247  .077      **.**:   .
 12   .790  .074        . :**.*************            12   .760  .077         . :**.************
 13  -.122  .074       .**:   .                         13  -.437  .077  ******.**:   .
 14  -.285  .074    ***.**:   .                        14  -.151  .077        ***:   .
 15  -.162  .073      ***:   .                         15  -.111  .077        .**:   .
 16   .011  .073        .   * .                        16  -.041  .077         . *:   .
 17   .067  .073        .  :* .                        17   .091  .077         .   :**.
 18   .033  .073        .  :* .                        18  -.045  .077         . *:   .
 19   .036  .072        .  :* .                        19  -.071  .077         . *:   .
 20   .005  .072        .   * .                        20  -.001  .077         .    * .
 21  -.129  .072      ***:   .                         21  -.070  .077         . *:   .
 22  -.253  .072     **.**:   .                        22  -.018  .077         .    * .
 23  -.100  .071       .**:   .                        23   .027  .077         .   :* .
 24   .731  .071        . :**.************            24   .065  .077         .   :* .
 25  -.117  .071       .**:   .                         25  -.074  .077         . *:   .
 26  -.245  .071     **.**:   .                        26   .048  .077         .   :* .
 27  -.140  .070      ***:   .                         27  -.054  .077         . *:   .
 28   .036  .070        .  :* .                        28  -.011  .077         .    * .
 29   .114  .070        .  :**.                        29   .041  .077         .   :* .
 30   .053  .070        .  :* .                        30  -.046  .077         . *:   .
 31   .029  .069        .  :* .                        31  -.045  .077         . *:   .
 32   .009  .069        .   * .                        32  -.009  .077         .    * .
 33  -.091  .069       .**:   .                         33   .066  .077         .   :* .
 34  -.223  .069      *.**:   .                         34   .002  .077         .    * .
 35  -.101  .068       .**:   .                         35  -.077  .077        .**:   .
 36   .662  .068        . :**.**********               36  -.018  .077         .    * .
```

Plot Symbols: Autocorrelations *   Two Standard Error Limits .

Total cases: 168   Computable first lags after differencing: 166

```
Autocorrelations:   IP_ALL              Partial Autocorrelations:   IP_ALL

Transformations:  seasonal difference (1 at 12)  Transformations:  seasonal difference (1 at 12)

      Auto- Stand.                              Pr-Aut- Stand.
Lag  Corr.  Err. -.25   0  .25  .5  .75   1    Lag  Corr.  Err.-.5 -.25   0  .25  .5  .75   1
                --+----+----+----+----+----+                   -+----+----+----+----+----+----+
  1   .958  .079    .  :**.****************     1   .958  .080       .  :**.****************
  2   .880  .079    .  :**.***************      2  -.457  .080  ******.**:   .
  3   .776  .079    .  :**.**************       3  -.219  .080       *.**:   .
  4   .658  .079    .  :**.***********          4  -.062  .080       . *:   .
  5   .536  .078    .  :**.********             5  -.032  .080       . *:   .
  6   .412  .078    .  :**.*****               6  -.062  .080       . *:   .
  7   .291  .078    .  :**.***                 7  -.076  .080       .**:   .
  8   .173  .077    .  :***                    8  -.055  .080       . *:   .
  9   .064  .077    .  :* .                    9  -.011  .080       . *   .
 10  -.034  .077    . *:  .                   10  -.040  .080       . *:   .
 11  -.122  .077    .**:  .                   11  -.032  .080       . *:   .
 12  -.199  .076   *.**:  .                   12  -.066  .080       . *:   .
 13  -.244  .076  **.**:  .                   13   .303  .080       .  :**.***
 14  -.267  .076  **.**:  .                   14  -.032  .080       . *:   .
 15  -.269  .076  **.**:  .                   15  -.026  .080       . *:   .
 16  -.259  .075  **.**:  .                   16  -.073  .080       . *:   .
 17  -.241  .075  **.**:  .                   17  -.025  .080       . *:   .
 18  -.220  .075   *.**:  .                   18  -.033  .080       . *:   .
 19  -.196  .075   *.**:  .                   19  -.013  .080       . *   .
 20  -.171  .074    ***:  .                   20  -.022  .080       . *   .
 21  -.148  .074    ***:  .                   21  -.057  .080       . *:   .
 22  -.125  .074    ***:  .                   22   .052  .080       . :*   .
 23  -.101  .073    .**:  .                   23   .030  .080       . :*   .
 24  -.077  .073    .**:  .                   24  -.055  .080       . *:   .
 25  -.055  .073    . *:  .                   25   .048  .080       . :*   .
 26  -.037  .073    . *:  .                   26  -.025  .080       . *:   .
 27  -.032  .072    . *:  .                   27  -.109  .080       .**:   .
 28  -.036  .072    . *:  .                   28  -.044  .080       . *:   .
 29  -.052  .072    . *:  .                   29  -.087  .080       .**:   .
 30  -.077  .071    .**:  .                   30  -.087  .080       .**:   .
 31  -.103  .071    .**:  .                   31   .074  .080       . :*   .
 32  -.129  .071    ***:  .                   32   .003  .080       . *   .
 33  -.151  .071    ***:  .                   33  -.019  .080       . *   .
 34  -.171  .070    ***:  .                   34  -.061  .080       . *:   .
 35  -.191  .070   *.**:  .                   35  -.031  .080       . *:   .
 36  -.210  .070   *.**:  .                   36  -.014  .080       . *   .

Plot Symbols:      Autocorrelations *     Two Standard Error Limits .

Total cases:  168     Computable first lags after differencing:  155
```

Autocorrelations: IP_ALL   Partial Autocorrelations: IP_ALL

Transformations: difference (1), seasonal difference (1 at 12)

```
     Auto- Stand.                                    Pr-Aut- Stand.
Lag  Corr.  Err.  -.25  0  .25  .5  .75   1    Lag  Corr.  Err.  -.25  0  .25  .5  .75   1
                  --+----+----+----+----+----+                   --+----+----+----+----+----+
 1   .604   .080      . :**.********       1    .604   .080      . :**.********
 2   .429   .079      . :**.******         2    .101   .080      . :**.
 3   .288   .079      . :**.***            3   -.010   .080      . *  .
 4   .184   .079      . :**.*              4   -.020   .080      . *  .
 5   .060   .079      . :*  .              5   -.094   .080      .**: .
 6   .033   .078      . :*  .              6    .034   .080      . :* .
 7  -.018   .078      . *   .              7   -.040   .080      . *: .
 8  -.069   .078      . *:  .              8   -.059   .080      . *: .
 9  -.060   .077      . *:  .              9    .031   .080      . :* .
10  -.121   .077      .**:  .             10   -.112   .080      .**: .
11  -.214   .077    *.**:  .              11   -.151   .080     ***: .
12  -.409   .077*****.**:  .              12   -.332   .080 ****.**: .
13  -.284   .076  ***.**:  .              13    .200   .080      . :**.*
14  -.286   .076  ***.**:  .              14   -.061   .080      . *: .
15  -.181   .076    *.**:  .              15    .101   .080      . :**.
16  -.120   .076      .**:  .             16   -.000   .080      . *  .
17  -.052   .075      . *:  .             17   -.021   .080      . *  .
18  -.044   .075      . *:  .             18   -.018   .080      . *  .
19  -.020   .075      . *   .             19   -.057   .080      . *: .
20   .012   .074      . *   .             20    .042   .080      . :* .
21  -.034   .074      . *:  .             21   -.063   .080      . *: .
22  -.047   .074      . *:  .             22   -.063   .080      . *: .
23   .006   .074      . *   .             23    .043   .080      . :* .
24  -.024   .073      . *   .             24   -.269   .080   **.**: .
25  -.004   .073      . *   .             25    .156   .080      . :***
26   .083   .073      . :**.              26    .016   .080      . *  .
27   .039   .073      . :* .              27   -.007   .080      . *  .
28   .072   .072      . :* .              28    .113   .080      . :**.
29   .133   .072      . :***              29    .077   .080      . :**.
30   .075   .072      . :* .              30   -.110   .080      .**: .
31   .038   .071      . :* .              31   -.040   .080      . *: .
32   .046   .071      . :* .              32    .050   .080      . :* .
33   .066   .071      . :* .              33    .030   .080      . :* .
34   .001   .071      . *  .              34   -.158   .080     ***: .
35  -.025   .070      . *: .              35    .035   .080      . :* .
36   .025   .070      . *  .              36   -.068   .080      . *: .
```

Plot Symbols: Autocorrelations *   Two Standard Error Limits .

Total cases: 168   Computable first lags after differencing: 154

It is clear that both first regular and first seasonal differencing is required. Comparing the ACF and the PACF of the first regular and first seasonal differences indicates that, at the nonseasonal level only one AR term is required, while at the seasonal level, two SARs will be required. Thus portions of the results for the ARIMA(1,1,0)(2,1,0) are shown below.

ARIMA(1,1,0)(2,1,0)

Standard error	1.5104803
Log likelihood	-285.4181
AIC	576.8362
SBC	585.96648

Variables in the Model:

	B	SEB	T-RATIO	APPROX. PROB.
AR1	.61379165	.06315115	9.7194057	0.0
SAR1	-.60829507	.08123317	-7.4882596	0.0
SAR2	-.33443982	.08161536	-4.0977560	.00006787

Forecasts

Case#	IP_ALL	FIT
163	147.00	145.19
164	153.30	154.01
165	158.40	156.51
166	158.40	158.67
167	154.70	155.97
168	151.40	149.99
169	.	152.37
170	.	158.06
171	.	159.42
172	.	159.02
173	.	160.03
174	.	164.57
175	.	160.18
176	.	165.32
177	.	167.66
178	.	165.79
179	.	161.33
180	.	156.61

****

7.19 The accompanying table shows 132 monthly observations on total consumer credit outstanding, in billions of dollars, in the United States. Fit an appropriate seasonal ARIMA model to the logarithms of these data, and predict credit outstanding for the next twelve months.

------- Answer to 7.19 -------

To find out which models might be appropriate, the autocorrelation and partial autocorrelation functions for the undifferenced, first differences, first seasonal differences, and first differences of the first seasonal differences of this series are necessary. The following output is from SPSS:

Graph Accompanying Exercise 7.19
Credit Outstanding

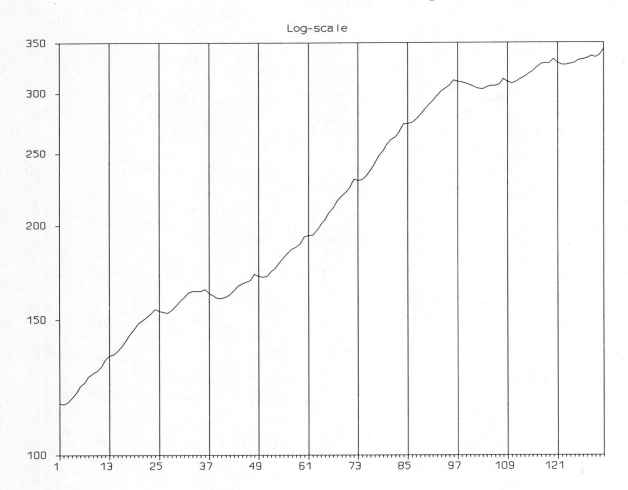

Autocorrelations: CREDITOS   Partial Autocorrelations: CREDITOS
Transformations: natural log   Transformations: natural log

```
      Auto- Stand.                                        Pr-Aut- Stand.
Lag   Corr.  Err.  -.25   0   .25  .5   .75   1   Lag  Corr.  Err.  -.25   0   .25  .5   .75   1
                   ---+----+----+----+----+----+                    ---+----+----+----+----+----+
 1    .980   .086     . :**.*****************      1    .980   .087     . :**.*****************
 2    .960   .086     . :**.****************       2   -.019   .087     . *  .
 3    .939   .085     . :**.****************       3   -.019   .087     . *  .
 4    .918   .085     . :**.***************        4   -.017   .087     . *  .
 5    .897   .085     . :**.***************        5   -.009   .087     . *  .
 6    .877   .084     . :**.***************        6   -.003   .087     . *  .
 7    .856   .084     . :**.**************         7   -.016   .087     . *  .
 8    .836   .084     . :**.**************         8   -.002   .087     . *  .
 9    .815   .083     . :**.*************          9   -.015   .087     . *  .
10    .794   .083     . :**.*************         10   -.017   .087     . *  .
11    .773   .083     . :**.************          11   -.015   .087     . *  .
12    .753   .082     . :**.************          12   -.011   .087     . *  .
13    .731   .082     . :**.************          13   -.031   .087     . *: .
14    .709   .082     . :**.***********           14   -.016   .087     . *  .
15    .687   .081     . :**.***********           15   -.017   .087     . *  .
16    .665   .081     . :**.**********            16   -.012   .087     . *  .
17    .644   .081     . :**.**********            17   -.000   .087     . *  .
18    .623   .080     . :**.*********             18    .005   .087     . *  .
19    .603   .080     . :**.*********             19   -.005   .087     . *  .
20    .583   .080     . :**.*********             20    .002   .087     . *  .
21    .564   .079     . :**.********              21   -.011   .087     . *  .
22    .545   .079     . :**.********              22   -.007   .087     . *  .
23    .525   .079     . :**.********              23   -.008   .087     . *  .
24    .506   .078     . :**.*******               24   -.015   .087     . *  .
25    .486   .078     . :**.*******               25   -.043   .087     . *: .
26    .465   .077     . :**.******                26   -.016   .087     . *  .
27    .444   .077     . :**.******                27   -.024   .087     . *  .
28    .423   .077     . :**.*****                 28   -.015   .087     . *  .
29    .402   .076     . :**.*****                 29   -.009   .087     . *  .
30    .382   .076     . :**.*****                 30   -.006   .087     . *  .
31    .361   .076     . :**.****                  31   -.015   .087     . *  .
32    .341   .075     . :**.****                  32   -.012   .087     . *  .
33    .321   .075     . :**.***                   33   -.024   .087     . *  .
34    .299   .074     . :**.***                   34   -.028   .087     . *: .
35    .278   .074     . :**.***                   35   -.027   .087     . *: .
36    .256   .074     . :**.**                    36   -.022   .087     . *  .
```

Plot Symbols: Autocorrelations *   Two Standard Error Limits .

Total cases: 132   Computable first lags: 131

```
Autocorrelations:   CREDITOS              Partial Autocorrelations:   CREDITOS
Transformations:  natural log, difference (1)   Transformations:  natural log, difference (1)

     Auto- Stand.                                   Pr-Aut- Stand.
Lag  Corr.  Err.   -.25  0  .25  .5  .75  1    Lag  Corr.  Err.  -.5 -.25  0  .25  .5  .75  1
            --+----+----+----+----+----+              --+----+----+----+----+----+----+
 1   .490  .086    . :**.*******                 1   .490  .087      . :**.*******
 2   .298  .086    . :**.***                      2   .076  .087      . :**.
 3   .286  .086    . :**.***                      3   .150  .087      . :***
 4   .236  .085    . :**.**                       4   .046  .087      . :* .
 5   .075  .085    . :**.                         5  -.123  .087      .**: .
 6   .125  .085    . :**.                         6   .109  .087      . :**.
 7   .032  .084    . :* .                         7  -.117  .087      .**: .
 8   .141  .084    . :***                         8   .211  .087      . :**.*
 9   .137  .084    . :***                         9   .004  .087      . * .
10   .063  .083    . :* .                        10  -.060  .087      . *: .
11   .213  .083    . :**.*                        11   .273  .087      . :**.**
12   .583  .083    . :**.*********                12   .504  .087      . :**.*******
13   .162  .082    . :***                         13  -.557  .087   *******.**: .
14   .025  .082    . :* .                         14  -.123  .087      .**: .
15   .028  .082    . :* .                         15  -.050  .087      . *: .
16   .024  .081    .  *                           16   .062  .087      . :* .
17  -.128  .081   ***: .                          17  -.102  .087      .**: .
18  -.076  .081    .**: .                         18  -.036  .087      . *: .
19  -.163  .080   ***: .                          19  -.032  .087      . *: .
20  -.047  .080    . *: .                         20   .003  .087      . * .
21  -.082  .079    .**: .                         21  -.081  .087      .**: .
22  -.130  .079   ***: .                          22   .118  .087      . :**.
23   .020  .079    . *                            23   .009  .087      . * .
24   .332  .078    . :**.****                      24   .031  .087      . :* .
25  -.004  .078    . *  .                          25  -.063  .087      . *: .
26  -.152  .078   ***: .                          26  -.206  .087     *.**: .
27  -.134  .077   ***: .                          27   .009  .087      . * .
28  -.114  .077    .**: .                          28  -.012  .087      . * .
29  -.278  .077  ***.**: .                         29  -.115  .087      .**: .
30  -.235  .076   **.**: .                         30  -.047  .087      . *: .
31  -.312  .076  ***.**: .                         31  -.075  .087      . *: .
32  -.224  .075    *.**: .                         32  -.103  .087      .**: .
33  -.236  .075   **.**: .                         33   .110  .087      . :**.
34  -.242  .075   **.**: .                         34   .013  .087      . * .
35  -.103  .074    .**: .                          35  -.010  .087      . * .
36   .181  .074    . :**.*                         36  -.041  .087      . *: .
```

Plot Symbols: Autocorrelations *   Two Standard Error Limits .

Total cases: 132   Computable first lags after differencing: 130

```
Autocorrelations:    CREDITOS                Partial Autocorrelations:   CREDITOS
Transformations:  natural log, seasonal difference (1 at 12)


      Auto- Stand.                                      Pr-Aut- Stand.
Lag   Corr.  Err. -.5 -.25  0  .25  .5  .75  1    Lag   Corr.  Err. -.5 -.25  0  .25  .5  .75  1
                  -+----+----+----+----+----+----+                  -+----+----+----+----+----+----+
  1   .984  .090         .  :***.***************     1   .984  .091        .   :***.***************
  2   .954  .090         .  :***.**************      2  -.429  .091   *****.***:      .
  3   .912  .089         .  :***.*************       3  -.251  .091       *.***:      .
  4   .863  .089         .  :***.************        4  -.066  .091        .  *:      .
  5   .807  .089         .  :***.***********         5  -.074  .091        .  *:      .
  6   .747  .088         .  :***.**********          6  -.044  .091        .  *:      .
  7   .683  .088         .  :***.*********           7  -.071  .091        .  *:      .
  8   .616  .087         .  :**.*********            8  -.041  .091        .  *:      .
  9   .548  .087         .  :**.********             9  -.002  .091        .   *      .
 10   .479  .087         .  :**.*******             10  -.063  .091        .  *:      .
 11   .412  .086         .  :**.*****               11   .028  .091        .   :*     .
 12   .346  .086         .  :**.****                12  -.002  .091        .   *      .
 13   .286  .085         .  :**.***                 13   .106  .091        .   :**    .
 14   .229  .085         .  :**.**                  14  -.039  .091        .  *:      .
 15   .175  .085         .  :**.*                   15  -.076  .091        . **:      .
 16   .124  .084         .  :**.                    16  -.071  .091        .  *:      .
 17   .072  .084         .  :* .                    17  -.096  .091        . **:      .
 18   .022  .083         .  * .                     18  -.064  .091        .  *:      .
 19  -.029  .083         . *: .                     19  -.082  .091        . **:      .
 20  -.082  .083         .**: .                     20  -.119  .091        . **:      .
 21  -.135  .082        ***: .                      21  -.069  .091        .  *:      .
 22  -.187  .082       *.**: .                      22   .012  .091        .   *      .
 23  -.237  .081      **.**: .                       23   .031  .091        .   :*     .
 24  -.284  .081     ***.**: .                      24   .021  .091        .   *      .
 25  -.327  .081    ****.**: .                      25   .038  .091        .   :*     .
 26  -.367  .080    ****.**: .                      26  -.072  .091        .  *:      .
 27  -.404  .080   *****.**: .                      27   .016  .091        .   *      .
 28  -.435  .079  ******.**: .                      28   .007  .091        .   *      .
 29  -.462  .079  ******.**: .                      29  -.042  .091        .  *:      .
 30  -.485  .078 *******.**: .                      30  -.046  .091        .  *:      .
 31  -.504  .078 *******.**: .                      31  -.051  .091        .  *:      .
 32  -.516  .078 *******.**: .                      32   .018  .091        .   *      .
 33  -.523  .077 *******.**: .                      33  -.009  .091        .   *      .
 34  -.526  .077 ********.**: .                      34  -.043  .091        .  *:      .
 35  -.525  .076 ********.**: .                      35  -.023  .091        .   *      .
 36  -.522  .076 *******.**: .                      36  -.040  .091        .  *:      .

Plot Symbols:      Autocorrelations *     Two Standard Error Limits .

Total cases:  132     Computable first lags after differencing:  119
```

Autocorrelations: CREDITOS   Partial Autocorrelations: CREDITOS
Transformations: natural log, difference (1), seasonal difference (1 at 12)

```
      Auto- Stand.                                Pr-Aut- Stand.
Lag   Corr.  Err. -.25  0  .25  .5  .75  1    Lag  Corr.  Err. -.25  0  .25  .5  .75  1
                  --+----+----+----+----+----+                 --+----+----+----+----+----+
  1   .761  .091      . :*** .**********          1   .761  .092      .  :*** .**********
  2   .652  .090      . :*** .********            2   .174  .092      .  :***.
  3   .536  .090      . :*** .*******             3  -.014  .092      .   *  .
  4   .423  .089      . :*** .****                4  -.058  .092      .  *:  .
  5   .358  .089      . :*** .***                 5   .043  .092      .  :*  .
  6   .260  .089      . :***.*                    6  -.079  .092      . **:  .
  7   .176  .088      . :****                     7  -.063  .092      .  *:  .
  8   .093  .088      . :** .                     8  -.061  .092      .  *:  .
  9   .093  .087      . :**.                      9   .138  .092      .  :***.
 10  -.020  .087      .  * .                      10 -.224  .092      ****:  .
 11  -.087  .087      .**: .                       11 -.076  .092      . **:  .
 12  -.172  .086      ***: .                       12 -.108  .092      . **:  .
 13  -.155  .086      ***: .                       13  .194  .092      .  :****
 14  -.085  .085      .**: .                       14  .166  .092      .  :***.
 15  -.095  .085      .**: .                       15 -.088  .092      . **:  .
 16  -.099  .085      .**: .                       16 -.103  .092      . **:  .
 17  -.061  .084      . *: .                       17  .154  .092      .  :***.
 18  -.066  .084      . *: .                       18 -.107  .092      . **:  .
 19  -.070  .083      . *: .                       19 -.070  .092      .  *:  .
 20  -.063  .083      . *: .                       20 -.019  .092      .  *   .
 21  -.151  .082      ***: .                       21 -.136  .092      .***:  .
 22  -.175  .082      ***: .                       22 -.091  .092      . **:  .
 23  -.151  .082      ***: .                       23  .027  .092      .  :*  .
 24  -.164  .081      ***: .                       24 -.015  .092      .  *   .
 25  -.162  .081      ***: .                       25  .071  .092      .  :*  .
 26  -.155  .080      ***: .                       26  .033  .092      .  :*  .
 27  -.169  .080      ***: .                       27 -.061  .092      . *:   .
 28  -.121  .079      .**: .                        28  .075  .092      .  :*  .
 29  -.124  .079      .**: .                        29 -.049  .092      . *:   .
 30  -.156  .079      ***: .                        30 -.091  .092      . **:  .
 31  -.136  .078      ***: .                        31 -.002  .092      .  *   .
 32  -.122  .078      .**: .                        32  .013  .092      .  *   .
 33  -.123  .077      .**: .                        33 -.145  .092      .***:  .
 34  -.115  .077      .**: .                        34 -.110  .092      . **:  .
 35  -.161  .076      ***: .                        35 -.085  .092      . **:  .
 36  -.209  .076      *.**: .                       36 -.034  .092      . *:   .
```

Plot Symbols: Autocorrelations *   Two Standard Error Limits .

Total cases: 132   Computable first lags after differencing: 118

The appropriate level of differencing is just first differencing. Taking seasonal differences as well just seems to eliminate significant seasonality in the ACFs and PACFs. The autocorrelations of the first differences of the logs of the data seems to suggest an ARIMA(1,1,0)(1,0,0). Among other models tried the ARIMA(1,1,0)(2,1,0) proved to be interesting. In fact not only are all its parameters significant at the 5% level, its AIC and SBC statistics are lower than for the ARIMA(1,1,0)(1,0,0).

ARIMA(1,1,0)(1,0,0)

```
Standard error        .00443335
Log likelihood        476.03101
AIC                   -948.06201
SBC                   -942.50377
```

Variables in the Model:

	B	SEB	T-RATIO	APPROX. PROB.
AR1	.78147919	.05755997	13.576783	0.0
SAR1	-.27718605	.09175323	-3.020995	.00309465

Autocorrelations: ERR#1

```
      Auto- Stand.
Lag   Corr.  Err.  -.25    0    .25
                   --+----+----+--
  1  -.192   .091   ****:    .
  2   .136   .090   .  :*** .
  3   .119   .090   .  :**  .
  4  -.104   .089   . **:    .
  5   .128   .089   .  :*** .
  6   .000   .089   .   *   .
  7   .039   .088   .  :*   .
  8  -.115   .088   . **:    .
  9   .238   .087   .  :** .**
 10  -.110   .087   .**:    .
 11   .018   .087   .   *   .
 12   .004   .086   .   *   .
 13  -.183   .086   *.**:    .
 14   .191   .085   .  :** .*
 15  -.055   .085   . *:    .
 16  -.084   .085   .**:    .
 17   .109   .084   .  :**  .
 18  -.044   .084   . *:    .
 19  -.025   .083   . *:    .
 20   .162   .083   .  :***
 21  -.096   .082   .**:    .
 22  -.112   .082   .**:    .
 23   .078   .082   .  :**  .
 24  -.189   .081   *.**:    .
 25  -.002   .081   .  *    .
 26   .018   .080   .  *    .
 27  -.161   .080   ***:    .
 28   .089   .079   .  :**  .
 29   .037   .079   .  :*   .
 30  -.136   .079   ***:    .
 31  -.026   .078   . *:    .
 32   .013   .078   .   *   .
 33  -.101   .077   .**:    .
 34   .083   .077   .  :**  .
 35  -.035   .076   . *:    .
 36  -.230   .076   **.**:    .
```

ARIMA(1,1,0)(2,0,0)

Standard error	.00433206
Log likelihood	520.03067
AIC	-1034.0613
SBC	-1025.4358

Variables in the Model:

	B	SEB	T-RATIO	APPROX. PROB.
AR1	.77138933	.05374903	14.351688	0.0
SAR1	.65700145	.08452659	7.772719	0.0
SAR2	.21109414	.08997147	2.346234	.02050017

Autocorrelations: ERR#1

Lag	Auto-Corr.	Stand. Err.	-.25 0 .25
1	-.121	.086	.**: .
2	.151	.086	. :***
3	.113	.086	. :**.
4	-.023	.085	. * .
5	.092	.085	. :**.
6	.060	.085	. :* .
7	.075	.084	. :* .
8	-.039	.084	. *: .
9	.237	.084	. :**.**
10	-.104	.083	.**: .
11	.041	.083	. :* .
12	-.027	.083	. *: .
13	-.195	.082	*.**: .
14	.137	.082	. :***
15	-.047	.082	. *: .
16	-.031	.081	. *: .
17	-.005	.081	. * .
18	.033	.081	. :* .
19	-.115	.080	.**: .
20	.149	.080	. :***
21	-.125	.079	.**: .
22	-.144	.079	***: .
23	.037	.079	. :* .
24	-.115	.078	.**: .
25	-.010	.078	. * .
26	-.027	.078	. *: .
27	-.122	.077	.**: .
28	.049	.077	. :* .
29	-.064	.077	. *: .
30	-.081	.076	.**: .
31	-.069	.076	. *: .
32	-.001	.075	. * .
33	-.091	.075	.**: .
34	.036	.075	. :* .
35	-.027	.074	. *: .
36	-.144	.074	***: .

Forecasts

Case#	CREDITOS	F110100	F110200
121	328.80	330.06	330.32
122	327.40	326.18	326.01
123	327.10	328.75	328.17
124	328.30	328.16	327.75
125	329.30	329.15	328.91
126	331.90	331.51	331.27
127	332.50	333.67	333.84
128	333.80	334.86	334.96
129	335.90	335.30	335.14
130	334.90	335.58	335.84
131	337.00	333.90	334.09
132	343.40	342.06	342.41
133	.	341.99	341.76
134	.	342.45	341.89
135	.	343.47	343.17
136	.	345.51	345.49
137	.	347.13	347.32
138	.	349.99	350.39
139	.	350.96	351.72
140	.	352.44	353.83
141	.	354.54	356.37
142	.	353.86	355.97
143	.	355.86	357.60
144	.	361.60	363.11

****

7.20 The accompanying table shows 156 monthly observations on end of month retailers'
      inventories in durable goods stores, in billions of dollars, in the United States. Fit an
      appropriate seasonal ARIMA model to this series, and forecast inventories for the next
      twelve months.

------- Answer to 7.20 -------

Graph Accompanying Exercise 7.20
End of Month Retailers' Inventories

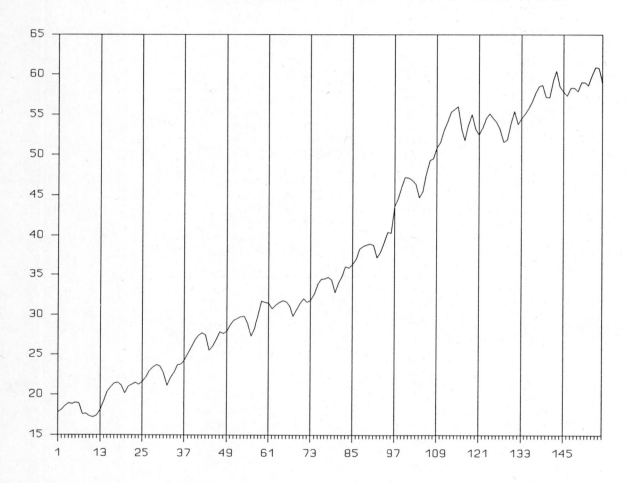

To find out which models might be appropriate, the autocorrelation and partial
autocorrelation functions for the undifferenced, first differences, first seasonal differences,
and first differences of the first seasonal differences of this series are necessary. The
following output is from SPSS:

```
Autocorrelations:     DURA_INV              Partial Autocorrelations:   DURA_INV

      Auto- Stand.                              Pr-Aut- Stand.
Lag   Corr.  Err.  -.25  0  .25  .5  .75  1    Lag  Corr.  Err.  -.25  0  .25  .5  .75  1
                   ---+----+----+----+----+----+              ---+----+----+----+----+----+
  1   .984  .079      . :**.******************    1   .984  .080      . :**.******************
  2   .965  .079      . :**.*****************     2  -.089  .080      .**: .
  3   .948  .079      . :**.*****************     3   .021  .080      .  * .
  4   .931  .079      . :**.****************      4   .035  .080      .  :* .
  5   .915  .078      . :**.****************      5  -.008  .080      .  * .
  6   .899  .078      . :**.***************       6  -.014  .080      .  * .
  7   .883  .078      . :**.***************       7  -.010  .080      .  * .
  8   .866  .077      . :**.**************        8  -.014  .080      .  * .
  9   .849  .077      . :**.**************        9  -.031  .080      . *: .
 10   .832  .077      . :**.**************       10   .004  .080      .  * .
 11   .816  .077      . :**.*************        11   .019  .080      .  * .
 12   .799  .076      . :**.*************        12  -.056  .080      . *: .
 13   .778  .076      . :**.*************        13  -.105  .080      .**: .
 14   .756  .076      . :**.************         14  -.043  .080      . *: .
 15   .736  .076      . :**.************         15   .056  .080      .  :* .
 16   .719  .075      . :**.***********          16   .040  .080      .  :* .
 17   .701  .075      . :**.***********          17  -.035  .080      . *: .
 18   .682  .075      . :**.***********          18  -.033  .080      . *: .
 19   .663  .075      . :**.**********           19  -.010  .080      .  * .
 20   .643  .074      . :**.**********           20  -.013  .080      .  * .
 21   .625  .074      . :**.*********            21   .024  .080      .  * .
 22   .608  .074      . :**.*********            22   .021  .080      .  * .
 23   .592  .073      . :**.*********            23   .008  .080      .  * .
 24   .575  .073      . :**.*********            24  -.028  .080      . *: .
 25   .556  .073      . :**.********             25  -.061  .080      . *: .
 26   .535  .073      . :**.********             26  -.046  .080      . *: .
 27   .517  .072      . :**.*******              27   .045  .080      .  :* .
 28   .501  .072      . :**.*******              28   .032  .080      .  :* .
 29   .484  .072      . :**.*******              29  -.028  .080      . *: .
 30   .467  .071      . :**.******               30  -.034  .080      . *: .
 31   .448  .071      . :**.******               31  -.043  .080      . *: .
 32   .427  .071      . :**.******               32  -.063  .080      . *: .
 33   .406  .071      . :**.*****                33  -.024  .080      .  * .
 34   .387  .070      . :**.*****                34   .015  .080      .  * .
 35   .369  .070      . :**.****                 35   .031  .080      .  :* .
 36   .352  .070      . :**.****                 36  -.007  .080      .  * .

Plot Symbols:     Autocorrelations *     Two Standard Error Limits .

Total cases:  156    Computable first lags:  155
```

```
Autocorrelations:     DURA_INV              Partial Autocorrelations:   DURA_INV
Transformations:  difference (1)            Transformations:  difference (1)

      Auto- Stand.                               Pr-Aut- Stand.
Lag   Corr.  Err.  -.25  0  .25  .5   .75   1   Lag  Corr.  Err.  -.25  0  .25  .5   .75   1
                   ---+----+----+----+----+----+                  ---+----+----+----+----+----+
  1    .248  .080        .  :**.**               1    .248  .080        .  :**.**
  2   -.206  .079     *.**:  .                    2   -.285  .080    ***.**:  .
  3   -.214  .079     *.**:  .                    3   -.090  .080       .**:  .
  4    .048  .079        . :*  .                   4    .093  .080       .  :**.
  5   -.060  .079        . *:  .                   5   -.202  .080     *.**:  .
  6   -.054  .078        . *:  .                   6    .030  .080       .  :*  .
  7   -.068  .078        . *:  .                   7   -.092  .080       .**:  .
  8    .015  .078        .  *  .                   8   -.011  .080       .  *  .
  9   -.204  .077     *.**:  .                    9   -.272  .080    **.**:  .
 10   -.172  .077     ***:  .                    10   -.093  .080       .**:  .
 11    .158  .077        .  :***                  11    .188  .080       .  :**.*
 12    .663  .077        .  :**.*********         12    .549  .080       .  :**.********
 13    .100  .076        .  :**.                  13   -.279  .080    ***.**:  .
 14   -.217  .076     *.**:  .                    14    .062  .080       .  :*  .
 15   -.195  .076     *.**:  .                    15   -.062  .080       . *:  .
 16    .081  .076        .  :**.                  16    .027  .080       .  :*  .
 17   -.066  .075        . *:  .                   17   -.099  .080       .**:  .
 18   -.032  .075        . *:  .                   18    .068  .080       .  :*  .
 19   -.076  .075        .**:  .                   19   -.105  .080       .**:  .
 20   -.025  .074        .  *  .                   20   -.041  .080       . *:  .
 21   -.195  .074     *.**:  .                    21   -.030  .080       . *:  .
 22   -.158  .074     ***:  .                     22   -.093  .080       .**:  .
 23    .113  .074        .  :**.                  23    .032  .080       .  :*  .
 24    .598  .073        .  :**.*********         24    .269  .080       .  :**.**
 25    .121  .073        .  :**.                  25   -.058  .080       . *:  .
 26   -.215  .073     *.**:  .                    26   -.054  .080       . *:  .
 27   -.216  .073     *.**:  .                    27   -.048  .080       . *:  .
 28    .076  .072        .  :**.                  28   -.026  .080       . *:  .
 29   -.035  .072        . *:  .                   29    .015  .080       .  *  .
 30   -.032  .072        . *:  .                   30   -.060  .080       . *:  .
 31   -.039  .071        . *:  .                   31    .119  .080       .  :**.
 32    .003  .071        .  *  .                   32   -.047  .080       . *:  .
 33   -.175  .071     *.**:  .                    33   -.007  .080       .  *  .
 34   -.151  .071     ***:  .                     34   -.061  .080       . *:  .
 35    .034  .070        . :*  .                   35   -.116  .080       .**:  .
 36    .450  .070        .  :**.******            36   -.026  .080       . *:  .
```

Plot Symbols: Autocorrelations *   Two Standard Error Limits .

Total cases: 156   Computable first lags after differencing: 154

```
Autocorrelations:   DURA_INV             Partial Autocorrelations:   DURA_INV
  Transformations:  seasonal difference (1 at 12)

      Auto- Stand.                                Pr-Aut- Stand.
Lag   Corr.  Err.  -.25  0  .25  .5  .75  1   Lag  Corr.  Err.  -.25  0  .25  .5  .75  1
             ---+----+----+----+----+----+                   ---+----+----+----+----+----+
  1   .941  .082     . :**.****************     1   .941  .083     .  :**.****************
  2   .848  .082     . :**.***************      2  -.334  .083   ****.**:  .
  3   .761  .082     . :**.************         3   .104  .083     .  :**.
  4   .682  .082     . :**.***********          4  -.037  .083     . *:  .
  5   .604  .081     . :**.*********            5  -.063  .083     . *:  .
  6   .518  .081     . :**.*******              6  -.108  .083     .**:  .
  7   .432  .081     . :**.******               7  -.021  .083     . *   .
  8   .346  .080     . :**.****                 8  -.075  .083     .**:  .
  9   .266  .080     . :**.**                   9  -.009  .083     . *   .
 10   .183  .080     . :**.*                   10  -.126  .083   ***:  .
 11   .099  .080     . :**.                    11  -.034  .083     . *:  .
 12   .030  .079     . :* .                    12   .060  .083     . :*  .
 13   .004  .079     . *  .                    13   .285  .083     . :**.***
 14  -.003  .079     . *  .                    14  -.072  .083     . *:  .
 15  -.011  .078     . *  .                    15   .001  .083     . *   .
 16  -.026  .078     . *: .                    16  -.065  .083     . *:  .
 17  -.042  .078     . *: .                    17  -.016  .083     . *   .
 18  -.049  .077     . *: .                    18  -.008  .083     . *   .
 19  -.064  .077     . *: .                    19  -.168  .083   ***:  .
 20  -.080  .077     .**: .                    20   .031  .083     . :*  .
 21  -.087  .076     .**: .                    21   .057  .083     . :*  .
 22  -.087  .076     .**: .                    22  -.038  .083     . *:  .
 23  -.084  .076     .**: .                    23  -.018  .083     . *   .
 24  -.088  .076     .**: .                    24  -.027  .083     . *:  .
 25  -.108  .075     .**: .                    25  -.049  .083     . *:  .
 26  -.138  .075   ***: .                      26  -.033  .083     . *:  .
 27  -.162  .075   ***: .                      27   .002  .083     . *   .
 28  -.172  .074   ***: .                      28   .041  .083     . :*  .
 29  -.182  .074   *.**: .                      29  -.087  .083     .**:  .
 30  -.196  .074   *.**: .                      30   .007  .083     . *   .
 31  -.199  .073   *.**: .                      31   .028  .083     . :*  .
 32  -.207  .073   *.**: .                      32  -.138  .083   ***:  .
 33  -.218  .073   *.**: .                      33   .036  .083     . :*  .
 34  -.229  .072  **.**: .                      34   .002  .083     . *   .
 35  -.238  .072  **.**: .                      35  -.012  .083     . *   .
 36  -.236  .072  **.**: .                      36   .034  .083     . :*  .

Plot Symbols:      Autocorrelations *      Two Standard Error Limits .

Total cases:  156      Computable first lags after differencing:  143
```

```
Autocorrelations:   DURA_INV              Partial Autocorrelations:   DURA_INV
Transformations:  difference (1), seasonal difference (1 at 12)

      Auto- Stand.                             Pr-Aut- Stand.
Lag   Corr.  Err.  -.25   0  .25  .5  .75   1  Lag  Corr.  Err.  -.25   0  .25  .5  .75   1
                   --+----+----+----+----+----+               --+----+----+----+----+----+
  1   .387  .083        . :** .*****            1   .387  .084        . :** .*****
  2   .010  .082        . *    .                2  -.164  .084        ***:   .
  3  -.042  .082        . *:   .                3   .021  .084        . *    .
  4  -.030  .082        . *:   .                4  -.021  .084        . *    .
  5   .034  .082        . :*   .                5   .058  .084        . :*   .
  6   .008  .081        . *    .                6  -.041  .084        . *:   .
  7  -.004  .081        . *    .                7   .015  .084        . *    .
  8   .027  .081        . :*   .                8   .030  .084        . :*   .
  9   .080  .080        . :**  .                9   .070  .084        . :*   .
 10   .007  .080        . *    .               10  -.066  .084        . *:   .
 11  -.131  .080        ***:   .               11  -.118  .084        .**:   .
 12  -.413  .079   *****.**:   .               12  -.379  .084   *****.**:   .
 13  -.206  .079        *.**:  .               13   .128  .084        . :***
 14   .008  .079        . *    .               14  -.021  .084        . *    .
 15   .065  .079        . :*   .               15   .063  .084        . :*   .
 16   .018  .078        . *    .               16  -.064  .084        . *:   .
 17  -.102  .078        .**:   .               17  -.071  .084        . *:   .
 18   .021  .078        . *    .               18   .121  .084        . :**.
 19  -.069  .077        . *:   .               19  -.190  .084        *.**:  .
 20  -.150  .077        ***:   .               20  -.058  .084        . *:   .
 21  -.065  .077        . *:   .               21   .085  .084        . :**.
 22   .028  .076        . :*   .               22   .021  .084        . *    .
 23   .089  .076        . :**  .               23   .021  .084        . *    .
 24   .124  .076        . :**  .               24  -.119  .084        .**:   .
 25   .103  .075        . :**  .               25   .112  .084        . :**.
 26  -.069  .075        . *:   .               26  -.147  .084        ***:   .
 27  -.134  .075        ***:   .               27  -.049  .084        . *:   .
 28  -.052  .074        . *:   .               28   .040  .084        . :*   .
 29   .015  .074        . *    .               29  -.090  .084        .**:   .
 30  -.043  .074        . *:   .               30   .035  .084        . :*   .
 31   .061  .073        . :*   .               31   .012  .084        . *    .
 32   .093  .073        . :**. .               32  -.067  .084        . *:   .
 33   .016  .073        . *    .               33   .015  .084        . *    .
 34  -.013  .073        . *    .               34  -.023  .084        . *    .
 35  -.129  .072        ***:   .               35  -.038  .084        . *:   .
 36  -.068  .072        . *:   .               36  -.019  .084        . *    .
```

Plot Symbols: Autocorrelations *   Two Standard Error Limits .

Total cases: 156   Computable first lags after differencing: 142

The appropriate level of differencing is first regular differences and first seasonal differences. The autocorrelations and partial autocorrelations of the first regular and seasonal differences suggest that either an ARIMA(1,1,0)(1,1,0) or an ARIMA(0,1,1)(0,1,1) or some model close to this (with just one regular term and one seasonal term) will be best.

ARIMA(1,1,0)(1,1,0)

```
Standard error        .6220586
Log likelihood       -135.46212
AIC                   274.92425
SBC                   280.84994
```

Variables in the Model:

	B	SEB	T-RATIO	APPROX. PROB.
AR1	.37975378	.07721432	4.9181783	.00000243
SAR1	-.45136004	.08101447	-5.5713512	.00000013

Autocorrelations: ERR#1

```
      Auto- Stand.
Lag   Corr.  Err.  -1  -.75  -.5  -.25   0   .25   .5   .75
                   +----+----+----+----+----+----+----+-
  1   .056   .083                       . :* .
  2  -.142   .082                       ***: .
  3  -.003   .082                       . * .
  4  -.013   .082                       . * .
  5   .002   .082                       . * .
  6   .013   .081                       . * .
  7  -.005   .081                       . * .
  8  -.074   .081                       . *: .
  9   .078   .080                       . :**.
 10   .022   .080                       . * .
 11   .078   .080                       . :**.
 12  -.072   .079                       . *: .
 13  -.042   .079                       . *: .
 14   .001   .079                       . * .
 15  -.001   .079                       . * .
 16   .053   .078                       . :* .
 17  -.158   .078                       ***: .
 18   .091   .078                       . :**.
 19  -.010   .077                       . * .
 20  -.143   .077                       ***: .
 21  -.013   .077                       . * .
 22   .074   .076                       . :* .
 23   .004   .076                       . * .
 24  -.122   .076                       .**: .
 25   .128   .075                       . :***
 26  -.093   .075                       .**: .
 27  -.062   .075                       . *: .
 28   .056   .074                       . :* .
 29   .038   .074                       . :* .
 30  -.107   .074                       .**: .
 31  -.004   .073                       . * .
 32   .025   .073                       . * .
 33  -.033   .073                       . *: .
 34   .076   .073                       . :**.
 35  -.160   .072                       ***: .
 36  -.093   .072                       .**: .
```

ARIMA(0,1,1)(1,1,0)

```
Standard error        .61427587
Log likelihood       -133.65936
AIC                   271.31873
SBC                   277.24441
```

Variables in the Model:

	B	SEB	T-RATIO	APPROX. PROB.
MA1	-.43893547	.07540571	-5.8209848	.00000004
SAR1	-.44669026	.08056045	-5.5447837	.00000014

Autocorrelations: ERR#1

```
       Auto- Stand.
Lag   Corr.  Err.  -1  -.75  -.5  -.25   0   .25   .5   .75   1
                   +----+----+----+----+----+----+----+----+
  1    .010   .083                       .  *  .
  2    .014   .082                       .  *  .
  3   -.005   .082                       .  *  .
  4   -.009   .082                       .  *  .
  5    .009   .082                       .  *  .
  6   -.003   .081                       .  *  .
  7    .020   .081                       .  *  .
  8   -.084   .081                       .**:  .
  9    .097   .080                       .  :**.
 10   -.012   .080                       .  *  .
 11    .087   .080                       .  :**.
 12   -.080   .079                       .**:  .
 13   -.031   .079                       . *:  .
 14    .005   .079                       .  *  .
 15   -.038   .079                       . *:  .
 16    .079   .078                       .  :**.
 17   -.177   .078                     *.**:  .
 18    .094   .078                       .  :**.
 19   -.037   .077                       . *:  .
 20   -.116   .077                       .**:  .
 21   -.010   .077                       .  *  .
 22    .028   .076                       .  :* .
 23    .029   .076                       .  :* .
 24   -.138   .076                     ***:  .
 25    .136   .075                       .  :***
 26   -.116   .075                       .**:  .
 27   -.030   .075                       . *:  .
 28    .021   .074                       .  *  .
 29    .040   .074                       .  :* .
 30   -.105   .074                       .**:  .
 31   -.003   .073                       .  *  .
 32    .021   .073                       .  *  .
 33   -.066   .073                       . *:  .
 34    .076   .073                       .  :**.
 35   -.162   .072                     ***:  .
 36   -.078   .072                       .**:  .
```

ARIMA(0,1,1)(0,1,1)

```
Standard error        .59150834
Log likelihood       -129.78278
AIC                   263.56557
SBC                   269.49126
```

Variables in the Model:

	B	SEB	T-RATIO	APPROX. PROB.
MA1	-.46864135	.07309081	-6.4117686	0.0
SMA1	.61216274	.07875190	7.7733077	0.0

Autocorrelations: ERR#1

```
      Auto- Stand.
 Lag  Corr.  Err. -1  -.75  -.5 -.25   0   .25  .5  .75   1
                  +----+----+----+----+----+----+----+----+
   1   .012  .083                      . * .
   2   .015  .082                      . * .
   3  -.014  .082                      . * .
   4  -.038  .082                      . *: .
   5  -.010  .082                      . * .
   6  -.006  .081                      . * .
   7  -.006  .081                      . * .
   8  -.071  .081                      . *: .
   9   .079  .080                      . :** .
  10  -.004  .080                      . * .
  11   .044  .080                      . :* .
  12  -.014  .079                      . * .
  13  -.011  .079                      . * .
  14  -.007  .079                      . * .
  15   .007  .079                      . * .
  16   .086  .078                      . :**.
  17  -.155  .078                    ***: .
  18   .062  .078                      . :* .
  19  -.029  .077                      . *: .
  20  -.111  .077                     .**: .
  21  -.014  .077                      . * .
  22   .031  .076                      . :* .
  23   .004  .076                      . * .
  24   .031  .076                      . :* .
  25   .095  .075                      . :**.
  26  -.098  .075                     .**: .
  27  -.034  .075                      . *: .
  28   .034  .074                      . :* .
  29   .051  .074                      . :* .
  30  -.078  .074                     .**: .
  31   .032  .073                      . :* .
  32   .011  .073                      . * .
  33  -.069  .073                      . *: .
  34   .041  .073                      . :* .
  35  -.147  .072                    ***: .
  36  -.081  .072                     .**: .
```

ARIMA(1,1,0)(0,1,1)

Standard error	.60154189
Log likelihood	-132.09459
AIC	268.18917
SBC	274.11486

Variables in the Model:

	B	SEB	T-RATIO	APPROX. PROB.
AR1	.39850093	.07608378	5.2376592	.00000059
SMA1	.60757367	.07816025	7.7734357	0.0

Autocorrelations: ERR#1

```
       Auto- Stand.
Lag    Corr.  Err.  -1  -.75  -.5 -.25   0   .25  .5   .75  1
                     +----+----+----+----+----+----+----+----+
  1    .068  .083                     .   :*  .
  2   -.154  .082                   ***:   .
  3   -.010  .082                     .  *  .
  4   -.043  .082                     . *:  .
  5   -.013  .082                     .  *  .
  6    .012  .081                     .  *  .
  7   -.028  .081                     . *:  .
  8   -.064  .081                     . *:  .
  9    .072  .080                     .   :*  .
 10    .019  .080                     .  *  .
 11    .035  .080                     .   :*  .
 12   -.011  .079                     .  *  .
 13   -.018  .079                     .  *  .
 14   -.018  .079                     .  *  .
 15    .041  .079                     .   :*  .
 16    .070  .078                     .   :*  .
 17   -.144  .078                   ***:   .
 18    .056  .078                     .   :*  .
 19   -.004  .077                     .  *  .
 20   -.136  .077                   ***:   .
 21   -.014  .077                     .  *  .
 22    .049  .076                     .   :*  .
 23   -.006  .076                     .  *  .
 24    .046  .076                     .   :*  .
 25    .101  .075                     .   :**  .
 26   -.106  .075                    .**:   .
 27   -.066  .075                     . *:  .
 28    .066  .074                     .   :*  .
 29    .047  .074                     .   :*  .
 30   -.080  .074                    .**:   .
 31    .032  .073                     .   :*  .
 32    .019  .073                     .  *  .
 33   -.044  .073                     . *:  .
 34    .045  .073                     .   :*  .
 35   -.143  .072                   ***:   .
 36   -.093  .072                    .**:   .
```

Forecasts

Case#	DURA_INV	F110110	F011110	F011011	F110011
145	57.87	58.41	58.44	58.71	58.71
146	57.37	58.29	58.29	58.15	58.06
147	58.34	57.83	57.87	58.02	57.92
148	58.35	59.06	59.24	59.26	59.09
149	57.93	58.44	58.31	58.42	58.55
150	58.98	57.89	58.02	57.96	57.83
151	59.01	58.96	59.09	59.26	59.10
152	58.62	57.64	57.47	57.17	57.38
153	59.86	59.15	59.23	59.34	59.19
154	60.94	62.32	62.17	61.99	62.23
155	60.81	61.95	61.77	61.79	61.96
156	58.90	58.40	58.55	58.91	58.77
157	.	58.88	59.06	59.06	58.88
158	.	58.83	59.01	59.28	59.02
159	.	59.65	59.84	60.28	59.98
160	.	60.01	60.20	60.75	60.44
161	.	60.29	60.47	60.89	60.58
162	.	61.26	61.44	61.46	61.15
163	.	61.36	61.54	61.35	61.04
164	.	60.47	60.65	60.15	59.84
165	.	61.14	61.34	60.66	60.36
166	.	62.66	62.84	62.23	61.93
167	.	63.15	63.33	63.01	62.70
168	.	61.19	61.37	61.39	61.07

****

7.21 The accompanying table shows 168 monthly observations on an index of newspaper advertising. Fit an appropriate seasonal ARIMA model, and obtain forecasts for the next twelve months.

------- Answer to 7.21 -------

To find out which models might be appropriate, the autocorrelation and partial autocorrelation functions for the undifferenced, first differences, first seasonal differences, and first differences of the first seasonal differences of this series are necessary. The following output is from SPSS:

Graph Accompanying Exercise 7.21
Index of Newspaper Advertising

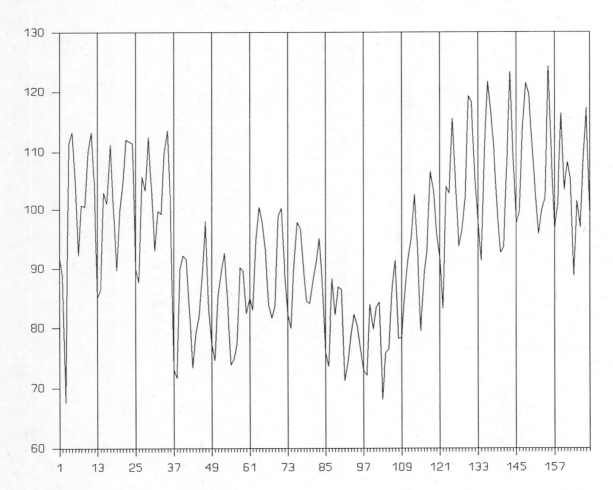

```
Autocorrelations:   NEWSADV              Partial Autocorrelations:   NEWSADV

      Auto- Stand.                              Pr-Aut- Stand.
Lag   Corr.  Err.  -.25   0   .25  .5  .75  1   Lag  Corr.  Err.  -.25   0   .25  .5  .75  1
            ---+----+----+----+----+----+            ---+----+----+----+----+----+
  1   .703  .076      . :**.***********            1   .703  .077      . :**.***********
  2   .407  .076      . :**.*****                  2  -.172  .077      ***: .
  3   .288  .076      . :**.***                    3   .151  .077      . :***
  4   .391  .076      . :**.*****                  4   .335  .077      . :**.****
  5   .639  .076      . :**.**********             5   .475  .077      . :**.*******
  6   .739  .075      . :**.************           6   .236  .077      . :**.**
  7   .602  .075      . :**.*********              7   .030  .077      . :* .
  8   .319  .075      . :**.***                    8  -.248  .077      **.**: .
  9   .184  .075      . :**.*                      9  -.119  .077      .**: .
 10   .295  .074      . :**.***                   10  -.007  .077      . * .
 11   .543  .074      . :**.********              11   .191  .077      . :**.*
 12   .681  .074      . :**.***********           12   .203  .077      . :**.*
 13   .481  .074      . :**.*******              13  -.202  .077      *.**: .
 14   .199  .073      . :**.*                    14  -.166  .077      ***: .
 15   .071  .073      . :* .                     15  -.118  .077      .**: .
 16   .167  .073      . :***                     16  -.092  .077      .**: .
 17   .386  .073      . :**.*****               17  -.040  .077      . *: .
 18   .469  .072      . :**.******              18  -.036  .077      . *: .
 19   .345  .072      . :**.****                19   .074  .077      . :* .
 20   .077  .072      . :**.                    20  -.032  .077      . *: .
 21  -.087  .072      .**: .                    21  -.141  .077      ***: .
 22   .016  .071      . * .                      22  -.055  .077      . *: .
 23   .235  .071      . :**.**                   23  -.026  .077      . *: .
 24   .326  .071      . :**.****                 24  -.042  .077      . *: .
 25   .174  .071      . :***                     25  -.005  .077      . * .
 26  -.054  .071      . *: .                     26   .097  .077      . :**.
 27  -.177  .070      *.**: .                    27   .040  .077      . :* .
 28  -.083  .070      .**: .                     28   .046  .077      . :* .
 29   .124  .070      . :**.                     29   .013  .077      . * .
 30   .205  .070      . :**.*                    30  -.028  .077      . *: .
 31   .099  .069      . :**.                     31   .007  .077      . * .
 32  -.138  .069      ***: .                     32  -.031  .077      . *: .
 33  -.265  .069      **.**: .                   33   .026  .077      . :* .
 34  -.134  .068      ***: .                     34   .149  .077      . :***
 35   .042  .068      . :* .                     35  -.065  .077      . *: .
 36   .148  .068      . :***                     36   .092  .077      . :**.
```

Plot Symbols: Autocorrelations *   Two Standard Error Limits .

Total cases: 168   Computable first lags: 167

```
Autocorrelations:    NEWSADV            Partial Autocorrelations:   NEWSADV
Transformations:  difference (1)        Transformations:  difference (1)

      Auto- Stand.                            Pr-Aut- Stand.
Lag   Corr.  Err.5 -.25  0  .25 .5  .75  1   Lag  Corr.  Err. .5 -.25  0  .25  .5  .75  1
                ---+----+----+----+----+----+                   +----+----+----+----+----+----+
 1  -.008  .077        .   *   .               1  -.008  .077        .   *   .
 2  -.300  .076    ***.**:   .                 2  -.300  .077    ***.**:   .
 3  -.362  .076   ****.**:   .                 3  -.404  .077   *****.**:   .
 4  -.245  .076     **.**:   .                 4  -.509  .077 *******.**:   .
 5   .252  .076        .:**.**                 5  -.253  .077     **.**:   .
 6   .391  .076        .:**.*****              6  -.051  .077        . *:   .
 7   .248  .075        .:**.**                 7   .242  .077        .:**.**
 8  -.248  .075     **.**:   .                 8   .110  .077        .:**.
 9  -.416  .075  *****.**:   .                 9  -.009  .077        . *   .
10  -.226  .075     **.**:   .                10  -.210  .077     *.**:   .
11   .184  .074        .:**.*                 11  -.222  .077     *.**:   .
12   .563  .074        .:**.********          12   .172  .077        .:***
13   .133  .074        .:***                  13   .139  .077        .:***
14  -.249  .074     **.**:   .                14   .111  .077        .:**.
15  -.379  .073  *****.**:   .                15   .070  .077        .:* .
16  -.205  .073     *.**:   .                 16   .022  .077        . *   .
17   .226  .073        .:**.**                17   .001  .077        . *   .
18   .345  .073        .:**.****              18  -.109  .077        .**:   .
19   .243  .072        .:**.**                19  -.008  .077        . *   .
20  -.176  .072     *.**:   .                 20   .100  .077        .:**.
21  -.446  .072******.**:   .                 21   .022  .077        . *   .
22  -.191  .072     *.**:   .                 22  -.004  .077        . *   .
23   .215  .071        .:**.*                 23   .012  .077        . *   .
24   .405  .071        .:**.*****             24  -.027  .077        . *:   .
25   .122  .071        .:**.                  25  -.135  .077     ***:   .
26  -.168  .071     ***:   .                  26  -.074  .077        . *:   .
27  -.364  .070   ****.**:   .                27  -.077  .077        .**:   .
28  -.187  .070     *.**:   .                 28  -.031  .077        . *:   .
29   .207  .070        .:**.*                 29   .014  .077        . *   .
30   .313  .070        .:**.***               30  -.020  .077        . *   .
31   .219  .069        .:**.*                 31   .017  .077        . *   .
32  -.188  .069     *.**:   .                 32  -.049  .077        . *:   .
33  -.428  .069******.**:   .                 33  -.180  .077     *.**:   .
34  -.072  .069        . *:   .               34   .030  .077        . :*   .
35   .116  .068        .:**.                  35  -.120  .077        .**:   .
36   .369  .068        .:**.****              36   .014  .077        . *   .
```

Plot Symbols: Autocorrelations *   Two Standard Error Limits .

Total cases: 168   Computable first lags after differencing: 166

```
Autocorrelations:   NEWSADV              Partial Autocorrelations:   NEWSADV
Transformations:  seasonal difference (1 at 12)  Transformations:  seasonal difference (1 at 12)

     Auto- Stand.                             Pr-Aut- Stand.
Lag  Corr.  Err.  -.25  0  .25  .5  .75  1   Lag  Corr.  Err.  -.25  0  .25  .5  .75  1
              ---+----+----+----+----+----+                    ---+----+----+----+----+----+
  1   .643  .079        .:**.**********         1   .643  .080        .:**.**********
  2   .594  .079        .:**.*********          2   .308  .080        .:**.***
  3   .589  .079        .:**.*********          3   .239  .080        .:**.**
  4   .513  .079        .:**.*******            4   .042  .080        .:*.
  5   .490  .078        .:**.*******            5   .062  .080        .:*.
  6   .451  .078        .:**.******             6   .014  .080        . *.
  7   .406  .078        .:**.*****              7  -.005  .080        . *.
  8   .336  .077        .:**.****               8  -.083  .080        .**:.
  9   .303  .077        .:**.***                9  -.029  .080        . *:.
 10   .241  .077        .:**.**                10  -.073  .080        . *:.
 11   .182  .077        .:**.*                 11  -.069  .080        . *:.
 12   .125  .076        .:**.                  12  -.084  .080        .**:.
 13   .139  .076        .:***                  13   .078  .080        . :**.
 14   .074  .076        . :* .                 14  -.044  .080        . *:.
 15   .036  .076        . :* .                 15  -.022  .080        . * .
 16  -.013  .075        .  *  .                16  -.079  .080        .**:.
 17  -.034  .075        . *: .                 17   .007  .080        . * .
 18  -.046  .075        . *: .                 18   .012  .080        . * .
 19  -.064  .075        . *: .                 19   .017  .080        . * .
 20  -.075  .074        .**: .                 20  -.001  .080        . * .
 21  -.173  .074       ***: .                  21  -.164  .080       ***:.
 22  -.247  .074      **.**: .                 22  -.203  .080      *.**:.
 23  -.220  .073      *.**: .                  23   .009  .080        . * .
 24  -.336  .073    ****.**: .                 24  -.203  .080      *.**:.
 25  -.289  .073     ***.**: .                 25   .094  .080        . :**
 26  -.232  .073      **.**: .                 26   .148  .080        . :***
 27  -.271  .072      **.**: .                 27   .058  .080        . :*.
 28  -.244  .072      **.**: .                 28   .069  .080        . :*.
 29  -.265  .072      **.**: .                 29  -.020  .080        . * .
 30  -.236  .071      **.**: .                 30   .055  .080        . :* .
 31  -.239  .071      **.**: .                 31  -.018  .080        . * .
 32  -.206  .071      *.**: .                  32  -.009  .080        . * .
 33  -.215  .071      *.**: .                  33  -.109  .080        .**:.
 34  -.133  .070       ***: .                  34   .113  .080        . :**.
 35  -.127  .070       ***: .                  35   .009  .080        . * .
 36  -.107  .070       .**: .                  36  -.001  .080        . * .
```

Plot Symbols: Autocorrelations *   Two Standard Error Limits .

Total cases: 168   Computable first lags after differencing: 155

Autocorrelations: NEWSADV   Partial Autocorrelations: NEWSADV
Transformations: difference (1), seasonal difference (1 at 12)

Lag	Auto-Corr.	Stand. Err.	-.5 -.25 0 .25 .5 .75 1
1	-.431	.080	******.**: .
2	-.020	.079	. * .
3	.057	.079	. :* .
4	-.058	.079	. *: .
5	-.002	.079	. * .
6	.018	.078	. * .
7	.031	.078	. :* .
8	-.056	.078	. *: .
9	.061	.077	. :* .
10	-.007	.077	. * .
11	.002	.077	. * .
12	-.103	.077	.**: .
13	.112	.076	. :**.
14	-.046	.076	. *: .
15	.029	.076	. :* .
16	-.045	.076	. *: .
17	-.011	.075	. * .
18	.005	.075	. * .
19	-.008	.075	. * .
20	.115	.074	. :**.
21	-.025	.074	. *: .
22	-.136	.074	***: .
23	.186	.074	. :**.*
24	-.234	.073	**.**: .
25	-.012	.073	. * .
26	.119	.073	. :**.
27	-.088	.073	.**: .
28	.068	.072	. :* .
29	-.062	.072	. *: .
30	.049	.072	. :* .
31	-.060	.071	. *: .
32	.084	.071	. :**.
33	-.148	.071	***: .
34	.116	.071	. :**.
35	-.026	.070	. *: .
36	.017	.070	. * .

Lag	Pr-Aut-Corr.	Stand. Err.	-.5 -.25 0 .25 .5
1	-.431	.080	******.**: .
2	-.253	.080	**.**: .
3	-.083	.080	.**: .
4	-.090	.080	.**: .
5	-.078	.080	.**: .
6	-.040	.080	. *: .
7	.027	.080	. :* .
8	-.033	.080	. *: .
9	.033	.080	. :* .
10	.038	.080	. :* .
11	.047	.080	. :* .
12	-.110	.080	.**: .
13	.015	.080	. * .
14	-.009	.080	. * .
15	.038	.080	. :* .
16	-.049	.080	. *: .
17	-.059	.080	. *: .
18	-.052	.080	. *: .
19	-.039	.080	. *: .
20	.109	.080	. :**.
21	.129	.080	. :***
22	-.094	.080	.**: .
23	.106	.080	. :**.
24	-.185	.080	*.**: .
25	-.213	.080	*.**: .
26	-.086	.080	.**: .
27	-.109	.080	.**: .
28	-.026	.080	. *: .
29	-.107	.080	.**: .
30	-.034	.080	. *: .
31	-.034	.080	. *: .
32	.084	.080	. :**.
33	-.128	.080	***: .
34	-.008	.080	. * .
35	.008	.080	. * .
36	-.005	.080	. * .

Plot Symbols: Autocorrelations *   Two Standard Error Limits .

Total cases: 168   Computable first lags after differencing: 154

It seems that the appropriate level of differenceing is first regular, and first seasonal differencing. It is clear that the nonseasonal portion of the movement of this data can be represented by an MA(1). As for the seasonal portion, the appropriate model has "to take care of" the significant lag at 24 (both autocorrelation and partial autocorrelation) with no other seasonal aspect. Thus two models are tried the ARIMA(0,1,1)(2,1,0) and the ARIMA(0,1,1)(0,1,2). The better of the two (looking for the smaller standard error, AIC, and BIC) is the ARIMA(0,1,1)(0,1,2). Forecasts are shown below for both models.

ARIMA(0,1,1)(2,1,0)

```
Standard error      6.2482565
Log likelihood     -505.71703
AIC                 1017.4341
SBC                 1026.5643
```

Variables in the Model:

	B	SEB	T-RATIO	APPROX. PROB.
MA1	.63959850	.06266965	10.205873	0.0
SAR1	-.21590140	.08655280	-2.494447	.01368493
SAR2	-.46141854	.07402125	-6.233596	0.0

Autocorrelations: ERR#1

```
      Auto- Stand.
Lag   Corr.  Err.  -1  -.75  -.5 -.25   0   .25   .5   .75   1
                   +----+----+----+----+----+----+----+----+
  1   -.010  .080                      . *  .
  2   -.061  .079                      . *: .
  3    .026  .079                      . :* .
  4   -.001  .079                      . *  .
  5    .005  .079                      . *  .
  6    .058  .078                      . :* .
  7    .026  .078                      . :* .
  8   -.015  .078                      . *  .
  9    .002  .077                      . *  .
 10   -.030  .077                      . *: .
 11   -.018  .077                      . *  .
 12    .003  .077                      . *  .
 13    .021  .076                      . *  .
 14   -.004  .076                      . *  .
 15    .016  .076                      . *  .
 16   -.057  .076                      . *: .
 17   -.039  .075                      . *: .
 18   -.029  .075                      . *: .
 19    .048  .075                      . :* .
 20    .101  .074                      . :**.
 21   -.056  .074                      . *: .
 22   -.120  .074                      .**: .
 23   -.016  .074                      . *  .
 24    .024  .073                      . *  .
 25   -.042  .073                      . *: .
 26    .015  .073                      . *  .
 27   -.063  .073                      . *: .
 28    .033  .072                      . :* .
 29   -.084  .072                      .**: .
 30   -.041  .072                      . *: .
 31   -.050  .071                      . *: .
 32   -.019  .071                      . *  .
 33   -.118  .071                      .**: .
 34    .076  .071                      . :**.
 35    .019  .070                      . *  .
 36   -.074  .070                      . *: .
```

ARIMA(0,1,1)(0,1,2)

```
Standard error        6.0260807
Log likelihood       -502.96476
AIC                   1011.9295
SBC                   1021.0598
```

Variables in the Model:

	B	SEB	T-RATIO	APPROX. PROB.
MA1	.62670349	.06229909	10.059593	0.0
SMA1	.35154412	.10692031	3.287908	.00125400
SMA2	.45000853	.09753304	4.613908	.00000842

Autocorrelations: ERR#1

```
      Auto- Stand.
Lag  Corr.  Err.  -1  -.75  -.5 -.25   0   .25   .5   .75   1
                  +----+----+----+----+----+----+----+----+
  1   .008  .080                      .  *  .
  2  -.036  .079                      . *:  .
  3   .007  .079                      .  *  .
  4  -.005  .079                      .  *  .
  5  -.024  .079                      .  *  .
  6   .012  .078                      .  *  .
  7   .001  .078                      .  *  .
  8  -.015  .078                      .  *  .
  9   .003  .077                      .  *  .
 10  -.008  .077                      .  *  .
 11  -.012  .077                      .  *  .
 12   .050  .077                      .  :* .
 13   .022  .076                      .  *  .
 14  -.022  .076                      .  *  .
 15  -.020  .076                      .  *  .
 16  -.047  .076                      . *:  .
 17  -.055  .075                      . *:  .
 18  -.034  .075                      . *:  .
 19   .018  .075                      .  *  .
 20   .092  .074                      .  :**.
 21  -.055  .074                      . *:  .
 22  -.127  .074                    ***:  .
 23  -.019  .074                      .  *  .
 24   .037  .073                      .  :* .
 25  -.069  .073                      . *:  .
 26  -.005  .073                      .  *  .
 27  -.075  .073                      . *:  .
 28   .015  .072                      .  *  .
 29  -.084  .072                      .**:  .
 30  -.033  .072                      . *:  .
 31  -.071  .071                      . *:  .
 32  -.020  .071                      .  *  .
 33  -.119  .071                      .**:  .
 34   .070  .071                      .  :* .
 35   .014  .070                      .  *  .
 36   .082  .070                      .  :**.
```

<u>Forecasts</u>

Case#	NEWSADV	F011210	F011012
157	96.60	100.82	99.32
158	101.00	98.60	98.45
159	116.40	116.46	113.16
160	103.60	118.12	117.67
161	108.30	118.54	115.99
162	105.40	104.37	104.64
163	88.80	96.24	95.75
164	101.60	91.03	92.19
165	96.90	100.52	100.09
166	109.10	105.11	103.77
167	117.30	119.69	117.93
168	98.80	105.46	105.43
169	.	91.76	92.07
170	.	91.64	93.38
171	.	108.57	106.87
172	.	102.36	101.60
173	.	104.13	105.18
174	.	101.41	101.74
175	.	85.19	86.04
176	.	93.69	96.30
177	.	89.46	93.43
178	.	105.11	107.35
179	.	113.15	111.52
180	.	95.58	96.72

****

Chapter 8

ECONOMETRIC FORECASTING MODELS, LEADING INDICATORS, AND EXPECTATIONS

Contents of Chapter 8

Answers to questions at end of chapter.

8.1   Distinguish between the members of the following pairs:
       (a)   "Structural form" and "reduced form"
       (b)   "Endogenous variables" and "exogenous variables"
       (c)   "Conditional forecasts" and "unconditional forecasts"

------- Answer to 8.1 --------

(a)   (From the text) "The structural form of an econometric model is that form which would be postulated by an economist on the basis of theory." while ". . . the reduced form of the model is obtained by solving these equations expressed as a function of all the exogenous variables, and an error term".

(b)   Endogenous variables are dependent variables (those determined by the model); while exogenous variables are independent or predetermined variables (variables which drive the system, and are not driven by any variable in the system).

(c)   Conditional forecasts arise from a regression in which the dependent variable is forecasted given a set of values (or given a particular "economic situation"/state); while unconditional forecasts do not depend on a particular scenario occurring.

****

8.2   (a)   Carefully explain what is meant by "the identification problem" in the context of simultaneous equations econometric models.
      (b)   Explain why the method of ordinary least squares is often not employed in the estimation of a regression equation that is part of a simultaneous equations econometric system.

------- Answer to 8.2 --------

(a)   See the first section of 8.2.

(b)   Ordinary least squares is often not used to estimate parameters of structural form equation, since if more than one endogenous (dependent) variable exists in the equation, then the estimates will be "inconsistent". This is the errors-in-variables problem - that is, where not all variables on the right-hand-side of the equation are uncorrelated with the error term. See an econometrics text.

****

8.3   Consider the pair of equations (8.2.2), which constitute a demand/supply system.
      (a)   Write down the reduced form equations, expressing their parameters as functions of the parameters of the structural equations.
      (b)   Explain how the supply equation (8.2.2b) can be estimated by the method of two-stage least squares.
      (c)   Explore the consequences of attempting to apply the method two-stage least squares to the estimation of the parameters of the demand equation (8.2.2a).

------- Answer to 8.3 --------

(a)   The structural equations (8.2) are:

$$Y_{1t} = \alpha_1 + \beta_{12} Y_{2t} + \gamma_{11} X_{1t} + \epsilon_{1t} \tag{1}$$

$$Y_{1t} = \alpha_2 + \beta_{22} Y_{2t} + \epsilon_{2t} \tag{2}$$

Setting the right-hand-sides of equations (1) and (2):

$$\alpha_1 + \beta_{12} Y_{2t} + \gamma_{11} X_{1t} + \epsilon_{1t} = Y_{1t} = \alpha_2 + \beta_{22} Y_{2t} + \epsilon_{2t}$$

Re-arranging this:

$$Y_{2t} (\beta_{12} - \beta_{22}) = (\alpha_2 - \alpha_1) - \gamma_{11} X_{1t} - \epsilon_{1t} + \epsilon_{2t}$$

$$Y_{2t} = (\alpha_2 - \alpha_1)/(\beta_{12} - \beta_{22}) - \gamma_{11}/(\beta_{12} - \beta_{22}) X_{1t} + (\epsilon_{2t} - \epsilon_{1t})/(\beta_{12} - \beta_{22}) \tag{3}$$

Substitute (3) into (2):

$$Y_{1t} = \alpha_2 + \beta_{22} (\alpha_2 - \alpha_1)/(\beta_{12} - \beta_{22}) - \beta_{22} \gamma_{11}/(\beta_{12} - \beta_{22}) X_{1t}$$

$$+ (\epsilon_{2t} - \epsilon_{1t}) \beta_{22} /(\beta_{12} - \beta_{22}) + \epsilon_{2t}$$

Or

$$Y_{1t} = (\alpha_2 \beta_{12} - \alpha_1 \beta_{22})/(\beta_{12} - \beta_{22}) - \beta_{22} \gamma_{11}/(\beta_{12} - \beta_{22}) X_{1t}$$

$$+ (\beta_{12} \epsilon_{2t} - \beta_{22} \epsilon_{1t})/(\beta_{12} - \beta_{22}) \tag{4}$$

Equations (3) and (4) consistitute the reduced form equations for the set of structural equations (1) and (2).

(b) Step 1:   Estimate the reduced form equation (3), above, and from this estimate, find $\hat{Y}_{2t}$, the estimates of Y_2.

Step 2:   Replace Y_2 with $\hat{Y}_{2t}$ in equation (2) above. Then estimate equation (2) with ordinary least squares.

(c) If one wanted to try to apply two-stage least squares to equation (1) above, and would proceed the same way.

Step 1:   Estimate the reduced form equation (3), above, and from this estimate, find $\hat{Y}_{2t}$, the estimates of Y_2.

Then proceeding to step 2:

Step 2:   Replace Y_2 with $\hat{Y}_{2t}$ in equation (1) above. Then estimate equation (2) with ordinary least squares.

Then $\hat{Y}_{2t}$ is simply a linear equation of X_{1t}. Hence $\hat{Y}_{2t}$ is perfectly correlated with X_{1t}. Hence the least squares estimates of the regression of Y_1 on $\hat{Y}_{2t}$ and X_{1t} does not exist.

****

8.4   Consider the pair of equations (8.2.6), which constitute a demand/supply system. Set out the reduced form equations, expressing the parameters and error terms in those equations as functions of the parameters and error terms of the structural form equations.

------- Answer to 8.4 --------

$$Y_{1t} = \alpha_1 + \beta_{12}\, Y_{2t} + \gamma_{11}\, X_{1t} + \gamma_{13}\, X_{3t} + \epsilon_{1t} \tag{1}$$

$$Y_{1t} = \alpha_2 + \beta_{22}\, Y_{2t} + \gamma_{22}\, X_{2t} + \epsilon_{2t} \tag{2}$$

Writing this is (semi) matrix form:

$$\begin{bmatrix} 1 & -\beta_{12} \\ 1 & -\beta_{22} \end{bmatrix} \begin{bmatrix} Y_{1t} \\ Y_{2t} \end{bmatrix} = \begin{bmatrix} V_1 \\ V_2 \end{bmatrix}$$

where $V_1 = \alpha_1 + \gamma_{11}\, X_{1t} + \gamma_{13}\, X_{3t} + \epsilon_{1t}$
and $V_2 = \alpha_2 + \gamma_{22}\, X_{2t} + \epsilon_{2t}$

Inverting the matrix on the left-hand-side, we get that

$$\begin{bmatrix} Y_{1t} \\ Y_{2t} \end{bmatrix} = \begin{bmatrix} 1 & -\beta_{12} \\ 1 & -\beta_{22} \end{bmatrix}^{-1} \begin{bmatrix} V_1 \\ V_2 \end{bmatrix} = (\beta_{12} - \beta_{22})^{-1} \begin{bmatrix} -\beta_{22} & \beta_{12} \\ -1 & 1 \end{bmatrix} \begin{bmatrix} V_1 \\ V_2 \end{bmatrix}$$

Thus

$$Y_{1t} = (\beta_{12}\alpha_2 - \beta_{22}\alpha_1)/(\beta_{12} - \beta_{22}) - (\gamma_{11}\beta_{22}(\beta_{12} - \beta_{22}))\, X_{1t}$$

$$+ (\gamma_{22}\beta_{12}/(\beta_{12} - \beta_{22}))\, X_{2t} - (\gamma_{13}\beta_{22}/(\beta_{12} - \beta_{22}))\, X_{3t}$$

$$+ (\beta_{12}\epsilon_2 - \beta_{22}\epsilon_1)/(\beta_{12} - \beta_{22})$$

and

$$Y_{2t} = (\alpha_2 - \alpha_1)/(\beta_{12} - \beta_{22}) - (\gamma_{11}/(\beta_{12} - \beta_{22}))\, X_{1t}$$

$$+ (\gamma_{22}/(\beta_{12} - \beta_{22}))\, X_{2t} - (\gamma_{13}/(\beta_{12} - \beta_{22}))\, X_{3t} + (\epsilon_2 - \epsilon_1)/(\beta_{12} - \beta_{22})$$

These last two equations are the reduced form equations for the two structural equations in the text (8.2.6).

****

8.5   The following two-equations model was estimated as an aid to the prediction of local advertising expenditures, using annual observations.

$$Y_{1t} = -41.9 + 0.48\,Y_{1,t-1} + 0.019\,Y_{2t} + \epsilon_{1t}$$

$$Y_{2t} = 1922 + 0.38\,X_t + \epsilon_{2t}$$

where Y_{1t} = Real local advertising expenditures per household
         Y_{2t} = Real value of retail sales per household
         X_t = Real disposable income per household

Real local advertising expenditures per household in the current year are $Y_{1n} = 155.7$

If real disposable income per household in the next thre years is expected to be

$$X_{n+1} = 12{,}798;\ X_{n+2} = 12{,}962;\ X_{n+3} = 13{,}216$$

obtain point forecasts of real local advertising expenditures per household in these three years.

------- Answer to 8.5 --------

To forecast Y_{1t} for periods n, $n+1$, and $n+2$ one needs forecasts of Y_{2t} which can be derived from the second equation. Thus, since the best forecast of $\epsilon_{2,n+1}$ is zero

$$\hat{Y}_{2,n+1} = 1922 + 0.38\,X_{n+1} = 1922 + 0.38\times12{,}798 = 6{,}785.24.$$

Similarly, since the best forecast of $\epsilon_{1,n+1}$ is zero, then

$$\hat{Y}_{1,n+1} = -41.9 + 0.48\,Y_{1n} + 0.019\,\hat{Y}_{2,n+1} = -41.9 + 0.48\times155.7 + 0.019\times6{,}785.24 = 161.76$$

Then for period $n+2$:

$$\hat{Y}_{2,n+2} = 1922 + 0.38\,X_{n+2} = 1922 + 0.38\times12{,}962 = 6{,}847.56\ \text{ and}$$

$$\hat{Y}_{1,n+2} = -41.9 + 0.48\,Y_{1,n+1} + 0.019\,\hat{Y}_{2,n+2} = -41.9 + 0.48\times161.76 + 0.019\times6{,}847.56 = 165.85$$

And finally for period $n+3$:

$$\hat{Y}_{2,n+3} = 1922 + 0.38\,X_{n+3} = 1922 + 0.38\times13{,}216 = 6{,}944.08\ \text{ and}$$

$$\hat{Y}_{1,n+3} = -41.9 + 0.48\,Y_{1,n+2} + 0.019\,\hat{Y}_{2,n+3} = -41.9 + 0.48\times165.85 + 0.019\times6{,}944.08 = 169.64$$

These results are easy to reproduce using a spreadsheet.

****

8.6   Consider the following simple two-equations model for price and wage inflation.

$$Y_{1t} = 3.1 + 0.80\, Y_{2t} - 0.62\, X_{1t}$$

$$Y_{2t} = 2.2 + 0.65\, Y_{1t} - 0.33\, X_{2t}$$

where Y_{1t} = Annual percentage change in prices
Y_{2t} = Anual percentage change in wages
X_{1t} = Anual percentage change in productivity
X_{2t} = Percentage of the labor force unemployed

Suppose that next year annual percentage change in productivity and percentage of the labor force unemployed are expected to be $X_{1,n+1} = 2.5$; $X_{2,n+1} = 6.4$

Find point forecasts for percentage changes in prices and wages.

------- Answer to 8.6 --------

It is expected that this exercise is done by first finding the reduced form of this two equation system.

Substitute the second equation into the first to get

$$Y_{1t} = 3.1 + 0.8\,(2.2 + 0.65\, Y_{1t} - 0.33\, X_{2t}) - 0.62\, X_{1t}$$

$$Y_{1t} = 4.86 + 0.52\, Y_{1t} - 0.264\, X_{2t} - 0.62\, X_{1t}$$

$$Y_{1t} = 4.86/0.48 - (0.264/0.48)\, X_{2t} - (0.62/0.48)\, X_{1t}$$

$$Y_{1t} = 10.125 - 1.29167\, X_{1t} - 0.55\, X_{2t}$$

Substitute the first structural equation into the second:

$$Y_{2t} = 2.2 + 0.65\,(3.1 + 0.8\, Y_{2t} - 0.62\, X_{1t}) - 0.33\, X_{2t}$$

$$Y_{2t} = 4.215 + 0.52\, Y_{2t} - 0.403\, X_{1t} - 0.33\, X_{2t}$$

$$Y_{2t} = 4.215/0.48 - (0.403/0.48)\, X_{1t} - (0.33/0.48)\, X_{2t}$$

$$Y_{2t} = 8.78125 - 0.899583\, X_{1t} - 0.6875\, X_{2t}$$

And so the reduced form of this system for period $n+1$ is:

$$Y_{1,n+1} = 10.125 - 1.29167\, X_{1,n+1} - 0.55\, X_{2,n+1}$$

$$Y_{2,n+1} = 8.78125 - 0.899583\, X_{1,n+1} - 0.6875\, X_{2,n+1}$$

Thus the point forecasts for period $n+1$ are:

$$Y_{1,n+1} = 10.125 - 1.29167{\times}2.5 - 0.55{\times}6.4 = 3.38$$

$$Y_{2,n+1} = 8.78125 - 0.899583{\times}2.5 - 0.6875{\times}6.4 = 2.28$$

****

8.7   Carefully explain the philosophical distinctions between the econometric model building and leading indicators approaches in macroeconomic forecasting.

------- Answer to 8.7 --------

The essential difference between econometric model building and the use of leading indicators in forecasting is that any regression using leading indicators is based on little or no economic theory, just the expectation that leading indicators lead some economic activity and that this fact can be exploited in forecasting

****

8.8   Continue, using more recent data, the analysis of Figure 8.3. Obtain data for all years after 1984 on the United States indices of industrial production and leading indicators. Graph these data, and provide a written summary of your findings. What has been revealed about the ability of the index of leading economic indicators to warn of turning points in the economy?

------- Answer to 8.8 --------

This exercise obviously needs to be attacked by the students. The data industrial production and the leading economic indicators are published monthly in the "Business Conditions Digest" of the Department of Commerce.

****

Chapter 9

REGRESSION MODELS, EXPONENTIAL SMOOTHING ALGORITHMS AND ARIMA MODELS: RELATIONSHIPS AND EXTENSIONS

Contents of Chapter 9

Answers to questions at end of chapter.

9.1   Suppose that the time series X_t is generated by the ARIMA(0,1,1) model

$$X_t - X_{t-1} = a_t - 0.3\, a_{t-1}$$

where a_t is white noise. Is there an exponential smoothing algorithm that yields the same forecasts as this model? If so, write down the recurrence form of that algorithm.

------- Answer to 9.1 --------

From section 9.2 of the text, the exponential smoothing algorithm that yields the same forecasts is the simple exponential smoothing algorithm:

$$L_t = 0.7\, X_t + 0.3\, L_{t-1}$$

****

9.2   Suppose that the time series X_t is generated by the ARIMA(0,2,2) model

$$(1 - B)^2 X_t = a_t - 1.4\, a_{t-1} + 0.6\, a_{t-2}$$

where B is the back-shift operator, and a_t is white noise. Is there an exponential smoothing algorithm that yields the same forecasts as this model? If so, write down the recurrence form of that algorithm.

-------- Answer to 9.2 --------

From section 9.3 of the text, from equations (9.3.1) to (9.3.9), we find that the Holt's linear trend algorithm yields the same forecasts as the ARIMA(0,2,2) model. In the above ARIMA(0,2,2), $\theta_1 = 1.4$ and $\theta_2 = -0.6$. Using equations (9.3.8) we have that $\theta_1 = 2 - \alpha - \alpha\beta$ and $\theta_2 = -(1 - \alpha)$.

Thus: $1 - \alpha = 0.6$ or $\alpha = 0.4$

Therefore: $1.4 = 2 - 0.4 - 0.4\beta$ or $\beta = 0.5$;

where α and β are the smoothing constants of Holt's linear trend algorithm:

$$L_t = \alpha X_t + (1 - \alpha)(L_{t-1} + T_{t-1})$$

$$T_t = \beta(L_t - L_{t-1}) + (1 - \beta)T_{t-1}$$

****

9.3   Consider the damped trend algorithm

$$L_t = \alpha X_t + (1 - \alpha)(L_{t-1} + \phi T_{t-1})$$

$$T_t = \beta(L_t - L_{t-1}) + (1 - \beta)\phi T_{t-1}$$

with forecasts derived from

$$\hat{X_t}(h) = L_t + \sum_{i=1}^{h}\phi^i\, T_t$$

Prove that the same forecasts follow from the ARIMA(1,1,2) model

$$(1 - \phi B)(1 - B)X_t = (1 - \theta_1 B - \theta_2 B_2)a_t$$

where B is the back-shift operator, and a_t is white noise, and

$$\theta_1 = 1 + \phi - \alpha - \phi\alpha\beta \quad ; \quad \theta_2 = -\phi(1 - \alpha)$$

------- Answer to 9.3 --------

The damped trend algorithm is

$$L_t = \alpha X_t + (1 - \alpha)(L_{t-1} + \phi T_{t-1}) \tag{1}$$

$$T_t = \beta(L_t - L_{t-1}) + (1 - \beta)\phi T_{t-1} \tag{2}$$

where one-period ahead forecasts are: $\hat{X}_{t-1}(1) = L_{t-1} + \phi T_{t-1}$

so that the one-period ahead forecast errors are:

$$e_t = X_t - \hat{X}_{t-1}(1) = X_t - L_{t-1} - \phi T_{t-1}$$

so that

$$X_t = L_{t-1} + \phi T_{t-1} + e_t \tag{3}$$

Substitute the value for X_t in equation (3) into equation (1):

$$L_t = \alpha L_{t-1} + \alpha\phi T_{t-1} + \alpha e_t + L_{t-1} - \alpha L_{t-1} + \phi T_{t-1} - \alpha\phi T_{t-1}$$

$$L_t = L_{t-1} + \phi T_{t-1} + \alpha e_t$$

$$L_t - L_{t-1} = \phi T_{t-1} + \alpha e_t \tag{4}$$

Substitute $(L_t - L_{t-1})$ in equation (5) into equation (2):

$$T_t = \beta\phi T_{t-1} + \alpha\beta e_t + \phi T_{t-1} - \beta\phi T_{t-1}$$

$$T_t = \phi T_{t-1} + \alpha\beta e_t \tag{5}$$

From equation (4) we have that:

$$(L_t - L_{t-1}) - (L_{t-1} - L_{t-2}) = (\phi T_{t-1} + \alpha e_t) - \phi(\phi T_{t-2} + \alpha e_{t-1})$$

$$= \phi T_{t-1} - \phi^2 T_{t-2} + \alpha e_t - \alpha\phi e_{t-1}$$

$$= \phi(T_{t-1} - \phi T_{t-2}) + \alpha e_t - \alpha\phi e_{t-1}$$

From equation (5) we have that:

$$(T_t - \phi T_{t-1}) - (T_{t-1} - \phi T_{t-2}) = \alpha\beta e_t - \alpha\beta e_{t-1}$$

Thus $(X_t - X_{t-1}) - \phi(X_{t-1} - X_{t-2})$

$$= (L_{t-1} - L_{t-2}) - \phi(L_{t-2} - L_{t-3}) + \phi[(T_{t-1} - \phi T_{t-2}) - (T_{t-2} - \phi T_{t-3})]$$

$$+ (e_t - e_{t-1}) - \phi(e_{t-1} - e_{t-2})$$

$$= \alpha e_{t-1} + \alpha\beta\phi e_{t-2} - \alpha\phi e_{t-2} + \alpha\beta\phi e_{t-1} - \alpha\phi e_{t-2} + e_t - e_{t-1} - \phi e_{t-1} + \phi e_{t-2}$$

$$= e_t - (1 + \phi - \alpha\beta\phi - \alpha)e_{t-1} - (-\phi + \alpha\phi)e_{t-2}$$

or

$$(1 - \phi B)(1 - B)X_t = (1 - \theta_1 B - \theta_2 B^2)a_t$$

where $a_t = e_t$, $\theta_1 = (1 + \phi - \alpha\beta\phi - \alpha)$, and $\theta_2 = -\phi(1 - \alpha)$.

****

9.4   Suppose that the time series X_t is generated by the ARIMA(1,1,2) model

$$(1 - 0.8B)(1 - B)\, X_t \; = \; (1 - 1.2B + 0.4B^2)a_t$$

where B is the back-shift operator, and a_t is white noise. Is there an exponential smoothing algorithm that yields the same forecasts as this model? If so, write down the recurrence form of that algorithm.

------- Answer to 9.4 --------

From the previous exercise the damped trend algorithm yields the same forecasts as the ARIMA(1,1,2). The values of the parameters for the damped trend algorithm are: $\phi = 0.8$

$$1.2 = \theta_1 = (1 + \phi - \alpha\beta\phi - \alpha), \quad \text{and} \tag{1}$$

$$-0.4 = \theta_2 = - \phi(1 - \alpha) \tag{2}$$

From (2), $-0.4 = -0.8(1 - \alpha)$, and so $\alpha = 0.5$

Then (1) becomes, $1.2 = 1 + 0.8 - 0.5{\times}0.8\,\beta$, and so $\beta = .25$.

****

9.5   Consider the additive seasonal variant of the Holt-Winters algorithm, with smoothing constants α, β, and γ. Prove that the same forecasts can be obtained from the ARIMA model defined by (9.4.1) and (9.4.2).

------- Answer to 9.5 --------

This exercise asks for the omitted proof in section 9.4 of the text. The additive variant of Holt-Winters algorithm is:

$$L_t = \alpha(X_t - F_{t-s}) + (1 - \alpha)(L_{t-1} + T_{t-1}) \tag{1}$$

$$T_t = \beta(L_t - L_{t-1}) + (1 - \beta)T_{t-1} \tag{2}$$

$$F_t = \gamma(X_t - L_t) + (1 - \gamma)F_{t-s} \tag{3}$$

where the one period ahead forecast is: $\hat{X}_{t-1}(1) = L_t + T_t + F_{t+1-s}$

so that the one period ahead forecast error is:

$$e_t = X_t - \hat{X}_{t-1}(1) = X_t - L_{t-1} - T_{t-1} - F_{t-s}$$

or that $\qquad\qquad X_t = L_{t-1} + T_{t-1} + F_{t-s} + e_t \tag{4}$

Substitute the value for X_t in equation (4) into equation (1):

$$L_t = \alpha L_{t-1} + \alpha T_{t-1} + \alpha F_{t-s} + \alpha e_t - \alpha F_{t-s} + L_{t-1} - \alpha L_{t-1} + T_{t-1} - \alpha T_{t-1}$$

$$L_t - L_{t-1} = T_{t-1} + \alpha e_t \tag{5}$$

Substitute $(L_t - L_{t-1})$ in equation (5) into equation (2):

$$T_t = \beta(T_{t-1} + \alpha e_t) + (1 - \beta)T_{t-1}$$

$$T_t = \beta T_{t-1} + \alpha\beta e_t + T_{t-1} - \beta T_{t-1}$$

$$T_t - T_{t-1} = \alpha\beta e_t \qquad (6)$$

Substitute the value of X_t in equation (4) into equation (3):

$$F_t = \gamma(L_{t-1} + T_{t-1} + F_{t-s} + e_t - L_t) + (1 - \gamma)F_{t-s}$$

$$F_t = \gamma L_{t-1} + \gamma T_{t-1} + \gamma F_{t-s} + \gamma e_t - \gamma L_t + F_{t-s} - \gamma F_{t-s}$$

$$F_t = -(L_t - L_{t-1}) + \gamma T_{t-1} + F_{t-s} + \gamma e_t$$

where by using equation (5)

$$F_t = -\gamma(T_{t-1} + \alpha e_t) + \gamma T_{t-1} + F_{t-s} + \gamma e_t$$

$$F_t - F_{t-s} = \gamma(1 - \alpha)e_t \qquad (7)$$

By using equation (4) we have:

$$(X_t - X_{t-1}) - (X_{t-s} - X_{t-s-1})$$

$$= (L_{t-1} - L_{t-2}) - (L_{t-s-1} - L_{t-s-2}) + (T_{t-1} - T_{t-2}) - (T_{t-s-1} - T_{t-s-2})$$

$$+ (F_{t-s} - F_{t-2s}) - (F_{t-s-1} - F_{t-2s-1}) + (e_t - e_{t-1}) - (e_{t-s} - e_{t-s-1})$$

where by using equations (5), (6), and (7):

$$(X_t - X_{t-1}) - (X_{t-s} - X_{t-s-1})$$

$$= T_{t-2} + \alpha e_{t-1} - T_{t-s-2} - \alpha e_{t-s-1} + \alpha\beta e_{t-1} - \alpha\beta e_{t-s-1}$$

$$+ \gamma(1 - \alpha)e_{t-s} - \gamma(1 - \alpha)e_{t-s-1} + (e_t - e_{t-1}) - (e_{t-s} - e_{t-s-1})$$

Since $(T_{t-2} - T_{t-s-2}) = (T_{t-2} - T_{t-3}) + (T_{t-3} - T_{t-4}) + (T_{t-4} - T_{t-5}) +$

$$\ldots + (T_{t-s} - T_{t-s-1}) + (T_{t-s-1} - T_{t-s-2})$$

$$= \alpha\beta(e_{t-2} + e_{t-3} + e_{t-4} + e_{t-5} + \ldots + e_{t-s} + e_{t-s-1})$$

thus: $(X_t - X_{t-1}) - (X_{t-s} - X_{t-s-1})$

$$= \alpha e_{t-1} - \alpha e_{t-s-1} + \alpha\beta e_{t-1} - \alpha\beta e_{t-s-1} + \gamma(1 - \alpha)e_{t-s} - \gamma(1 - \alpha)e_{t-s-1}$$

$$+ e_t - e_{t-1} - e_{t-s} + e_{t-s-1}$$

$$+ \alpha\beta e_{t-2} + \alpha\beta e_{t-3} + \alpha\beta e_{t-4} + \alpha\beta e_{t-5} + \ldots + \alpha\beta e_{t-s} + \alpha\beta e_{t-s-1}$$

And so $(1 - B)(1 - B^2)X_t$

$$= e_t - (1 - \alpha - \alpha\beta)e_{t-1} - [1 - \alpha\beta - \gamma(1 - \alpha)]e_{t-s} -$$

$$[-1 + \alpha + \gamma(1 - \alpha)]e_{t-s-1} + \alpha\beta e_{t-2} + \alpha\beta e_{t-3} + \ldots + \alpha\beta e_{t+1-s}$$

or $(1 - B)(1 - B^2)X_t = a_t - \theta_1 a_{t-1} + \theta_2 a_{t-2} - \ldots - \theta_s a_{t-s} - \theta_{s+1} a_{t-s-1}$

where $a_t = e_t$; $\theta_1 = 1 - \alpha - \alpha\beta$; $\theta_j = -\alpha\beta$ (for $j = 2, \ldots, s - 1$)

$$\theta_s = 1 - \alpha\beta - \gamma(1 - \alpha);   \theta_{s+1} = -1 + \alpha + \gamma(1 - \alpha)$$

****

9.6   Carefully explain why we say that in practice, when applied to monthly data, the additive seasonal variant of the Holt-Winters algorithm and the Box-Jenkins ARIMA model building methodology will not yield the same forecasts.

------- Answer to 9.6 --------

The above exercise shows that the additive variant of the Holt-Winters model will yield the same forecasts as a particular ARIMA model with severe constraints as the values of the parameters. If one would be estimating an ARIMA model of the same form of (text) equations (9.4.1) and (9.4.2), one would not (nor could one) constrain the values of the parameters in the way that would make it equivalent to the additive variant of the Holt-Winters algorithm. The constraints implied by the usual multiplicative seasonal ARIMA models are quite different.

****

9.7   Let Y_t be a dependent variable and X_t an independent variable whose relationship can be represented by the model

$$Y_t = \alpha + \beta X_t + \epsilon_t$$

$$\epsilon_t = a_t - \theta a_{t-1}$$

where α, β and θ are fixed parameters, and a_t is white noise. Given a sample of 50 pairs of observations on (X_t, Y_t) explain how in practice you would arrive at this model from an analysis of the available data.

------- Answer to 9.7 --------

This exercise will be answered with the aid of data from Table 4.4 which contains data on bank borrowing (Y) and the difference (X) between the discount rate and the U.S. Treasury bill rate. When regression is carried out on this data one finds significant autocorrelation. Although the purpose of this exercise is to solicit interest in possible different ARIMA models for the errors of a regression, we are not concerned here with the appropriate model for the error in that regression. It is interesting enough for the MA(1) model on the errors of a regression model.

Exposition of the process one could follow to find estimates of the parameters of the model is done with a LOTUS 123 spreadsheet, printed below. Since the above model has three parameters (α, β, and θ) and since it is easier to carry out a two parameter grid search, the deviations of the data (columns C and D) were used instead of the raw data (Columns A and B). Cells B47 and C47 contain the averages of the Ys and Xs. A regression on the deviations of the data eliminates the coefficient of the constant term, α. α can later be calculated, as it is below in cell B2.

The first step in the estimation procedure, is to find "good" initial estimates for the parameters of the model. The easiest way is to find the OLS estimate of β (here in cell D2) and let θ's initial estimate be zero (which would be fine if the errors could in no way be modelled by an MA(1)). (Later, we are going to do a grid search, not for β directly, but on a proportion or scale factor of the OLS estimate of β. Thus the OLS estimate is held in cell D2 and its scale factor held in cell C2. The initial scale factor is 1 (one).)

Once the OLS estimate of β is found, one calculates the estimates of a_t (and its square) – here in columns E and F. The mean error sum of squares, MSE, is calculated in cell G3. The estimates of a_t are derived as follows: $a_t = y_t - \beta x_t + \theta a_{t-1}$.
One needs an estimate of a_0. The easiest is zero – see cell F6.

The next step is carry out an appropriate grid search over values of β and θ. Here a /Data Table 2 was done to effect a grid search for the scale factor of the OLS estimate of β and θ. Actually we did this several times to fine tune our search. Our final estimates, after three successive grid searches are shown above. The three grids were as follows:
(1)   (0.5 to 2.0, in increments of 0.1) for the proportion of OLS estimate of β; and (−0.9 to 0.9 in increments of 0.2) for θ which yields the minimum MSE at estimates of β and θ of 0.8 and −0.5;
(2)   (0.7 to 0.9, in increments of 0.025) for the proportion of OLS estimate of β; and (−0.7 to −0.3 in increments of 0.025) for θ which yields the minimum MSE at estimates of β and θ of 0.8 and −0.425;
(3)   (0.775 to 0.825, in increments of 0.005) for the proportion of OLS estimate of β; and (−0.45 to −0.4 in increments of 0.005) for θ which yields the minimum MSE at estimates of β and θ of 0.805 and −0.43.

Compare this to the SPSS estimates of the parameters below the spreadsheet. SPSS uses exact maximum likelihood, while we did not!

	A	B	C	D	E	F	G
1	Alpha	672.4114					
2	Beta	-457.393	0.805	-568.191			
3	Theta	-0.43					60094.98
4							
5	t	Y(t)	X(t)	y(t)	x(t)	a(t)	a(t)²
6	0					0	
7	1	242	0.32	-341.512	0.125641	-284.045	80681.77
8	2	170	0.30	-413.512	0.105641	-243.053	59075.12
9	3	338	0.12	-245.512	-0.07435	-175.011	30628.86
10	4	657	0.02	73.48717	-0.17435	68.99119	4759.785
11	5	307	0.16	-276.512	-0.03435	-321.894	103616.1
12	6	579	0.05	-4.51282	-0.14435	67.87295	4606.737
13	7	683	0.04	99.48717	-0.15435	-0.30104	0.090627
14	8	1593	-0.34	1009.487	-0.53435	765.2040	585537.2
15	9	1202	-0.01	618.4871	-0.20435	195.9768	38406.93
16	10	423	-0.11	-160.512	-0.30435	-383.994	147452.0
17	11	468	0.21	-115.512	0.015641	56.75906	3221.590
18	12	441	0.40	-142.512	0.205641	-72.8602	5308.618
19	13	189	0.62	-394.512	0.425641	-168.497	28391.33
20	14	146	0.86	-437.512	0.665641	-60.5988	3672.218
21	15	67	0.49	-516.512	0.295641	-355.230	126189.0
22	16	246	0.36	-337.512	0.165641	-109.000	11881.07
23	17	464	0.22	-119.512	0.025641	-60.9146	3710.592
24	18	146	0.34	-437.512	0.145641	-344.704	118820.9
25	19	849	0.18	265.4871	-0.01435	407.1422	165764.8
26	20	839	-0.04	255.4871	-0.23435	-26.7783	717.0810
27	21	993	0.25	409.4871	0.055641	446.4517	199319.1
28	22	769	0.26	185.4871	0.065641	23.53673	553.9778
29	23	792	0.16	208.4871	-0.03435	182.6507	33361.31
30	24	688	-0.21	104.4871	-0.40435	-159.003	25282.27
31	25	834	-0.08	250.4871	-0.27435	193.3687	37391.48
32	26	1005	-0.29	421.4871	-0.48435	116.7957	13641.25
33	27	988	-0.03	404.4871	-0.22435	251.6445	63324.99
34	28	710	-0.04	126.4871	-0.23435	-88.9143	7905.762
35	29	138	0.95	-445.512	0.755641	-61.6540	3801.221
36	30	142	0.92	-441.512	0.725641	-83.0977	6905.243
37	31	476	-0.44	-107.512	-0.63435	-361.932	130995.2
38	32	557	-0.27	-26.5128	-0.46435	-83.2767	6935.013
39	33	601	0.20	17.48717	0.005641	55.87634	3122.165
40	34	921	0.29	337.4871	0.095641	357.2059	127596.1
41	35	903	-0.04	319.4871	-0.23435	58.69424	3445.014
42	36	906	-0.49	322.4871	-0.68435	-15.7729	248.7866
43	37	635	0.69	51.48717	0.495641	284.9727	81209.46
44	38	425	1.04	-158.512	0.845641	105.7399	11180.93
45	39	225	0.52	-358.512	0.325641	-255.034	65042.73
46							
47		583.5128	0.194358				
48							
49							
50							

SPSS output for the model. (The shaded portion directs attention to the estimates).

```
FINAL PARAMETERS:

Number of residuals   39
Standard error        254.69832
Log likelihood        -269.99499
AIC                   545.98997
SBC                   550.98066


              Analysis of Variance:

          DF  Adj. Sum of Squares     Residual Variance
Residuals  36              2347466.0              64871.234

          Variables in the Model:

                  B         SEB       T-RATIO    APPROX. PROB.
MA1            -.42726       .15212   -2.808808    .00798493
X          -457.42532    125.66802   -3.639950    .00084961
CONSTANT    667.63265     62.81569   10.628437   0.0


          ******************************
```

9.8   The relationship between a dependent variable Y_t and an independent variable X_t is given by the transfer function-noise model

$$Y_t = \alpha + \frac{\omega_0 + \omega_1 B}{1 - \delta_1 B} X_t + \epsilon_t$$

$$\phi(B)(1 - B)^d \epsilon_t = \theta(B) a_t$$

Write $$V(B) = V_0 + V_1 B + V_2 B^2 + \ldots = \frac{\omega_0 + \omega_1 B}{1 - \delta_1 B}$$

so that $$(1 - \delta_1 B)(V_0 + V_1 B + V_2 B^2 + \ldots) = \omega_0 + \omega_1 B$$

Hence find $V_0, V_1, V_2, \ldots$ as functions of $\omega_0, \omega_1, \delta_1$, and discuss the expected behavior of current and future values of the dependent variable resulting from a one unit increase in the dependent variable.

------- Answer to 9.8 --------

If $$(1 - \delta_1 B)(V_0 + V_1 B + V_2 B^2 + \ldots) = \omega_0 + \omega_1 B$$

then $\omega_0 + \omega_1 B = V_0 + (V_1 - \delta_1 V_0)B + (V_2 - \delta_1 V_1)B^2 + (V_3 - \delta_1 V_2)B^3 + \ldots$

Therefore $V_0 = \omega_0$

$$\omega_1 = V_1 - \delta_1 V_0 = V_1 - \delta_1 \omega_0 \qquad \text{or} \qquad V_1 = \omega_1 + \delta_1 \omega_0$$

$$0 = V_2 - \delta_1 V_1 \qquad \text{or} \qquad V_2 = \delta_1(\omega_1 + \delta_1 \omega_0)$$

$$0 = V_3 - \delta_1 V_2 \qquad \text{or} \qquad V_3 = \delta_1^2(\omega_1 + \delta_1 \omega_0)$$

Similarly for all $s > 1$

$$0 = V_s - \delta_1 V_{s-1} \qquad \text{or} \qquad V_s = \delta_1^{s-1}(\omega_1 + \delta_1 \omega_0)$$

Given the above, a one unit increase in the independent variable X at time t will lead to increases in Y of ω_0 units at time t, a $(\omega_1 + \delta_1 \omega_0)$ unit increase at time $t+1$, a $\delta_1(\omega_1 + \delta_1 \omega_0)$ unit increase at time $t+2$, a $\delta_1^2(\omega_1 1+ \delta_1 \omega_0)$ unit increase at time $t+3$, etc..

****

Chapter 10

SOME OTHER QUANTITATIVE FORECASTING METHODS

Contents of Chapter 10

Answers to questions at end of chapter.

10.1 Consider the nonseasonal variant of the basic structural model

$$X_t = T_t + a_t \tag{1}$$

$$T_t = T_{t-1} + \beta_{t-1} + a_{1t} \tag{2}$$

$$\beta_t = \beta_{t-1} + a_{2t} \tag{3}$$

where a_t, a_{1t}, a_{2t} are independent white noise processes.

(a) Show that it follows from this specification that we can write

$$(1 - B)^2 X_t = a_t - 2a_{t-1} + a_{t-2} + a_{1t} - a_{1,t-1} + a_{2,t-1}$$

where B is the back shift operator.

(b) Let $\qquad Z_t = a_t - 2a_{t-1} + a_{t-2} + a_{1t} - a_{1,t-1} + a_{2,t-1}$

Show that all autocorrelations beyond the second of Z_t are zero. Hence deduce that the nonseasonal variant of the basic structural model is equivalent to a subset of the ARIMA(0,2,2) models.

------- Answer to 10.1 --------

(a)   From equation (3) above, $\beta_t - \beta_{t-1} = a_{2t}$ (4)

Similarly, equation (2) can be written as: $T_t - T_{t-1} = \beta_{t-1} + a_{1t}$ (5)

Taking the first differences of equation (5)

$$(1 - B)^2 T_t = (T_t - T_{t-1}) - (T_{t-1} - T_{t-2}) = \beta_{t-1} - \beta_{t-2} + a_{1t} - a_{1,t-1} \qquad (6)$$

Substitute the first lag of equation (4) into (6):

$$(1 - B)^2 T_t = a_{2,t-1} + a_{1t} - a_{1,t-1} \qquad (7)$$

Multiply equation (1) by $(1 - B)^2$ (or, taking second differences)

$$(1 - B)^2 X_t = (1 - B)^2 T_t + (1 - B)^2 a_t$$

Substitute equation (7) into this last equation to get

$$(1 - B)^2 X_t = (1 - B)^2 a_t + a_{2,t-1} + a_{1t} - a_{1,t-1}$$

(b)   First let's find the expressions for the first two autocorrelations of Z_t (the second differences of the raw data, X_t). After this it will be obvious the all further autocorrelations are zero.

First we need to find the variance of Z_t. To do this we need to just square Z_t and take expectations of the result. When expectations of the terms are taken, only those that are of the form a_i^2 will remain -- the expectations of all cross-product terms are zero since the errors are all independent of each other.

Since $Z_t = a_t - 2a_{t-1} + a_{t-2} + a_{1t} - a_{1,t-1} + a_{2,t-1}$

then $Z_t^2 = a_t^2 + 4a_{t-1}^2 + a_{t-2}^2 + a_{1t}^2 + a_{1,t-1}^2 + a_{2,t-1}^2 + \text{cross product terms}$

Thus $E(Z_t^2) = 6\sigma^2 + 2\sigma_1^2 + \sigma_2^2$

where $\sigma^2 = E(a_t^2) = Var(a_t)$, $\sigma_1^2 = Var(a_{1t})$, and $\sigma_2^2 = Var(a_{2t})$.

For the first autocorrelation, we need $E(Z_t Z_{t-1})$. Again, we only need to concern ourselves with squared terms, and not cross-products.

$$Z_t Z_{t-1} = -2a_{t-1}^2 - 2a_{t-2}^2 - a_{1,t-1}^2 + \text{cross-product terms}$$

Thus $E(Z_t Z_{t-1}) = -4\sigma^2 - \sigma_1^2$

Therefore, the first autocorrelation of Z_t is

$$\gamma_1 = E(Z_t Z_{t-1})/E(Z_t^2) = (-4\sigma^2 - \sigma_1^2)/(6\sigma^2 + 2\sigma_1^2 + \sigma_2^2)$$

We can write $\sigma_1^2 = A_1\sigma^2$, and $\sigma_2^2 = A_2\sigma^2$

Thus
$$\gamma_1 = (-4 - A_1)/(6 + 2A_1 + A_2)$$

For the second autocorrelation, we need $E(Z_t Z_{t-2})$.

$$Z_t Z_{t-2} = a_{t-2}^2 + \text{cross-product terms}$$

and so
$$E(Z_t Z_{t-2}) = \sigma^2.$$

Therefore, the second autocorrelation of Z_t is

$$\gamma_2 = E(Z_t Z_{t-2})/E(Z_t^2) = \sigma^2/(6\sigma^2 + 2\sigma_1^2 + \sigma_2^2) = 1/(6 + 2A_1 + A_2)$$

One can similarly show that the first and second autocorrelations for an MA(2) process are:

$$\gamma_1 = (\theta_1\theta_2 - \theta_2)/(1 + \theta_1^2 + \theta_2^2) \quad \text{and} \quad \gamma_2 = -\theta_2/(1 + \theta_1^2 + \theta_2^2)$$

These autocorrelations can be made equivalent to the first two autocorrelations of the nonseasonal variant of the basic structural model:

$$\gamma_1 = (-4 - A_1)/(6 + 2A_1 + A_2) \quad \text{and} \quad \gamma_2 = 1/(6 + 2A_1 + A_2)$$

Although the relationship is nonlinear, one can express A_1 and A_2 as functions of θ_1 and θ_2. Finally, the covariance between Z_t and Z_{t-j} is zero for $j > 2$.

****

10.2 Consider the basic structural model defined by equations (10.3.1)– (10.3.4), where a_t, a_{1t}, a_{2t}, a_{3t} are white noise processes

(a) Show that (10.3.4) implies $\quad (1 - B^s)S_t = a_{3t} - a_{3,t-1}$

(b) Hence show that the basic structural model specification implies

$$(1 - B)(1 - B^s)X_t = a_t - a_{t-1} - a_{t-s} + a_{t-s-1} + a_{1t} - a_{1,t-s}$$

$$+ a_{2,t-1} + a_{2,t-2} + \ldots + a_{2,t-s} + a_{3t} - a_{3,t-1} + a_{3,t-2}$$

Deduce that $(1 - B)(1 - B^s)X_t$ obeys a moving average model of order $s + 1$. Discuss the likelihood of this particular specification being identified by the ARIMA model building methodology of Section 7.11.

------- Answer to 10.2 --------

(a)

$$X_t = T_t + S_t + a_t \tag{10.3.1}$$

$$T_t = T_{t-1} + \beta_{t-1} + a_{1t} \tag{10.3.2}$$

$$\beta_t = \beta_{t-1} + a_{2t} \tag{10.3.3}$$

$$\sum_{i=1}^{s-1} S_{t-j} = a_{3t} \tag{10.3.4}$$

From (10.3.4) $a_{3t} = S_t + S_{t-1} + S_{t-2} + \ldots + S_{t-s+2} + S_{t-s+1}$

and $a_{3,t-1} = S_{t-1} + S_{t-2} + S_{t-3} + \ldots + S_{t-s+1} + S_{t-s}$

Thus: $a_{3t} - a_{3,t-1} = S_t - S_{t-s}$

(b)   Let $Z_t = a_t - a_{t-1} - a_{t-s} + a_{t-s-1} + a_{1t} - a_{1,t-s}$

$$+ a_{2,t-1} + a_{2,t-2} + \ldots + a_{2,t-s} + a_{3t} - a_{3,t-1} + a_{3,t-2}$$

Similarly to Exercise 10.1 above, one can show that this obeys a moving average model of order $s+1$ by showing that all autocorrelations beyond the $s+1^{\text{th}}$ are zero. This can easily be done by, say, writing down the expression for Z_{t-s-1}.

$$Z_{t-s-1} = a_{t-s-1} - a_{t-s-2} - a_{t-2s-1} + a_{t-2s-2} + a_{1t-s-1} - a_{1,t-2s-1}$$

$$+ a_{2,t-s-2} + a_{2,t-s-3} + \ldots + a_{2,t-2s-1} + a_{3t-s-1} - a_{3,t-s-2} + a_{3,t-s-3}$$

When one finds the product of Z_t and Z_{t-s-1}, one finds that the only term that does not involve cross-products (and hence the only term that will survive taking expectations) is a_{t-s-1}^2. This autocorrelation at lag $s+1$ is the last non-zero autocorrelation.

As discussed in Exercise 9.6, it is extremely unlikely that one would choose to fit as many parameters in an in ARIMA model as is needed to make an ARIMA model equivalent to the one describe by equations (10.3.1)– (10.3.4).

****

10.3   Discuss the differences between Bayesian forecasting and the incorporation of intervention analysis into the ARIMA model building framework.

------- Answer to 10.3 --------

See the first two paragraphs of section 10.4. Essentially intervention analysis is useful in situations in which the time series experiences discrete qualitative changes at one or a small number of known points in time; whereas Bayesian forecasting continuously allows for possibility of such structural changes (rather than having to be told as in intervention analysis).

****

10.4 Consider the data of Exercise 7.12 on prices received by farmers for all crops. Fit ARIMA models to the transformed series, $X_t(\lambda)$ defined by (10.6.1), for $\lambda = 0, 0.2, 0.4, 0.8, 1$. Choose the most appropriate λ, and forecast the next six values of the series.

------- Answer to 10.4 --------

Equation (10.6.1) is the Box-Cox transformation:

$$X_t(\lambda) = (X_t^\gamma - 1)/\lambda \qquad \text{if } \lambda \neq 0$$

and
$$X_t(\lambda) = \log X_t \qquad \text{if } \lambda \neq 0$$

In Exercise 7.12, it was found that the ARIMA(0,1,1) model on the log of the data worked best - though the ARIMA(2,1,0) model worked well. Thus, here both models were tried for each λ. The criterion $g(\lambda)$ (from the text, section 10.6) was calculated for each estimation. They are shown after all the estimations.

The MINITAB output is as follows:

```
MTB > let c2 = loge(c1)                      MTB > diff 1 c2 c12
MTB > let c3 = (c1**.2 - 1)/.2               MTB > diff 1 c3 c13
MTB > let c4 = (c1**.4 - 1)/.4               MTB > diff 1 c4 c14
MTB > let c5 = (c1**.6 - 1)/.6               MTB > diff 1 c5 c15
MTB > let c6 = (c1**.8 - 1)/.8               MTB > diff 1 c6 c16
MTB > let c7 = (c1**1. - 1)/1.               MTB > diff 1 c6 c17
                                             MTB >
MTB > acf 5 c2                               MTB > pacf 5 c2
```

```
ACF of C2                                    PACF of C2

      -1.0 -0.8 -0.6 -0.4 -0.2  0.0  0.2  0.4  0.6  0.8  1.0         -1.0 -0.8 -0.6 -0.4 -0.2  0.0  0.2  0.4  0.6  0.8  1.0
      +----+----+----+----+----+----+----+----+----+----+           +----+----+----+----+----+----+----+----+----+----+
  1  0.932                      XXXXXXXXXXXXXXXXXXXXXXXX         1  0.932                      XXXXXXXXXXXXXXXXXXXXXXXX
  2  0.835                      XXXXXXXXXXXXXXXXXXXXXX           2  -0.263            XXXXXXX
  3  0.750                      XXXXXXXXXXXXXXXXXXX             3  0.100                      XXXX
  4  0.680                      XXXXXXXXXXXXXXXXX              4  0.013                      X
  5  0.627                      XXXXXXXXXXXXXXXX              5  0.075                      XXX
```

```
MTB > acf 5 c3                               MTB > pacf 5 c3
```

```
ACF of C3                                    PACF of C3

      -1.0 -0.8 -0.6 -0.4 -0.2  0.0  0.2  0.4  0.6  0.8  1.0         -1.0 -0.8 -0.6 -0.4 -0.2  0.0  0.2  0.4  0.6  0.8  1.0
      +----+----+----+----+----+----+----+----+----+----+           +----+----+----+----+----+----+----+----+----+----+
  1  0.932                      XXXXXXXXXXXXXXXXXXXXXXXX         1  0.932                      XXXXXXXXXXXXXXXXXXXXXXXX
  2  0.835                      XXXXXXXXXXXXXXXXXXXXXX           2  -0.255            XXXXXXX
  3  0.751                      XXXXXXXXXXXXXXXXXXX             3  0.094                      XXX
  4  0.680                      XXXXXXXXXXXXXXXXX              4  0.005                      X
  5  0.624                      XXXXXXXXXXXXXXXX              5  0.061                      XXX
```

```
MTB > acf 5 c4                               MTB > pacf 5 c4
```

```
ACF of C4                                    PACF of C4

      -1.0 -0.8 -0.6 -0.4 -0.2  0.0  0.2  0.4  0.6  0.8  1.0         -1.0 -0.8 -0.6 -0.4 -0.2  0.0  0.2  0.4  0.6  0.8  1.0
      +----+----+----+----+----+----+----+----+----+----+           +----+----+----+----+----+----+----+----+----+----+
  1  0.930                      XXXXXXXXXXXXXXXXXXXXXXXX         1  0.930                      XXXXXXXXXXXXXXXXXXXXXXXX
  2  0.832                      XXXXXXXXXXXXXXXXXXXXXX           2  -0.252            XXXXXXX
  3  0.746                      XXXXXXXXXXXXXXXXXXX             3  0.095                      XXX
  4  0.674                      XXXXXXXXXXXXXXXXX              4  -0.002                     X
  5  0.616                      XXXXXXXXXXXXXXXX              5  0.053                      XX
```

```
MTB > acf 5 c5                               MTB > pacf 5 c5
```

```
ACF of C5                                    PACF of C5

      -1.0 -0.8 -0.6 -0.4 -0.2  0.0  0.2  0.4  0.6  0.8  1.0         -1.0 -0.8 -0.6 -0.4 -0.2  0.0  0.2  0.4  0.6  0.8  1.0
      +----+----+----+----+----+----+----+----+----+----+           +----+----+----+----+----+----+----+----+----+----+
  1  0.928                      XXXXXXXXXXXXXXXXXXXXXXXX         1  0.928                      XXXXXXXXXXXXXXXXXXXXXXXX
  2  0.825                      XXXXXXXXXXXXXXXXXXXXXX           2  -0.254            XXXXXXX
  3  0.738                      XXXXXXXXXXXXXXXXXXX             3  0.102                      XXXX
  4  0.664                      XXXXXXXXXXXXXXXXX              4  -0.007                     X
  5  0.604                      XXXXXXXXXXXXXXXX              5  0.051                      XX
```

```
MTB > acf 5 c6                               MTB > pacf 5 c6
```

```
ACF of C6                                    PACF of C6

      -1.0 -0.8 -0.6 -0.4 -0.2  0.0  0.2  0.4  0.6  0.8  1.0         -1.0 -0.8 -0.6 -0.4 -0.2  0.0  0.2  0.4  0.6  0.8  1.0
      +----+----+----+----+----+----+----+----+----+----+           +----+----+----+----+----+----+----+----+----+----+
  1  0.924                      XXXXXXXXXXXXXXXXXXXXXXXX         1  0.924                      XXXXXXXXXXXXXXXXXXXXXXXX
  2  0.817                      XXXXXXXXXXXXXXXXXXXXXX           2  -0.261            XXXXXXX
  3  0.726                      XXXXXXXXXXXXXXXXXXX             3  0.112                      XXXX
  4  0.650                      XXXXXXXXXXXXXXXXX              4  -0.010                     X
  5  0.589                      XXXXXXXXXXXXXXXX              5  0.052                      XX
```

```
MTB > acf 5 c7                               MTB > pacf 5 c7
```

```
ACF of C7                                    PACF of C7

      -1.0 -0.8 -0.6 -0.4 -0.2  0.0  0.2  0.4  0.6  0.8  1.0         -1.0 -0.8 -0.6 -0.4 -0.2  0.0  0.2  0.4  0.6  0.8  1.0
      +----+----+----+----+----+----+----+----+----+----+           +----+----+----+----+----+----+----+----+----+----+
  1  0.921                      XXXXXXXXXXXXXXXXXXXXXXXX         1  0.921                      XXXXXXXXXXXXXXXXXXXXXXXX
  2  0.806                      XXXXXXXXXXXXXXXXXXXXXX           2  -0.269            XXXXXXX
  3  0.712                      XXXXXXXXXXXXXXXXXXX             3  0.124                      XXXX
  4  0.634                      XXXXXXXXXXXXXXXXX              4  -0.011                     X
  5  0.573                      XXXXXXXXXXXXXXXX              5  0.058                      XX
```

```
MTB > acf 5 c12

ACF of C12

          -1.0 -0.8 -0.6 -0.4 -0.2  0.0  0.2  0.4  0.6  0.8  1.0
           +----+----+----+----+----+----+----+----+----+----+
   1   0.378                         XXXXXXXXX
   2  -0.098                      XXX
   3  -0.175                     XXXX
   4  -0.194                    XXXXXX
   5  -0.044                       XX


MTB > acf 5 c13

ACF of C13

          -1.0 -0.8 -0.6 -0.4 -0.2  0.0  0.2  0.4  0.6  0.8  1.0
           +----+----+----+----+----+----+----+----+----+----+
   1   0.371                         XXXXXXXXX
   2  -0.094                      XXX
   3  -0.156                    XXXXX
   4  -0.163                    XXXXX
   5  -0.019                         X


MTB > acf 5 c14

ACF of C14

          -1.0 -0.8 -0.6 -0.4 -0.2  0.0  0.2  0.4  0.6  0.8  1.0
           +----+----+----+----+----+----+----+----+----+----+
   1   0.358                         XXXXXXXXX
   2  -0.098                      XXX
   3  -0.141                    XXXXX
   4  -0.134                     XXXX
   5   0.005                         X


MTB > acf 5 c15

ACF of C15

          -1.0 -0.8 -0.6 -0.4 -0.2  0.0  0.2  0.4  0.6  0.8  1.0
           +----+----+----+----+----+----+----+----+----+----+
   1   0.340                         XXXXXXXXX
   2  -0.110                     XXXX
   3  -0.132                     XXXX
   4  -0.111                     XXXX
   5   0.028                        XX


MTB > acf 5 c16

ACF of C16

          -1.0 -0.8 -0.6 -0.4 -0.2  0.0  0.2  0.4  0.6  0.8  1.0
           +----+----+----+----+----+----+----+----+----+----+
   1   0.319                         XXXXXXXXX
   2  -0.124                     XXXX
   3  -0.130                     XXXX
   4  -0.097                      XXX
   5   0.047                        XX


MTB > acf 5 c17

ACF of C17

          -1.0 -0.8 -0.6 -0.4 -0.2  0.0  0.2  0.4  0.6  0.8  1.0
           +----+----+----+----+----+----+----+----+----+----+
   1   0.319                         XXXXXXXXX
   2  -0.124                     XXXX
   3  -0.130                     XXXX
   4  -0.097                      XXX
   5   0.047                        XX
```

```
MTB > pacf 5 c12

PACF of C12

          -1.0 -0.8 -0.6 -0.4 -0.2  0.0  0.2  0.4  0.6  0.8  1.0
           +----+----+----+----+----+----+----+----+----+----+
   1   0.378                         XXXXXXXXX
   2  -0.281                   XXXXXXX
   3  -0.027                        XX
   4  -0.161                    XXXXX
   5   0.077                       XXX


MTB > pacf 5 c13

PACF of C13

          -1.0 -0.8 -0.6 -0.4 -0.2  0.0  0.2  0.4  0.6  0.8  1.0
           +----+----+----+----+----+----+----+----+----+----+
   1   0.371                         XXXXXXXXX
   2  -0.268                   XXXXXXX
   3  -0.015                         X
   4  -0.137                     XXXX
   5   0.083                       XXX


MTB > pacf 5 c14

PACF of C14

          -1.0 -0.8 -0.6 -0.4 -0.2  0.0  0.2  0.4  0.6  0.8  1.0
           +----+----+----+----+----+----+----+----+----+----+
   1   0.358                         XXXXXXXXX
   2  -0.259                   XXXXXXX
   3  -0.004                         X
   4  -0.116                     XXXX
   5   0.089                       XXX


MTB > pacf 5 c15

PACF of C15

          -1.0 -0.8 -0.6 -0.4 -0.2  0.0  0.2  0.4  0.6  0.8  1.0
           +----+----+----+----+----+----+----+----+----+----+
   1   0.340                         XXXXXXXXX
   2  -0.254                   XXXXXXX
   3   0.002                         X
   4  -0.101                     XXXX
   5   0.095                       XXX


MTB > pacf 5 c16

PACF of C16

          -1.0 -0.8 -0.6 -0.4 -0.2  0.0  0.2  0.4  0.6  0.8  1.0
           +----+----+----+----+----+----+----+----+----+----+
   1   0.319                         XXXXXXXXX
   2  -0.251                   XXXXXXX
   3  -0.000                         X
   4  -0.091                      XXX
   5   0.101                       XXXX


MTB > pacf 5 c17

PACF of C17

          -1.0 -0.8 -0.6 -0.4 -0.2  0.0  0.2  0.4  0.6  0.8  1.0
           +----+----+----+----+----+----+----+----+----+----+
   1   0.319                         XXXXXXXXX
   2  -0.251                   XXXXXXX
   3  -0.000                         X
   4  -0.091                      XXX
   5   0.101                       XXXX
```

```
MTB > arima 0 1 1 c2 c30;                      MTB > arima 2 1 0 c2 c30;
SUBC> fore 6.                                  SUBC> fore 6.

Estimates at each iteration                    Estimates at each iteration
Iteration      SSE      Parameters             Iteration      SSE      Parameters
   0         1.37176      0.100                    0         1.21346    0.100    0.100
   1         1.21361     -0.050                    1         1.07546    0.250   -0.036
   2         1.09987     -0.200                    2         0.99772    0.400   -0.173
   3         1.02329     -0.350                    3         0.97944    0.508   -0.274
   4         0.98305     -0.500                    4         0.97937    0.514   -0.281
   5         0.97897     -0.553                    5         0.97937    0.514   -0.282
   6         0.97890     -0.559                    6         0.97937    0.514   -0.282
   7         0.97890     -0.560
   8         0.97890     -0.560
Relative change in each estimate less than  0.0010   Relative change in each estimate less than  0.0010

Final Estimates of Parameters                  Final Estimates of Parameters
Type     Estimate    St. Dev.   t-ratio       Type     Estimate    St. Dev.   t-ratio
MA   1    -0.5600      0.1080     -5.19        AR   1     0.5143      0.1260     4.08
                                               AR   2    -0.2816      0.1263    -2.23

Differencing: 1 regular difference             Differencing: 1 regular difference
No. of obs.: Original series 62, after differencing 61   No. of obs.: Original series 62, after differencing 61
Residuals:   SS = 0.978643  (backforecasts excluded)     Residuals:   SS = 0.978156  (backforecasts excluded)
             MS = 0.016311  DF = 60                                    MS = 0.016579  DF = 59

Modified Box-Pierce chisquare statistic        Modified Box-Pierce chisquare statistic
Lag           12          24         36          48   Lag          12          24         36          48
Chisquare   4.6(DF=11)  11.3(DF=23)  21.2(DF=35)  39.9(DF=47)   Chisquare  4.0(DF=10)  11.6(DF=22)  22.7(DF=34)  40.2(DF=46)


Forecasts from period 62                       Forecasts from period 62
                  95 Percent Limits                               95 Percent Limits
Period   Forecast    Lower      Upper    Actual   Period   Forecast    Lower      Upper    Actual
  63     6.18960    5.93923   6.43997               63     6.18863    5.93621   6.44105
  64     6.18960    5.72567   6.65352               64     6.17975    5.72169   6.63781
  65     6.18960    5.58316   6.79604               65     6.19571    5.60188   6.78953
  66     6.18960    5.46827   6.91092               66     6.20641    5.52258   6.89024
  67     6.18960    5.36932   7.00987               67     6.20742    5.45226   6.96259
  68     6.18960    5.28109   7.09811               68     6.20493    5.38410   7.02575

MTB > acf 5 c30                                MTB > acf 5 c30

ACF of C30                                     ACF of C30

        -1.0 -0.8 -0.6 -0.4 -0.2  0.0  0.2  0.4  0.6  0.8  1.0          -1.0 -0.8 -0.6 -0.4 -0.2  0.0  0.2  0.4  0.6  0.8  1.0
        +----+----+----+----+----+----+----+----+----+----+           +----+----+----+----+----+----+----+----+----+----+
 1  -0.034                        XX                        1  -0.025                        XX
 2  -0.046                        XX                        2  -0.058                        XX
 3  -0.088                       XXX                        3   0.066                        XXX
 4  -0.151                     XXXXX                        4  -0.145                     XXXXX
 5  -0.008                         X                        5  -0.022                        XX
```

```
MTB > arima 0 1 1 c3 c30;                          MTB > arima 2 1 0 c3 c30;
SUBC> fore 6.                                       SUBC> fore 6.

Estimates at each iteration                         Estimates at each iteration
Iteration    SSE      Parameters                    Iteration    SSE      Parameters
    0      10.3385    0.100                              0      9.12889   0.100    0.100
    1       9.1505   -0.050                              1      8.12685   0.250   -0.033
    2       8.3025   -0.200                              2      7.56665   0.400   -0.168
    3       7.7341   -0.350                              3      7.43985   0.505   -0.265
    4       7.4307   -0.500                              4      7.43936   0.511   -0.271
    5       7.3928   -0.557                              5      7.43936   0.511   -0.272
    6       7.3914   -0.568                              6      7.43936   0.511   -0.272
    7       7.3914   -0.570
    8       7.3914   -0.570
Relative change in each estimate less than 0.0010   Relative change in each estimate less than 0.0010

Final Estimates of Parameters                       Final Estimates of Parameters
Type     Estimate    St. Dev.   t-ratio             Type     Estimate    St. Dev.   t-ratio
MA   1    -0.5702     0.1077     -5.29              AR   1     0.5114     0.1271      4.02
                                                    AR   2    -0.2720     0.1276     -2.13


Differencing: 1 regular difference                  Differencing: 1 regular difference
No. of obs.:  Original series 62, after differencing 61   No. of obs.:  Original series 62, after differencing 61
Residuals:    SS = 7.39007 (backforecasts excluded)  Residuals:   SS = 7.43127 (backforecasts excluded)
              MS = 0.12317  DF = 60                              MS = 0.12595  DF = 59

Modified Box-Pierce chisquare statistic             Modified Box-Pierce chisquare statistic
Lag            12          24          36        48  Lag          12          24          36        48
Chisquare  4.5(DF=11)  11.5(DF=23) 23.2(DF=35) 45.3(DF=47) Chisquare 4.1(DF=10) 11.9(DF=22) 25.1(DF=34) 45.8(DF=46)


Forecasts from period 62                            Forecasts from period 62
                   95 Percent Limits                                   95 Percent Limits
Period   Forecast   Lower      Upper     Actual     Period   Forecast   Lower      Upper     Actual
  63     12.2326   11.5446    12.9206                  63     12.2377   11.5420    12.9334
  64     12.2326   10.9518    13.5135                  64     12.2053   10.9445    13.4662
  65     12.2326   10.5570    13.9082                  65     12.2579   10.6208    13.8950
  66     12.2326   10.2390    14.2263                  66     12.2936   10.4040    14.1832
  67     12.2326    9.9651    14.5002                  67     12.2975   10.2070    14.3881
  68     12.2326    9.7209    14.7444                  68     12.2899   10.0152    14.5645

MTB > acf 5 c30                                      MTB > acf 5 c30

ACF of C30                                           ACF of C30

      -1.0 -0.8 -0.6 -0.4 -0.2 0.0 0.2 0.4 0.6 0.8 1.0        -1.0 -0.8 -0.6 -0.4 -0.2 0.0 0.2 0.4 0.6 0.8 1.0
      +----+----+----+----+----+----+----+----+----+----+     +----+----+----+----+----+----+----+----+----+----+
 1 -0.045                    XX                      1 -0.024                    XX
 2 -0.044                    XX                      2 -0.061                   XXX
 3 -0.072                   XXX                      3  0.068                    XXX
 4 -0.145                  XXXXX                     4 -0.136                  XXXX
 5  0.031                    XX                      5  0.018                    X

                                                    MTB >
```

```
MTB > arima 0 1 1 c4 c30;                          MTB > arima 2 1 0 c4 c30;
SUBC> fore 6.                                      SUBC> fore 6.

Estimates at each iteration                        Estimates at each iteration
Iteration      SSE    Parameters                   Iteration      SSE    Parameters
    0       83.1821    0.100                            0       73.6354    0.100    0.100
    1       73.7913   -0.050                            1       65.7485    0.250   -0.035
    2       67.1203   -0.200                            2       61.4107    0.400   -0.170
    3       62.6455   -0.350                            3       60.5099    0.499   -0.262
    4       60.1841   -0.500                            4       60.5065    0.504   -0.269
    5       59.7828   -0.565                            5       60.5065    0.505   -0.269
    6       59.7543   -0.580                            6       60.5065    0.505   -0.269
    7       59.7517   -0.585
    8       59.7515   -0.587
    9       59.7514   -0.587
Relative change in each estimate less than  0.0010  Relative change in each estimate less than  0.0010

Final Estimates of Parameters                      Final Estimates of Parameters
Type      Estimate   St. Dev.   t-ratio            Type      Estimate   St. Dev.   t-ratio
MA   1     -0.5870    0.1070     -5.49              AR   1     0.5048     0.1283     3.93
                                                   AR   2    -0.2690     0.1290    -2.09


Differencing: 1 regular difference                 Differencing: 1 regular difference
No. of obs.: Original series 62, after differencing 61   No. of obs.: Original series 62, after differencing 61
Residuals:   SS = 59.7463  (backforecasts excluded)  Residuals:   SS = 60.4524  (backforecasts excluded)
             MS =  0.9958  DF = 60                               MS = 1.0246  DF = 59

Modified Box-Pierce chisquare statistic            Modified Box-Pierce chisquare statistic
Lag            12        24        36        48    Lag            12        24        36        48
Chisquare   5.6(DF=11) 12.5(DF=23) 24.9(DF=35) 47.9(DF=47)  Chisquare   5.1(DF=10) 12.8(DF=22) 26.9(DF=34) 48.7(DF=46)


Forecasts from period 62                           Forecasts from period 62
                   95 Percent Limits                                   95 Percent Limits
Period   Forecast    Lower      Upper     Actual   Period   Forecast    Lower      Upper     Actual
  63     27.1515    25.1952    29.1077             63     27.2087    25.2243    29.1930
  64     27.1515    23.4820    30.8210             64     27.1017    23.5164    30.6869
  65     27.1515    22.3448    31.9582             65     27.2865    22.6387    31.9344
  66     27.1515    21.4294    32.8736             66     27.4086    22.0464    32.7708
  67     27.1515    20.6414    33.6616             67     27.4205    21.4878    33.3532
  68     27.1515    19.9390    34.3640             68     27.3937    20.9377    33.8497

MTB > acf 5 c30                                    MTB > acf 5 c30

ACF of C30                                         ACF of C30

       -1.0 -0.8 -0.6 -0.4 -0.2  0.0  0.2  0.4  0.6  0.8  1.0        -1.0 -0.8 -0.6 -0.4 -0.2  0.0  0.2  0.4  0.6  0.8  1.0
       +----+----+----+----+----+----+----+----+----+----+          +----+----+----+----+----+----+----+----+----+----+
  1  -0.062                     XXX                  1  -0.023                     XX
  2  -0.049                     XX                   2  -0.066                    XXX
  3  -0.057                     XX                   3   0.074                       XXX
  4  -0.142                   XXXXX                  4  -0.129                    XXXX
  5   0.067                     XXX                  5   0.052                       XX

                                                   MTB >
```

```
MTB > arima 0 1 1 c5 c30;                        MTB > arima 2 1 0 c5 c30;
SUBC> fore 6.                                    SUBC> fore 6.

Estimates at each iteration                      Estimates at each iteration
Iteration      SSE      Parameters               Iteration      SSE      Parameters
     0      715.108      0.100                         0      637.092      0.100      0.100
     1      636.908     -0.050                         1      569.842      0.250     -0.039
     2      581.523     -0.200                         2      533.815      0.400     -0.180
     3      544.291     -0.350                         3      527.328      0.490     -0.266
     4      523.136     -0.500                         4      527.304      0.494     -0.271
     5      518.721     -0.571                         5      527.304      0.495     -0.272
     6      518.169     -0.595                         6      527.304      0.495     -0.272
     7      518.086     -0.603
     8      518.073     -0.607
     9      518.071     -0.608
    10      518.071     -0.609
Relative change in each estimate less than  0.0010   Relative change in each estimate less than  0.0010

Final Estimates of Parameters                    Final Estimates of Parameters
Type    Estimate    St. Dev.  t-ratio            Type    Estimate    St. Dev.  t-ratio
MA   1   -0.6086     0.1057    -5.76              AR   1    0.4947     0.1295     3.82
                                                 AR   2   -0.2719     0.1306    -2.08

Differencing: 1 regular difference               Differencing: 1 regular difference
No. of obs.: Original series 62, after differencing 61   No. of obs.: Original series 62, after differencing 61
Residuals:   SS = 518.060  (backforecasts excluded)      Residuals:   SS = 526.941  (backforecasts excluded)
             MS =   8.634  DF = 60                                     MS =   8.931  DF = 59

Modified Box-Pierce chisquare statistic          Modified Box-Pierce chisquare statistic
Lag            12          24          36          48    Lag            12          24          36          48
Chisquare    7.7(DF=11) 14.2(DF=23) 26.0(DF=35) 47.4(DF=47)   Chisquare   7.0(DF=10) 14.1(DF=22) 27.7(DF=34) 48.2(DF=46)


Forecasts from period 62                         Forecasts from period 62
                  95 Percent Limits                                95 Percent Limits
Period   Forecast    Lower      Upper     Actual  Period   Forecast    Lower      Upper     Actual
  63     66.2254    60.4650    71.9859             63     66.5872    60.7285    72.4458
  64     66.2254    55.3148    77.1361             64     66.2699    55.7338    76.8060
  65     66.2254    51.9110    80.5398             65     66.9572    53.3581    80.5562
  66     66.2254    49.1737    83.2772             66     67.3834    51.7404    83.0265
  67     66.2254    46.8187    85.6322             67     67.4074    50.1256    84.6893
  68     66.2254    44.7200    87.7308             68     67.3034    48.5076    86.0993

MTB > acf 5 c30                                   MTB > acf 5 c30

ACF of C30                                        ACF of C30

      -1.0 -0.8 -0.6 -0.4 -0.2 0.0 0.2 0.4 0.6 0.8 1.0          -1.0 -0.8 -0.6 -0.4 -0.2 0.0 0.2 0.4 0.6 0.8 1.0
      +----+----+----+----+----+----+----+----+----+----+       +----+----+----+----+----+----+----+----+----+----+
 1  -0.083                        XXX               1  -0.023                        XX
 2  -0.057                        XX                2  -0.072                       XXX
 3  -0.044                        XX                3   0.079                       XXX
 4  -0.143                      XXXXX               4  -0.125                      XXXX
 5   0.098                        XXX               5   0.081                       XXX

                                                 MTB >
```

```
MTB > arima 0 1 1 c6 c30;                    MTB > arima 2 1 0 c6 c30;
SUBC> fore 6.                                SUBC> fore 6.

Estimates at each iteration                 Estimates at each iteration
Iteration       SSE      Parameters         Iteration       SSE      Parameters
    0        6537.08     0.100                  0        5877.17     0.100    0.100
    1        5853.23    -0.050                  1        5261.40     0.250   -0.047
    2        5370.44    -0.200                  2        4944.13     0.400   -0.195
    3        5046.21    -0.350                  3        4898.30     0.477   -0.273
    4        4858.25    -0.500                  4        4898.14     0.481   -0.278
    5        4812.50    -0.574                  5        4898.14     0.481   -0.278
    6        4803.61    -0.604                  6        4898.14     0.481   -0.278
    7        4801.63    -0.618
    8        4801.18    -0.624
    9        4801.08    -0.627
   10        4801.06    -0.629
   11        4801.05    -0.630
   12        4801.05    -0.630
Relative change in each estimate less than  0.0010     Relative change in each estimate less than  0.0010

Final Estimates of Parameters               Final Estimates of Parameters
Type    Estimate    St. Dev.  t-ratio       Type    Estimate    St. Dev.  t-ratio
MA   1   -0.6298     0.1042    -6.05         AR   1    0.4813     0.1308    3.68
                                            AR   2   -0.2781     0.1323   -2.10

Differencing: 1 regular difference          Differencing: 1 regular difference
No. of obs.: Original series 62, after differencing 61     No. of obs.: Original series 62, after differencing 61
Residuals:   SS = 4801.05  (backforecasts excluded)        Residuals:   SS = 4895.67  (backforecasts excluded)
             MS =   80.02  DF = 60                                       MS =   82.98  DF = 59

Modified Box-Pierce chisquare statistic     Modified Box-Pierce chisquare statistic
Lag             12        24        36        48     Lag             12        24        36        48
Chisquare   10.5(DF=11)  16.3(DF=23)  26.7(DF=35)  44.7(DF=47)   Chisquare   9.0(DF=10)  15.4(DF=22)  27.5(DF=34)  45.0(DF=46)

Forecasts from period 62                    Forecasts from period 62
                   95 Percent Limits                            95 Percent Limits
Period   Forecast    Lower     Upper    Actual     Period   Forecast    Lower     Upper    Actual
  63     173.304    155.768   190.840              63     175.137    157.279   192.995
  64     173.304    139.772   206.836              64     174.325    142.409   206.241
  65     173.304    129.244   217.364              65     176.950    136.021   217.878
  66     173.304    120.786   225.822              66     178.439    131.573   225.306
  67     173.304    113.512   233.096              67     178.426    126.771   230.081
  68     173.304    107.032   239.576              68     178.005    121.876   234.135

MTB > acf 5 c30                             MTB > acf 5 c30

ACF of C30                                  ACF of C30

        -1.0 -0.8 -0.6 -0.4 -0.2  0.0  0.2  0.4  0.6  0.8  1.0          -1.0 -0.8 -0.6 -0.4 -0.2  0.0  0.2  0.4  0.6  0.8  1.0
        +----+----+----+----+----+----+----+----+----+----+           +----+----+----+----+----+----+----+----+----+----+
 1  -0.104                     XXXX                          1  -0.025                      XX
 2  -0.066                      XXX                          2  -0.075                     XXX
 3  -0.035                       XX                          3   0.081                      XXX
 4  -0.150                    XXXXX                          4  -0.125                     XXXX
 5   0.124                       XXXX                        5   0.104                      XXXX

                                            MTB >
```

```
MTB > arima 0 1 1 c7 c30;                          MTB > arima 2 1 0 c7 c30;
SUBC> fore 6.                                       SUBC> fore 6.

Estimates at each iteration                        Estimates at each iteration
Iteration      SSE       Parameters                Iteration      SSE       Parameters
   0        62986.7       0.100                        0        57228.4     0.100    0.100
   1        56748.2      -0.050                         1        51446.6     0.244   -0.050
   2        52368.5      -0.200                         2        48487.4     0.386   -0.200
   3        49453.7      -0.350                         3        48053.6     0.461   -0.280
   4        47773.8      -0.500                         4        48052.1     0.465   -0.285
   5        47362.8      -0.570                         5        48052.1     0.465   -0.285
   6        47252.7      -0.604                         6        48052.1     0.465   -0.285
   7        47219.7      -0.621
   8        47209.7      -0.631
   9        47206.6      -0.636
  10        47205.7      -0.639
  11        47205.5      -0.640
  12        47205.4      -0.641
  13        47205.4      -0.642
Relative change in each estimate less than 0.0010  Relative change in each estimate less than 0.0010

Final Estimates of Parameters                      Final Estimates of Parameters
Type    Estimate    St. Dev.   t-ratio             Type     Estimate    St. Dev.   t-ratio
MA   1   -0.6416     0.1036     -6.19               AR   1    0.4647     0.1322     3.52
                                                    AR   2   -0.2849     0.1342    -2.12

Differencing: 1 regular difference                 Differencing: 1 regular difference
No. of obs.: Original series 62, after differencing 61    No. of obs.: Original series 62, after differencing 61
Residuals:   SS = 47205.1  (backforecasts excluded)       Residuals:   SS = 48035.1  (backforecasts excluded)
             MS =   786.8  DF = 60                                      MS =   814.2  DF = 59

Modified Box-Pierce chisquare statistic            Modified Box-Pierce chisquare statistic
Lag            12          24          36       48 Lag            12          24          36       48
Chisquare  13.2(DF=11) 18.4(DF=23) 27.0(DF=35) 40.9(DF=47) Chisquare  10.9(DF=10) 16.5(DF=22) 26.5(DF=34) 40.3(DF=46)

Forecasts from period 62                           Forecasts from period 62
                  95 Percent Limits                                  95 Percent Limits
Period  Forecast    Lower     Upper     Actual     Period  Forecast    Lower     Upper     Actual
  63    477.388   422.401   532.376                   63    485.297   429.360   541.234
  64    477.388   371.692   583.085                   64    483.730   384.525   582.934
  65    477.388   338.392   616.385                   65    493.742   367.500   619.984
  66    477.388   311.654   643.123                   66    498.842   355.032   642.651
  67    477.388   288.666   666.111                   67    498.359   340.252   656.466
  68    477.388   268.189   686.588                   68    496.682   325.024   668.339

MTB > acf 5 c30                                     MTB > acf 5 c30

ACF of C30                                          ACF of C30

     -1.0 -0.8 -0.6 -0.4 -0.2 0.0 0.2 0.4 0.6 0.8 1.0      -1.0 -0.8 -0.6 -0.4 -0.2 0.0 0.2 0.4 0.6 0.8 1.0
     +----+----+----+----+----+----+----+----+----+----+       +----+----+----+----+----+----+----+----+----+----+
1  -0.121                      XXXX                 1  -0.028                       XX
2  -0.074                      XXX                  2  -0.074                      XXX
3  -0.031                      XX                   3   0.077                        XXX
4  -0.159                     XXXXX                 4  -0.128                      XXXX
5   0.143                         XXXXX             5   0.122                        XXXX
```

ARIMA(0,1,1)   ARIMA(2,1,0)

λ	$g(\lambda)$	$g(\lambda)$
0.0	201.06	201.56
0.2	198.00	198.69
0.4	197.06	197.94
0.6	198.29	199.34
0.8	201.58	202.71
1.0	206.71	207.77

The best models occur with $\lambda = 0.4$, and as before in Exercise 7.12, the ARIMA(0,1,1) model is somewhat beter than the ARIMA(2,1,0) model.

****

10.5   Consider the data of Exercise 7.13 on the United Kingdom-United States exchange rate. Fit ARIMA models to the transformed series, $X_t(\lambda)$ defined by (10.6.1), for $\lambda = 0, 0.2, 0.4, 0.8, 1$. Choose the most appropriate λ, and forecast the next five values of the series.

------- Answer to 10.5 --------

Equation (10.6.1) is the Box-Cox transformation:

$$X_t(\lambda) = (X_t^\gamma - 1)/\lambda \quad \text{if } \lambda \neq 0$$

and
$$X_t(\lambda) = \log X_t \quad \text{if } \lambda \neq 0$$

In Exercise 7.13 it was found that an ARIMA(1,1,0) was slightly better than an ARIMA(0,1,1). Thus both models were tried here for each λ. The criterion $g(\lambda)$ (from section 10.6 of the text) was calculated for each estimation. These values follow in a table after the estimations.

The MINITAB output is as follows:

```
MTB > let c2 = loge(c1)                          MTB > diff 1 c2 c12
MTB > let c3 = (c1**.2 - 1)/.2                    MTB > diff 1 c3 c13
MTB > let c4 = (c1**.4 - 1)/.4                    MTB > diff 1 c4 c14
MTB > let c5 = (c1**.6 - 1)/.6                    MTB > diff 1 c5 c15
MTB > let c6 = (c1**.8 - 1)/.8                    MTB > diff 1 c6 c16
MTB > let c7 = (c1**1. - 1)/1.                    MTB > diff 1 c6 c17
MTB >                                             MTB >

MTB > acf 5 c2                                    MTB > pacf 5 c2

ACF of C2                                         PACF of C2

      -1.0 -0.8 -0.6 -0.4 -0.2 0.0 0.2 0.4 0.6 0.8 1.0          -1.0 -0.8 -0.6 -0.4 -0.2 0.0 0.2 0.4 0.6 0.8 1.0
      +----+----+----+----+----+----+----+----+----+----+       +----+----+----+----+----+----+----+----+----+----+
  1  0.963                    XXXXXXXXXXXXXXXXXXXXXXXXX      1   0.963                    XXXXXXXXXXXXXXXXXXXXXXXXX
  2  0.923                    XXXXXXXXXXXXXXXXXXXXXXXX       2  -0.069                    XXX
  3  0.879                    XXXXXXXXXXXXXXXXXXXXXXX        3  -0.074                    XXX
  4  0.837                    XXXXXXXXXXXXXXXXXXXXXX         4   0.000                    X
  5  0.796                    XXXXXXXXXXXXXXXXXXXXX          5   0.013                    X


MTB > acf 5 c3                                    MTB > pacf 5 c3

ACF of C3                                         PACF of C3

      -1.0 -0.8 -0.6 -0.4 -0.2 0.0 0.2 0.4 0.6 0.8 1.0          -1.0 -0.8 -0.6 -0.4 -0.2 0.0 0.2 0.4 0.6 0.8 1.0
      +----+----+----+----+----+----+----+----+----+----+       +----+----+----+----+----+----+----+----+----+----+
  1  0.965                    XXXXXXXXXXXXXXXXXXXXXXXXX      1   0.965                    XXXXXXXXXXXXXXXXXXXXXXXXX
  2  0.925                    XXXXXXXXXXXXXXXXXXXXXXXX       2  -0.081                    XXX
  3  0.882                    XXXXXXXXXXXXXXXXXXXXXXX        3  -0.073                    XXX
  4  0.839                    XXXXXXXXXXXXXXXXXXXXXX         4  -0.001                    X
  5  0.799                    XXXXXXXXXXXXXXXXXXXXX          5   0.008                    X


MTB > acf 5 c4                                    MTB > pacf 5 c4

ACF of C4                                         PACF of C4

      -1.0 -0.8 -0.6 -0.4 -0.2 0.0 0.2 0.4 0.6 0.8 1.0          -1.0 -0.8 -0.6 -0.4 -0.2 0.0 0.2 0.4 0.6 0.8 1.0
      +----+----+----+----+----+----+----+----+----+----+       +----+----+----+----+----+----+----+----+----+----+
  1  0.966                    XXXXXXXXXXXXXXXXXXXXXXXXX      1   0.966                    XXXXXXXXXXXXXXXXXXXXXXXXX
  2  0.927                    XXXXXXXXXXXXXXXXXXXXXXXX       2  -0.093                    XXX
  3  0.884                    XXXXXXXXXXXXXXXXXXXXXXX        3  -0.073                    XXX
  4  0.842                    XXXXXXXXXXXXXXXXXXXXXX         4  -0.002                    X
  5  0.802                    XXXXXXXXXXXXXXXXXXXXX          5   0.002                    X


MTB > acf 5 c5                                    MTB > pacf 5 c5

ACF of C5                                         PACF of C5

      -1.0 -0.8 -0.6 -0.4 -0.2 0.0 0.2 0.4 0.6 0.8 1.0          -1.0 -0.8 -0.6 -0.4 -0.2 0.0 0.2 0.4 0.6 0.8 1.0
      +----+----+----+----+----+----+----+----+----+----+       +----+----+----+----+----+----+----+----+----+----+
  1  0.967                    XXXXXXXXXXXXXXXXXXXXXXXXX      1   0.967                    XXXXXXXXXXXXXXXXXXXXXXXXX
  2  0.928                    XXXXXXXXXXXXXXXXXXXXXXXX       2  -0.105                    XXXX
  3  0.886                    XXXXXXXXXXXXXXXXXXXXXXX        3  -0.072                    XXX
  4  0.844                    XXXXXXXXXXXXXXXXXXXXXX         4  -0.004                    X
  5  0.804                    XXXXXXXXXXXXXXXXXXXXX          5  -0.003                    X


MTB > acf 5 c6                                    MTB > pacf 5 c6

ACF of C6                                         PACF of C6

      -1.0 -0.8 -0.6 -0.4 -0.2 0.0 0.2 0.4 0.6 0.8 1.0          -1.0 -0.8 -0.6 -0.4 -0.2 0.0 0.2 0.4 0.6 0.8 1.0
      +----+----+----+----+----+----+----+----+----+----+       +----+----+----+----+----+----+----+----+----+----+
  1  0.968                    XXXXXXXXXXXXXXXXXXXXXXXXX      1   0.968                    XXXXXXXXXXXXXXXXXXXXXXXXX
  2  0.930                    XXXXXXXXXXXXXXXXXXXXXXXX       2  -0.116                    XXXX
  3  0.888                    XXXXXXXXXXXXXXXXXXXXXXX        3  -0.071                    XXX
  4  0.846                    XXXXXXXXXXXXXXXXXXXXXX         4  -0.005                    X
  5  0.805                    XXXXXXXXXXXXXXXXXXXXX          5  -0.009                    X


MTB > acf 5 c7                                    MTB > pacf 5 c7

ACF of C7                                         PACF of C7

      -1.0 -0.8 -0.6 -0.4 -0.2 0.0 0.2 0.4 0.6 0.8 1.0          -1.0 -0.8 -0.6 -0.4 -0.2 0.0 0.2 0.4 0.6 0.8 1.0
      +----+----+----+----+----+----+----+----+----+----+       +----+----+----+----+----+----+----+----+----+----+
  1  0.969                    XXXXXXXXXXXXXXXXXXXXXXXXX      1   0.969                    XXXXXXXXXXXXXXXXXXXXXXXXX
  2  0.931                    XXXXXXXXXXXXXXXXXXXXXXXX       2  -0.128                    XXXX
  3  0.889                    XXXXXXXXXXXXXXXXXXXXXXX        3  -0.071                    XXX
  4  0.848                    XXXXXXXXXXXXXXXXXXXXXX         4  -0.007                    X
  5  0.807                    XXXXXXXXXXXXXXXXXXXXX          5  -0.014                    X
```

```
MTB > acf 5 c12                                    MTB > pacf 5 c12

ACF of C12                                         PACF of C12

        -1.0 -0.8 -0.6 -0.4 -0.2  0.0  0.2  0.4  0.6  0.8  1.0          -1.0 -0.8 -0.6 -0.4 -0.2  0.0  0.2  0.4  0.6  0.8  1.0
        +----+----+----+----+----+----+----+----+----+----+            +----+----+----+----+----+----+----+----+----+----+
  1  0.401                       XXXXXXXXXXX        1  0.401                       XXXXXXXXXXX
  2  0.114                       XXXX               2 -0.056                     XX
  3  0.021                       XX                 3 -0.006                     X
  4  0.036                       XX                 4  0.043                       XX
  5  0.112                       XXXX               5  0.100                       XXX


MTB > acf 5 c13                                    MTB > pacf 5 c13

ACF of C13                                         PACF of C13

        -1.0 -0.8 -0.6 -0.4 -0.2  0.0  0.2  0.4  0.6  0.8  1.0          -1.0 -0.8 -0.6 -0.4 -0.2  0.0  0.2  0.4  0.6  0.8  1.0
        +----+----+----+----+----+----+----+----+----+----+            +----+----+----+----+----+----+----+----+----+----+
  1  0.402                       XXXXXXXXXXX        1  0.402                       XXXXXXXXXXX
  2  0.114                       XXXX               2 -0.057                     XX
  3  0.019                       X                  3 -0.008                     X
  4  0.034                       XX                 4  0.042                       XX
  5  0.104                       XXXX               5  0.093                       XXX
MTB > acf 5 c14                                    MTB > pacf 5 c14

ACF of C14                                         PACF of C14

        -1.0 -0.8 -0.6 -0.4 -0.2  0.0  0.2  0.4  0.6  0.8  1.0          -1.0 -0.8 -0.6 -0.4 -0.2  0.0  0.2  0.4  0.6  0.8  1.0
        +----+----+----+----+----+----+----+----+----+----+            +----+----+----+----+----+----+----+----+----+----+
  1  0.403                       XXXXXXXXXXX        1  0.403                       XXXXXXXXXXX
  2  0.114                       XXXX               2 -0.057                     XX
  3  0.018                       X                  3 -0.009                     X
  4  0.032                       XX                 4  0.041                       XX
  5  0.097                       XXX                5  0.086                       XXX


MTB > acf 5 c15                                    MTB > pacf 5 c15

ACF of C15                                         PACF of C15

        -1.0 -0.8 -0.6 -0.4 -0.2  0.0  0.2  0.4  0.6  0.8  1.0          -1.0 -0.8 -0.6 -0.4 -0.2  0.0  0.2  0.4  0.6  0.8  1.0
        +----+----+----+----+----+----+----+----+----+----+            +----+----+----+----+----+----+----+----+----+----+
  1  0.402                       XXXXXXXXXXX        1  0.402                       XXXXXXXXXXX
  2  0.115                       XXXX               2 -0.056                     XX
  3  0.019                       X                  3 -0.009                     X
  4  0.031                       XX                 4  0.039                       XX
  5  0.091                       XXX                5  0.079                       XXX


MTB > acf 5 c16                                    MTB > pacf 5 c16

ACF of C16                                         PACF of C16

        -1.0 -0.8 -0.6 -0.4 -0.2  0.0  0.2  0.4  0.6  0.8  1.0          -1.0 -0.8 -0.6 -0.4 -0.2  0.0  0.2  0.4  0.6  0.8  1.0
        +----+----+----+----+----+----+----+----+----+----+            +----+----+----+----+----+----+----+----+----+----+
  1  0.401                       XXXXXXXXXXX        1  0.401                       XXXXXXXXXXX
  2  0.115                       XXXX               2 -0.055                     XX
  3  0.019                       X                  3 -0.009                     X
  4  0.030                       XX                 4  0.037                       XX
  5  0.084                       XXX                5  0.072                       XXX


MTB > acf 5 c17                                    MTB > pacf 5 c17

ACF of C17                                         PACF of C17

        -1.0 -0.8 -0.6 -0.4 -0.2  0.0  0.2  0.4  0.6  0.8  1.0          -1.0 -0.8 -0.6 -0.4 -0.2  0.0  0.2  0.4  0.6  0.8  1.0
        +----+----+----+----+----+----+----+----+----+----+            +----+----+----+----+----+----+----+----+----+----+
  1  0.401                       XXXXXXXXXXX        1  0.401                       XXXXXXXXXXX
  2  0.115                       XXXX               2 -0.055                     XX
  3  0.019                       X                  3 -0.009                     X
  4  0.030                       XX                 4  0.037                       XX
  5  0.084                       XXX                5  0.072                       XXX
```

```
MTB > arima 1 1 0 c2 c30;                          MTB > arima 0 1 1 c2 c30;
SUBC> fore 6.                                      SUBC> fore 6.


Estimates at each iteration                        Estimates at each iteration
Iteration      SSE      Parameters                 Iteration      SSE      Parameters
    0      0.0724513     0.100                          0      0.0861288     0.100
    1      0.0663730     0.250                          1      0.0752777    -0.050
    2      0.0636665     0.400                          2      0.0685188    -0.200
    3      0.0635130     0.442                          3      0.0651515    -0.350
    4      0.0635119     0.445                          4      0.0647947    -0.428
    5      0.0635119     0.445                          5      0.0647791    -0.414
Relative change in each estimate less than 0.0010      6      0.0647788    -0.416
                                                       7      0.0647788    -0.415
                                                   Relative change in each estimate less than 0.0010


Final Estimates of Parameters                      Final Estimates of Parameters
Type    Estimate   St. Dev.  t-ratio               Type    Estimate   St. Dev.  t-ratio
AR  1    0.4454     0.0763     5.83                 MA  1   -0.4154     0.0780    -5.33

Differencing: 1 regular difference                 Differencing: 1 regular difference
No. of obs.: Original series 144, after differencing 143    No. of obs.: Original series 144, after differencing 143
Residuals:   SS = 0.0633032 (backforecasts excluded)        Residuals:   SS = 0.0646073 (backforecasts excluded)
             MS = 0.0004458  DF = 142                                     MS = 0.0004550  DF = 142

Modified Box-Pierce chisquare statistic            Modified Box-Pierce chisquare statistic
Lag            12        24        36        48     Lag            12        24        36        48
Chisquare  6.9(DF=11) 20.3(DF=23) 34.8(DF=35) 64.2(DF=47)  Chisquare  8.3(DF=11) 22.4(DF=23) 39.4(DF=35) 65.8(DF=47)


Forecasts from period 144                          Forecasts from period 144
                95 Percent Limits                                  95 Percent Limits
Period  Forecast    Lower      Upper     Actual     Period  Forecast    Lower      Upper     Actual
145    0.147455  0.106063   0.188846               145    0.146672  0.104857   0.188488
146    0.138281  0.065531   0.211030               146    0.146672  0.074206   0.219139
147    0.134195  0.034588   0.233801               147    0.146672  0.053109   0.240236
148    0.132375  0.009650   0.255099               148    0.146672  0.035961   0.257384
149    0.131564 -0.011395   0.274524               149    0.146672  0.021134   0.272211
150    0.131203 -0.029794   0.292201               150    0.146672  0.007882   0.285463

MTB > acf 5 c30                                     MTB > acf 5 c30

ACF of C30                                          ACF of C30

      -1.0 -0.8 -0.6 -0.4 -0.2 0.0 0.2 0.4 0.6 0.8 1.0        -1.0 -0.8 -0.6 -0.4 -0.2 0.0 0.2 0.4 0.6 0.8 1.0
      +----+----+----+----+----+----+----+----+----+----+    +----+----+----+----+----+----+----+----+----+----+
 1  -0.005                      X                      1   0.024                        XX
 2  -0.069                     XXX                     2   0.111                        XXXX
 3  -0.053                     XX                      3  -0.024                        XX
 4  -0.009                      X                      4   0.025                        XX
 5   0.099                      XXX                    5   0.083                        XXX

                                                   MTB >
```

```
MTB > arima 1 1 0 c3 c30;                    MTB > arima 0 1 1 c3 c30;
SUBC> fore 6.                                SUBC> fore 6.

Estimates at each iteration                  Estimates at each iteration
Iteration    SSE       Parameters            Iteration    SSE       Parameters
    0      0.0942509    0.100                     0      0.112052     0.100
    1      0.0863515    0.250                     1      0.097928    -0.050
    2      0.0828526    0.400                     2      0.089133    -0.200
    3      0.0826627    0.440                     3      0.084781    -0.350
    4      0.0826611    0.444                     4      0.084347    -0.426
    5      0.0826611    0.444                     5      0.084327    -0.411
Relative change in each estimate less than       6      0.084327    -0.413
0.0010                                           7      0.084327    -0.413
                                             Relative change in each estimate less than  0.0010


Final Estimates of Parameters               Final Estimates of Parameters
Type    Estimate    St. Dev.   t-ratio      Type    Estimate    St. Dev.   t-ratio
AR   1   0.4442     0.0762      5.83         MA   1  -0.4129     0.0777     -5.31

Differencing: 1 regular difference          Differencing: 1 regular difference
No. of obs.:  Original series 144, after    No. of obs.:  Original series 144, after
differencing 143                            differencing 143
Residuals:    SS = 0.0823660 (backforecasts Residuals:    SS = 0.0840864 (backforecasts
              excluded)                                   excluded)
              MS = 0.0005800  DF = 142                    MS = 0.0005922  DF = 142

Modified Box-Pierce chisquare statistic     Modified Box-Pierce chisquare statistic
Lag          12      24      36      48      Lag          12      24      36      48
Chisquare  6.8(DF=11) 20.0(DF=23) 34.7(DF=35) 63.6(DF=47)  Chisquare  8.2(DF=11) 22.0(DF=23) 39.2(DF=35) 65.4(DF=47)


Forecasts from period 144                   Forecasts from period 144
                  95 Percent Limits                           95 Percent Limits
Period  Forecast   Lower      Upper    Actual  Period  Forecast   Lower      Upper    Actual
145    0.149563   0.102349   0.196778          145    0.148837   0.101132   0.196542
146    0.140081   0.057143   0.223019          146    0.148837   0.066262   0.231412
147    0.135869   0.022354   0.249384          147    0.148837   0.042247   0.255427
148    0.133998  -0.005828   0.273824          148    0.148837   0.022725   0.274949
149    0.133167  -0.029684   0.296017          149    0.148837   0.005844   0.291830
150    0.132797  -0.050578   0.316173          150    0.148837  -0.009245   0.306919

MTB > acf 5 c30                             MTB > acf 5 c30

ACF of C30                                  ACF of C30


       -1.0 -0.8 -0.6 -0.4 -0.2 0.0 0.2 0.4 0.6 0.8 1.0          -1.0 -0.8 -0.6 -0.4 -0.2 0.0 0.2 0.4 0.6 0.8 1.0
       +----+----+----+----+----+----+----+----+----+----+      +----+----+----+----+----+----+----+----+----+----+
 1 -0.004                     X                           1  0.026                        XX
 2 -0.067                    XXX                          2  0.112                        XXXX
 3 -0.055                    XX                           3 -0.027                        XX
 4 -0.009                     X                           4  0.024                        XX
 5  0.092                     XXX                         5  0.076                        XXX

                                             MTB >
```

```
MTB > arima 1 1 0 c4 c30;                          MTB > arima 0 1 1 c4 c30;
SUBC> fore 6.                                      SUBC> fore 6.

Estimates at each iteration                        Estimates at each iteration
Iteration       SSE      Parameters                Iteration       SSE      Parameters
    0         0.123290    0.100                         0         0.146536    0.100
    1         0.112997    0.250                         1         0.128088   -0.050
    2         0.108475    0.400                         2         0.116614   -0.200
    3         0.108244    0.439                         3         0.110984   -0.350
    4         0.108242    0.442                         4         0.110459   -0.422
    5         0.108242    0.443                         5         0.110436   -0.408
Relative change in each estimate less than  0.0010     6         0.110435   -0.410
                                                       7         0.110435   -0.410
                                                   Relative change in each estimate less than  0.0010


Final Estimates of Parameters                      Final Estimates of Parameters
Type      Estimate     St. Dev.  t-ratio           Type      Estimate     St. Dev.  t-ratio
AR   1     0.4425      0.0760     5.82              MA   1    -0.4101      0.0776    -5.29

Differencing: 1 regular difference                 Differencing: 1 regular difference
No. of obs.:  Original series 144, after differencing 143   No. of obs.:  Original series 144, after differencing 143
Residuals:    SS = 0.107826  (backforecasts excluded)       Residuals:    SS = 0.110098  (backforecasts excluded)
              MS = 0.000759  DF = 142                                      MS = 0.000775  DF = 142

Modified Box-Pierce chisquare statistic            Modified Box-Pierce chisquare statistic
Lag              12        24        36        48  Lag              12        24        36        48
Chisquare   6.6(DF=11) 19.6(DF=23) 34.4(DF=35) 62.6(DF=47)  Chisquare   8.0(DF=11) 21.5(DF=23) 38.8(DF=35) 64.6(DF=47)


Forecasts from period 144                          Forecasts from period 144
                      95 Percent Limits                                  95 Percent Limits
Period   Forecast     Lower      Upper     Actual  Period   Forecast     Lower      Upper     Actual
 145     0.151737    0.097716   0.205757           145     0.151061    0.096474   0.205648
 146     0.141960    0.047140   0.236779           146     0.151061    0.056697   0.245424
 147     0.137633    0.007926   0.267340           147     0.151061    0.029285   0.272836
 148     0.135718   -0.023992   0.295429           148     0.151061    0.006998   0.295124
 149     0.134871   -0.051090   0.320832           149     0.151061   -0.012276   0.314397
 150     0.134496   -0.074863   0.343855           150     0.151061   -0.029504   0.331626

MTB > acf 5 c30                                    MTB > acf 5 c30

ACF of C30                                         ACF of C30

        -1.0 -0.8 -0.6 -0.4 -0.2 0.0 0.2 0.4 0.6 0.8 1.0            -1.0 -0.8 -0.6 -0.4 -0.2 0.0 0.2 0.4 0.6 0.8 1.0
        +----+----+----+----+----+----+----+----+----+----+        +----+----+----+----+----+----+----+----+----+----+

  1  -0.004                     X                    1   0.027                     XX
  2  -0.065                    XXX                   2   0.114                     XXXX
  3  -0.055                    XX                    3  -0.028                     XX
  4  -0.009                     X                    4   0.023                     XX
  5   0.087                    XXX                   5   0.070                     XXX

                                          MTB >
```

```
MTB > arima 1 1 0 c5 c30;                        MTB > arima 0 1 1 c5 c30;
SUBC> fore 6.                                    SUBC> fore 6.

Estimates at each iteration                      Estimates at each iteration
Iteration      SSE      Parameters               Iteration      SSE      Parameters
    0       0.162113      0.100                       0       0.192570      0.100
    1       0.148669      0.250                       1       0.168393     -0.050
    2       0.142823      0.400                       2       0.153384     -0.200
    3       0.142550      0.436                       3       0.146091     -0.350
    4       0.142548      0.440                       4       0.145463     -0.418
    5       0.142548      0.440                       5       0.145436     -0.405
Relative change in each estimate less than  0.0010   6       0.145435     -0.407
                                                     7       0.145435     -0.407
                                                 Relative change in each estimate less than  0.0010


Final Estimates of Parameters                    Final Estimates of Parameters
Type     Estimate    St. Dev.   t-ratio          Type     Estimate    St. Dev.   t-ratio
AR   1    0.4404      0.0759      5.80            MA   1   -0.4071      0.0775     -5.25

Differencing: 1 regular difference               Differencing: 1 regular difference
No. of obs.:  Original series 144, after differencing 143    No. of obs.:  Original series 144, after differencing 143
Residuals:    SS = 0.141960  (backforecasts excluded)        Residuals:    SS = 0.144963  (backforecasts excluded)
              MS = 0.001000  DF = 142                                       MS = 0.001021  DF = 142

Modified Box-Pierce chisquare statistic          Modified Box-Pierce chisquare statistic
Lag                12          24          36          48      Lag                12          24          36          48
Chisquare    6.5(DF=11)  19.2(DF=23)  34.1(DF=35)  61.2(DF=47) Chisquare    7.8(DF=11)  21.0(DF=23)  38.4(DF=35)  63.6(DF=47)


Forecasts from period 144                        Forecasts from period 144
                   95 Percent Limits                                95 Percent Limits
Period   Forecast     Lower       Upper    Actual Period   Forecast     Lower       Upper    Actual
 145    0.153972    0.091987    0.215956           145    0.153344    0.090707    0.215980
 146    0.143909    0.035219    0.252600           146    0.153344    0.045218    0.261469
 147    0.139478   -0.009105    0.288060           147    0.153344    0.013849    0.292839
 148    0.137526   -0.045342    0.320395           148    0.153344   -0.011661    0.318348
 149    0.136666   -0.076189    0.349522           149    0.153344   -0.033724    0.340411
 150    0.136288   -0.103293    0.375869           150    0.153344   -0.053446    0.360134

MTB > acf 5 c30                                  MTB > acf 5 c30

ACF of C30                                       ACF of C30

         -1.0 -0.8 -0.6 -0.4 -0.2  0.0  0.2  0.4  0.6  0.8  1.0            -1.0 -0.8 -0.6 -0.4 -0.2  0.0  0.2  0.4  0.6  0.8  1.0
         +----+----+----+----+----+----+----+----+----+----+           +----+----+----+----+----+----+----+----+----+----+
  1  -0.005                      X                        1   0.027                        XX
  2  -0.063                     XXX                       2   0.115                        XXXX
  3  -0.054                     XX                        3  -0.029                      XX
  4  -0.009                      X                        4   0.023                        XX
  5   0.081                      XXX                      5   0.065                        XXX

                                                 MTB >
```

```
MTB > arima 1 1 0 c6 c30;              MTB > arima 0 1 1 c6 c30;
SUBC> fore 6.                          SUBC> fore 6.

Estimates at each iteration            Estimates at each iteration
Iteration    SSE      Parameters       Iteration    SSE      Parameters
    0      0.214194    0.100                0      0.254225    0.100
    1      0.196591    0.250                1      0.222438   -0.050
    2      0.189035    0.400                2      0.202752   -0.200
    3      0.188719    0.434                3      0.193297   -0.350
    4      0.188716    0.437                4      0.192551   -0.414
    5      0.188716    0.438                5      0.192521   -0.402
Relative change in each estimate            6      0.192520   -0.404
less than  0.0010                           7      0.192520   -0.404
                                       Relative change in each estimate less than  0.0010

Final Estimates of Parameters          Final Estimates of Parameters
Type    Estimate   St. Dev.  t-ratio   Type    Estimate   St. Dev.  t-ratio
AR   1   0.4378     0.0759     5.77     MA   1   -0.4039    0.0774    -5.22

Differencing: 1 regular difference     Differencing: 1 regular difference
No. of obs.: Original series 144, after differencing 143      No. of obs.: Original series 144, after differencing 143
Residuals:   SS = 0.187890 (backforecasts excluded)           Residuals:   SS = 0.191859 (backforecasts excluded)
             MS = 0.001323  DF = 142                                        MS = 0.001351  DF = 142

Modified Box-Pierce chisquare statistic    Modified Box-Pierce chisquare statistic
Lag            12         24         36         48    Lag            12         24         36         48
Chisquare   6.4(DF=11) 18.7(DF=23) 33.6(DF=35) 59.6(DF=47)  Chisquare   7.7(DF=11) 20.4(DF=23) 37.8(DF=35) 62.3(DF=47)

Forecasts from period 144              Forecasts from period 144
                95 Percent Limits                      95 Percent Limits
Period  Forecast    Lower      Upper    Actual    Period  Forecast    Lower      Upper    Actual
145    0.156280   0.084970   0.227590            145    0.155688   0.083628   0.227747
146    0.145952   0.021064   0.270839            146    0.155688   0.031485   0.279890
147    0.141430  -0.029149   0.312010            147    0.155688  -0.004500   0.315875
148    0.139451  -0.070368   0.349270            148    0.155688  -0.033769   0.345144
149    0.138585  -0.105540   0.382710            149    0.155688  -0.059085   0.370460
150    0.138205  -0.136490   0.412901            150    0.155688  -0.081717   0.393093

MTB > acf 5 c30                        MTB > acf 5 c30

ACF of C30                             ACF of C30

       -1.0 -0.8 -0.6 -0.4 -0.2  0.0  0.2  0.4  0.6  0.8  1.0              -1.0 -0.8 -0.6 -0.4 -0.2  0.0  0.2  0.4  0.6  0.8  1.0
       +----+----+----+----+----+----+----+----+----+----+                +----+----+----+----+----+----+----+----+----+----+
 1 -0.005                         X                         1  0.027                          XX
 2 -0.061                        XXX                        2  0.115                          XXXX
 3 -0.053                        XX                         3 -0.029                          XX
 4 -0.009                         X                         4  0.022                          XX
 5  0.076                        XXX                        5  0.060                          XX

                                       MTB >
```

```
MTB > arima 1 1 0 c7 c30;
SUBC> fore 6.


Estimates at each iteration
Iteration       SSE        Parameters
     0       0.284283      0.100
     1       0.261180      0.250
     2       0.251416      0.400
     3       0.251060      0.431
     4       0.251056      0.434
     5       0.251056      0.435
Relative change in each estimate less than  0.0010



Final Estimates of Parameters
Type      Estimate      St. Dev.  t-ratio
AR   1     0.4348        0.0759    5.73

Differencing: 1 regular difference
No. of obs.: Original series 144, after differencing 143
Residuals:   SS = 0.249896  (backforecasts excluded)
             MS = 0.001760  DF = 142

Modified Box-Pierce chisquare statistic
Lag            12          24          36            48
Chisquare   6.3(DF=11)  18.3(DF=23)  33.1(DF=35)  57.8(DF=47)


Forecasts from period 144
                        95 Percent Limits
Period     Forecast     Lower        Upper        Actual
145       0.158652     0.076413     0.240892
146       0.148067     0.004240     0.291893
147       0.143464    -0.052799     0.339727
148       0.141463    -0.099790     0.382717
149       0.140593    -0.139978     0.421165
150       0.140215    -0.175388     0.455818


MTB > acf 5 c30

ACF of C30

        -1.0 -0.8 -0.6 -0.4 -0.2 0.0 0.2 0.4 0.6 0.8 1.0
         +----+----+----+----+----+----+----+----+----+----+
  1  -0.006                         X
  2  -0.059                        XX
  3  -0.050                        XX
  4  -0.008                         X
  5   0.071                         XXX
```

```
MTB > arima 0 1 1 c7 c30;
SUBC> fore 6.


Estimates at each iteration
Iteration       SSE        Parameters
     0       0.337056      0.100
     1       0.295137     -0.050
     2       0.269249     -0.200
     3       0.256977     -0.350
     4       0.256103     -0.410
     5       0.256069     -0.399
     6       0.256068     -0.401
     7       0.256068     -0.400
Relative change in each estimate less than  0.0010


Final Estimates of Parameters
Type      Estimate      St. Dev.  t-ratio
MA   1    -0.4005        0.0774    -5.18

Differencing: 1 regular difference
No. of obs.: Original series 144, after differencing 143
Residuals:   SS = 0.255145  (backforecasts excluded)
             MS = 0.001797  DF = 142

Modified Box-Pierce chisquare statistic
Lag            12          24          36            48
Chisquare   7.5(DF=11)  19.9(DF=23)  37.2(DF=35)  60.7(DF=47)


Forecasts from period 144
                        95 Percent Limits
Period     Forecast     Lower        Upper        Actual
145       0.158093     0.074994     0.241191
146       0.158093     0.015093     0.301092
147       0.158093    -0.026278     0.342463
148       0.158093    -0.059935     0.376120
149       0.158093    -0.089051     0.405236
150       0.158093    -0.115080     0.431265


MTB > acf 5 c30

ACF of C30

        -1.0 -0.8 -0.6 -0.4 -0.2 0.0 0.2 0.4 0.6 0.8 1.0
         +----+----+----+----+----+----+----+----+----+----+
  1   0.027                          XX
  2   0.115                          XXXX
  3  -0.028                         XX
  4   0.022                          XX
  5   0.055                          XX
```

	ARIMA(1,1,0)	ARIMA(0,1,1)
λ	$g(\lambda)$	$g(\lambda)$
0.0	-144.18	-143.54
0.2	-155.02	-154.38
0.4	-165.68	-165.04
0.6	-176.14	-175.49
0.8	-186.46	-185.81
1.0	-196.62	-195.97

The values for $g(\lambda)$ are very similar at each level of λ, and it is clear that the value of $g(\lambda)$ is smallest when $\lambda = 1$.

****

10.6 Carefully discuss the problem of calendar effects in the analysis and forecasting of monthly time series. List as many possible effects of this sort as you can, and suggest possible time series for which you would expect them to be important.

------- Answer to 10.6 --------

See section 10.7 of the text.
(1)   number of days in the month;
(2)   number of weekends in the month;
(3)   what day Christmas falls - in contrast to the what the text says, it sometimes matters whether Christmas is on a Saturday or a Monday. It is possible that if it is on a Saturday, that many people will be forced to take-off from work to do their last minute shopping, or indeed, be forced to skip some of it. The conjunction of which days Thanksgiving (in the U.S.), Christmas and New Year fall matter as to how much work gets done.
(4)   which month Easter falls
       Calendar effects are important in sales, employment (see first instance *The Conference Board*'s help wanted index), and production.

****

Chapter 11

JUDGMENTAL METHODS
AND TECHNOLOGICAL FORECASTS

Contents of Chapter 11

Given the content of this chapter and the nature of the two questions, no attempt will be made to show answers.

11.1 How good are your friends at judgmental extrapolation? Find a time series, and, holding out a few values at the end, graph the remaining observations. Invite a sample of your friends to project the series forward. Note the extent of the diversity of their projections. Now, use a formal approach - either build an ARIMA model, or employ an exponential smoothing algorithm. Compare the judgmental and quantitative forecasts with the actual outcomes.

11.2 (a) From among your friends, assemble a Delphi panel. Choose a possible future event, and try to obtain an assessment of if and when it will occur. Discuss any movement towards consensus that is observed during the Delphi iterations.

    (b) Look at the same forecasting problem as in part (a), but now through constituting from among your friends a jury of executive opinion, with yourself as chairperson. Compare and contrast the processes through which the final prediction was achieved in these two cases.

****

It might be interesting for the instructor to ask the members of the class to judgmentally forecast a set of time series. Give them a listing and graph of the time series to be forecast. You can later use these forecasts to show both evaluation and combination.

****

Chapter 12

THE COMBINATION OF FORECASTS

Contents of Chapter 12

Answers to questions at end of chapter.

12.1 Why is the combination of forecasts often an attractive option in practice? Develop a realistic example of a case where an analyst might opt for combination of individual forecasts.

------- Answer to 12.1 --------

See section 12.1.

****

12.2 When individual forecasts are combined, a weighted average is frequently used. Explain why this is so.

------- Answer to 12.2 --------

(It is important to understand that a "weighted" average is being discussed here – not a simple average). Different weights are useful when one series of forecasts is better than the other series of forecasts under consideration.

****

12.3 Let f_{1t} and f_{2t} be two unbiased forecasts of X_t, with errors e_{1t} and e_{2t}. Denote by σ_1^2 and σ_2^2 the two error variances, and by ρ the correlation between these errors. Let the weighted average composite forecast be

$$f_{ct} = w_1 f_1 + (1 - w_1)f_{2t}$$

with error $\qquad e_{ct} = X_t - f_{ct} = w_1 e_{1t} + (1 - w_1)e_{2t}$

(a) Show that the variance of the error of the composite forecast is

$$\sigma_c^2 = w_1^2 \sigma_1^2 + (1 - w_1)^2 \sigma_2^2 + 2\rho w_1(1 - w_1)\sigma_1 \sigma_2$$

(b) Show that this expression for the variance of the error of the composite forecast can be written as

$$\sigma_c^2 = (\sigma_1^2 + \sigma_2^2 - 2\rho\sigma_1\sigma_2)w_1^2 - 2(\sigma_2^2 - \rho\sigma_1\sigma_2)w_1 + \sigma_2^2$$

$$= (\sigma_1^2 + \sigma_2^2 - 2\rho\sigma_1\sigma_2)\{w_1 - [\sigma_2^2 - \rho\sigma_1\sigma_2]/[\sigma_1^2 + \sigma_2^2 - 2\rho\sigma_1\sigma_2]\}^2$$

$$+ [\sigma_1^2\sigma_2^2(1 - \rho^2)]/[\sigma_1^2 + \sigma_2^2 - 2\rho\sigma_1\sigma_2]$$

(c) Using the result in (b), show that the value of the weight w_1 for which the variance of the error of the composite forecast is the smallest is

$$w_1 = [\sigma_2^2 - \rho\sigma_1\sigma_2]/[\sigma_1^2 + \sigma_2^2 - 2\rho\sigma_1\sigma_2]$$

(d) The value of w_1 in (c) is often called the "optimal weight". In practice it cannot be found, since σ_1^2, σ_2^2 and ρ will not be known.
   (i) Show that the regression-based weight (12.2.5) follows from substituting for σ_1^2, σ_2^2 and ρ their natural sample estimates based on the last n sets of forecast errors.
   (ii) Show that the weight (12.2.4) follows from substituting zero for ρ and the natural estimates based on the last n sets of forecast errors for σ_1^2 and σ_2^2.

(e) Using the result of (b), show that if the "optimal weight" w_1 of (c) is used, the variance of the error of the composite forecast is

$$\sigma_c^2 = [\sigma_1^2\sigma_2^2(1 - \rho^2)]/[\sigma_1^2 + \sigma_2^2 - 2\rho\sigma_1\sigma_2]$$

(f) Using the result of (e), show that if the "optimal weight" w_1 is used,

$$\sigma_c^2 < \sigma_1^2$$

except in the special cases

$$\sigma_1^2 = 0$$
$$\sigma_1^2 = \sigma_2^2, \quad \text{and} \quad \rho = 1$$
$$\rho = \sigma_1/\sigma_2$$

(a)   Since $\qquad\qquad\qquad\qquad\qquad e_{ct} = w_1 e_{1t} + (1 - w_1)e_{2t}$

then squaring both sides, one gets

$$e_{ct}^2 = w_1^2 \sigma_1^2 + (1 - w_1)^2 e_{2t}^2 + 2w_1(1 - w_1)e_{1t}e_{2t}$$

Then, taking expectations of both sides:

$$\sigma_c^2 = w_1^2 \sigma_1^2 + (1 - w_1)^2 \sigma_2^2 + 2w_1(1 - w_1)Cov(e_{1t},e_{2t})$$

and since $\rho = Cov(e_{1t},e_{2t})/\sigma_1\sigma_2$

$$\sigma_c^2 = w_1^2 \sigma_1^2 + (1 - w_1)^2 \sigma_2^2 + 2\rho w_1(1 - w_1)\sigma_1\sigma_2$$

(b)   Multiplying out several terms in the last equation

$$\sigma_c^2 = w_1^2 \sigma_1^2 + (1 - 2w_1 + w_1^2)\sigma_2^2 + 2\rho(w_1 - w_1^2)\sigma_1\sigma_2$$

$$= w_1^2 \sigma_1^2 + \sigma_2^2 - 2w_1\sigma_2^2 + w_1^2\sigma_2^2 + 2\rho\sigma_1\sigma_2 w_1 - 2\rho\sigma_1\sigma_2 w_1^2$$

$$= (\sigma_1^2 + \sigma_2^2 - 2\rho\sigma_1\sigma_2)w_1^2 - 2(\sigma_2^2 - \rho\sigma_1\sigma_2)w_1 + \sigma_2^2$$

$$= (\sigma_1^2 + \sigma_2^2 - 2\rho\sigma_1\sigma_2) \{w_1^2 - 2(\sigma_2^2 - \rho\sigma_1\sigma_2)w_1/[\sigma_1^2 + \sigma_2^2 - 2\rho\sigma_1\sigma_2]\} + \sigma_2^2$$

$$= (\sigma_1^2 + \sigma_2^2 - 2\rho\sigma_1\sigma_2)$$

$$\times\{w_1^2 - 2(\sigma_2^2 - \rho\sigma_1\sigma_2)w_1/[\sigma_1^2 + \sigma_2^2 - 2\rho\sigma_1\sigma_2] + (\sigma_2^2 - \rho\sigma_1\sigma_2)^2/[\sigma_1^2 + \sigma_2^2 - 2\rho\sigma_1\sigma_2]^2\}$$

$$- (\sigma_2^2 - \rho\sigma_1\sigma_2)^2/[\sigma_1^2 + \sigma_2^2 - 2\rho\sigma_1\sigma_2] + \sigma_2^2$$

where the last two terms of the above equation:

$$- (\sigma_2^2 - \rho\sigma_1\sigma_2)^2/[\sigma_1^2 + \sigma_2^2 - 2\rho\sigma_1\sigma_2] + \sigma_2^2$$

$$= (\sigma_1^2 + \sigma_2^2 - 2\rho\sigma_1\sigma_2)^{-1} [-(\sigma_2^2 - \rho\sigma_1\sigma_2)^2 + \sigma_2^2(\sigma_1^2 + \sigma_2^2 - 2\rho\sigma_1\sigma_2)]$$

$$= (\sigma_1^2 + \sigma_2^2 - 2\rho\sigma_1\sigma_2)^{-1} [-\sigma_2^4 + 2\rho\sigma_1\sigma_2^3 - \rho^2\sigma_1^2\sigma_2^2 + \sigma_1^2\sigma_2^2 + \sigma_2^4 - 2\rho\sigma_1\sigma_2^3]$$

$$= \sigma_1^2\sigma_2^2(1 - \rho^2)/(\sigma_1^2 + \sigma_2^2 - 2\rho\sigma_1\sigma_2)$$

Thus $\sigma_c^2 = (\sigma_1^2 + \sigma_2^2 - 2\rho\sigma_1\sigma_2)$

$$\times\{w_1^2 - 2(\sigma_2^2 - \rho\sigma_1\sigma_2)w_1/[\sigma_1^2 + \sigma_2^2 - 2\rho\sigma_1\sigma_2] + (\sigma_2^2 - \rho\sigma_1\sigma_2)^2/[\sigma_1^2 + \sigma_2^2 - 2\rho\sigma_1\sigma_2]^2\}$$

$$+ \sigma_1^2\sigma_2^2(1 - \rho^2)/(\sigma_1^2 + \sigma_2^2 - 2\rho\sigma_1\sigma_2)$$

$$= (\sigma_1^2 + \sigma_2^2 - 2\rho\sigma_1\sigma_2) \{w_1 - [\sigma_2^2 - \rho\sigma_1\sigma_2]/[\sigma_1^2 + \sigma_2^2 - 2\rho\sigma_1\sigma_2]\}^2$$

$$+ [\sigma_1^2\sigma_2^2(1 - \rho^2)]/[\sigma_1^2 + \sigma_2^2 - 2\rho\sigma_1\sigma_2]$$

(c)   Since σ_1^2, σ_2^2, and ρ are fixed, clearly the value if w_1 that minimizes σ_c^2 is

$$w_1 = [\sigma_2^2 - \rho\sigma_1\sigma_2]/[\sigma_1^2 + \sigma_2^2 - 2\rho\sigma_1\sigma_2]$$

(d)(i)   The regression-based weight 12.2.5 is essentially:

$$\hat{w}_1 = (\Sigma e_{2t}^2 - \Sigma e_{1t}e_{2t}) \, / \, (\Sigma e_{1t}^2 + \Sigma e_{2t}^2 - 2\Sigma e_{1t}e_{2t}) \qquad\qquad 12.2.5$$

Since $w_1 = [\sigma_2^2 - \rho\sigma_1\sigma_2]/[\sigma_1^2 + \sigma_2^2 - 2\rho\sigma_1\sigma_2]$

or, as $\rho\sigma_1\sigma_2 = Cov(e_{1t},e_{2t})$; $w_1 = [\sigma_2^2 - Cov(e_{1t},e_{2t})]/[\sigma_1^2 + \sigma_2^2 - 2\rho\sigma_1\sigma_2]$

The natural sample estimates of $\sigma_1^2 = \Sigma e_{1t}^2/n$; $\sigma_2^2 = \Sigma e_{2t}^2/n$; and $Cov(e_{1t},e_{2t}) = \Sigma e_{1t}e_{2t}/n$ where all summations are over the last n forecast errors. Thus substituting these sample estimates into the above expression for w_1 yields:

$$\hat{w}_1 = (\Sigma e_{2t}^2 - \Sigma e_{1t}e_{2t}) \, / \, (\Sigma e_{1t}^2 + \Sigma e_{2t}^2 - 2\Sigma e_{1t}e_{2t})$$

------- Answer to 12.3dii --------

(d)(ii)   The weight 12.2.4 is essentially:

$$\hat{w}_1 = (\Sigma e_{2t}^2) \, / \, (\Sigma e_{1t}^2 + \Sigma e_{2t}^2) \qquad\qquad 12.2.4$$

Using the results from above, if $\rho = 0$, then the optimal weight is

$$w_1 = \sigma_2^2/(\sigma_1^2 + \sigma_2^2)$$

so, as above substituting the sample estimates of $\sigma_1^2 = \Sigma e_{1t}^2/n$ and $\sigma_2^2 = \Sigma e_{2t}^2/n$ gives

$$\hat{w}_1 = (\Sigma e_{2t}^2) \, / \, (\Sigma e_{1t}^2 + \Sigma e_{2t}^2) \qquad\qquad 12.2.4$$

where the summations agains are over the last n forecasts errors.

(e)   Quite simply, if the optimal weight

$$w_1 = [\sigma_2^2 - \rho\sigma_1\sigma_2]/[\sigma_1^2 + \sigma_2^2 - 2\rho\sigma_1\sigma_2]$$

is used, then, the variance of the composite forecast, which from above is

$$\sigma_c^2 = (\sigma_1^2 + \sigma_2^2 - 2\rho\sigma_1\sigma_2) \, \{w_1 - [\sigma_2^2 - \rho\sigma_1\sigma_2]/[\sigma_1^2 + \sigma_2^2 - 2\rho\sigma_1\sigma_2]\}^2$$
$$+ \, [\sigma_1^2\sigma_2^2(1 - \rho^2)]/[\sigma_1^2 + \sigma_2^2 - 2\rho\sigma_1\sigma_2]$$

becomes $\sigma_c^2 = [\sigma_1^2\sigma_2^2(1 - \rho^2)]/[\sigma_1^2 + \sigma_2^2 - 2\rho\sigma_1\sigma_2]$

since the first term becomes zero.

(f)   Let's see what $\sigma_c^2 < \sigma_1^2$ means. If $\sigma_c^2 < \sigma_1^2$ then

$$\sigma_1^2 > [\sigma_1^2\sigma_2^2(1 - \rho^2)]/[\sigma_1^2 + \sigma_2^2 - 2\rho\sigma_1\sigma_2]$$

or $$\sigma_1^4 + \sigma_1^2\sigma_2^2 - 2\rho\sigma_1^3\sigma_2 > \sigma_1^2\sigma_2^2 - \rho^2\sigma_1^2\sigma_2^2$$

or $$\sigma_1^4 - 2\rho\sigma_1^3\sigma_2 + \rho^2\sigma_1^2\sigma_2^2 > 0$$

or $$\sigma_1^2(\sigma_1^2 - 2\rho\sigma_1\sigma_2 + \rho^2\sigma_2^2) > 0$$

or $$\sigma_1^2(\sigma_1 - \rho\sigma_2)^2 > 0$$

Summarizing: if $\sigma_c^2 < \sigma_1^2$ then $\sigma_1^2(\sigma_1 - \rho\sigma_2)^2 > 0$

$\sigma_1^2(\sigma_1 - \rho\sigma_2)_2 > 0$ as long as the the left-hand-side is not zero; or as long as the following are **not** true:

(1) $\sigma_1^2 = 0$

(2) $\sigma_1 = \rho\sigma_2$.

Condition (2) can hold in two situations:

(2a) $\rho = \sigma_1/\sigma_2$ and

(2b) $\sigma_1^2 = \sigma_2^2$, and $\rho = 1$

$$\text{*****************************}$$

12.4 The accompanying table shows product sales for six consecutive months, together with two sets of one month ahead forecasts of these sales. Also shown are forecasts for a seventh month. Assume that both sets of forecasts are unbiased. [See the text or the solution below for data].
   (a)   Find the composite forecast for month seven based on equal weights.
   (b)   Find the composite forecast for month seven based on weights inversely proportional to the sums of squares of the last six sets of forecast errors.
   (c)   Find the composite forecast for month seven based on a regression approach using the last six sets of forecast errors.

------- Answer to 12.4 --------

The spreadsheet below contains the data and calculations for the solution of this exercise.

	A	B	C	D	E	F	G
1	t	X(t)	f(1t)	f(2t)	e(1t)²	e(2t)²	e(1t)*e(2t)
2	1	1282	1075	1120	42849	26244	33534
3	2	1043	1169	1097	15876	2916	6804
4	3	923	882	973	1681	2500	-2050
5	4	1146	1253	1341	11449	38025	20865
6	5	1562	1469	1397	8649	27225	15345
7	6	1347	1293	1370	2916	529	-1242
8	7		1087	1205			
9					83420	97439	73256
10		Forecasts for t=7			Sum	Sum	Sum
11	(a)	1146.00 : equal weights					
12	(b)	1141.43			0.538756 = w1 from (12.2.4)		
13	(c)	1121.92			0.704078 = w1 from (12.2.5)		

(a)   The composite forecast for month seven based on equal weights = $(1{,}087 + 1{,}205)/2 = 1{,}146$.

(b)   The sums of squares of the last six sets of forecast errors are 83,420 and 97,439 for f_{1t} and f_{2t} respectively.

Thus the weight w_1 calculated using equation 12.2.4 is

$$\hat{w}_1 = (\Sigma e_{2t}^2) / (\Sigma e_{1t}^2 + \Sigma e_{2t}^2)$$

$$= 97{,}439/(83{,}420 + 97{,}439) = 0.5388$$

Therefore the composite forecast for month seven is

$$\hat{X}_7 = 0.5388 \times 1{,}087 + (1 - 0.5388) \times 1{,}205 = 1141.43$$

(c)   Assuming that the forecasts are unbiased, the regression based weight to be used is given in equation 12.2.5.

$$\hat{w}_1 = (\Sigma e_{2t}^2 - \Sigma e_{1t}e_{2t}) / (\Sigma e_{1t}^2 + \Sigma e_{2t}^2 - 2\Sigma e_{1t}e_{2t})$$

$$= (97{,}439 - 73{,}256)/(83{,}420 + 97{,}439 - 2 \times 73{,}256) = 0.7041$$

Therefore the composite forecast for month seven is

$$\hat{X}_7 = 0.7041 \times 1{,}087 + (1 - 0.7041) \times 1{,}205 = 1121.92$$

****

12.5 The accompanying table shows demand for a product over six consecutive months, together with two sets of one-month ahead forecasts. Also shown are forecasts for the next month. Assume that both sets of forecasts are unbiased. [See the text or the solution below for data].

(a) Find the composite forecast for month seven based on equal weights.

(b) Find the composite forecast for month seven based on weights inversely proportional to the sums of squares of the last six sets of forecast errors.

(c) Using the regression-based approach with the last six sets of forecast errors, find a composite forecast for month seven.

------- Answer to 12.5 --------

The spreadsheet below contains the data and calculations for the solution of this exercise.

	A	B	C	D	E	F	G
1	t	X(t)	f(1t)	f(2t)	e(1t)²	e(2t)²	e(1t)*e(2t)
2	1	682	627	589	3025	8649	5115
3	2	739	763	782	576	1849	1032
4	3	843	891	927	2304	7056	4032
5	4	792	763	779	841	169	377
6	5	647	680	691	1089	1936	1452
7	6	673	659	663	196	100	140
8	7		792	848			
9					8031	19759	12148
10		Forecasts for t=7			Sum	Sum	Sum
11	(a)	820.00 : equal weights					
12	(b)	808.18			0.711011 = w1 from (12.2.4)		
13	(c)	726.01			2.178305 = w1 from (12.2.5)		
14					(f2 is consistently larger than f1)		

(a) The composite forecast for month seven based on equal weights = $(792+848)/2 = 820$.

(b) The sums of squares of the last six sets of forecast errors are 8,031 and 19,759 for f_{1t} and f_{2t} respectively.

Thus the weight w_1 calculated using equation 12.2.4 is

$$\hat{w}_1 = (\Sigma e_{2t}^2) / (\Sigma e_{1t}^2 + \Sigma e_{2t}^2)$$

$$= 19{,}759/(8{,}031+19{,}759) = 0.7110$$

Therefore the composite forecast for month seven is

$$\hat{X}_7 = 0.7110 \times 792 + (1 - 0.7110) \times 848 = 808.18$$

(c)   Assuming that the forecasts are unbiased, the regression based weight to be used is given in equation 12.2.5.

$$\hat{w}_1 = (\Sigma e_{2t}^2 - \Sigma e_{1t}e_{2t}) / (\Sigma e_{1t}^2 + \Sigma e_{2t}^2 - 2\Sigma e_{1t}e_{2t})$$

$$= (19{,}759 - 12{,}148)/(8{,}031 + 19{,}759 - 2\times12{,}148) = 2.1783$$

Therefore the composite forecast for month seven is

$$\hat{X}_7 = 2.1783\times792 + (1 - 2.1783)\times848 = 726.01$$

It is expected that weights will be between zero and one. Since the forecasts f_{1t} and f_{2t} are, on average, above the actual data (ie, biased in this sample), the regression weight compensates for this, thus forcing the weight to be larger than one.

Graph Accompanying Exercise 12.5

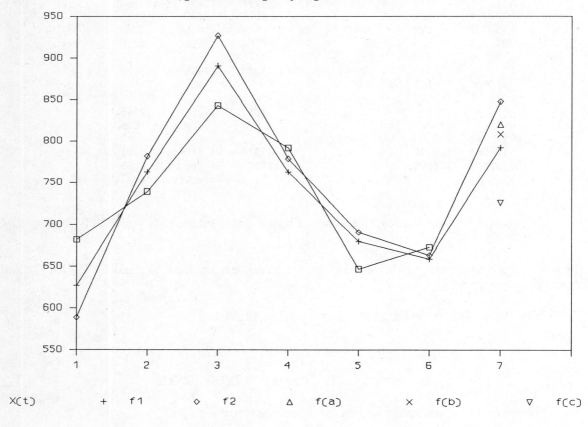

X(t)   +   f1   ◇   f2   △   f(a)   ×   f(b)   ▽   f(c)

****

12.6 Discuss the relative advantage of equal weights, weights inversely proportional to the sum of squared forecast errors, and regression-based weights in the combination of forecasts.

------- Answer to 12.6 --------

When sufficient (and consistent) history of forecasts is available, regression-based weights are always more desireable than the other two, provided that one believes that the performance history is stationary. Thus, equal weights, and weights inversely proportional to the sum of squared forecast errors are useful when no history is available, or very little history is available. To be a little clearer, equal weights would be used if one had no way of knowing the qualities of all, or all-but-one of the forecasts; and "inverse weights" when one has very few observations on the relative performance of the forecasts (too few degrees of freedom for a regression).

****

12.7 The accompanying table shows earnings per share (in dollars) of a corporation over eight consecutive quarters, together with forecasts made one quarter earlier by two financial analysts. Also shown are the analysts' forecasts for the next quarter. Assume that both sets of forecasts are unbiased. [See the text or the solution below for data].

(a) Find the composite forecast for quarter nine based on equal weights.
(b) Find the composite forecast for quarter nine based on weights inversely porportional to the sums of squares of the last four sets of forecast errors.
(c) Find the composite forecast for quarter nine based on weights inversely porportional to the sums of squares of the last eight sets of forecast errors.
(d) Find the composite forecast for quarter nine based on the regression approach using the last four sets of forecast errors.
(e) Find the composite forecast for quarter nine based on the regression approach using the last eight sets of forecast errors.
(f) How would you proceed if you suspected that the individual forecasts were biased.

------- Answer to 12.7 --------

The spreadsheet below contains the data and calculations for the solution of this exercise.

	A	B	C	D	E	F	G	H
1	t	X(t)	f(1t)	f(2t)	e(1t)²	e(2t)²	e(1t)*e(2t)	
2	1	10.25	9.50	8.75	0.5625	2.2500	1.1250	
3	2	14.75	13.50	12.25	1.5625	6.2500	3.1250	
4	3	15.50	16.75	16.25	1.5625	0.5625	0.9375	
5	4	12.00	12.50	13.25	0.2500	1.5625	0.6250	
6	5	15.50	14.25	14.25	1.5625	1.5625	1.5625	
7	6	19.25	18.50	17.50	0.5625	3.0625	1.3125	
8	7	16.50	17.75	17.25	1.5625	0.5625	0.9375	
9	8	14.75	15.50	16.75	0.5625	4.0000	1.5000	
10	9		13.75	12.50				
11					8.1875	19.8125	11.1250	< SUM (8)
12					4.2500	9.1875	5.3125	< SUM (4)
13	(a)	13.1250	equal	weights				
14	(b)	13.3547			0.6837			
15	(c)	13.3845			0.7076			
16	(d)	14.2222			1.3778			
17	(e)	14.3886			1.5109			
18	(f)	14.5362			2.2315	1.4323	-0.5911	
19								
20								
21			Regression	Output:				
22		Constant			2.231509			
23		Std Err of Y Est			1.004919			
24		R Squared			0.903304			
25		No. of Observations			8			
26		Degrees of Freedom			5			
27				f(1t)	f(2t)			
28		X Coefficient(s)		1.432261	-0.59111			
29		Std Err of Coef.		0.448321	0.439980			

(a)   The composite forecast for quarter nine based on equal weights = $(13.75+12.50)/2 = 13.125$

(b)   The sums of squares of the last four sets of forecast errors are 4.25 and 9.1875 for f_{1t} and f_{2t} respectively.

Thus the weight w_1 calculated using equation 12.2.4 is

$$\hat{w}_1 = (\Sigma e_{2t}^2) / (\Sigma e_{1t}^2 + \Sigma e_{2t}^2)$$

$$= 9.1875/(4.25+9.1875) = 0.6837$$

Therefore the composite forecast for quarter nine is = $0.6837 \times 13.75 + (1 - 0.6837) \times 12.5 = 13.3547$

(c)   The sums of squares of the last eight sets of forecast errors are 8.1875 and 19.8125 for f_{1t} and f_{2t} respectively.

Thus the weight w_1 calculated using equation 12.2.4 is

$$\hat{w}_1 = (\Sigma e_{2t}^2) / (\Sigma e_{1t}^2 + \Sigma e_{2t}^2)$$

$$= 19.8125/(8.1875 + 19.8125) = 0.7076$$

Therefore the composite forecast for quarter nine is

$$\hat{X}_9 = 0.7076 \times 13.75 + (1 - 0.7076) \times 12.5 = 13.3845$$

(d)   Assuming that the forecasts are unbiased, the regression based weight to be used is given in equation 12.2.5.
For the last four sets of forecast errors, $\Sigma e_{1t}^2 = 4.25$, $\Sigma e_{2t}^2 = 9.1875$, and $\Sigma e_{1t}e_{2t} = 5.3125$

$$\hat{w}_1 = (\Sigma e_{2t}^2 - \Sigma e_{1t}e_{2t}) / (\Sigma e_{1t}^2 + \Sigma e_{2t}^2 - 2\Sigma e_{1t}e_{2t})$$

$$= (9.1875 - 5.3125)/(4.25 + 9.1875 - 2 \times 5.3125) = 1.3778$$

(Again might prefer $\hat{w}_1 = 1$).

Therefore the composite forecast for quarter nine is

$$\hat{X}_9 = 1.3778 \times 13.75 + (1 - 1.3778) \times 12.5 = 14.2222$$

(e)   For the last four sets of forecast errors, $\Sigma e_{1t}^2 = 8.1875$, $\Sigma e_{2t}^2 = 19.8125$, and $\Sigma e_{1t}e_{2t} = 11.125$

$$\hat{w}_1 = (\Sigma e_{2t}^2 - \Sigma e_{1t}e_{2t}) / (\Sigma e_{1t}^2 + \Sigma e_{2t}^2 - 2\Sigma e_{1t}e_{2t})$$

$$= (19.8125 - 11.125)/(8.1875 + 19.8125 - 2 \times 11.125) = 1.5109$$

(Again might prefer $\hat{w}_1 = 1$).

Therefore the composite forecast for quarter nine is

$$\hat{X}_9 = 1.5109 \times 13.75 + (1 - 1.5109) \times 12.5 = 14.3886$$

(f)   If one suspected that the forecasts were biased one would run a regression of X_t on f_{1t} and f_{2t} without constraining the intercept to zero, nor that the coefficients of f_{1t} and f_{2t} to add to one. This results of this regression are shown in the range B20..E29.

****

12.8 The accompanying table shows product sales for six consecutive months, together with three sets of one-month ahead forecasts. Also shown are forecasts for a seventh month. Assume that all three sets of forecasts are unbiased. [See the text or the solution below for data].

(a) Find the composite forecast for month seven based on equal weights.
(b) Find the composite forecast for month seven based on weights inversely proportional to the sums of squares of the last six sets of forecast errors.
(c) Using the regression-based approach with the last six sets of forecast errors, find a composite forecast for month seven.

------- Answer to 12.8 --------

The spreadsheet below contains the data and calculations for the solution of this exercise.

	A	B	C	D	E	F	G	H	I	J	K
1	t	X(t)	f(1t)	f(2t)	f(3t)	e(1t)²	e(2t)²	e(3t)²	X-f3	f1-f3	f2-f3
2	1	1872	1681	1963	1716	36481	8281	24336	156	-35	247
3	2	1639	1725	1701	1649	7396	3844	100	-10	76	52
4	3	1281	1131	1087	1349	22500	37636	4624	-68	-218	-262
5	4	1394	1210	1498	1307	33856	10816	7569	87	-97	191
6	5	1168	1015	1278	1109	23409	12100	3481	59	-94	169
7	6	1340	1531	1438	1280	36481	9604	3600	60	251	158
8	7		1683	1509	1745						
9											
10						160123	82281	43710			
11						MSE1	MSE2	MSE3			
12											
13	(a)	1645.7		0.3333	0.3333	0.3333			Regression Output:		
14	(b)	1666.1		0.1513	0.2944	0.5543			Constant		0
15	(c)	1647.6		-0.1171	0.4437	0.6735			Std Err of Y Est		31.9141
16									R Squared		0.86539
17									No. of Observations		6
18									Degrees of Freedom		4
19											
20									X Coefficient(s)-0.1171 0.44365		
21									Std Err of Coef.0.09181 0.07174		

(a)   The composite forecast for month seven based on equal weights = $(1{,}683 + 1{,}509 + 1{,}745)/3 = 1645.7$

(b)   The sums of squares of the last six sets of forecast errors are 160123, 82281, and 43710 for f_{1t}, f_{2t} and f_{3t} respectively.

Thus the weight w_1 calculated using equation 12.2.3 is

$$\hat{w}_1 = (\Sigma e_{1t}^2)^{-1} / [(\Sigma e_{1t}^2)^{-1} + (\Sigma e_{2t}^2)^{-1} + (\Sigma e_{3t}^2)^{-1}]$$

$$\hat{w}_1 = 160123^{-1}/(160123^{-1} + 82281^{-1} + 43710^{-1}) = 0.1513$$

Similarly $\hat{w}_2 = 82281^{-1}/(160123^{-1} + 82281^{-1} + 43710^{-1}) = 0.2944$

and $\hat{w}_3 = 43710^{-1}/(160123^{-1} + 82281^{-1} + 43710^{-1}) = 0.5543$

Therefore the composite forecast for month seven is

$$\hat{X}_7 = 0.1513 \times 1{,}683 + 0.2944 \times 1{,}509 + 0.5543 \times 1{,}745 = 1666.1$$

(c)   Assuming that the forecasts are unbiased, the regression based weights are estimated with a regression of $(X_t - f_{3t})$ on $(f_{1t} - f_{3t})$ and $(f_{2t} - f_{3t})$. The regression is shown in the above spreadsheet in the range H13..K21.

The estimated weights are then $\hat{w}_1 = -0.1171$, $\hat{w}_2 = 0.4437$, and $\hat{w}_3 = (1 - \hat{w}_1 - \hat{w}_2) = 0.6735$

Therefore the composite forecast for month seven is

$$\hat{X}_7 = -0.1171 \times 1{,}683 + 0.4437 \times 1{,}509 + 0.6735 \times 1{,}745 = 1647.6$$

****

12.9   The accompanying table shows demand for a product over 12 consecutive months, together with three sets of one-month ahead forecasts. Also shown are forecasts for the next month. Assume that all three sets of forecasts are unbiased. [See the text or the solution below for data].

(a)   Find the composite forecast for month 13 based on equal weights.
(b)   Find the composite forecast for month 13 based on weights inversely porportional to the sums of squares of the last six sets of forecast errors.
(c)   Find the composite forecast for month 13 based on weights inversely porportional to the sums of squares of the last 12 sets of forecast errors.
(d)   Find the composite forecast for month 13 based on the regression approach using the last six sets of forecast errors.
(e)   Find the composite forecast for month 13 based on the regression approach using the last 12 sets of forecast errors.
(f)   How would you proceed if you suspected that the individual forecasts were biased.

------- Answer to 12.9 --------

The spreadsheet below contains the data and calculations for the solution of this exercise.

	A	B	C	D	E	F	G	H	I	J	K
1	t	X(t)	f(1t)	f(2t)	f(3t)	e(1t)²	e(2t)²	e(3t)²	X-f3	f1-f3	f2-f3
2	1	971	901	989	998	4900	324	729	70	-18	-27
3	2	1129	1056	1042	1087	5329	7569	1764	73	87	42
4	3	1135	1191	1183	1079	3136	2304	3136	-56	-48	56
5	4	1362	1280	1395	1423	6724	1089	3721	82	-33	-61
6	5	1287	1359	1327	1186	5184	1600	10201	-72	-40	101
7	6	1079	1010	1031	1143	4761	2304	4096	69	48	-64
8	7	1120	1035	1080	991	7225	1600	16641	85	40	129
9	8	986	923	995	1067	3969	81	6561	63	-9	-81
10	9	923	959	902	1015	1296	441	8464	-36	21	-92
11	10	834	729	875	806	11025	1681	784	105	-41	28
12	11	898	795	843	930	10609	3025	1024	103	55	-32
13	12	875	806	821	810	4761	2916	4225	69	54	65
14	13		982	871	998						
15											
16						68919	24934	61346	<SUM(12)		
17						38885	9744	37699	<SUM(6)		
18				w1	w2	w3					
19	(a)	950.3		0.3333	0.3333	0.3333					
20	(b)	911.2		0.1661	0.6627	0.1713					
21	(c)	922.9		0.2046	0.5655	0.2299					
22	(d)	952.8		0.6042	0.2798	0.1160					
23	(e)	998.6		0.7427	-0.0982	0.3555					
24	(f)	958.6	112.66	0.2628	0.4521	0.1945					

```
            Regression Output:
Constant                      0
Std Err of Y Est        87.7992
R Squared               -1.2565 SIC!
No. of Observations           6
Degrees of Freedom            4

X Coefficient(s)0.60420 0.27980
Std Err of Coef.0.91573 0.46555


            Regression Output:
Constant                      0
Std Err of Y Est        73.9649
R Squared               -0.2649 SIC!
No. of Observations          12
Degrees of Freedom           10

X Coefficient(s)0.74266 -0.0982
Std Err of Coef.0.46854 0.29871


            Regression Output:
Constant                112.661
Std Err of Y Est        39.0929
R Squared               0.95918
No. of Observations          12
Degrees of Freedom            8

X Coefficient(s)0.26282 0.45206 0.19452
Std Err of Coef.0.19367 0.23255 0.14806
```

(a)   The composite forecast for month 13 based on equal weights $= (982+871+998)/3 = 950.3$

(b)   The sums of squares of the last six sets of forecast errors are 38885, 9744, and 37699 for f_{1t}, f_{2t} and f_{3t} respectively.

Thus the weight w_1 calculated using equation 12.2.3 is

$$\hat{w}_1 = (\Sigma e_{1t}^2)^{-1} / [(\Sigma e_{1t}^2)^{-1} + (\Sigma e_{2t}^2)^{-1} + (\Sigma e_{3t}^2)^{-1}]$$

$$\hat{w}_1 = 38885^{-1}/(38885^{-1} + 9744^{-1} + 37699^{-1}) = 0.1661$$

Similarly $\hat{w}_2 = 9744^{-1}/(38885^{-1} + 9744^{-1} + 37699^{-1}) = 0.6627$

and $\hat{w}_3 = 37699^{-1}/(38885^{-1} + 9744^{-1} + 37699^{-1}) = 0.1713$

Therefore the composite forecast for month 13 is

$$\hat{X}_{13} = 0.1661 \times 982 + 0.6627 \times 871 + 0.1713 \times 998 = 911.2$$

(c)   The sums of squares of the last 12 sets of forecast errors are 68919, 24934, and 61346 for f_{1t}, f_{2t} and f_{3t} respectively.

Thus the weight w_1 calculated using equation 12.2.3 is

$$\hat{w}_1 = (\Sigma e_{1t}^2)^{-1} / [(\Sigma e_{1t}^2)^{-1} + (\Sigma e_{2t}^2)^{-1} + (\Sigma e_{3t}^2)^{-1}]$$

$$\hat{w}_1 = 68919^{-1}/(68919^{-1} + 24934^{-1} + 61346^{-1}) = 0.2046$$

Similarly $\hat{w}_2 = 24934^{-1}/(68919^{-1} + 24934^{-1} + 61346^{-1}) = 0.5655$

and $\hat{w}_3 = 61346^{-1}/(68919^{-1} + 24934^{-1} + 61346^{-1}) = 0.2299$

Therefore the composite forecast for month 13 is

$$\hat{X}_{13} = 0.2046 \times 982 + 0.5655 \times 871 + 0.2299 \times 998 = 922.9$$

(d)   Assuming that the forecasts are unbiased, the regression based weights are estimated with a regression of $(X_t - f_{3t})$ on $(f_{1t} - f_{3t})$ and $(f_{2t} - f_{3t})$. The regression on the last six sets of forecasts is shown in the above spreadsheet in the range B27..E32.

The estimated weights are then $\hat{w}_1 = 0.6042$, $\hat{w}_2 = 0.2798$, and $\hat{w}_3 = (1 - \hat{w}_1 - \hat{w}_2) = 0.1160$

Therefore the composite forecast for month 13 is

$$= 0.6042 \times 982 + 0.2798 \times 871 + 0.1160 \times 998 = 952.8$$

(e)   The regression on the last 12 sets of forecasts is shown in the above spreadsheet in the range B38..E43.

The estimated weights are then $\hat{w}_1 = 0.7427$, $\hat{w}_2 = -0.0982$, and $\hat{w}_3 = (1 - \hat{w}_1 - \hat{w}_2) = 0.3555$

Therefore the composite forecast for month 13 is

$$\hat{X}_{13} = 0.7427 \times 982 - 0.0982 \times 871 + 0.3555 \times 998 = 998.6$$

(f)   If one suspects that the forecasts are biased, one estimates a regression of X_t, on f_{1t}, f_{2t} and f_{3t} without any restrictions. The regression on the last 12 sets of forecasts is shown in the above spreadsheet in the range B49..F57.

The estimated equation is: $X_t = 122.66 + 0.2628f_{1t} + 0.4521f_{2t} + 0.1945f_{3t}$

and so the forecast for month 13 is

$X_{13} = 122.66 + 0.2628 \times 982 + 0.4521 \times 871 + 0.1945 \times 998 = 958.6$

****

12.10 The accompanying table shows U.S. unemployment rate over 33 consecutive quarters, together with five sets of one-quarter ahead forecasts, made respectively by the U.C.L.A. Business Forecasting Project, Merrill Lynch Economics Inc., The Conference Board, Data Resources Inc., and Wharton E.F.A. Inc.. Also shown are forecasts for the next quarter. Assume that all five sets of forecasts are unbiased. [See the text or the solution below for data].

(a)   Find all composite forecasts based on equal weights for 1980 I through 1988 II.
(b)   Find the sums of squared forecast errors for all individual forecasts and the equal wieghts composite forecasts over the period 1980 I through 1988 I. Comment on your findings.
(c)   Find all composite forecasts based on weights inversely proportional to the sums of squares of the last eight sets of forecast errors for 1982 I through 1988 II.
(d)   Find the sums of squared forecast errors for all individual forecasts and the composite forecasts of part (c) over the period 1982 I through 1988 I. Comment on your findings.
(e)   Find the composite forecast for 1988 II based on the regression approach, using all information from the previous 33 quarters.

-------- Answer to 12.10 --------

(a)   See the accompanying spreadsheet, column *I*.

(b)   The sums of squares for the individual forecasts are in the range *K39..O39*,   while that
       for the equal weights composite forecasts is in *J39*.

       For the period under consideration the sum of squares for the composite forecasts is
       lower than the sum of squares for all of the individual forecasts, except that for forecast
       f_{3t}.   One might be surprised that the composite is not better than the individual forecasts.
       One is tempted to go back to the text and find the section discussing the relative
       performance of composite forecasts (Section 1. of 12.2).

       One should realize that there are cases in which the composite will fare worse than one
       or more of the individual forecasts that it is made up of.   Let's show this with a situation
       where the composite is a equal weighted average of two forecasts.   Following the algebra
       of section 12.2, one has that

$$\sigma_c^2 = (\sigma_1^2 + \sigma_2^2 + 2Cov_{12})/4$$

Let $\sigma_1^2 < \sigma_2^2$ so that $\sigma_2^2 = b^2\sigma_1^2$ where b is some constant, $b > 1$.   Then,

since $\rho = Cov_{12}/\sigma_1\sigma_2$, $Cov_{12} = \rho\sigma_1\sigma_2 = \rho b\sigma_1^2$

$$\sigma_c^2 = (\sigma_1^2 + b^2\sigma_1^2 + 2\rho b\sigma_1^2)/4$$

Thus $\sigma_c^2 > \sigma_1^2$ when $(\sigma_1^2 + b^2\sigma_1^2 + 2\rho b\sigma_1^2)/4 > \sigma_1^2$

or   when $(1 + b^2 + 2\rho b) > 4$

or   when $b^2 + 2\rho b - 3 > 0$

If one studies this quadratic, one will find that although it is true for most values of b and
ρ, it is not always true.   For example, let's use the data for f_{2t} and f_{3t} from this exercise.
Since f_{3t} has the lowest forecast error sum of squares, it will correspond to the first
forecast in the formulas above.   Thus since the forecast error sum of squares for f_{3t} and
f_{2t} are 2.92 and 4.39 respectively, $b^2 = 4.39/2.92 = 1.503$, or $b = 1.226$.   Also, one can
find that the correlation between f_{3t} and f_{2t}, $\rho = .426$.   Putting these two values into the
left-hand-side of the last equation above, yields

$$b^2 + 2\rho b - 3 = 1.503 + 2\times0.426\times1.226 - 3 = -0.452$$

which obviously is not positive, and thus for such a situation the composite based on equal
weights will not fare better than the best of the individual forecasts.

(c)   The composite forecasts based on weights inversely proportional to the sums of squares
       are contained in column *U*.   The weights used for the calculation of these forecasts are
       contained in columns *P* through *T*.   The weights in the first calculated row, row 12 or
       1982 II, are based on the error sums of squares in the range *K4..O11*;   the weights in row
       13 are based on the error sums of squares in the range *K5..O12*;   etc..

Weights inversely proportional to the sums of squares of the last eight set of forecast errors

		C	D	E	F	G	H	I	J	K	L	M	N	O	P	Q	R	S	T	U	V
A	B	X(t)	f(1t)	f(2t)	f(3t)	f(4t)	f(5t)	Avg (a)	(X-avg)²	(X-f1)²	(X-f2)²	(X-f3)²	(X-f4)²	(X-f5)²	SSE1	SSE2	SSE3	SSE4	SSE5	Avg (c)	(X-Avg)² (c)
80	I	6.1	6.6	6.4	6.3	6.1	6.3	6.34	0.058	0.250	0.090	0.040	0.000	0.040						8.97	0.029
80	II	7.5	7.2	7.2	7.3	6.6	6.5	6.96	0.292	0.090	0.090	0.040	0.810	1.000						9.32	0.033
80	III	7.6	7.9	8.3	8.2	7.9	8.1	8.08	0.230	0.090	0.490	0.360	0.090	0.250						9.65	0.064
80	IV	7.5	8.2	7.9	7.4	7.8	7.7	7.80	0.090	0.490	0.160	0.010	0.090	0.040						10.33	0.140
81	I	7.3	7.7	7.5	7.8	7.7	7.6	7.66	0.130	0.160	0.040	0.250	0.160	0.090						10.85	0.205
81	II	7.4	7.5	7.8	7.5	7.4	7.4	7.52	0.014	0.010	0.160	0.010	0.000	0.000						10.21	0.012
81	III	7.2	7.6	7.8	7.7	7.6	7.6	7.66	0.212	0.160	0.360	0.250	0.160	0.160						9.66	0.069
81	IV	8.3	8.0	7.7	7.8	8.0	8.1	7.92	0.144	0.090	0.360	0.250	0.090	0.040						8.91	0.170
82	I	8.8	9.3	8.0	8.9	9.2	9.3	8.94	0.020	0.250	0.640	0.010	0.160	0.250	0.215	0.164	0.238	0.206	0.178	7.95	0.003
82	II	9.5	9.2	9.5	9.5	9.2	9.2	9.32	0.032	0.090	0.000	0.000	0.090	0.090	0.232	0.135	0.264	0.199	0.170	7.67	0.029
82	III	9.9	9.7	9.7	9.7	9.6	9.6	9.66	0.058	0.040	0.040	0.040	0.090	0.090	0.171	0.104	0.201	0.273	0.250	6.95	0.064
82	IV	10.7	10.4	10.2	10.5	10.3	10.2	10.32	0.144	0.090	0.250	0.040	0.160	0.250	0.153	0.112	0.241	0.235	0.260	7.32	0.298
83	I	10.4	11.0	10.9	10.6	11.0	10.8	10.86	0.212	0.360	0.250	0.040	0.360	0.160	0.226	0.109	0.237	0.221	0.207	7.19	0.049
83	II	10.1	10.2	10.3	10.2	10.2	10.2	10.22	0.014	0.010	0.040	0.010	0.010	0.010	0.190	0.101	0.324	0.187	0.199	7.33	0.012
83	III	9.4	9.6	9.4	9.8	9.6	9.7	9.62	0.048	0.040	0.000	0.160	0.040	0.090	0.190	0.106	0.323	0.184	0.197	7.31	0.001
83	IV	8.5	9.0	9.1	8.7	8.9	9.1	8.96	0.212	0.250	0.360	0.040	0.160	0.360	0.187	0.115	0.330	0.182	0.185	7.16	0.045
84	I	7.9	8.1	8.2	7.8	8.1	8.0	8.04	0.020	0.040	0.090	0.010	0.040	0.010	0.144	0.103	0.477	0.152	0.125	6.92	0.026
84	II	7.5	7.6	7.7	7.7	7.6	7.7	7.66	0.026	0.010	0.040	0.040	0.010	0.040	0.155	0.139	0.420	0.150	0.135	6.86	0.031
84	III	7.5	6.9	7.3	6.9	6.9	6.9	6.98	0.270	0.360	0.040	0.360	0.360	0.360	0.173	0.136	0.382	0.167	0.144	7.16	0.113
84	IV	7.1	7.3	7.1	7.5	7.3	7.3	7.30	0.040	0.040	0.000	0.160	0.040	0.040	0.177	0.191	0.293	0.180	0.160	6.98	0.066
85	I	7.3	7.1	7.3	7.2	7.2	7.1	7.18	0.014	0.040	0.000	0.010	0.010	0.040	0.171	0.232	0.232	0.187	0.178	6.86	0.032
85	II	7.3	7.3	7.2	7.4	7.4	7.4	7.34	0.002	0.000	0.010	0.010	0.010	0.010	0.185	0.257	0.185	0.218	0.154	6.61	0.025
85	III	7.1	7.1	7.4	7.3	7.3	7.2	7.30	0.040	0.000	0.090	0.040	0.040	0.010	0.185	0.267	0.182	0.215	0.152	6.03	0.171
85	IV	7.0	7.1	7.2	7.1	7.2	7.2	7.16	0.026	0.010	0.040	0.010	0.040	0.040	0.183	0.227	0.213	0.213	0.164	6.02	0.001
86	I	7.1	7.1	6.9	6.7	6.9	7.0	6.92	0.032	0.000	0.040	0.160	0.040	0.010	0.180	0.314	0.152	0.177	0.177	6.02	0.016
86	II	7.2	6.4	6.9	7.1	7.0	7.0	6.88	0.102	0.640	0.090	0.010	0.040	0.040	0.186	0.358	0.118	0.169	0.169	5.61	0.105
86	III	6.9	7.0	7.2	7.3	7.0	7.2	7.14	0.058	0.010	0.090	0.160	0.010	0.090	0.099	0.360	0.147	0.192	0.203		
86	IV	6.8	6.9	6.9	7.1	6.9	7.1	6.98	0.032	0.010	0.010	0.090	0.010	0.090	0.093	0.202	0.130	0.316	0.259		
87	I	6.7	6.8	6.8	7.2	6.8	6.8	6.88	0.032	0.010	0.010	0.250	0.010	0.010	0.095	0.192	0.145	0.354	0.215		
87	II	6.2	6.6	6.7	6.3	6.6	6.7	6.58	0.144	0.160	0.250	0.010	0.160	0.250	0.101	0.192	0.100	0.364	0.243		
87	III	6.0	6.0	6.7	6.0	6.1	6.0	6.02	0.000	0.000	0.000	0.000	0.010	0.000	0.129	0.183	0.155	0.324	0.210		
87	IV	5.9	6.2	6.0	6.0	6.0	6.0	6.04	0.020	0.090	0.010	0.010	0.010	0.010	0.125	0.198	0.152	0.328	0.198		
88	I	5.7	6.3	6.2	5.9	5.9	6.0	6.06	0.130	0.360	0.250	0.040	0.040	0.090	0.109	0.200	0.145	0.345	0.200		
88	II		5.9	5.5	5.4	5.7	5.6	5.62							0.086	0.154	0.192	0.378	0.189		

| | | | | | | | | 2.898 | 4.290 | 4.390 | 2.920 | 3.350 | 4.060 | | | | | | | 1.742 |
| | | | | | | | | 1.728 | 2.950 | 2.640 | 1.710 | 1.950 | 2.440 | | | | | | | |

<-- SSE 80I to 88I

<-- SSE 82I to 88I -->

EXERCISE 12.10: Spreadsheet

(d)   The sums of squared forecast errors for all individual forecasts and the composite forecasts of part (c) over the period 1982 I through 1988 I are contained in the range *K40..O40* for the individual forecasts, and in cell *V40* for the composite forecasts of part (c). For comparison, although not asked for, the sum of squared forecast errors for the equal weighted composite forecasts for the period 1982 I through 1988 I is shown in cell *J40*.

Similar to the equal weight composite, the composite forecasts of part (c) over the period 1982 I through 1988 I is not as good as f_{3t}.   Further the composite forecasts of part (c) are not as good as the equal weighted composite. Given the comments in the answer to (b) above, one imagine that conditions exist that this will happen – but hopefully it is rare.

(e)   When one does a regression of $(X_t - f_{5t})$ on $(f_{1t} - f_{5t})$, $(f_{2t} - f_{5t})$, $(f_{3t} - f_{5t})$, and $(f_{4t} - f_{5t})$ on all the given data and forcing the intercept to zero, one arrives at the equation:

$$(X_t - f_{5t}) = 0.053(f_{1t} - f_{5t}) + 0.131(f_{2t} - f_{5t}) + 0.587(f_{3t} - f_{5t}) + 0.898(f_{4t} - f_{5t})$$

Thus the regression-based forecast for period 33 is

$$\hat{X}_{33} = 0.053\times5.9 + 0.131\times5.5 + 0.587\times5.4 + 0.898\times5.7 + [1 - (0.053+0.131+0.587+0.898)]\times5.6$$

$$= 5.575$$

****

12.11 The accompanying table shows annualized U.S. percentage growth in gross national product over 33 consecutive quarters, together with five sets of one-quarter ahead forecasts, made respectively by the U.C.L.A. Business Forecasting Project, Merrill Lynch Economics Inc., The Conference Board, Data Resources Inc., and Wharton E.F.A. Inc.. Also shown are forecasts for the next quarter. Assume that all five sets of forecasts are unbiased. [See the text or the solution below for data].

(a)   Find all composite forecasts based on equal weights for 1980 I through 1988 II.
(b)   Find the sums of squared forecast errors for all individual forecasts and the equal wieghts composite forecasts over the period 1980 I through 1988 I. Comment on your findings.
(c)   Find all composite forecasts based on weights inversely proportional to the sums of squares of the last eight sets of forecast errors for 1982 I through 1988 II.
(d)   Find the sums of squared forecast errors for all individual forecasts and the composite forecasts of part (c) over the period 1982 I through 1988 I. Comment on your findings.
(e)   Find the composite forecast for 1988 II based on the regression approach, using all information from the previous 33 quarters.

Weights inversely proportional to the sums of squares of the last eight set of forecast errors (columns SSE1–SSE5).

Row	A	B	C X(t)	D f(1t)	E f(2t)	F f(3t)	G f(4t)	H f(5t)	I Avg (a)	J (X–avg)²	K (X–f1)²	L (X–f2)²	M (X–f3)²	N (X–f4)²	O (X–f5)²	P SSE1	Q SSE2	R SSE3	S SSE4	T SSE5	U Avg (c)	V (X–Avg)² (c)
4	80	I	1.1	-5.0	-2.3	1.0	-0.9	-1.7	-1.78	8.294	37.210	11.560	0.010	4.000	7.840							
5	80	II	-9.1	-2.4	-5.1	-8.5	-4.9	-2.5	-4.68	19.536	44.890	16.000	0.360	17.640	43.560							
6	80	III	1.0	-4.7	-5.0	-6.0	-3.6	-5.1	-4.88	34.574	32.490	36.000	49.000	21.160	37.210							
7	80	IV	5.0	-0.3	0.4	3.0	1.3	2.2	1.32	13.542	28.090	21.160	4.000	13.690	7.840							
8	81	I	6.5	0.7	-1.1	-1.6	-0.9	0.6	-0.46	48.442	33.640	57.760	65.610	54.760	34.810							
9	81	II	-1.9	-0.1	-2.5	1.5	0.4	0.4	-0.06	3.386	3.240	0.360	11.560	5.290	5.290							
10	81	III	-0.6	-0.9	-1.3	-3.0	-0.8	0.1	-1.18	0.336	0.090	0.490	5.760	0.040	0.490							
11	81	IV	-5.2	-5.3	0.8	-4.0	-3.4	-1.8	-2.74	6.052	0.010	36.000	1.440	3.240	11.560							
12	82	I	-3.9	-5.0	-2.5	-2.2	-2.8	-3.4	-3.18	0.518	1.210	1.960	2.890	1.210	0.250	0.166	0.167	0.217	0.249	0.201	-3.11	0.630
13	82	II	1.7	-1.7	2.0	-0.7	-1.4	2.2	0.08	2.624	11.560	0.090	5.760	9.610	0.250	0.196	0.165	0.200	0.240	0.199	-0.04	3.024
14	82	III	0.8	1.5	3.5	0.3	2.1	3.1	2.10	1.690	0.490	7.290	0.250	1.690	5.290	0.217	0.155	0.164	0.219	0.245	2.14	1.789
15	82	IV	-2.5	0.7	2.8	1.0	2.1	2.2	1.76	18.148	10.240	28.090	12.250	21.160	22.090	0.222	0.139	0.179	0.195	0.265	1.72	17.772
16	83	I	3.1	3.1	4.1	4.8	2.8	4.1	3.78	0.462	0.000	1.000	2.890	0.090	1.000	0.293	0.134	0.168	0.183	0.222	3.69	0.344
17	83	II	8.7	4.5	3.8	6.9	3.7	5.4	4.86	14.746	17.640	24.010	3.240	25.000	10.890	0.313	0.111	0.196	0.198	0.182	4.90	14.460
18	83	III	7.9	7.0	7.3	7.1	6.8	8.0	7.24	0.436	0.810	0.360	0.640	1.210	0.010	0.245	0.102	0.294	0.163	0.195	7.22	0.459
19	83	IV	4.5	5.1	4.9	8.5	5.4	6.2	6.02	2.310	0.360	0.160	16.000	0.810	2.890	0.231	0.098	0.330	0.153	0.189	6.45	3.821
20	84	I	8.3	6.1	5.1	6.2	5.6	5.4	5.68	6.864	4.840	10.240	4.410	7.290	8.410	0.231	0.155	0.223	0.161	0.229	5.73	6.627
21	84	II	7.5	5.2	2.5	2.8	3.8	3.7	3.60	15.210	5.290	25.000	22.090	13.690	14.440	0.235	0.152	0.238	0.162	0.213	3.67	14.647
22	84	III	2.7	5.8	5.2	5.2	5.3	6.1	5.52	7.952	9.610	6.250	6.250	6.760	11.560	0.310	0.128	0.199	0.173	0.189	5.57	8.258
23	84	IV	3.9	2.5	4.5	3.0	2.3	3.3	3.12	0.608	1.960	0.360	0.810	2.560	0.360	0.281	0.144	0.202	0.180	0.192	3.01	0.797
24	85	I	1.3	5.0	4.5	2.9	3.2	4.6	4.04	7.508	13.690	10.240	2.560	3.610	10.890	0.260	0.156	0.187	0.184	0.213	4.11	7.915
25	85	II	1.7	5.1	3.5	3.7	3.2	3.1	3.72	4.080	11.560	3.240	4.000	2.250	1.960	0.223	0.158	0.216	0.199	0.204	3.76	4.242
26	85	III	3.3	5.0	3.5	3.1	3.5	3.9	3.80	0.250	2.890	0.040	0.040	0.040	0.360	0.203	0.175	0.172	0.256	0.194	3.81	0.263
27	85	IV	2.4	3.2	2.1	3.3	2.0	2.2	2.56	0.026	0.640	0.090	0.810	0.160	0.040	0.195	0.176	0.174	0.264	0.192	2.52	0.013
28	86	I	3.2	2.5	4.8	4.3	2.7	2.8	3.42	0.048	0.490	2.560	1.210	0.250	0.160	0.179	0.163	0.221	0.249	0.188	3.38	0.032
29	86	II	1.1	5.0	3.8	2.8	2.6	2.9	3.42	5.382	15.210	7.290	2.890	2.250	3.240	0.169	0.170	0.206	0.266	0.196	3.30	4.845
30	86	III	2.9	3.3	1.6	2.0	2.6	2.5	2.40	0.250	0.160	1.690	0.810	0.090	0.160	0.091	0.138	0.275	0.286	0.179	2.31	0.347
31	86	IV	1.7	3.7	1.9	2.3	2.6	1.2	2.34	0.410	4.000	0.040	0.360	0.810	0.250	0.075	0.131	0.268	0.314	0.205	2.22	0.270
32	87	I	4.3	3.9	1.6	1.2	2.5	3.0	2.44	3.460	0.160	7.290	9.610	3.240	1.690	0.068	0.124	0.260	0.348	0.193	2.24	4.261
33	87	II	2.3	3.1	0.7	2.8	2.2	0.9	1.94	0.130	0.640	2.560	0.250	0.010	1.960	0.079	0.110	0.140	0.304	0.352	1.71	0.347
34	87	III	3.8	5.5	2.3	3.8	3.2	1.6	3.28	0.270	2.890	2.250	0.000	0.360	4.840	0.098	0.115	0.148	0.345	0.300	2.93	0.750
35	87	IV	4.2	-1.4	3.2	2.0	2.3	1.4	1.50	7.290	31.360	1.000	4.840	3.610	7.840	0.113	0.160	0.171	0.380	0.221	1.74	6.072
36	88	I	2.3	-7.2	-0.8	1.5	0.4	-0.2	-1.26	12.674	90.250	9.610	0.640	3.610	6.250	0.072	0.158	0.198	0.373	0.197	-0.24	6.453
37	88	II		-3.6	3.1	2.8	1.5	1.6	1.08							0.035		0.258	0.358	0.191	1.93	
38	88	III								247.51	417.61	332.04	243.24	231.19	265.68							108.44
39	88	IV								113.35	237.95	152.71	105.50	111.37	117.08							

<— SSE 80I to 88I (row 38)

<— SSE 82I to 88I —> (row 39)

EXERCISE 12.11: Spreadsheet

------- Answer to 12.11 --------

(a)   See the accompanying spreadsheet, column I.

(b)   The sums of squares for the individual forecasts are in the range $K39..O39$, while that for the equal weights composite forecasts is in $J39$.

The individual forecasts f_{4t} are better than all the other individual forecasts and the equal weighted composite.

(c)   The composite forecasts based on weights inversely proportional to the sums of squares are contained in column U. The weights used for the calculation of these forecasts are contained in columns P through T. The weights in the first calculated row, row 12 or 1982 II, are based on the error sums of squares in the range $K4..O11$; the weights in row 13 are based on the error sums of squares in the range $K5..O12$; etc..

(d)   The sums of squared forecast errors for all individual forecasts and the composite forecasts of part (c) over the period 1982 I through 1988 I are contained in the range $K40..O40$ for the individual forecasts, and in cell $V40$ for the composite forecasts of part (c). For comparison, although not asked for, the sum of squared forecast errors for the equal weighted composite forecasts for the period 1982 I through 1988 I is shown in cell $J40$.

Again, as in Exercise 12.10, the composite of part (c) is worse than the equal weighted composite.

(e)   When one does a regression of $(X_t - f_{5t})$ on $(f_{1t} - f_{5t})$, $(f_{2t} - f_{5t})$, $(f_{3t} - f_{5t})$, and $(f_{4t} - f_{5t})$ on all the given data and forcing the intercept to zero, one arrives at the equation:

$$(X_t - f_{5t}) = -0.153(f_{1t} - f_{5t}) - 0.459(f_{2t} - f_{5t}) + 0.377(f_{3t} - f_{5t}) + 0.737(f_{4t} - f_{5t})$$

Thus the regression-based forecast for period 33 is

$$\hat{X}_{33} = -0.153\times(-3.6) - 0.459\times3.1 + 0.377\times2.8 + 0.737\times1.5 +$$

$$[1 - (-0.153 - 0.459 + 0.377 + 0.737)]\times1.6 = 2.089$$

****

Chapter 13

THE EVALUATION OF FORECASTS

Contents of Chapter 13

Answers to questions at end of chapter.

13.1 We have analyzed the forecasts of Table 13.1. Consider now, based on these data, the actual and predicted changes in this time series.
  (a)   (i)   Plot a graph of predicted change against actual change.
        (ii)   Find the correlation between the predicted change and actual change.
        (iii) Fit by least squares the regression of actual changes on predicted change.
  (b)   Compare the results in part (a) with those found in this chapter relating actual and predicted levels.

------- Answer to 13.1 --------

(a)

(ii)   The correlation between the predicted change and the actual change is 0.5245.

(iii) The least squares equation is $(X_t - X_{t-1}) = 0.5137 + 0.7760 \, (f_{1t} - X_{t-1}) + e_t$

where this equation, and the sample correlation above, are significant.

Graph Accompanying Exercise 13.1

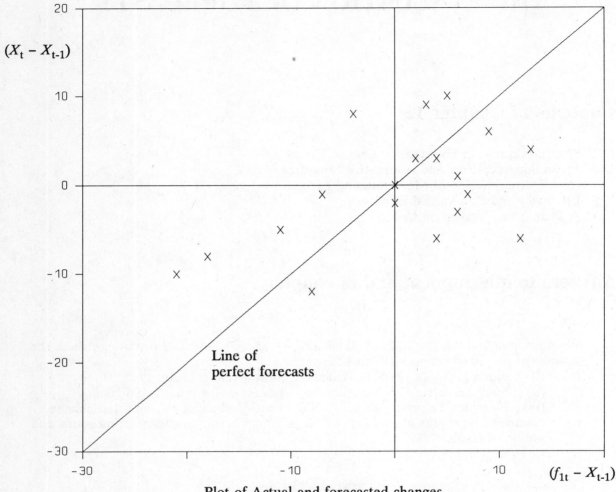

Plot of Actual and forecasted changes

(b)   Anytime comparisons of forecasts of the raw data with those of changes (or percentage changes) one is bound to be disappointed.

****

13.2   The table shows 21 observations and one-step forecasts for the last 20 of these.
   (a)   Find and interpret the mean squared error, the mean absolute error, and the mean absolute percentage error for these forecasts.
   (b)   Compare these forecasts with the naïve "no change" forecasts through Theil's U statistic.
   (c)   Find and interpret Theil's decomposition of mean squared error.
   (d)   Estimate the regression of X_t on f_{1t} and discuss your findings. In particular interpret the coefficient of determination and the Durbin-Watson statistic, and test for Mincer-Zarnowitz efficiency.
   (e)   Let f_{2t} denote the series of naïve "no change" forecasts. By considering weighted averages of f_{1t} and f_{2t}, test whether the forecasts f_{1t} are conditionally efficient with respect to the forecasts f_{2t}.
   (f)   Test jointly for Mincer-Zarnowitz efficiency and conditional efficiency of the forecasts f_{1t} with respect to the forecasts f_{2t}.

------- Answer to 13.2 --------

See the accompanying graph and spreadsheet.

(a)   MSE = 278.0, (RMSE = 16.67), MAE = 14.60, and MAPE = 2.58.

The MSE of 278 means that the average squared error is 278 units; while the MAE of 14.6 means that the average absolute error is 14.6 (the RMSE is similar to this in concept, and value); and the MAPE of 2.58 means that the average absolute percentage error is 2.58%.

(b)   Theil's U statistic provides a measure of the extent to which a set of forecasts is superior to the naïve "no change" forecasts.

$$U = \{\Sigma(X_t - f_{1t})^2 / \Sigma(X_t - X_{t-1})^2\}^{½}$$

$$U = (278.0/382.6)^{½} = .8524$$

so that the f_{1t} forecasts have a mean squared error that is 85.24% of the MSE of the naïve (no change) forecasts.

(c)   Theil's decomposition of MSE:

$$UM = (\bar{f} - \bar{X})^2/MSE = (567.05 - 568.65)^2/278.0 = 0.0092$$

$$UR = (S_f - rS_x)^2/MSE = (16.71 - 0.4457×14.63)^2/278.0 = 0.3736$$

$$UD = (1 - r^2)S_x^2/MSE = (1 - 0.4457^2)/278.0 = 0.6172$$

Remember that "the analyst is looking ideally for very small values of UM and UR." Certainly UM (the *bias proportion*) is small (implying little bias), but UR (the *regression proportion*) is not. This means that the slope of the regression line (see part (d)) is different from one (implying too much variability in the forecasts - see the accompanying graph).

(d)   The regression of X_t on f_{1t} was carried out on the accompanying LOTUS 123 spreadsheet. The results are contained in the range A35..D44. The "Y range" is B3..B22 and the "X range" C3..C22. The regression equation is:

$$X_t = 347.4 + 0.3903f_{1t} + a_t$$
std error $\qquad\qquad\qquad$ (0.1847)

with an R^2 = 19.87% and DW = 2.05. Calculations of the DW for this regression are contained columns I and J.

The DW of about 2 tells us that there is no significant information held in the forecast errors. It is obvious from the following graph that these forecasts are quite poor. (Actually without the point at the left (f_{11} = 508, X_1 = 539, the regression is insignificant). Thus there is little to no significant correlation between the forecasts and the actual data.

EXERCISE 13.2: Spreadsheet

t	X(t)	f1(t)	e(t)²	|e(t)|	|%e(t)|	(X(t)-X(t-1))²	a(t)	a(t)²	(a(t)-a(t-1))²	X-f1	f2-f1	e3(t)²
0	502											
1	539	508	961	31	5.75	1369	-6.6	43.6		31	-6	56.3
2	561	553	64	8	1.43	484	-2.2	4.7	19.7	8	-14	0.6
3	549	568	361	19	3.46	144	-20.0	400.8	318.8	-19	-7	369.8
4	583	558	625	25	4.29	1156	17.9	319.8	1436.6	25	-9	349.8
5	594	576	324	18	3.03	121	21.9	477.7	15.8	18	7	433.9
6	571	586	225	15	2.63	529	-5.0	25.5	723.7	-15	8	35.5
7	576	569	49	7	1.22	25	6.6	43.4	135.4	7	2	37.3
8	592	575	289	17	2.87	256	20.2	410.0	186.6	17	1	402.5
9	568	589	441	21	3.70	576	-9.2	84.9	868.1	-21	3	87.0
10	559	568	81	9	1.61	81	-10.0	100.4	0.6	-9	0	104.9
11	561	556	25	5	0.89	4	-3.3	11.1	44.7	5	3	18.5
12	573	560	169	13	2.27	144	7.1	50.4	109.0	13	1	42.6
13	570	568	4	2	0.35	9	1.0	1.0	37.5	2	5	0.0
14	589	575	196	14	2.38	361	17.2	297.5	264.7	14	-5	321.5
15	561	586	625	25	4.46	784	-15.0	226.4	1042.8	-25	3	232.1
16	543	570	729	27	4.97	324	-26.8	718.3	138.2	-27	-9	659.0
17	570	560	100	10	1.75	729	4.1	16.8	955.0	10	-17	37.6
18	564	566	4	2	0.35	36	-4.2	18.0	69.6	-2	4	25.9
19	582	570	144	12	2.06	324	12.2	148.8	270.2	12	-6	166.3
20	568	580	144	12	2.11	196	-5.7	32.5	320.5	-12	2	34.9

Summary statistics:

	X(t)	f1(t)	e(t)²	|e(t)|	|%e(t)|	(X(t)-X(t-1))²		a(t)²	(a(t)-a(t-1))²			e3(t)²
	568.65	567.05	278.00	14.60	2.58	382.60		171.58				170.80
	X bar	f1 bar	MSE	MAE	MAPE	MSE(2)		MSE				S3
	14.63	16.71	16.67						2.05			
	S(X)	S(f1)	RMSE						DW			

r = 0.4457

U = 0.8524
UM = 0.0092
UR = 0.3736
UD = 0.6172
Sum = 1.0000

M-Z test
F = 5.58
F(2,18) = 3.55
Reject Ho

MZ & cond eff test
F = 3.56
F(3,17) = 3.20
Reject Ho

Regression Output:

	f1
Constant	347.4
Std Err of Y Est	13.81
R Squared	0.1987
No. of Observations	20
Degrees of Freedom	18
X Coefficient(s)	0.3903
Std Err of Coef.	0.1847
t value	2.1126 Sig at 5%

Regression Output:

	(f2-f1)
Constant	0
Std Err of Y Est	16.62
R Squared	0.0473
No. of Observations	20
Degrees of Freedom	19
X Coefficient(s)	-0.563 = w
Std Err of Coef.	0.530
t value	-1.063 insignificant

Cannot reject Ho of conditional efficiency

Regression Output:

	f1	f2
Constant	362.2	
Std Err of Y Est	14.18	
R Squared	0.2023	
No. of Observations	20	
Degrees of Freedom	17	
X Coefficient(s)	0.2200	0.1445
Std Err of Coef.	0.6394	0.5182
t value	0.3441	0.2788

Reject Ho of MZ and conditional efficiency

Mincer-Zarnowitz test for efficiency:

$$H_0: \ X_t = f_{1t} \quad \text{or, said differently} \quad \alpha = 0, \ \beta = 1$$

This null hypothesis is to be rejected if the F statistic is above the critical value on an F distribution with $(2, n - 2)$ degrees of freedom.

$$F = [S_1 - S_2)/2] \ / \ [S_2/(n-2)] \ = \ [(278.0 - 171.58)/2] \ / \ [171.58/18] \ = \ 5.58$$

Since the calculated F of 5.58 is above the critical value on the F distribution with $(2, 18)$ degrees of freedom of 3.55, then the null hypothesis is rejected. These forecasts are not Mincer-Zarnowitz efficient.

Graph Accompanying Exercise 13.2

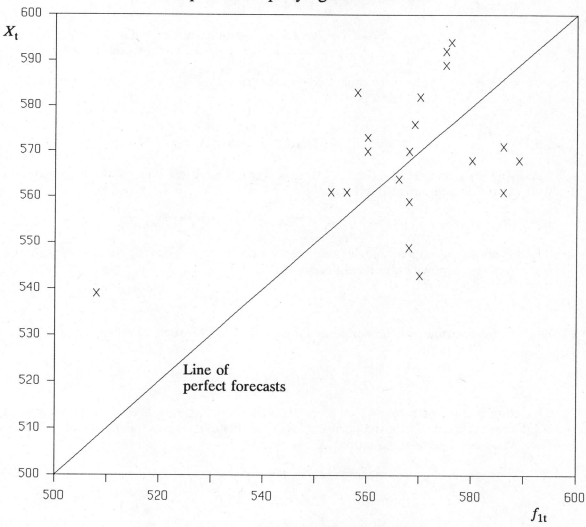

Plot of Actual Data and Forecasts

(e)   Test for conditional efficiency of the forecasts f_{1t} with respect to the no-change forecasts f_{2t}:

H_0: $w = 0$ (that is, the no-change forecasts f_{2t} do not help improve the forecasts f_{1t})

The regression results are on the spreadsheet in the range F35..I43. The equation is:

$$(X_t - f_{1t}) = -0.563(f_{2t} - f_{1t})$$

std error   (0.530)

Obviously, the estimated value of w of -0.563 is not significantly greater than 0. Thus the no-change forecasts do not significantly improve the forecasts f_{1t}.

(f)   Joint test of Mincer-Zarnowitz efficiency and conditional efficiency:

For the regression $X_t = \alpha + \beta_1 f_{1t} + \beta_2 f_{2t} + \epsilon_t$ test

H_0: $\alpha = 0, \beta_1 = 1, \beta_2 = 0$ (that is f_1 contains all information in f_2, and the expectations of f_{1t} are equal to the actual data)

The regression results are contained in the range K35..N43 of the accompanying spreadsheet. The regression is:

$$X_t = 362.2 + 0.2200\, f_{1t} + 0.1445\, f_{2t}$$

std error   (0.6394)   (0.5182)

The hypothesis is rejected if the F statistic is above the critical value of the F distribution with $(3, n - 3)$ degrees of freedom.

$$F = [(S_1 - S_3)/3] / [S_3/(n - 3)] = [(278.0 - 170.8)/3] / [170.8/17] = 3.56$$

which is above the critical value of 3.20 (using an α of 5%). Thus the forecasts f_{1t} are not both Mincer-Zarnowitz and conditionally efficient.

****

13.3 Discuss the relevance of the combination of forecasts in forecast evaluation.

------- Answer to 13.3 --------

The combination of forecasts in forecast evaluation has relevance in the concept of conditional efficiency. See the portion of section 10.3 in the text on conditional efficiency (two paragraphs prior to equation 13.3.4).

****

13.4 The table shows 26 observations and one-step forecasts for the last 25 of these.

  (a) Find and interpret the mean squared error, the mean absolute error, and the mean absolute percentage error for these forecasts.
  (b) Compare these forecasts with the naïve "no change" forecasts through Theil's U statistic.
  (c) Find and interpret Theil's decomposition of mean squared error.
  (d) Estimate the regression of X_t on f_{1t} and discuss your findings. In particular interpret the coefficient of determination and the Durbin-Watson statistic, and test for Mincer-Zarnowitz efficiency.
  (e) Let f_{2t} denote the series of naïve "no change" forecasts. By considering weighted averages of f_{1t} and f_{2t}, test whether the forecasts f_{1t} are conditionally efficient with respect to the forecasts f_{2t}.
  (f) Test jointly for Mincer-Zarnowitz efficiency and conditional efficiency of the forecasts f_{1t} with respect to the forecasts f_{2t}.

------- Answer to 13.4 --------

(a) MSE = 497.92 (RMSE = 22.31), MAE = 19.36, and MAPE = 2.54.

The MSE of 497.92 means that the average squared error is 497.92 units; while the MAE of 19.36 means that the average absolute error is 19.36 (the RMSE is similar to this in concept, and value); and the MAPE of 2.54 means that the average absolute percentage error is 2.54%.

(b) Theil's U statistic provides a measure of the extent to which a set of forecasts is superior to the naïve "no change" forecasts.

$$U = \{\Sigma(X_t - f_{1t})^2 / \Sigma(X_t - X_{t-1})^2\}^{\frac{1}{2}}$$

$$U = (278.0/382.6)^{\frac{1}{2}} = .7765$$

so that the f_{1t} forecasts have a mean squared error that is 77.65% of the MSE of the naïve (no change) forecasts.

(c) Theil's decomposition of MSE:

$$UM = (\bar{f} - \bar{X})^2/MSE = (763.36 - 763.84)^2/497.92 = 0.0005$$

$$UR = (S_f - rS_x)^2/MSE = (42.67 - 0.8644 \times 43.00)^2/497.92 = 0.0607$$

$$UD = (1 - r^2)S_x^2/MSE = (1 - 0.8644^2)/497.92 = 0.9388$$

Remember that "the analyst is looking ideally for very small values of UM and UR." In this case both the UM (the *bias proportion*) is small (implying little bias), and the UR (the *regression proportion*) is also small (implying little deviation from the regression of X on f_1). See the accompanying graph.

	A	B	C	D	E	F	G	H	I	J	K	L	M	N
	t	X(t)	f1(t)	e(t)²	|e(t)|	|%e(t)|	(X(t)−X(t−1))²	a(t)	a(t)²	(a(t)−a(t−1))²	X−f1	f2−f1	e3(t)²	
	0	729												
	1	763	721	1764	42	5.50	1156	36.1	1300.5		42	8	1451.8	
	2	744	753	81	9	1.21	361	−10.8	117.0	2197.5	−9	10	61.1	
	3	728	736	64	8	1.10	256	−12.0	144.1	1.4	−8	8	95.9	
	4	683	729	2116	46	6.73	2025	−50.9	2591.5	1513.4	−46	−1	2643.3	
	5	674	692	324	18	2.67	81	−27.7	765.9	539.8	−18	−9	958.4	
	6	699	691	64	8	1.14	625	−1.8	3.3	669.3	8	−17	55.4	
	7	711	698	169	13	1.83	144	4.1	16.8	3.3	13	1	14.6	
	8	759	729	900	30	3.95	2304	25.1	629.7	440.8	30	−18	384.2	
	9	723	736	169	13	1.80	1296	−17.0	289.2	1772.3	−13	23	108.0	
	10	769	741	784	28	3.64	2116	24.6	607.1	1734.2	28	−18	372.0	
	11	783	771	144	12	1.53	196	12.5	156.4	147.3	12	−2	148.7	
	12	819	800	361	19	2.32	1296	23.2	540.1	115.3	19	−17	356.1	
	13	802	831	841	29	3.62	289	−20.8	431.2	1936.5	−29	−12	543.2	
	14	815	818	9	3	0.37	169	3.6	12.7	591.7	−3	−16	0.1	
	15	782	791	81	9	1.15	1089	−5.9	35.0	89.8	−9	24	2.7	
	16	753	769	256	16	2.12	841	−15.8	248.2	96.7	−16	13	136.6	
	17	766	743	529	23	3.00	169	19.9	395.9	1270.9	23	10	518.9	
	18	740	731	81	9	1.22	676	4.4	18.9	241.7	9	35	208.1	
	19	783	768	225	15	1.92	1849	15.1	228.5	115.9	15	−28	51.1	
	20	798	790	64	8	1.00	225	11.0	120.0	17.4	8	−7	88.3	
	21	823	802	441	21	2.55	625	25.5	650.2	211.6	21	−4	623.2	
	22	841	821	400	20	2.38	324	26.9	726.1	2.1	20	2	806.2	
	23	802	838	1296	36	4.49	1521	−26.9	721.6	2895.5	−36	3	621.3	
	24	779	810	961	31	3.98	529	−25.5	648.8	1.9	−31	−8	733.6	
	25	757	775	324	18	2.38	484	−17.0	288.3	72.1	−18	4	239.7	
		763.84	763.36	497.92	19.36	2.54	825.84		467.47				448.90	
		X bar	f1 bar	MSE	MAE	MAPE	MSE(2)		MSE				S3	

	43.00	42.67	22.31		1.61
	S(X)	S(f1)	RMSE		DW

U =	0.7765
UM =	0.0005
UR =	0.0607
UD =	0.9388
Sum =	1.0000

r = 0.8644

M-Z test
F = 0.75
F(2,23) = 3.42
Accept Ho

MZ & cond eff test
F = 0.80
F(3,22) = 3.44
Accept Ho

Regression Output:

Constant	98.83
Std Err of Y Est	22.54
R Squared	0.7472
No. of Observations	25
Degrees of Freedom	23

	f1
X Coefficient(s)	0.8712
Std Err of Coef.	0.1057
t value	8.2443 Sig at 5%

Regression Output:

Constant	0
Std Err of Y Est	22.46
R Squared	0.0266
No. of Observations	25
Degrees of Freedom	24

	(f2−f1)
X Coefficient(s)	−0.248 = w
Std Err of Coef.	0.303
t value	−0.816 insignificant

Cannot reject Ho of conditional efficiency

Regression Output:

Constant	107.55
Std Err of Y Est	22.59
R Squared	0.7572
No. of Observations	25
Degrees of Freedom	22

	f1	f2
X Coefficient(s)	1.1528	−0.2933
Std Err of Coef.	0.3135	0.3074
t value	3.6765	−0.9541

Cannot reject Ho of MZ and conditional efficiency

EXERCISE 13.4: Spreadsheet

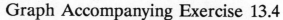

Graph Accompanying Exercise 13.4

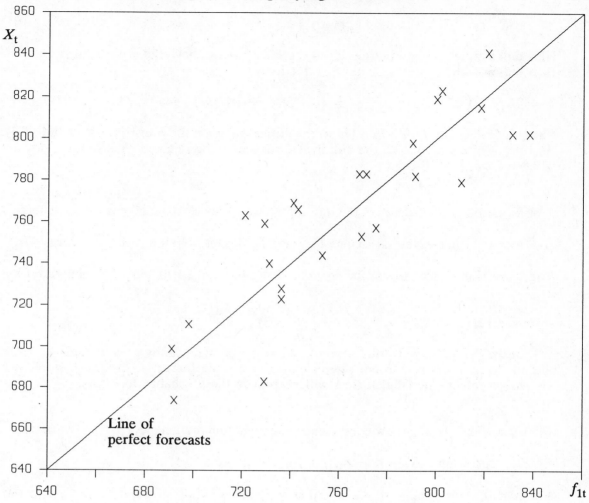

Plot of Actual Data and Forecasts

(d)   The regression of X_t on f_{1t} was carried out on the accompanying LOTUS 123 spreadsheet. The results are contained in the range A40..D48. The "Y range" is B3..B27 and the "X range" C3..C27. The regression equation is:

$$X_t = 98.83 + 0.8712 f_{1t} + a_t$$
std error   (0.1847)

with an R^2 = 74.72% and DW = 1.61 (implying no significant autocorrelation, as the DW of 1.61 > d_U of 1.45. Calculations of the DW for this regression are contained columns I and J. Since there is no significant autocorrelation there is no significant information held in the forecast errors. It is obvious from the following graph that these forecasts are quite poor.

Mincer-Zarnowitz test for efficiency:

$$H_0: \ X_t = f_{1t} \quad \text{or, said differently} \quad \alpha = 0, \ \beta = 1$$

This null hypothesis is to be rejected if the F statistic is above the critical value on an F distribution with $(2, n - 2)$ degrees of freedom.

$$F = [(S_1 - S_2)/2] \ / \ [S_2/(n - 2)] \ = \ [(497.92 - 467.47)/2] \ / \ [467.47/23] \ = \ 0.75$$

Since the calculated F of 0.75 is below the critical value on the F distribution with $(2, 23)$ degrees of freedom of 3.42, the null hypothesis cannot be rejected. These forecasts are Mincer-Zarnowitz efficient.

(e)   Test for conditional efficiency of the forecasts f_{1t} with respect to the no-change forecasts f_{2t}:

$$H_0: \ w = 0 \quad \text{(that is, the no-change forecasts } f_{2t} \text{ do not help improve the forecasts } f_{1t})$$

The regression results are on the spreadsheet in the range F40..I48. The equation is:

$$(X_t - f_{1t}) \ = \ -0.248(f_{2t} - f_{1t})$$

std error $\qquad\qquad\qquad\qquad\qquad$ (0.303)

Obviously, the estimated value of w of -0.248 is not significantly greater than 0. Thus the no-change forecasts do not significantly improve the forecasts f_{1t}. The f_{1t} forecasts are therefore conditionally efficient with respect to the no-change forecasts.

(f)   Joint test of Mincer-Zarnowitz efficiency and conditional efficiency:

For the regression $\quad X_t = \alpha + \beta_1 f_{1t} + \beta_2 f_{2t} + \epsilon_t \quad$ test

$H_0: \ \alpha = 0, \beta_1 = 1, \beta_2 = 0 \qquad$ (that is f_1 contains all information in f_2, and the expectations of f_{1t} are equal to the actual data)

The regression results are contained in the range K40..N48 of the accompanying spreadsheet. The regression is:

$$X_t = 107.55 + 1.1528 \ f_{1t} - 0.2933 \ f_{2t}$$

std error $\qquad\qquad\qquad\qquad$ (0.3135) $\qquad$ (0.3074)

The hypothesis is rejected if the F statistic is above the critical value of the F distribution with $(3, n - 3)$ degrees of freedom.

$$F = [(S_1 - S_3)/3] \ / \ [S_3/(n - 3)] \ = \ [(497.92 - 448.9)/3] \ / \ [448.9/22] \ = \ 0.80$$

which is below the critical value of 3.44 (using an α of 5%). Thus the forecasts f_{1t} are both Mincer-Zarnowitz and conditionally efficient.

****

13.5 Optimally, the errors for h-steps ahead forecasts should follow a moving average of order $(h - 1)$. Explain why this is so, and discuss the consequences for forecast evaluation.

------- Answer to 13.5 --------

Let e_t ($t = 1, 2, \ldots, n$) be a set of h–step forecast errors. Consider e_t, the error made in forecasting X_t at time t–h. Now, if this forecast is optimal, e_t must be uncorrelated with any information available at the time the forecast is made (*i.e.* at time t–h). It therefore follows that

$$\text{Corr.}(e_t, e_{t-j}) = 0 \quad ; \quad j = h, h+1, h+2, \ldots$$

Hence it follows that the process e_t must be MA($h-1$). Note:– there is no requirement that e_t be uncorrelated with e_{t-j} ($j < h$). Indeed, typically these correlations will be non-zero for optimal forecasts. The implication is that the regression-based evaluation methods discussed in the text must be modified to allow for autocorrelated errors of the appropriate type when evaluating forecasts made beyond one step ahead.

****

13.6 In the regression $X_t = \alpha + \beta f_t + \epsilon_t$

the least squares estimates of α and β are

$$b = \Sigma(f_t - \bar{f})(X_t - \bar{X}) / \Sigma(f_t - \bar{f})^2$$

and $a = \bar{X} - b\bar{f}$

(a) Show that $b = 1$ if and only if $S_f = rS_x$

where S_f and S_x are the forecast and actual standard deviations, and r is the correlation between the predicted and actual values.

(b) Show that, if $b = 1$, $a = 0$ if and only if $\bar{X} = \bar{f}$

(c) Hence show that the bias proportion and regression proportion, UM and UR, in Theil's decomposition are both zero if and only if $a = 0$ and $b = 1$.

------- Answer to 13.6 --------

(a) One can write that $b = Cov(f, X)/S_f^2$

and similarly since $r = Cov(f, X)/S_f S_x$

therefore $b = rS_f S_x/S_f^2$

Hence $b = 1$, if and only if $S_f = rS_x$.

(b) If $b = 1$, then $a = \bar{X} - \bar{f}$

and hence $a = 0$, if and only if $\bar{X} = \bar{f}$.

(c) $UM = (\bar{f} - \bar{X})^2/\text{MSE}$ and $UR = (S_f - rS_x)^2/\text{MSE}$

UM and UR can only be zero if $\bar{X} = \bar{f}$ and $S_f = rS_x$, or thus can only be zero if $b = 1$ and $a = 0$.

****

13.7 Consider the regression of X_t on f_t (13.3.1), and the notation (13.2.1)–(13.2.3) of Theil's decomposition.
   (a) Show that the sum of squared residuals from the fitted regression (13.3.1) can be written

$$S_2 = \Sigma(X_t - a - bf_t)^2 = nS_x^2(1 - r^2)2$$

   (b) Hence show that the statistic (13.3.2) for testing Mincer-Zarnowitz efficiency can be written

$$F = [(S_1 - S_2)/2] / [S_2/(n - 2)] = [(UM + UR)/2] / [(1 - UM - UR)/(n - 2)]$$

------- Answer to 13.7 --------

(a)   Since $a = \bar{X} - b\bar{f}$

then $S_2 = \Sigma(X_t - \bar{X} + b\bar{f} - bf_t)^2$

and, if one lets $g_t = f_t - \bar{f}$ = the deviations of f_t from its mean, then

$$S_2 = \Sigma(x_t - bg_t)^2$$
$$= \Sigma x_t^2 - 2b\,\Sigma g_t x_t + b^2\,\Sigma g_t^2$$

Since $S_x^2 = \Sigma x_t^2/n$, $S_f^2 = \Sigma g_t^2/n$, and $Cov(f,X) = \Sigma g_t x_t/n$, then

$$S_2 = nS_x^2 - 2nb\,Cov(f,X) + nb^2S_f^2$$
$$= nS_x^2\,[1 - 2b\,Cov(f,X)/S_x^2 + b^2S_f^2/S_x^2]$$

Since $b = Cov(f,X)/S_f^2$, and $r = Cov(f,X)/S_fS_x$, then

the part of the second term in the parenthesis of the equation for S_2 above is

$$b\,Cov(f,X)/S_x^2 = Cov(f,X)^2/S_x^2S_f^2 = r^2,$$

and also the next term in the parenthesis is

$$b^2S_f^2/S_x^2 = Cov(f,X)^2S_f^2/S_x^2S_f^4 = Cov(f,X)^2/S_x^2S_f^2 = r^2$$

Thus $S_2 = nS_x^2\,[1 - 2r^2 + r^2] = nS_x^2(1 - r^2)$

(b) $F = [(S_1 - S_2)/2] / [S_2/(n - 2)]$

$= \{[n\text{MSE} - nS_x^2(1 - r^2)]/2\} / \{[nS_x^2(1 - r^2)/\text{MSE}]/(n - 2)\}$

$= [(1 - UD)/2] / [UD/(n - 2)] = [(UM + UR)/2] / [(1 - UM - UR)/(n - 2)]$

13.8 Refer to the data of Exercise 2 of Chapter 7, showing 120 observations on soybean meal price. Hold out the last 20 observations for forecasting purposes. fit an ARIMA model to the first 100 observations, and use the fitted model to generate series of forecasts one-step ahead, two-steps ahead, and so on. Evaluate these forecasts.

------- Answer to 13.8 --------

See the accompanying exhibit comprising portion of a LOTUS 123 spreadsheet, and graph.

Graph Accompanying Exercise 13.8

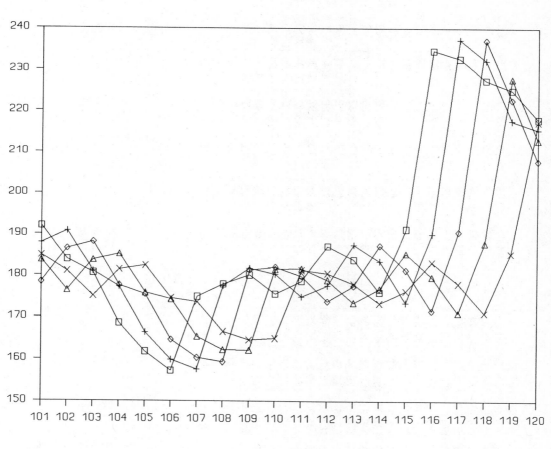

	A	B	C	D	E	F	G	H	I	J	K	L	M	N	O	P	Q	R
99	98	191.3	192.52															
100	99	184.8	189.57	190.84														
101	100	190.7	181.59	186.58	187.93													
102	101	192.0	187.99	178.44	183.70	184.86	16.1	4.01	2.09	183.8	13.56	7.06	68.9	8.30	4.32	50.9	7.14	3.72
103	102	183.9	190.75	186.55	176.50	181.03	47.0	6.85	3.73	7.0	2.65	1.44	54.8	7.40	4.03	8.2	2.87	1.56
104	103	180.7	181.03	188.21	183.79	175.11	0.1	0.33	0.18	56.4	7.51	4.16	9.5	3.09	1.71	31.2	5.59	3.09
105	104	168.6	177.36	177.70	185.27	181.45	76.7	8.76	5.19	82.8	9.10	5.40	277.8	16.67	9.89	165.2	12.85	7.62
106	105	161.8	166.36	175.54	175.91	182.43	20.8	4.56	2.82	188.9	13.74	8.49	199.0	14.11	8.72	425.6	20.63	12.75
107	106	157.2	159.85	164.63	174.30	174.61	7.0	2.65	1.68	55.2	7.43	4.73	292.4	17.10	10.88	303.1	17.41	11.08
108	107	175.0	157.54	160.31	165.35	173.69	305.0	17.46	9.98	215.8	14.69	8.39	93.2	9.65	5.52	1.7	1.31	0.75
109	108	178.0	177.60	159.30	162.22	166.56	0.2	0.40	0.22	349.8	18.70	10.51	249.1	15.78	8.87	130.8	11.44	6.43
110	109	180.2	181.80	181.39	162.11	164.63	2.6	1.60	0.89	1.4	1.19	0.66	327.2	18.09	10.04	242.4	15.57	8.64
111	110	175.7	180.38	182.06	181.62	165.00	21.9	4.68	2.66	40.5	6.36	3.62	35.1	5.92	3.37	114.5	10.70	6.09
112	111	178.7	175.04	179.95	181.72	181.34	13.4	3.66	2.05	1.6	1.25	0.70	9.1	3.02	1.69	7.0	2.64	1.48
113	112	187.2	177.70	173.87	179.04	180.57	90.2	9.50	5.07	177.7	13.33	7.12	66.6	8.16	4.36	44.0	6.63	3.54
114	113	183.9	187.57	177.62	173.59	178.04	13.5	3.67	2.00	39.4	6.28	3.41	106.4	10.31	5.61	34.3	5.86	3.19
115	114	176.1	183.53	187.38	176.90	173.42	55.2	7.43	4.22	127.2	11.28	6.41	0.6	0.80	0.45	7.2	2.68	1.52
116	115	191.3	173.55	181.33	185.39	176.35	315.2	17.75	9.28	99.3	9.97	5.21	34.9	5.91	3.09	223.5	14.95	7.82
117	116	234.7	190.13	171.53	179.72	183.22	1986.1	44.57	18.99	3991.1	63.17	26.92	3022.3	54.98	23.42	2649.9	51.48	21.93
118	117	232.7	237.34	190.63	171.03	178.11	21.6	4.64	2.00	1769.9	42.07	18.08	3802.7	61.67	26.50	2980.6	54.59	23.46
119	118	227.5	232.27	237.14	187.95	171.05	22.8	4.77	2.10	92.9	9.64	4.24	1564.5	39.55	17.39	3187.0	56.45	24.81
120	119	225.1	217.68	222.68	227.81	185.38	55.1	7.42	3.30	5.9	2.42	1.07	7.3	2.71	1.20	1577.5	39.72	17.64
121	120	218.0	215.56	207.78	213.05	217.47	6.0	2.44	1.12	104.5	10.22	4.69	24.5	4.95	2.27	0.3	0.53	0.24
122	t	X	f1	f2	f3	f4	e_1^2	|e1|	|e1/X1|	e_2^2	|e2|	|e2/X2|	e_3^2	|e3|	|e3/X3|	e_4^2	|e4|	|e4/X4|
124		190.42	187.55	184.20	181.35	178.72	153.81	7.86	3.98	379.55	13.23	6.62	512.30	15.41	7.67	609.26	17.05	8.37
125		X bar	f1 bar	f2 bar	f3 bar	f4 bar	MSE1	MAE1	MAPE1	MSE2	MAE2	MAPE2	MSE3	MAE3	MAPE3	MSE4	MAE4	MAPE4
127		23.17	21.33	18.69	15.07	10.78	12.40			19.48			22.63			24.68		
128		Sx	Sf1	Sf2	Sf3	Sf4	RMSE1			RMSE2			RMSE3			RMSE4		

C = 174.46

	UM / UR / UD	MSE1 column	MSE2 column	MSE3 column	MSE4 column
PHI1 = 1.0482	UM =	0.0532	0.1016	0.1604	0.2246
PHI2 = 0.0051	UR =	0.0146	0.0444	0.0311	0.0095
PHI3 = -0.210	UD =	0.9321	0.8538	0.8083	0.7658

$\dfrac{\text{MSE1}}{\text{MSE(no change)}} = 106.5\%$ $\dfrac{\text{MSE2}}{\text{MSE(no change)}} = 109.6\%$ $\dfrac{\text{MSE3}}{\text{MSE(no change)}} = 106.8\%$ $\dfrac{\text{MSE4}}{\text{MSE(no change)}} = 106.9\%$

X = f(f1) Regression Output:

Constant	16.046	
Std Err of Y Est	12.621	2867.3 = S2
R Squared	0.7328	0.6555 = F
No. of Observations	20	< 3.55 thus MZ efficient
Degrees of Freedom	18	

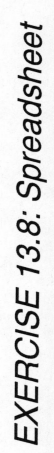

EXERCISE 13.8: Spreadsheet

	A	B	C	D	E	F
142						
143	X Coefficient(s)	0.9297				
144	Std Err of Coef.	0.1322				
145	t value	7.0273	significant			
146						
147	X = f(f2) Regression Output:					
148	Constant	46.700				
149	Std Err of Y Est	18.976	6481.6	= S2		
150	R Squared	0.3961	1.5404	= F		
151	No. of Observations	20	< 3.55 thus MZ efficient			
152	Degrees of Freedom	18				
153						
154	X Coefficient(s)	0.7801				
155	Std Err of Coef.	0.2270				
156	t value	3.4364	significant			
157						
158	X = f(f3) Regression Output:					
159	Constant	57.143				
160	Std Err of Y Est	21.450	8282.4	= S2		
161	R Squared	0.2283	2.1335	= F		
162	No. of Observations	20	< 3.55 thus MZ efficient			
163	Degrees of Freedom	18				
164						
165	X Coefficient(s)	0.7348				
166	Std Err of Coef.	0.3183				
167	t value	2.3082	significant			
168						
169	X = f(f4) Regression Output:					
170	Constant	51.595				
171	Std Err of Y Est	22.769	9331.9	= S2		
172	R Squared	0.1306	2.7516	= F		
173	No. of Observations	20	< 3.55 thus MZ efficient			
174	Degrees of Freedom	18				
175						
176	X Coefficient(s)	0.7767				
177	Std Err of Coef.	0.4723				
178	t value	1.6445	insignificant			

Columns: A B C D E F G H I J K L M N O P Q R

The wording of the exercise left it open as to how many steps ahead to compare - here up to four steps ahead were calculated. Also, the scope of the evaluation was left up to the reader. The following were carried out for the four forecast series: MSE, (RMSE), MAE, MAPE, MSE decomposition, comparison of MSE to the naïve no-change MSE, and a test for Minzer-Zarnowitz efficiency. An ARIMA(3,0,0) model (with constant) is the model used to generate the one-, two-, three-, and four-period ahead forecasts.

After looking at the graph of the forecasts and actual data, it is clear that the forecasts get increasingly worse the further ahead one is forecasting. Also, one might wonder, after looking at this graph, whether the naïve forecasts are better. Actually, this turns out to be true. (This may be caused by the ARIMA model chosen.)

The set of forecast criteria; MSE, MAE, and MAPE; tell a similar story, when comparing the one-, two-, three-, and four-period forecasts: the quality decreases substantially from the one-period to the two-period ahead forecasts, and then gets worse more slowly as we go further ahead.

Look at the decomposition of MSE: UM, UR, and UD. UM - the bias proportion - is somewhat large at 5.33% for the one-period ahead, and then it gets increasingly bad - to 22.5% for the four-period ahead forecasts. UR - the regression proportion - measures the extent that the slope of the regression of X on the forecast is different from one. It is reasonably low for the four different forecast series, and it has no tendency to get worse or better. UD - the disturbance proportion - is large (as desired) for the one-period ahead forecasts, but gets increasingly worse the further ahead one forecasts.

The comparison between the forecast MSE and the no-change MSE, is disheartening. One would expect the ratio to be below one. This is not true here. The four different forecast series are nearly all about 6% worse than the MSEs from the no-change forecasts. (Calculations for these MSEs are not shown on the spreadsheet. The no-change forecasts that were compared to the (for example) four-period forecasts: $X_n(4) = X_n$.)

The tests for Minzer-Zarnowitz efficiency all yielded the same result - one cannot reject the null hypothesis of Minzer-Zarnowitz efficiency. (As the text notes, and as one should learn from this example, not being able to reject the null of MZ efficiency does not always mean much.)

****

13.9 Refer to the data of Exercise 21 of Chapter 7, showing 168 observations on newspaper advertising. Hold out the last 24 observations for forecasting purposes. fit a seasonal ARIMA model to the first 144 observations, and use the fitted model to generate series of forecasts one-step ahead, two-steps ahead, and so on. Evaluate these forecasts, including a comparison with Holt-Winters forecasts of this series.

------- Answer to 13.9 --------

See the accompanying exhibits comprising portion of LOTUS 123 spreadsheets for the ARIMA and Holt-Winters forecasts, and graphs.

First Graph Accompanying Exercise 13.9

ARIMA forecasts

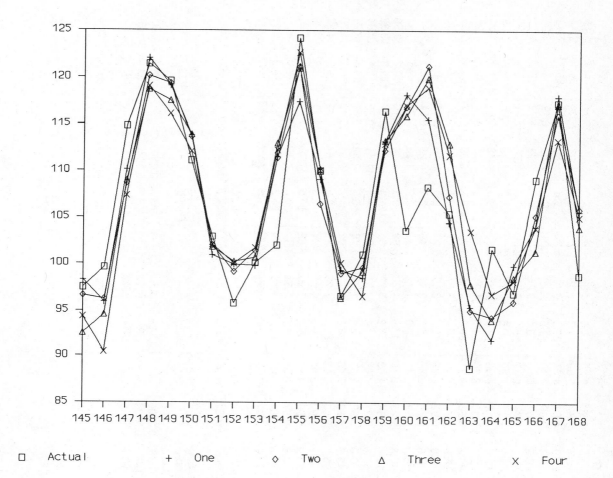

As with exercise 13.8 above, forecasts up to 4 periods ahead were calculated. The ARIMA model fitted to the first 144 observations is an ARIMA(0,1,1)(0,1,2)12 where MA1 = .61058, SMA1 = .39501, SMA2 = .39454. The Holt-Winters model is additive with parameters α = 0.31, β = 0.0, and γ = 0.92. These parameters minimized the sum of squared forecast errors for the one-period ahead forecasts for observations 25 through 144. One should note and realize that the same parameters were used for all the forecasts – that is, the parameters were not re-estimated with the addition of each new parameter.

After looking at both graphs of the forecasts (and after seeing the results for Exercise 13.8) one is pleased with the good fit of all the forecasts, although some are better than others.

As expected (but not as bad as in Exercise 13.8) all forecast criteria get worse for the further ahead forecasts – both for the ARIMA forecasts, and the Holt-Winters forecasts.

Look at the decomposition of MSE: UM, UR, and UD. UM - the bias proportion - stays relatively low at just over 2% for all the ARIMA forecasts, and is even lower for the Holt-Winters forecasts. UR - the regression proportion - measures the extent that the slope of the regression of X on the forecast is different from one. It is somewhat large for the

	A	B	C	D	E	F	G	H	I	J	K	L	M	N	O	P	Q	R
146	145	97.50	98.30	96.63	92.49	94.35	0.6	0.80	0.82	0.8	0.87	0.89	25.1	5.01	5.14	9.9	3.15	3.23
147	146	99.60	95.93	96.24	94.58	90.43	13.5	3.67	3.69	11.3	3.36	3.38	25.2	5.02	5.04	84.1	9.17	9.21
148	147	114.80	110.12	108.69	109.00	107.34	21.9	4.68	4.07	37.3	6.11	5.32	33.6	5.80	5.05	55.7	7.46	6.50
149	148	121.40	122.00	120.18	118.75	119.06	0.4	0.60	0.49	1.5	1.22	1.01	7.0	2.65	2.19	5.5	2.34	1.93
150	149	119.60	119.13	119.36	117.54	116.11	0.2	0.47	0.40	0.1	0.24	0.20	4.3	2.06	1.72	12.2	3.49	2.92
151	150	111.10	113.84	113.66	113.89	112.07	7.5	2.74	2.47	6.5	2.56	2.30	7.8	2.79	2.51	0.9	0.97	0.87
152	151	102.90	100.93	102.00	101.81	102.05	3.9	1.97	1.92	0.8	0.90	0.88	1.2	1.09	1.06	0.7	0.85	0.83
153	152	95.80	99.92	99.15	100.22	100.03	17.0	4.12	4.30	11.2	3.35	3.50	19.5	4.42	4.61	17.9	4.23	4.42
154	153	100.10	99.80	99.80	100.64	101.71	0.1	0.30	0.30	1.7	1.31	1.30	0.3	0.54	0.54	2.6	1.61	1.60
155	154	102.00	111.50	111.38	112.99	112.22	90.2	9.50	9.31	88.0	9.38	9.20	120.7	10.99	10.77	104.4	10.22	10.02
156	155	124.20	117.43	121.13	121.02	122.62	45.8	6.77	5.45	9.4	3.07	2.47	10.1	3.18	2.56	2.5	1.58	1.27
157	156	110.00	109.08	106.45	110.15	110.03	0.8	0.92	0.83	12.6	3.55	3.23	0.0	0.15	0.13	0.0	0.03	0.03
158	157	96.60	99.37	99.01	96.37	100.07	7.6	2.77	2.86	5.8	2.41	2.49	0.1	0.23	0.24	12.1	3.47	3.59
159	158	101.00	98.50	99.58	99.22	96.58	6.3	2.50	2.48	2.0	1.42	1.41	3.2	1.78	1.76	19.5	4.42	4.37
160	159	116.40	113.15	112.18	113.26	112.90	10.5	3.25	2.79	17.8	4.22	3.63	9.9	3.14	2.70	12.2	3.50	3.01
161	160	103.60	118.14	116.87	115.90	116.98	211.4	14.54	14.03	176.2	13.27	12.81	151.3	12.30	11.87	179.0	13.38	12.91
162	161	108.30	115.51	121.17	119.91	118.94	52.0	7.21	6.66	165.8	12.87	11.89	134.8	11.61	10.72	113.1	10.64	9.82
163	162	105.40	104.44	107.25	112.92	111.65	0.9	0.96	0.91	3.4	1.85	1.76	56.5	7.52	7.13	39.1	6.25	5.93
164	163	88.80	95.40	95.03	97.84	103.50	43.6	6.60	7.43	38.8	6.23	7.02	81.7	9.04	10.18	216.1	14.70	16.55
165	164	101.60	91.77	94.34	93.96	96.77	96.7	9.83	9.68	52.8	7.26	7.15	58.3	7.64	7.52	23.3	4.83	4.75
166	165	96.90	99.82	99.99	98.56	98.19	8.5	2.92	3.01	0.8	0.91	0.94	2.8	1.66	1.71	1.7	1.29	1.33
167	166	109.10	104.01	105.15	101.32	103.89	25.9	5.09	4.66	15.6	3.95	3.62	60.5	7.78	7.13	27.1	5.21	4.77
168	167	117.30	117.97	115.99	117.13	113.30	0.5	0.67	0.58	1.7	1.31	1.11	0.0	0.17	0.14	16.0	4.00	3.41
169	168	98.80	105.64	105.90	103.92	105.06	46.8	6.84	6.92	50.5	7.10	7.19	26.2	5.12	5.19	39.2	6.26	6.34
170	t	f1	f2	f3	f4		$e1^2$	$\lvert e1 \rvert$	$\lvert e1/X1 \rvert$	$e2^2$	$\lvert e2 \rvert$	$\lvert e2/X2 \rvert$	$e3^2$	$\lvert e3 \rvert$	$\lvert e3/X3 \rvert$	$e4^2$	$\lvert e4 \rvert$	$\lvert e4/X4 \rvert$
171																		
172	105.95	106.74	106.86	106.81	106.91	29.69	4.15	4.00	29.69	4.11	3.95	35.00	4.65	4.48	41.45	5.13	4.98
173	X bar	f1 bar	f2 bar	f3 bar	f4 bar	MSE1	MAE1	MAPE1	MSE2	MAE2	MAPE2	MSE3	MAE3	MAPE3	MSE4	MAE4	MAPE4
174																		
175	9.06	8.70	8.87	9.09	8.59	5.45			5.45			5.92			6.44		
176	Sx	Sf1	Sf2	Sf3	Sf4	RMSE1			RMSE2			RMSE3			RMSE4		

X = f(f1) Regression Output:

Constant	15.225	
Std Err of Y Est	5.4636	537.33 = S2
R Squared	0.6667	0.9457 = F
No. of Observations	24	< 3.44 thus MZ efficient
Degrees of Freedom	22	

UM = 0.0208, UR = 0.0574, UD = 0.9216

UM = 0.0281, UR = 0.0692, UD = 0.9026

UM = 0.0209, UR = 0.1046, UD = 0.8743

UM = 0.0222, UR = 0.0850, UD = 0.8926

62.1% MSE1/MSE(no change)

62.1% MSE2/MSE(no change)

73.2% MSE3/MSE(no change)

86.7% MSE4/MSE(no change)

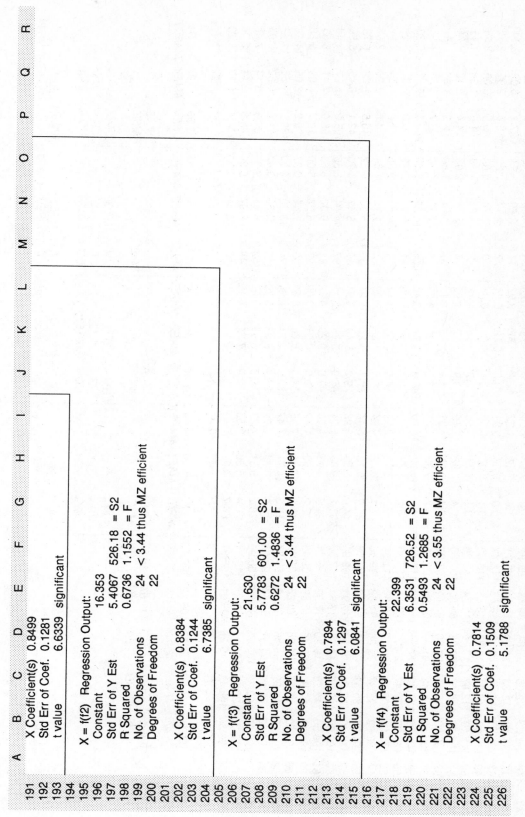

	A	B	C	D	E	F	G	H	I	J	K	L	M	N	O	P	Q	R
191	X Coefficient(s)	0.8499
192	Std Err of Coef.	0.1281
193	t value	6.6339	significant
194		
195	X = f(f2) Regression Output:
196	Constant			16.353
197	Std Err of Y Est			5.4067	526.18	= S2
198	R Squared			0.6736	1.1552	= F
199	No. of Observations			24	< 3.44 thus MZ efficient
200	Degrees of Freedom			22
201	
202	X Coefficient(s)	0.8384
203	Std Err of Coef.	0.1244
204	t value	6.7385	significant
205	
206	X = f(f3) Regression Output:
207	Constant			21.630
208	Std Err of Y Est			5.7783	601.00	= S2
209	R Squared			0.6272	1.4836	= F
210	No. of Observations			24	< 3.44 thus MZ efficient
211	Degrees of Freedom			22
212	
213	X Coefficient(s)	0.7894
214	Std Err of Coef.	0.1297
215	t value	6.0841	significant
216	
217	X = f(f4) Regression Output:
218	Constant			22.399
219	Std Err of Y Est			6.3531	726.52	= S2
220	R Squared			0.5493	1.2685	= F
221	No. of Observations			24	< 3.55 thus MZ efficient
222	Degrees of Freedom			22
223	
224	X Coefficient(s)	0.7814
225	Std Err of Coef.	0.1509
226	t value	5.1788	significant

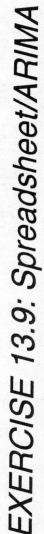

EXERCISE 13.9: Spreadsheet/ARIMA

	A	B	C	D	E	F	G	H	I	J	K	L	M	N	O	P	Q	R
146	145	97.50	96.96	94.55	90.32	92.58	0.3	0.54	0.55	8.7	2.95	3.02	51.5	7.18	7.36	24.2	4.92	5.04
147	146	99.60	92.03	91.86	89.45	85.22	57.3	7.57	7.60	59.9	7.74	7.77	103.0	10.15	10.19	206.8	14.38	14.44
148	147	114.80	113.63	111.28	111.11	108.71	1.4	1.17	1.02	12.4	3.52	3.07	13.6	3.69	3.21	37.1	6.09	5.31
149	148	121.40	121.34	120.98	118.63	118.47	0.0	0.06	0.05	0.2	0.42	0.34	7.7	2.77	2.28	8.6	2.93	2.42
150	149	119.60	119.24	119.23	118.86	116.52	0.1	0.36	0.30	0.1	0.37	0.31	0.5	0.74	0.62	9.5	3.08	2.58
151	150	111.10	112.87	112.76	112.74	112.38	3.1	1.77	1.59	2.7	1.66	1.49	2.7	1.64	1.48	1.6	1.28	1.15
152	151	102.90	100.38	100.93	100.81	100.80	6.4	2.52	2.45	3.9	1.97	1.92	4.3	2.09	2.03	4.4	2.10	2.04
153	152	95.80	97.64	96.86	97.41	97.30	3.4	1.84	1.93	1.1	1.06	1.11	2.6	1.61	1.68	2.2	1.50	1.57
154	153	100.10	101.42	101.99	101.21	101.75	1.7	1.32	1.31	3.6	1.89	1.89	1.2	1.11	1.10	2.7	1.65	1.65
155	154	102.00	117.30	117.71	118.28	117.50	234.2	15.30	15.00	246.9	15.71	15.40	265.1	16.28	15.96	240.3	15.50	15.20
156	155	124.20	122.47	127.21	127.62	128.19	3.0	1.73	1.39	9.1	3.01	2.43	11.7	3.42	2.76	15.9	3.99	3.22
157	156	110.00	106.72	106.19	110.93	111.34	10.7	3.28	2.98	14.5	3.81	3.47	0.9	0.93	0.85	1.8	1.34	1.22
158	157	96.60	96.37	95.36	94.82	99.56	0.1	0.23	0.24	1.5	1.24	1.29	3.2	1.78	1.84	8.8	2.96	3.07
159	158	101.00	95.81	95.74	94.72	94.18	27.0	5.19	5.14	27.7	5.26	5.21	39.4	6.28	6.22	46.5	6.82	6.75
160	159	116.40	112.61	111.00	110.93	109.91	14.4	3.79	3.26	29.2	5.40	4.64	30.0	5.47	4.70	42.1	6.49	5.58
161	160	103.60	120.43	119.25	117.64	117.57	283.1	16.83	16.24	245.0	15.65	15.11	197.1	14.04	13.55	195.2	13.97	13.48
162	161	108.30	113.28	118.50	117.32	115.71	24.8	4.98	4.60	104.0	10.20	9.42	81.4	9.02	8.33	55.0	7.41	6.85
163	162	105.40	103.90	105.45	110.67	109.49	2.2	1.50	1.42	0.0	0.05	0.05	27.7	5.27	5.00	16.7	4.09	3.88
164	163	88.80	95.15	94.68	96.23	101.45	40.3	6.35	7.15	34.6	5.88	6.63	55.2	7.43	8.37	159.9	12.65	14.24
165	164	101.60	86.89	88.86	88.40	89.94	216.3	14.71	14.47	162.3	12.74	12.54	174.3	13.20	12.99	135.9	11.66	11.47
166	165	96.90	96.13	91.57	93.54	93.08	0.6	0.77	0.79	28.4	5.33	5.50	11.3	3.36	3.47	14.6	3.82	3.95
167	166	109.10	103.79	103.55	98.99	100.96	28.2	5.31	4.87	30.8	5.55	5.09	102.2	10.11	9.27	66.3	8.14	7.46
168	167	117.30	126.16	124.51	124.27	119.71	78.4	8.86	7.55	52.0	7.21	6.15	48.6	6.97	5.94	5.8	2.41	2.06
169	168	98.80	108.11	110.86	109.21	108.97	86.7	9.31	9.42	145.3	12.06	12.20	108.3	10.41	10.53	103.4	10.17	10.29
170	t	X	$f1$	$f2$	$f3$	$f4$	$e1^2$	$|e1|$	$|e1/X1|$	$e2^2$	$|e2|$	$|e2/X2|$	$e3^2$	$|e3|$	$|e3/X3|$	$e4^2$	$|e4|$	$|e4/X4|$
171																		
172		105.95	106.69	106.70	106.42	106.30	46.83	4.80	4.64	51.00	5.45	5.25	55.99	6.04	5.82	58.56	6.22	6.04
173		X bar	$f1$ bar	$f2$ bar	$f3$ bar	$f4$ bar	MSE1	MAE1	MAPE1	MSE2	MAE2	MAPE2	MSE3	MAE3	MAPE3	MSE4	MAE4	MAPE4
174																		
175		9.06	10.81	11.33	11.54	10.81	6.84			7.14			7.48			7.65		
176		Sx	$Sf1$	$Sf2$	$Sf3$	$Sf4$	RMSE1			RMSE2			RMSE3			RMSE4		

X = f(1) Regression Output:

Constant	36.251	
Std Err of Y Est	5.9289	632.73 = S2
R Squared	0.6075	4.3214 = F
No. of Observations	24	> 3.44 thus not MZ efficient
Degrees of Freedom	22	

UM = 0.0117   UR = 0.3000   UD = 0.6881

UM = 0.0111   UR = 0.3573   UD = 0.6315

UM = 0.0039   UR = 0.3823   UD = 0.6136

UM = 0.0021   UR = 0.3168   UD = 0.6809

98.0% MSE1 / MSE(no change)

106.7% MSE2 / MSE(no change)

117.1% MSE3 / MSE(no change)

122.5% MSE4 / MSE(no change)

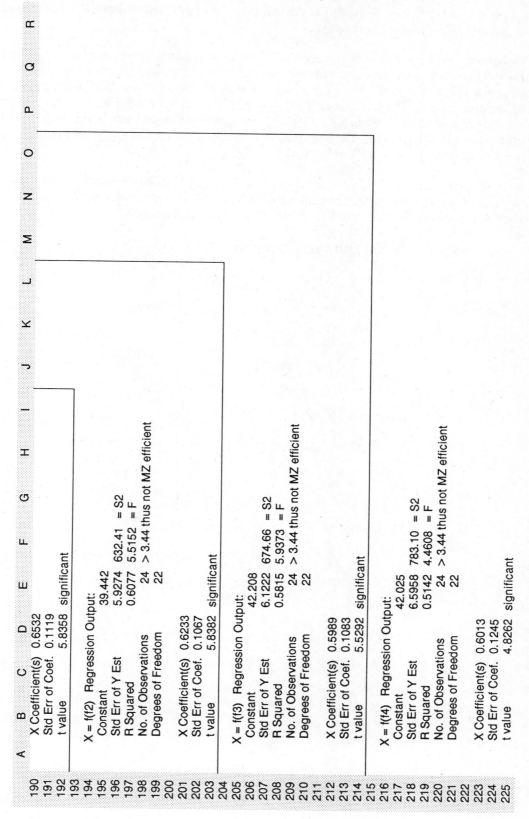

	A	B	C	D	E	F	G
190	X Coefficient(s)		0.6532				
191	Std Err of Coef.		0.1119				
192	t value		5.8358	significant			
193							
194	X = f(f2) Regression Output:						
195	Constant			39.442			
196	Std Err of Y Est			5.9274	632.41	= S2	
197	R Squared			0.6077	5.5152	= F	
198	No. of Observations			24	> 3.44 thus not MZ efficient		
199	Degrees of Freedom			22			
200							
201	X Coefficient(s)		0.6233				
202	Std Err of Coef.		0.1067				
203	t value		5.8382	significant			
204							
205	X = f(f3) Regression Output:						
206	Constant			42.208			
207	Std Err of Y Est			6.1222	674.66	= S2	
208	R Squared			0.5815	5.9373	= F	
209	No. of Observations			24	> 3.44 thus not MZ efficient		
210	Degrees of Freedom			22			
211							
212	X Coefficient(s)		0.5989				
213	Std Err of Coef.		0.1083				
214	t value		5.5292	significant			
215							
216	X = f(f4) Regression Output:						
217	Constant			42.025			
218	Std Err of Y Est			6.5958	783.10	= S2	
219	R Squared			0.5142	4.4608	= F	
220	No. of Observations			24	> 3.44 thus not MZ efficient		
221	Degrees of Freedom			22			
222							
223	X Coefficient(s)		0.6013				
224	Std Err of Coef.		0.1245				
225	t value		4.8262	significant			

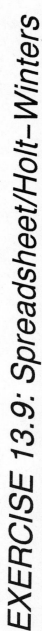

EXERCISE 13.9: Spreadsheet/Holt–Winters

ARIMA forecasts, and very large for the Holt-Winters forecasts. UD - the disturbance proportion - is large (as desired) for the ARIMA forecasts and is quite low (not good at all) for the Holt-Winters forecasts.

The comparison between the forecast MSE and the no-change MSE, is quite good for the ARIMA forecasts, and the Holt-Winters forecasts are worse than the no-change forecasts, except for the one-period ahead forecasts. (Calculations for these MSEs are not shown on the spreadsheet. The no-change forecasts are different from what was used in Exercise 13.8. Since this data is monthly and highly seasonal instead of using the last available observation for the forecast, the last available observation for the <u>same</u> month was used. Thus the no-change forecasts are: $X_n(h) = X_{n+h-12}$.)

The tests for Minzer-Zarnowitz efficiency all yielded the same result within sets of forecasts – one cannot reject the null hypothesis of Minzer-Zarnowitz efficiency for the ARIMA forecasts, but one can for all the Holt-Winters forecasts.

Second Graph Accompanying Exercise 13.9

Holt-Winters forecasts

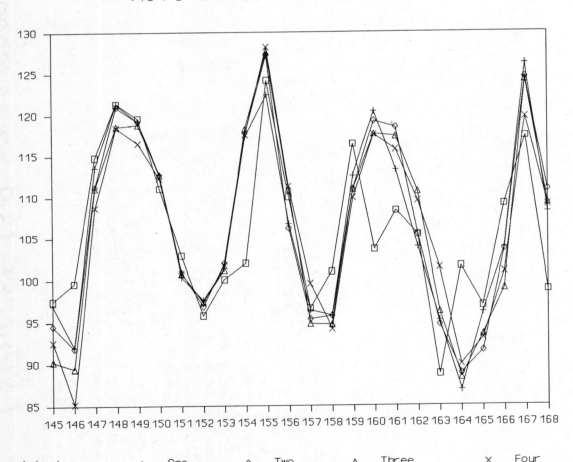

****

13.10 Refer to the data of Exercise 12.10, showing forecasts of the U.S. unemployment rate. Compare the mean squared errors of the two sets of forecasts f_{2t} and f_{3t}. Is either of these conditionally efficient with respect to the other?

-------- Answer to 13.10 --------

See the exhibit comprising a LOTUS 123 spreadsheet of the results of this exercise.

The MSE for f_{2t} is 0.1330, while the MSE for f_{3t} is much better at 0.0884. The MSE for the forecasts f_{2t} is about 50% worse than the MSE for f_{3t}.

The tests for conditionally efficiency of one forecast over the other involved running two regressions - the first with $(X_t - f_{2t})$ on $(f_{3t} - f_{2t})$, and the second $(X_t - f_{3t})$ on $(f_{2t} - f_{3t})$. These regressions are run without intercepts. Efficiency occurs if the slope (w) is zero, instead of being positive.

In the first regression $(X_t - f_{2t})$ on $(f_{3t} - f_{2t})$, the coefficient is clearly significantly positive, thus f_{2t} is not conditionally efficient with respect to f_{3t}.

In the second regression $(X_t - f_{3t})$ on $(f_{2t} - f_{3t})$, the coefficient is just as clearly not significantly greater than zero, and thus f_{3t} is conditionally efficient with respect to f_{2t}. Or, in other words, there is no significant gain by combining f_{2t} (the worse forecasts) with f_{3t} (the better forecasts).

****

13.11 Refer to the data of Exercise 12.11, showing forecasts of growth rates in U.S. gross national product. Compare the mean squared errors of the two sets of forecasts f_{4t} and f_{5t}. Is either of these conditionally efficient with respect to the other?

-------- Answer to 13.11 --------

See the exhibit comprising a LOTUS 123 spreadsheet of the results of this exercise. See the above exercise.

The MSE for f_{4t} is 7.01, while the MSE for f_{5t} is similar at 8.05.

In the first regression $(X_t - f_{4t})$ on $(f_{5t} - f_{4t})$, the coefficient is clearly not significantly positive, thus f_{4t} is conditionally efficient with respect to f_{5t}. Or, in other words, there is no significant gain by combining f_{5t} with f_{4t}.

In the second regression $(X_t - f_{5t})$ on $(f_{4t} - f_{5t})$, the coefficient is similarly not significantly greater than zero, and thus f_{5t} is conditionally efficient with respect to f_{4t}. Or, in other words, there is no significant gain by combining f_{4t} with f_{5t}.

****

	A	B	C X	D $f2$	E $f3$	F $e2^2$	G $e3^2$	H $X{-}f2$	I $f3{-}f2$	J $X{-}f3$	K $f2{-}f3$
1			X	$f2$	$f3$	$e2^2$	$e3^2$	$X{-}f2$	$f3{-}f2$	$X{-}f3$	$f2{-}f3$
2	80	I	6.1	6.4	6.3	0.09	0.04	-0.3	-0.1	-0.2	0.1
3	80	II	7.5	7.2	7.3	0.09	0.04	0.3	0.1	0.2	-0.1
4	80	III	7.6	8.3	8.2	0.49	0.36	-0.7	-0.1	-0.6	0.1
5	80	IV	7.5	7.9	7.4	0.16	0.01	-0.4	-0.5	0.1	0.5
6	81	I	7.3	7.5	7.8	0.04	0.25	-0.2	0.3	-0.5	-0.3
7	81	II	7.4	7.8	7.5	0.16	0.01	-0.4	-0.3	-0.1	0.3
8	81	III	7.2	7.8	7.7	0.36	0.25	-0.6	-0.1	-0.5	0.1
9	81	IV	8.3	7.7	7.8	0.36	0.25	0.6	0.1	0.5	-0.1
10	82	I	8.8	8.0	8.9	0.64	0.01	0.8	0.9	-0.1	-0.9
11	82	II	9.5	9.5	9.5	0.00	0.00	0.0	0.0	0.0	0.0
12	82	III	9.9	9.7	9.7	0.04	0.04	0.2	0.0	0.2	0.0
13	82	IV	10.7	10.2	10.5	0.25	0.04	0.5	0.3	0.2	-0.3
14	83	I	10.4	10.9	10.6	0.25	0.04	-0.5	-0.3	-0.2	0.3
15	83	II	10.1	10.3	10.2	0.04	0.01	-0.2	-0.1	-0.1	0.1
16	83	III	9.4	9.4	9.8	0.00	0.16	0.0	0.4	-0.4	-0.4
17	83	IV	8.5	9.1	8.7	0.36	0.04	-0.6	-0.4	-0.2	0.4
18	84	I	7.9	8.2	7.8	0.09	0.01	-0.3	-0.4	0.1	0.4
19	84	II	7.5	7.7	7.7	0.04	0.04	-0.2	0.0	-0.2	0.0
20	84	III	7.5	7.3	6.9	0.04	0.36	0.2	-0.4	0.6	0.4
21	84	IV	7.1	7.1	7.5	0.00	0.16	0.0	0.4	-0.4	-0.4
22	85	I	7.3	7.3	7.2	0.00	0.01	0.0	-0.1	0.1	0.1
23	85	II	7.3	7.2	7.4	0.01	0.01	0.1	0.2	-0.1	-0.2
24	85	III	7.1	7.4	7.3	0.09	0.04	-0.3	-0.1	-0.2	0.1
25	85	IV	7.0	7.2	7.1	0.04	0.01	-0.2	-0.1	-0.1	0.1
26	86	I	7.1	6.9	6.7	0.04	0.16	0.2	-0.2	0.4	0.2
27	86	II	7.2	6.9	7.1	0.09	0.01	0.3	0.2	0.1	-0.2
28	86	III	6.9	7.2	7.3	0.09	0.16	-0.3	0.1	-0.4	-0.1
29	86	IV	6.8	6.9	7.1	0.01	0.09	-0.1	0.2	-0.3	-0.2
30	87	I	6.7	6.8	7.2	0.01	0.25	-0.1	0.4	-0.5	-0.4
31	87	II	6.2	6.7	6.3	0.25	0.01	-0.5	-0.4	-0.1	0.4
32	87	III	6.0	6.0	6.0	0.00	0.00	0.0	0.0	0.0	0.0
33	87	IV	5.9	6.0	6.0	0.01	0.01	-0.1	0.0	-0.1	0.0
34	88	I	5.7	6.2	5.9	0.25	0.04	-0.5	-0.3	-0.2	0.3
35	88	II		5.5	5.4						
36	88	III									
37	88	IV				0.1330	0.0884				
38						MSE2	MSE3				

Dependent variable: X–f2
Regression Output:
Constant	0
Std Err of Y Est	0.2929
R Squared	0.3237
No. of Observations	33
Degrees of Freedom	32

Independent Variable: f3–f2
X Coefficient(s	0.754
Std Err of Coef	0.172
t value	4.377 *Is significantly different from zero*

Dependent variable: X–f3
Regression Output:
Constant	0
Std Err of Y Est	0.2929
R Squared	-0.037
No. of Observations	33
Degrees of Freedom	32

Independent Variable: f2–f3
X Coefficient(s	0.245
Std Err of Coef	0.172
t value	1.425 *Not significantly greater than zero*

EXERCISE 13.10: Spreadsheet

	A	B	C	D	E	F	G	H	I	J	K
1			X	f4	f5	e4²	e5²	X-f4	f5-f4	X-f5	f4-f5
2	80	I	1.1	-0.9	-1.7	4.0	7.8	2.0	-0.8	2.8	0.8
3	80	II	-9.1	-4.9	-2.5	17.6	43.6	-4.2	2.4	-6.6	-2.4
4	80	III	1.0	-3.6	-5.1	21.2	37.2	4.6	-1.5	6.1	1.5
5	80	IV	5.0	1.3	2.2	13.7	7.8	3.7	0.9	2.8	-0.9
6	81	I	6.5	-0.9	0.6	54.8	34.8	7.4	1.5	5.9	-1.5
7	81	II	-1.9	0.4	0.4	5.3	5.3	-2.3	0.0	-2.3	0.0
8	81	III	-0.6	-0.8	0.1	0.0	0.5	0.2	0.9	-0.7	-0.9
9	81	IV	-5.2	-3.4	-1.8	3.2	11.6	-1.8	1.6	-3.4	-1.6
10	82	I	-3.9	-2.8	-3.4	1.2	0.3	-1.1	-0.6	-0.5	0.6
11	82	II	1.7	-1.4	2.2	9.6	0.3	3.1	3.6	-0.5	-3.6
12	82	III	0.8	2.1	3.1	1.7	5.3	-1.3	1.0	-2.3	-1.0
13	82	IV	-2.5	2.1	2.2	21.2	22.1	-4.6	0.1	-4.7	-0.1
14	83	I	3.1	2.8	4.1	0.1	1.0	0.3	1.3	-1.0	-1.3
15	83	II	8.7	3.7	5.4	25.0	10.9	5.0	1.7	3.3	-1.7
16	83	III	7.9	6.8	8.0	1.2	0.0	1.1	1.2	-0.1	-1.2
17	83	IV	4.5	5.4	6.2	0.8	2.9	-0.9	0.8	-1.7	-0.8
18	84	I	8.3	5.6	5.4	7.3	8.4	2.7	-0.2	2.9	0.2
19	84	II	7.5	3.8	3.7	13.7	14.4	3.7	-0.1	3.8	0.1
20	84	III	2.7	5.3	6.1	6.8	11.6	-2.6	0.8	-3.4	-0.8
21	84	IV	3.9	2.3	3.3	2.6	0.4	1.6	1.0	0.6	-1.0
22	85	I	1.3	3.2	4.6	3.6	10.9	-1.9	1.4	-3.3	-1.4
23	85	II	1.7	3.2	3.1	2.3	2.0	-1.5	-0.1	-1.4	0.1
24	85	III	3.3	3.5	3.9	0.0	0.4	-0.2	0.4	-0.6	-0.4
25	85	IV	2.4	2.0	2.2	0.2	0.0	0.4	0.2	0.2	-0.2
26	86	I	3.2	2.7	2.8	0.3	0.2	0.5	0.1	0.4	-0.1
27	86	II	1.1	2.6	2.9	2.3	3.2	-1.5	0.3	-1.8	-0.3
28	86	III	2.9	2.6	2.5	0.1	0.2	0.3	-0.1	0.4	0.1
29	86	IV	1.7	2.6	1.2	0.8	0.3	-0.9	-1.4	0.5	1.4
30	87	I	4.3	2.5	3.0	3.2	1.7	1.8	0.5	1.3	-0.5
31	87	II	2.3	2.2	0.9	0.0	2.0	0.1	-1.3	1.4	1.3
32	87	III	3.8	3.2	1.6	0.4	4.8	0.6	-1.6	2.2	1.6
33	87	IV	4.2	2.3	1.4	3.6	7.8	1.9	-0.9	2.8	0.9
34	88	I	2.3	0.4	-0.2	3.6	6.2	1.9	-0.6	2.5	0.6
35	88	II		1.5	1.6						
36	88	III									
37	88	IV				7.01	8.05				
38						MSE4	MSE5				

Dependent variable: X-f4
Regression Output:

Constant	0
Std Err of Y Est	2.6826
R Squared	-0.041
No. of Observations	33
Degrees of Freedom	32

Independent variable: f5-f4

X Coefficient(s	0.138	
Std Err of Coef	0.389	
t value	0.356	Insignificantly greater than zero

Dependent variable: X-f5
Regression Output:

Constant	0
Std Err of Y Est	2.6826
R Squared	0.1301
No. of Observations	33
Degrees of Freedom	32

Independent variable: f4-f5

X Coefficient(s	0.862	
Std Err of Coef	0.389	
t value	2.218	Significantly greater than zero

EXERCISE 13.11: Spreadsheet

Chapter 14

AN OVERVIEW OF
BUSINESS FORECASTING METHODS

Contents of Chapter 14